THE
ENCHANTED
VOYAGER

THE LIFE OF
J.B. RHINE

THE ENCHANTED VOYAGER

THE LIFE OF J. B. RHINE

An Authorized Biography by

DENIS BRIAN

Prentice-Hall, Inc., Englewood Cliffs, N.J. 07632

The Enchanted Voyager: The Life of J. B. Rhine, by Denis Brian
© 1982 by Denis Brian
All rights reserved. No part of this book may be reproduced in any form or by any means, except for the inclusion of brief quotations in a review, without permission in writing from the publisher. Address inquiries to Prentice-Hall, Inc., Englewood Cliffs, N.J. 07632
Printed in the United States of America
Prentice-Hall International, Inc., London/Prentice-Hall of Australia, Pty. Ltd., Sydney/
Prentice-Hall of Canada, Ltd., Toronto/Prentice-Hall of India Private Ltd., New Delhi/
Prentice-Hall of Japan, Inc., Tokyo/Prentice-Hall of Southeast Asia, Pte. Ltd., Singapore/
Whitehall Books Limited, Wellington, New Zealand
10   9   8   7   6   5   4   3   2   1

ISBN 0-13-275107-0

Library of Congress Cataloging in Publication Data
Brian, Denis.
    Enchanted voyager.
    Includes bibliographical references and
index.
    1. Rhine, J. B. (Joseph Banks), 1895–1980.
    2. Psychical research—Biography.   I. Title.
BF1027.R48B74   133.8'092'4 [B]   81-12029
ISBN 0-13-275107-0   AACR2

To Martine, with all my love.

CONTENTS

ACKNOWLEDGMENTS

The jacket photograph of J. B. Rhine is published courtesy of N.E.T. WUNC-TV, Chapel Hill, North Carolina.

I wish to thank the following for their help: Virginia Lowell Mauck, The Lilly Library, Indiana University; the staff of the Perkins Library, Duke University; the staff of The American Society for Psychical Research; the staff of the Foundation for Research on the Nature of Man; Eileen Coly of the Parapsychology Foundation; Jean Shinoda Bolen, M.D., of *Psychic* magazine; Thomas R. Tietze, Dr. E. J. Dingwall, Martin Gardner, Milbourne Christopher, David Sinclair, Laura A. Dale, Rhea A. White, Alan Vaughan, Dr. Robert Ashby, Allan Angoff, Charles Angoff, Helen Dukas, Larry Rubin, Paul D. Allison, Professor H. A. Murray, Professor R. Laurence Moore, Mrs. Aldous Huxley, Jeremiah O'Leary, Dr. Lawrence Casler, Dr. Irvin L. Child, Dr. Ben Feather, Dr. George Evelyn Hutchinson, Dr. Ernest R. Hilgard, Dr. Robert Jastrow, Mrs. Hubert Pearce, Mrs. Dorothy Pope, Mrs. Gaither Pratt, Rosalind Heywood, Mrs. K. M. Goldney, Mrs. Fletcher V. Houchens, Arthur Koestler, Mrs. William Sloane, Dr. George Wald, and Dr. Theodore X. Barber.

I have also made use of these sources: C. G. Jung, *Letters*, ed. Gerhard Adler and Aniela Jaffé, translated by R. F. C. Hull, Bollingen Series XCV, Vol. 1: *1906–1950* copyright © 1971, 1973 by Princeton University Press; Vol. II: 1951–1961, copyright © 1953, 1955, 1961, 1963, 1968, 1971, 1972, 1974, 1975 by Princeton University Press. The following letters from C. G. Jung to J. B. Rhine: 27 November 1934; 20 May 1935; 5 November 1942; 18 September 1945; November 1945; 1 April 1948; 18 February 1953; 25 September 1953; and 9 August 1954; reproduced by permission of Princeton University Press.

Special thanks to my wife, Martine, and daughter, Danielle, for their enthusiastic and valuable assistance, and to my editor, Robert Sussman Stewart, for his advice and encouragement.

INTRODUCTION

While contemporary twentieth-century scientists split the atom, unraveled the secrets of the cell, and listened to the echoes of Creation, J. B. Rhine, the son of an itinerant schoolteacher, probed another world that could not be seen, heard, or touched. Because it seemed to lie beyond the senses and violated established laws of time and space, all but a few physical scientists thought he was wasting his time, chasing a myth.

But, in searching for this nonphysical or extrasensory world, Rhine kept open the possibility of its existence and staked claims no open-minded thinker can ignore. He did this against opposition that continued throughout his life, in the face of scorn and derision. He persevered for fifty years, putting "miracles" to the test in his North Carolina laboratory and announcing extraordinary discoveries which are still feverishly disputed. Today his name is synonymous with parapsychology and ESP, yet the man himself has largely escaped scrutiny.

Rhine, biologist turned psychologist, is so closely associated with parapsychology that writing about the subject—which I planned—while keeping him in the background is like trying to describe an elaborate house seen only in the dark. So, as I got to know him between 1968 and his death in 1980, I attempted to persuade him to talk about himself. He often and eagerly discussed his work, but continued to balk at personal revelation; at best his answers were oblique or parabolic. At times his attitude seemed paranoid. This only sharpened the appetites of writers whom he began to regard as vultures, myself probably included, waiting to pounce and scavenge his life. When they persisted with plans to write his biography, Rhine refused to cooperate or used delaying tactics that amounted to passive resistance, although to suggest Rhine was ever passive is like calling a tiger ticklish.

Why did Rhine continue to resist his would-be biographers? He was certainly battle-trained and scarred from fights with both

believers and skeptics. The battleground even spread to his laboratory. It was not uncommon for him to fight fiercely with his staff and
for the loser—never Rhine—to continue research elsewhere. Several
of these bruised ex-staffers had written of their work, but their
relationship with Rhine remained shrouded in mist, if not in mystery.
None of their books or articles tells what went on behind the scenes,
or the reasons for the fights. None indicates whether Rhine was
touched with greatness or was, as characterized by Sir Arthur Conan
Doyle, "a monumental ass."[1]

Rhine once mentioned to me with a wry laugh that he suspected several former associates were waiting for him to die before
bringing out books about him, implying they were afraid to publish
while he was alive.

By 1978 I had known him for ten years. At his request my wife
and I had investigated a woman living in our neighborhood who
claimed X-ray vision. An account in a local newspaper described how
she demonstrated this ability: identifying playing cards while in a
hypnotic trance and blindfolded. We caught her peeking under the
blindfold. Rhine approved our methods of investigation and conclusions. He and his wife and partner, Dr. Louisa Rhine, had by this
time given me many interviews about their work, but I had learned
next to nothing about Rhine himself. He explained one reason for his
reticence was that he had often been the victim of misquotation,
especially by journalists with a penchant for hyperbole, which gave
scientific critics fresh fuel for attack. Consequently they dismissed his
claims as not only impossible in an Einsteinian universe, but not
worth careful study; or mocked the tabloid press headlines that
paraphrased them into parody. And Rhine was determined to avoid a
biographer who might perpetuate the parody.

My arguments finally weakened his resistance. His biography
was inevitable with or without his cooperation, I told him. There was
growing evidence that the personality of the experimenter had a
crucial effect on results. Rhine's own success as an experimenter had
been outstanding, therefore it was necessary to reveal his personality
in describing his work. He kept an escape clause, though, reserving
the right to pull out at any time he felt I was distorting or misrepresenting. He agreed to allow me to use all the information he had
supplied up to that point of disillusion—if it was ever reached. Rhine
accepted the fact that I would seek and publish the negative opinions
of his most informed and vehement critics (characteristics sometimes

found in the same man), assured he would have a chance to rebut them.

Naturally I hoped he would be frank and open. And the first hint that he intended to give an uncensored version of his life came when he gave me unrestricted access to his correspondence. I started to interview him specifically for this biography in 1978: He read and approved about half the manuscript before his death in 1980. He did not see the more critical later chapters, although I had confronted him with the views of the critics quoted in those chapters and had obtained his answers.

His widow and fellow parapsychologist, Dr. Louisa Rhine, has seen the entire manuscript. The only changes and additions she suggested and which I made were matters of fact and responses to criticism. She wrote to me on May 28, 1980:

> I think the testimony of all these old (young) staff members, etc., is interesting. To an alert reader it should be a rather challenging puzzle to picture the character of the man behind it all. . . . I wondered whether you knew the real reason for the "do it my way" characteristic these various staff members complain of? The Lab, of course, was JB's creation, organized with and for a definite purpose by a trained scientist who intended to use only the best possible methods. But the field had no training school, no academic standing which could, in a way, have exercised a bit of pre-selection on those who wanted to work there. And so, the recruits were a diverse lot—from 13-year-old Honorton, to PhD's like some of them. But above all they were individualistic—or they wouldn't have ventured into so unconventional a field with no career promise or future of any tangible kind. And so, clashes of personality were a built-in consequence. And JB had to be a strong leader with an indomitable sense of purpose and direction to get anywhere. but the project was his creation, not theirs, and the slender funds that supported it he had raised by main effort. Therefore, those who wanted to play by their own rules, not his, were free to leave. They usually did not do it graciously however, and probably he did not take pains to be tactful, human nature being what it is.

For J. B. Rhine's biography I have interviewed and corresponded with J.B. and Dr. Louisa Rhine; his two brothers, three daughters, and son; his staff and ex-staff; his fellow parapsychologists;

his supporters and major critics, including several Nobel-prizewinning scientists. I have made use of the Rhines' books,* their *Journal of Parapsychology, The Journal of the American Society for Psychical Research,* Rhine's correspondence kept in the Duke University Perkins Library, and some five hundred books on psychic research and parapsychology. Most of the interviews, made in person and by telephone, have been tape-recorded for the sake of accuracy.

Rhine's quest was to discover by scientific methods the nature of man, his purpose and destiny. Can man transcend the physical, read minds, foretell the future, cure the incurable? Is this life on earth his only existence? Those were some of the questions he tried to answer. Rhine was not the first to test the infinite or probe into the depths of the unconscious mind. In fact, a few of the pioneer psychical researchers were still at work when he began his experiments in the 1920s. Rhine was the first to bring the mystery into the laboratory for sustained testing, profiting both from the mistakes and discoveries of the early researchers. Their active, organized efforts began on the heels of Charles Darwin's shattering evidence that man was closer to apes than angels; that the reality of angels was in serious doubt. Darwin is partly responsible for the work of Rhine and his predecessors, who accepted neither the spiritual view of man as revealed in the Bible, nor the Darwinian version which brought man down to earth with a bang.

J. B. Rhine's books are: Extra-Sensory Perception, *1934;* New Frontiers of the Mind, *1937;* The Reach of the Mind, *1947;* New World of the Mind, *1953. He and J. G. Pratt coauthored* Parapsychology: Frontier Science of the Mind, *1957. And with four staff members of his laboratory, Rhine wrote a critical survey and examination of the evidence of ESP:* Extra-Sensory Perception After Sixty Years, *1940. It was reprinted in 1966 with a foreword by Rhine.*

Dr. Louisa Rhine's books are: Hidden Channels of the Mind, *1961;* ESP in Life and Lab: Tracing Hidden Channels, *1967;* Mind Over Matter, Psychokinesis, *1970;* PSI: What Is It? The Story of ESP and PK, *1975;* The Invisible Picture, *1981.*

The Legacy

By a curious coincidence Charles Darwin died in 1882, the year the Society for Psychical Research was founded.* His theory of man's origin had demolished the biblical version, and by extension much else reported in the Bible, for many who had relied on it to inspire, console, and guide them. The kindly, mild-mannered Englishman had shaken their assurance that they were spiritual beings with immortal souls. And their doubts increased as nineteenth-century science remorselessly uncovered a mechanical universe, in which man emerged as a clever animal most probably destined, like his world, to ultimate and irrevocable death.

Could parts of the Bible be salvaged in a post-Darwinian age? Were the tales of miracles, for example, which testified to man's extrasensory, spiritual, or psychic nature simply written by deluded or deceitful men? Accounts had persisted down the ages, in life and literature, of miracle cures, haunted houses, apparitions, of people who saw the future. Were they all imaginary? Some who were not sustained by religious faith, yet still hoped there was more to man than the sum of his chemical elements, wondered if any aspect of man—his mind, perhaps—might transcend the physical and even outlast his body.

Spiritualists gave credence to such possibilities. Their movement swept through America and Europe at the end of the nineteenth century like a buoyant wave of renewed hope, leaving many supporters almost breathless with excitement. The source of optimism was usually a poorly educated man or woman able to go into a trance and become, it seemed, a channel for the voices of the dead. These messages from "the next world" were frequently banal, evasive, vague, or inaccurate; and the mediums, as they were called, often frauds. But among those who practiced this macabre ritual, a handful

---

*Darwin had discovered man's probable origin and evolution. Members of the SPR intended to probe man's nonphysical nature, and destiny—if any—beyond his earthly life.

brought intelligent, accurate, and even genuinely prophetic messages, and withstood rigorous investigations that went on for decades. They kept alive the faint possibility that the dead survived and could communicate with the living.

French psychiatrists offered scientific support for the mind's ability to rise above the physical when they reported that hypnotized patients had demonstrated supernormal abilities like mind reading. Some psychoanalysts, though not Freud, announced similar findings soon after they began the new therapy which encouraged patients to talk freely, without inhibition. And American psychologist Morton Prince, in a detailed study of a woman with multiple personalities, indicated that the mind's unconscious depths still defied a physical or mechanistic explanation.[1]

Encouraged by these reports, a small group of men and women began to investigate, with varying degrees of scientific exactitude, borderline beliefs that had fallen into disrepute, especially since Darwin. One of the most eager and persistent of these researchers was Frederic Myers, a lecturer in classics at Trinity College, Cambridge. He had lost faith in Christianity but had an almost desperate urge for reassurance that he lived in a benevolent universe and could look forward to immortality. Myers has been portrayed by friends as a saint, by critics as an overemotional libertine. Both may be describing the man at various stages of his life, because, according to his friend William James, the Harvard psychologist and philosopher, Myers "was made over again from the day when he took up psychical research seriously. He became learned in science . . . endlessly patient, and above all, happy."[2]

Myers and his friend Henry Sidgwick, professor of philosophy at Trinity, had been informally investigating mediums for several years before joining the Society for Psychical Research at its inception in London in 1882. Sidgwick was elected president, and both men endorsed the broad purpose of the society "to investigate that large body of debatable phenomena designated by such terms as mesmeric, psychical and spiritualistic, and to do so without prejudice or prepossession of any kind, and in the same spirit of exact and unimpassioned enquiry which has enabled Science to solve so many problems, ones not less obscure nor less hotly debated."[3]

The leaders of the group, scholars and scientists, included Sir Oliver Lodge, world-famed as an expert on electromagnetism; Sir William Barrett, also a physicist; psychologist Edmund Gurney, who became a leading authority on hypnosis; Henry's wife, Eleanor Sidgwick, and her brother Arthur James Balfour, a future British prime minister. All were comparatively young, with an average age of thirty-two (Rhine was thirty-one when he began his investigations) and exceptionally intelligent. The American Society for Psychical Research was formed in 1885, and William James, America's first major philosopher; Columbia University educator Professor James H. Hyslop; and an Australian, Dr. Richard Hodgson, with a doctorate in law were among its most active members. Psychical researchers soon formed a network in America, Britain, and Europe. They corresponded frequently and occasionally teamed up to test the latest psychic star. Many mediums, they discovered, used elaborate and ingenious tricks requiring the patience and combined skills of a psychiatrist, detective, and conjurer to expose them.

In some respects psychical research resembled the constant contest between cops and robbers in which the crooks changed the scene of their crimes or their modus operandi just before they could be caught in the act.

Two of the most spectacular mediums of those wild days were Neapolitan Eusapia Palladino and Scottish-American Daniel Dunglas Home. Dr. Ercole Chiaia of Naples was the first scientist to bring Palladino to the attention of the scientific community. He described her as an ignorant, invalid women of thirty who apparently was capable of defying natural laws.* She floated in the air, wrote Chiaia, as if lying on a couch, made furniture leave the ground, stay suspended for a while, then slowly descend to the floor. She grew taller or shorter at will, like a real-life Alice in Wonderland. At times, what looked like flashes of lightning shot from her body; and distant musical instruments played as though she had only to think of music for them to come to life.[4]

If anything, Daniel Dunglas Home exceeded even these "miracles" because he undertook more hazardous exploits, like floating out of a fourth-floor window of a London house and returning through the window of an adjoining room. Several apparently sane witnesses who had not been drinking or indulging in drugs, testified to this feat. Others told of Home holding red-hot coals in his bare hands without raising a blister. He also was said to change his height at will. William Crookes, a British chemist and physicist later knighted for his scientific work, announced in 1871 that he had tested Home and judged him to be genuine. Because of this endorsement, most other scientists regarded Crookes as a fool, a liar, or a lunatic. But, typically, none of those skeptics offered to put Home to the test. In fact, during a long career, Home was never publicly exposed. Some witnesses reported that Home was a trickster able to manipulate objects with his bare feet, but the evidence was inconclusive.

Palladino, however, was discovered cheating several times,

*In a letter to Italian psychiatrist and criminologist Dr. Cesar Lombroso.

most blatantly in New York City on April 17, 1910. Then two men in black tights crawled under chairs in the darkness and caught her trying to lift a table with her foot. Most leading researchers immediately dropped a medium who faked phenomena. A few made excuses for Palladino, explaining that while in a trance she might unconsciously cheat if her genuine powers temporarily failed. She agreed and angrily told the investigators, with some justification, that it was up to them to prevent her from cheating.

In any case, by this time researchers were more interested in mental mediums who wrote or spoke as if controlled or "possessed" by departed spirits. Professor William James had discovered one of the most outstanding of this breed, Mrs. Leonore Piper, a Boston housewife. James was familiar with talk about miracles at mealtime conversations in his home. His father, Henry James, Sr., had been a theology student and was a Swedenborgian, believing in Swedenborg's teaching that there is a spiritual or symbolic sense to the Bible which God revealed through him. Swedenborg (1688-1772), a Swedish scientist, philosopher, and mystic, declared that he had talked with the dead, "seen" living creatures on other planets, and clairvoyantly witnessed a fire three hundred miles away. James's own encounter with the "miraculous" happened nearer home, when he was professor of psychology at Harvard in 1885. His wife and other relatives greeted him with an awed account of a visit to Mrs. Piper. Her ability to tell them where to find a missing bank note, to read the contents of a hidden letter, and even describe a rocking chair that creaked mysteriously in the James's home, had astonished them. James, skeptical yet curious, went to test her for himself and returned baffled. After more visits to Leonore Piper, James concluded: "Taking everything I know of Mrs. Piper into account, the result is to make me feel absolutely certain as I am of any personal fact in the world that she knows things in her trances which she cannot possibly have heard in her waking state."[5]

James handed Mrs. Piper over to Dr. Richard Hodgson, recently arrived from England to be research officer for the ASPR. Three years before, in 1884, while working for the British SPR, he had exposed Madam Blavatsky, the founder of Theosophy, as a fraud. Hodgson had been so harsh in his exposure of some mediums that fellow SPR members had resigned in protest. His view was that most mediums were "vulgar tricksters more or less in league with one another."[6] Hodgson hired detectives to follow both Mrs. Piper and her husband and to report if they attempted to obtain information in advance about people who were to attend her séances. The detectives found nothing suspicious. As a rule, Hodgson made it impossible for her to know who was going to be at her séances by bringing sitters on the spur of the moment.

While in a trance, Mrs. Piper spoke in the gruff voice of a man who said he was the spirit of a French doctor called Phinuit. He claimed to be the source of the supernormal information produced by Mrs. Piper. Anxious to put her to more stringent tests, Hodgson sent Mrs. Piper to England to be interrogated by Sir Oliver Lodge and Frederic Myers in unfamiliar surroundings and among strangers. She gave Lodge so many details about the boyhood adventures of his uncles that he sent a detective to their hometown, Barking, to find out if the intimate family anecdotes Mrs. Piper had supplied might have been gathered by a persistent and curious investigator by normal methods. The detective admitted he had been unable to equal Mrs. Piper.* Few failed to be impressed if not overawed by Leonore Piper's powers. William James dubbed her his "one white crow," the one genuine medium among flocks of phonies. "To upset the conclusion that all crows are black," he explained, "there is no need to seek demonstration that no crow is black; it is sufficient to produce one white crow."[7]

Discovering Mrs. Piper and a score of other reputable and remarkable mediums was not the sole achievement of the psychical researchers. In 1886 Frederic Myers, Frank Podmore, and Edmund Gurney published *Phantasms of the Living*, a detailed account of their four years' intensive work and a guidebook for fellow psychical researchers. The trio described cases of spontaneous telepathy reported to the SPR, and successful telepathy experiments which they had directed or observed. They discussed the psychological conditions that seemed to favor paranormal activity and emphasized the unreliability of untrained witnesses. And they related how, joined by Mrs. Sidgwick and other volunteers, they had asked thousands of people the same question: Have you ever perceived an apparition? (An impression, voice, or figure of a person undergoing some crisis, especially death.) The team gathered 701 accounts of witnesses to apparitions, 21 of the ghostly appearances within hours of the individual's death. Gurney and his co-investigators concluded that "between death and apparitions a connection exists not due to chance alone. This we hold to be a fact."[8] Critics protested that 701 was too small a sample to support such a momentous conclusion. So the SPR undertook an international survey, and the 32,000 replies

---

British investigators even pricked, cut, and burned Mrs. Piper and held a bottle of ammonia under her nose to make sure she was really in a trance.

ruled out chance coincidence more emphatically than in the *Phantasms of the Living* survey. One of the unexpected achievements of the SPR was to make hypnosis respectable. Until Edmund Gurney's experiments with hypnosis, the conservative British Medical Association took at best a jaundiced view of the subject. But his extensive and successful use of hypnosis to test for telepathy helped to convince the staid body not only that hypnosis was a genuine phenomenon, but that it could be a useful therapeutic tool.

For almost twenty years Professor Henry Sidgwick had been the acknowledged leader of psychical researchers on both sides of the Atlantic. He was an intelligent, thoughtful, and compassionate man. He also endeared himself to them because of his almost childlike delight in life and his mild eccentricities. They remarked how he once skipped with excitement at a tennis match, and ran around the Cambridge streets for exercise still wearing his cap and gown. His intense absorption in conversation with a friend led him to walk into a church service absentmindedly holding a cup of tea. When Sidgwick wrote to fellow psychical researchers, by now his affectionate friends, that he was fatally ill, Richard Hodgson's response was typical. He replied that "even if I knew no more than that I was going into the dark, I would with absolute joy for your sake go out instead of you."[9]

Edmund Gurney's accidental death in 1888 at forty-one had devastated his colleagues, who had known him as a witty and sensitive man. Sidgwick died in August 1900, and Frederic Myers—he almost welcomed death as a wonderful adventure—six months after that. The ebullient workaholic Richard Hodgson dropped dead from a heart attack while playing handball in 1905. All had intimated that after their deaths they would try to communicate from "the next world," and it was hoped they would devise a vivid, convincing way to provide evidence for survival—if, in fact, they had survived.

Which is what seemed to happen. Several mediums in America, England, and India wrote to the SPR headquarters accounts of messages they had received apparently from the spirits of Myers and his dead colleagues. These strongly reflected their interest in classical scholarship, and when pieced together, appeared to have been arranged according to a clever, elaborate plan. In all, over the years the cross-correspondences—as they were called—grew to some three thousand messages. Professor Gardner Murphy, a leading psychologist and parapsychologist, considered them among the strongest evidence for survival.

Eleanor Sidgwick soon dispelled any fear that the deaths of the SPR's dynamic leaders meant the society's disintegration. Perhaps the greatest investigator of them all, the calm, cautious, and skeptical

Mrs. Sidgwick was elected president of the society in 1908 and secretary in 1910. She had received a good education in physical science; and had collaborated in several experiments with Lord Rayleigh, her brother-in-law and a Nobel-prizewinning physicist. No one devoted more time and energy to psychical research or was more awake to normal explanations for mysterious events. In 1915, when 73, she published a 657-page report on Leonore Piper, but still did not commit herself to an absolute Yes, Mrs. Piper has proved survival. "There is no doubt that Mrs. Sidgwick kept the S.P.R. to a high critical standard," wrote Alan Gauld in *The Founders of Psychical Research*. "Even among her own family it was said that it was impossible to convince Aunt Nora that anything in the world had ever happened." Eventually, even the skeptical Mrs. Sidgwick came to believe in survival.[10]

In 1927, optimistically appraising the 45-year-old history of the Society for Psychical Research, Sir Oliver Lodge stated that researchers had established hypnotism, telepathy, and clairvoyance as facts. He claimed that survival of the dead and their ability to communicate with the living had been demonstrated. Lodge admitted further investigation was needed to provide incontrovertible proof—but he was confident that with continued research such proof would ultimately be found.[11]

1

THE ULTIMATE MYSTERY 1895–1920

The scientific world rebuffed the claims of the pioneer psychical researchers: Their critics demanded more substantial proof.

William James wrote in his The Will to Believe: *Why do so few "scientists" ever look at the evidence for telepathy, so-called? Because they think as a leading biologist, now dead, once said to me, that even if such a thing were true, scientists ought to band together to keep it suppressed and concealed. It would undo the uniformity of nature and all sorts of other things without which scientists cannot carry on their pursuits.*

A young American biologist named J. B. Rhine was one of the few scientists who looked at the evidence for telepathy and was eager to investigate for himself. Reports by British researchers, especially Eleanor Sidgwick, Edmund Gurney, and Oliver Lodge, partly prepared him for the deceit, insults, betrayals, and frustrations he would encounter, as well as for the lure of the search itself. Their detailed, almost verbatim accounts of experiments and investigations were in a sense Rhine's Bible—but he brought the scene of operations out of the séance rooms into the laboratory and used the tools of twentieth-century science.

Was his urge to investigate ultimate mysteries an attempt to explore, confirm, or demolish the religious myths and old wives' tales he was exposed to as a child? He was always a questioning boy, unusually bright, incredibly stubborn—or strong-willed. It seemed clear that he would do something remarkable with his life. But why such an unusual preoccupation?

Joseph Banks Rhine, the second of five children and eldest of four brothers, was born in Waterloo, Pennsylvania, on September 29, 1895; his father was Samuel Ellis Rhine, his mother, Elizabeth Ellen (Vaughan). People in the mountains of that area accepted the reality of omens, prophetic warnings, and other supernatural happenings. His mother was inclined to believe, too; his father, to scoff.

"My father had some curiosity in the spiritualist movement, probably along with many young men in the community, and he told me once of attending a séance in which they did table tipping," said Rhine. "The medium influenced the table. Some of the people there tried to sit on the table. Nevertheless it moved. He was not taken in. He was always a bit of a skeptic. My mother was inclined to believe in the psychic stories and in omens and signs. She had less of the little bit of education available in the mountains. He'd been out to Harrisburg to a business college and worked for a while in one of the nearby cities. He was the more sophisticated of the two."

Rhine's father worked briefly as a public schoolteacher in Pennsylvania in the 1890s and then as a farmer and merchant in Pennsylvania, New Jersey, and Ohio in the early 1900s. The family didn't put down roots until they reached Ohio in 1910.

"My father was a teacher during the months of the year when the farmers let their children off the farm—for maybe four or five months," Rhine explained.

"When I was four years old, in 1899, my father took me to school with him and I started reading earlier than most of the kids in the mountains. My father taught all the subjects in the country school, he even taught us behavior with a hickory stick. Being his buddy as we went off to school in the morning, that kind of association encouraged me all along to go to school. He was proud of me.

"My mother wanted me to be a minister. I still remember going to the chapel with her when I was four years old to be baptized and she said to the preacher—there were three of us who got baptized: 'Preacher, this one is going to follow you. This one's going to be a preacher, too.' "

Rhine was not only a rarity among his peers for being able to read, he was one of the few to have books at hand. His was the one home in the area with a bookcase. "My father made a bookcase himself and he had a few shelves filled with books he'd buy from the traveling salesmen who came down the valley. He had a two-volume set of *Stanley's Travels in Darkest Africa*. That's about as much of a summa cum laude as you can give a farmer in the mountains!"[1]

Because there were no near neighbors, for the first five years of Rhine's life, his sister, Myra, two years older than he, was his only playmate. Consequently, he was, he says, "as shy as a wild turkey." He did not feel at home with people, but "I learned to love the big blue mountains, the rich dark woods, and the great brown hills."[2]

Rhine's brother Paul, nine years his junior, remembers their mother telling them that when J.B. was a lad in Pennsylvania he was interested in hypnotism. "You used to find some people hypnotizing others in the little towns throughout the valley," says Paul. "Mother warned J.B.: 'That's bad for you. Stay away from it.' I guess that's what made him more curious about it. Then, of course, he heard about the psychic things, like clairvoyance and telepathy—stories about psychic powers that have been handed down through the ages. Mother used to have omens—and we were fascinated by a story she told us about her brother, who was dying of cancer. And he heard the noise of a coffin being made. And he told her, 'That's my coffin they're making.' Somehow he sensed it would be his. And it was.

"That was one of the things that interested J.B.—the strange phenomena happening to everyday people, and he wanted to know all about it and if it could be done at will."[3]

Rhine also had personal experience of the mysterious aspects of the mind. He saw no ghosts, heard no disembodied voices, and had no premonitions, but he was subject to talking and walking in his sleep. And when he was later told of this unconscious activity, it fueled his growing interest in the subject.

His first memorable sleepwalk happened when he was ten and living with his family above a New Jersey grocery store his father ran, having left Pennsylvania and given up teaching as too poorly paid. J.B. had bruised his hand, which became poisoned and developed into an abscess. The doctor lanced it too soon and had a hard task stopping the bleeding. That night J.B. fell into a restless sleep while his father served late customers in the store below. Suddenly J.B. appeared on the stairs that led to the store, startling the customers with his shouting. He hammered his hand repeatedly against his leg and called out: "A thousand mules couldn't pull that hand off!" It took Rhine's father a long time to wake him and then he "just cried and cried" from the atrocious pain, says brother Thomas.[4]

Thomas, two years younger than J.B., recalls the fun they had in those days: "A neighbor in Auburn, New Jersey, had a whole field of ripe pumpkins. At the edge of the field was a deep bank into a pasture field. We broke the pumpkins off, rolled them down, and watched them go down over the bank. Man, when they hit the bottom they'd bust and fly in all directions! But Dad had to pay for the pumpkins. We didn't get such a kick out of it when he'd got done with us."[5]

That New Jersey neighbor must have been relieved to see the Rhines move soon afterward, in 1907. Their next brief stop was a return to Pennsylvania. Here J.B. so endeared himself to his teacher that she was visibly upset when the Rhines prepared to move once more and J.B. came to say good-bye. Thomas looked on as J.B. told the teacher this would be his last day. "Tears were streaming down her face," Thomas remembers. "She said to J.B.: 'You're either going to be an awfully bad boy or an awfully good one.' And he said: 'I'm going to be a good one. I often thought of that.'"[6]

In their search for greener pastures the Rhine family moved sixteen times, often right in the middle of a school term, so that all the youngsters started school at a disadvantage. Rhine, anxious to do well because he aimed to go to college as his father had done, found his own way to make up for the disruptive moves. When they settled in the sleepy village of Marshallville, Ohio, in 1910, he got up in the dark and left for school before his brothers were awake. As soon as the school opened he began to work on his own and stayed after class, studying until the janitor came to lock the doors. "He finished four years of high school in three years," says his brother Paul. "He took six subjects rather than the normal four or five. Although languages weren't taught at that school, he persuaded some of the teachers to help him with French, German, and Spanish, after school hours."[7]

In Marshallville, Rhine's father rented a farm from their neighbor, whose nineteen-year-old daughter, Louisa Ella Weckesser, taught in the local elementary school. She told J.B. with pride that her grandfather, a German immigrant, had been shipwrecked on Sandy Hook, clung to a mast all night, and lived to write a poem about it.[8]

Although Louisa and J.B. were merely acquaintances for several years, she eventually realized that if anyone could match her grandfather in endurance and determination, it was Joseph Banks Rhine. His brothers never doubted it. "If he had a mind set to something you might as well try to dynamite it loose, because he wouldn't change," says Thomas.[9]

In one encounter with brother Paul, J.B. gave a hint of his iron will. Having no indoor plumbing involved long trips to the outhouse. Paul, age eight, was afraid of the dark and J.B., then seventeen, volunteered one night to go with him, holding a lantern to light the way. On the way back, Rhine suggested Paul should carry the lantern. He refused.

"It was pitch dark and I was afraid of the dark," Paul admits, "but I wouldn't carry it."

They stayed there for the better part of an hour. Paul began to get cold, gave in, and carried the lantern back. "I wasn't quite as stubborn as he was and he was bigger, of course. I had to give in. But I didn't hold it against him. After all, he had done me a favor."[10]

All the Rhines caught the measles in 1915, except the father, who'd had it as a child. Again J.B. became delirious and walked —even ran—in his sleep, as he had done a few years before when he had a poisoned hand.

"I slept in the same room as J.B.," says Thomas. "Suddenly he jumped out of bed. It was the first part of May and cold—and all he had on were his shorts. He was gone a good while and when he finally came back I asked: 'Where in the world were you?'

"He said: 'I went clear up to the railroad. [About a quarter of a mile away.] I was dreaming that it just couldn't be reached. I was going to reach it.'

"So he said: 'If I jump out of bed like that again, catch me.'

"In about forty-five minutes, out he went again. I went after him and got him at the head of the stairs. I shook him and hollered and yelled. That got my other brother up and he helped me. We finally got him awake."[11]

Another time, while Rhine still had the measles, "He got out of his bed in his sleep and dressed and went out," says Paul. "He went past Mother and me in the kitchen and out the door. She was busy cooking and when he went out she asked me, 'Wasn't that Banks?' I said 'Yes.' And she said, 'Well, he's not supposed to be out of bed. He isn't even awake.' And I had to run—he was trotting—I had to run like crazy to catch him about a half mile up the road. Then I grabbed him by the arm. And he said, 'Oh, what's the matter?' I said, 'You're supposed to be back in bed.' Then he turned around and went back with me."[12]

The attack of measles left Rhine, then nineteen, with no sense of smell or taste. He lost some hearing in one ear, and the sight of one eye was impaired, but neither prevented him from developing into a formidable fighter.

Moving so often, Rhine's younger brothers sometimes fell victim to school bullies on the hunt for new prey. "He taught me how to handle them," says Paul. "When I was eleven, I was older than the bully but he was such a terrifically strong kid and was always getting the best of me. And J.B. showed me how to punch and he said, 'Now you try it on me.' He tried to defend himself and I waded right in and got to his solar plexus.

"And J.B. said, 'If you ever land a blow like that on that kid he'll never ask for another one. That's the way to do it. All you have to

do is come right in on him like you did me there. You might take a
couple, but that's all you'll take. Because if you land one of those on
him, he's not going to fight anymore.'

"That's exactly what happened. I battled the kid one time and
I only hit him once and that was the end of it. He didn't want me to hit
him again. J.B. had figured out how to fight for himself. He did his
own thinking."[13]

To put himself through his first year at college, Rhine worked
for a farmer north of town from daylight to dark for twenty-five
dollars a month. The farmer was a slave driver, but Rhine's brothers
never heard J.B. complain. Although when the farmer offered him a
job for the following summer, Rhine said, "I won't promise." He didn't
go back.

He was unhappy with the religious instruction at the first
college he attended, and in 1916, hearing that Louisa, his schoolteacher neighbor, was continuing her education at the College of
Wooster, he joined her. "We studied there side by side in the library
and the field," Rhine wrote, "and sat together in laboratory and pew.
Like myself, she had always been interested in new worlds to explore,
and new roads to travel."[14]

As they became friends she found him to be a youngster of
integrity and strong principles. "He wasn't a cutup like many young
men at his age," says Louisa. "I discovered after he was around a little
that he was very thoughtful and in the loose sense, philosophical; not
one of the nonsensical young men you occasionally meet. He was
quiet and self-confident, not one of those kids in class that always had
his hand up. He wasn't a show-off. But he was interested in learning
and he stood out."[15]

He also stood out because he didn't smoke or drink, and still
thought he was going to be a preacher. He hungered for music,
especially classical music, and taught himself to play the accordion
and mouth organ.

Above all he was determined that his life should mean something. "We went for long walks through the woods," says Louisa,
"discussing what we were going to do with our lives."[16] During their
frequent discussions on religion and their philosophical perplexities
they became attached to each other, and it seemed inevitable that
they should marry.

Rhine found the department of religion at Wooster too closed-
minded. Halfway through the year of preministerial training in
December 1917, when he was twenty-two, he quit. "I was on the way
to a pretty strong agnosticism when I left," he said. He was also eager

to fight for his country—the United States was already at war in Europe.[17]

Although he was six feet and solid, he spent too much time over books to be muscular. He realized that with his damaged hearing and sight, joining the Army wouldn't be easy. But at least he was determined to look the part. So he worked in the freight house at Cincinnati, building up his muscles. Then he reported to the Army. But they found two unexpected reasons to reject him—color blindness and hammertoes.

He tried the Navy. They turned him down, too.

He went straight to the Marines. No, again.

"J.B. decided something had to be done," recalls Paul. "He knew he could get through somehow. So he worked on the colors. And then he reported again. Instead of picking out all the greens and all the reds as they told him to, he picked out one of each color on the chart, two that he was sure were red and green.

"He said, 'I just proved to you I can pick out the colors. So why pick out all of them?' And they accepted that.

"Then the Marine doctor told him, 'You're hammertoed. We can't take you in the Marines.'

"J.B. said, 'I'll go on a hike with you and I'll walk until you drop. If I can't do it—you don't have to take me in the service.' The doctor passed him."[18]

A man of Rhine's spirit—despite physical flaws—was obviously Marine material. And he quickly showed he could overcome the damage measles had done. Even with impaired sight, he became a sharpshooter. He never got to use his prowess in the shooting war, however, being permanently stationed in Santo Domingo. Rhine was proud to be a Marine and felt the spirit among the men to be almost tangible. There was one exception—a sergeant who repeatedly picked on him. "And then they had an argument," says Rhine's brother Paul. "The sergeant said he'd give him a chance to prove himself—'Come to the gym and put on the gloves.' "

J.B.'s buddies were eager to see their sergeant on his back, so they pushed Rhine into the fight, saying they'd make a ring and find a referee. All he had to do was flatten the sergeant. Rhine soon found that wasn't going to be easy. The sergeant was a tough, tenacious fighter who landed several heavy blows in the first round and already looked like a winner. Rhine's pals cheered him on, but he stopped hearing them in the fifth round. That's when the sergeant knocked him unconscious—but not off his feet.

Rhine had no memory of what happened after that, but his

pals told him he kept fighting for round after round, giving a magnificent performance, until—they lost count of the rounds—J.B. finally
knocked out the sergeant. And the sergeant didn't stay on his feet.[19]

The story sounds apocryphal—a dramatic demonstration of
Rhine's incredible will directing his unconscious mind. Thomas
Rhine is convinced it's true. To Rhine, of course, like sleepwalking, it
was evidence of the mind's mysterious powers.

Soon after the war, when Rhine returned to the United States
as a sergeant, he was persuaded to enter a sharpshooting contest. The
Newark *Evening News* of August 22, 1919, reported how he became a
national champion:

*Fresh from two years of "badman hunting" in and about Santo
Domingo, where his rifle has been his constant companion, Sgt.
Joseph B. Rhine, Marine Corps, landed this week at the U.S. Navy rifle
range at Caldwell, outshot 700 or more expert riflemen at the President's Match, his first time in national competition, and earned the
title Military Rifle Champion of the country. Sgt. Rhine scored 289 out
of a possible 300, was but a point better than that of 3 others, but a
point is a big margin after shooting three days for the trophy. The
match was a triumph of youth and endurance over experience and
skill. A dozen of the best shots on the range led Sgt. Rhine over the
first two stages of the contest, but the final 20 shots at 1,000 yards
were the test. More than one expert rifleman who had made 99 or 100
on the 200 and 500 yard firing line found the going too hard on the
long range and failed to shoot up to the mark.*

*The final battle was between Sgt. Rhine, 23 years old, and a 17-
year-old marvel from Washington, Edward M. Newcomb. The latter
was one point behind Rhine.*

*Rhine was five points lower than the high man at the opening
of the 1,000 yards stage yesterday. Appreciating that he had a possible
chance to win, he was on the range early and tried to be one of the
first to shoot, as he declared the morning conditions were better
suited to him than any others. He got his chance and made good,
scoring 95 out of 100 and making his aggregate score 289. His
record stood as high all day, only three other contestants nearing
him. Newcomb had been tied with him before the last leg but was
unable to make more than 94 at the 1,000 yards.*

Today, that report is framed and hangs in the Florida home of
Rhine's son, Robert.

J.B. brought home a gold medal and an autographed letter of
congratulations on his sharpshooting from President Woodrow

Wilson. Louisa Ella Weckesser had waited for Rhine, and they were married on April 8, 1920, when he was twenty-five and she was twenty-nine. After much discussion they decided to continue their graduate studies together at the University of Chicago to prepare for careers in botany or forestry, hoping to wrest from Nature some of her still-hidden secrets.

University of Chicago— Battles With the Behaviorists 1920–1925

A fierce intellectual battle was raging when the Rhines arrived at the University of Chicago campus in 1920: The lines were drawn between those who believed man has an "immortal soul" or an "unconquerable mind," and the behaviorists, as they called themselves, who saw man as a machine and nothing more. The fight had been on for several years, but now an experimental psychologist had brought new, devastating ammunition for what looked like a final attack. His name was John Broadus Watson and he claimed that man was a machine, a robot that could be controlled by his environment, whose "mind" was a myth, simply another part of his body and equally subject to decay and death.

Most educated people had accepted Darwin's theory, pointing to man's animal nature, but millions still clung to the belief that man was a higher animal with free will and a transcendental mind or spirit. Many believed, scientists among them, that the mind or spirit survived bodily death.

To Watson this was hogwash, and he declared that his experiments indicated what man really was—a machine. He spelled out his views based on his experiments in *Psychology From the Standpoint of a Behaviorist*, published in 1919. Watson's theory impressed his contemporaries, especially fellow psychologists, who rallied to his side and joined in the attack.

Like Rhine, Watson had briefly contemplated a career as a minister of religion. But his work as an experimental psychologist led him to proclaim not the truth of the Bible, but the antithesis. How did

Watson know man was a machine when he had experimented only with rats? Because, replied Watson, people are just complicated rats.

Darwin had suggested that we evolved "like the animals and that animals were emotionally and mentally like man." Watson went much further, concluding that "all behavior, human and animal, is analyzable in terms of stimulus and response, and the only difference between man and animal . . . [is] in the complexity of behavior." Watson downgraded thought as "implicit laryngeal activity"—in other words, physical action. And he rejected introspective study of states of consciousness as a waste of time. The mind will be worth studying, claimed Dr. Watson, only when it can be analyzed and described in physical terms.[1]

Watson's boyhood teachers in Greenville, South Carolina, were astonished to learn of his reputation as the leader of a new school of psychology. They knew him as "indolent, argumentative, impatient of discipline," and content barely to pass his studies. He was twice arrested for fighting and for firing a gun within the town limits. At the same age he had been a striking contrast to the serious, studious, persevering young Rhine. After Watson's plan to become a minister fizzled out, he toyed with the idea of practicing medicine, but couldn't afford the education.

Then came a remarkable change. He got an M.A. degree from Furman University and in 1900, when he was twenty-two, started on his career as a psychologist by studying neurology, psychology, and physiology at the University of Chicago, paying his way by working as an assistant janitor, lab porter, waiter, messenger boy, and "private nurse to a cageful of white rats."

The lazy, contentious boy was now, a few years later, considered brilliant and tenacious and the coming man in psychology. What stimulus had worked on Watson to transform him? That was always a mystery. After earning his Ph.D. in psychology in 1903, he stayed on as an assistant in experimental psychology and then as an instructor. Johns Hopkins persuaded him to join the staff as a professor of psychology in 1908, and it was in Baltimore that Watson conducted experiments with rats in a maze that were to make his name and help to found a new school—the Watson Behaviorists.[2]

The intellectual climate to which Rhine was exposed during his student years in Chicago from 1920 to 1923 was clearly in favor of Watson's view of a man, and generations of students were to be brought up on his teachings.

Inevitably there was a strong religious backlash. Scientists met one evening to promote Watson's behaviorism; ministers booked the same hall the next evening to voice their belief that man is an immortal spirit and the word of God as revealed in the Bible the only truth. It was exciting, a time of ferment, as the battle raged for men's minds. "The culture was ready for something besides the old-time religion," Rhine explained. "Various movements—phrenology, hypnotism, the Christian Scientists, the Mormons—were spreading all over the country."[3]

As a biology student in a post-Darwinian world and devoted to the scientific method, which he would never abandon, Rhine thought Watson was probably right. Probably, but not unequivocally. It was still conceivable that the behaviorists were wrong about the nature of man. Rhine hoped so, because he considered Watson's narrow view—though persuasive—uninspiring, even repugnant.

To refute Watson's claims, Rhine might have turned for support to ancient philosophers or more modern schools of psychology. Plato believed the mind ruled the body. The French philosopher René Descartes agreed with Plato that the mind and body were separate realities. And several contemporary schools of psychology—Gestalt, phenomenology, psychoanalysis, among others—considered the mind as separate from the body, though not necessarily immortal on that account. For a time, Rhine hoped that the attempts of Shailer Mathews —then dean of the divinity school at the University of Chicago—and other religious leaders to enlist science in the service of religion would give the transcendental view of man scientific credibility. But when Rhine realized the outcome was almost a new religion, with science a god to be worshiped, he lost interest. Rhine was not yet ready to commit himself to any view or school. He stood "midway between the orthodoxies of science and religion," unable to accept man as either a clever ape or an angel in disguise. He needed more evidence.[4]

Then the spiritualists joined the battle. The movement saw its heyday in the nineteenth century, but now it was enjoying a new lease on life. If behaviorists could be thought of as supporting the extreme right-wing view of humanity, spiritualists were the extreme left-wingers, regarding man as a spirit in a temporary home—his body—and capable of the miracles reported in the Bible, from walking on water (levitation) to returning after death to communicate with the living. Promising eternal life, spiritualism offered extraordinary comfort to those bereaved by the recent war or distressed and disillusioned by the teachings of Darwin and Watson. Moreover, the spiritualists said that one had only to attend a séance with a gifted medium to discover their claims to be true

Spiritualism was an international phenomenon, but "it went wilder in the United States than anywhere else," said Rhine, who was curious, but in no mood to be caught up in the frenzy.[5]

Sir Arthur Conan Doyle, the world leader and chief propagandist of the spiritualist movement, was a persuasive man with tongue and typewriter. Many believed that Sherlock Holmes, the fictional detective he had created, was a real man, because Conan Doyle had the gift to bring the imaginary to life. Now he took on a greater challenge, to convince doubters that the dead live.

Himself absolutely convinced that he had talked with the spirits of the dead, Conan Doyle arrived in Chicago in May 1922, during an American tour, to spread the spiritualist gospel and to raise funds for the movement. He was to lecture on "Proofs of Immortality" in Orchestra Hall. Rhine and his wife were among the audience. Rhine had many doubts, remembered his father's skepticism, and shared his attitude. Though ready to scoff at Conan Doyle's claims, he was also willing to hear him out.

A striking contrast to the spirits he was trying to substantiate, Conan Doyle had the physique and confident air of a heavyweight boxing champion. He explained to a packed hall how he had traveled the road from Catholicism to atheism, then back partway to agnosticism and, gradually—through personal experiences which he found overwhelming—to spiritualism. He described his qualifications for investigating spiritualism as those of a physician trained to the scientific point of view "and some slight knowledge of detective work." He denied that success in such investigations depended on emotionalism, though adding: "Cold, calculating scientific investigation will never get very far, because the personal element is lacking."

After naming the scientists of world repute who shared his beliefs, several of them Nobel prizewinners, Conan Doyle told of conversations with his dead son, Kingsley, and how at a sitting with American medium Ada Bessinet, his own dead mother appeared. "I swear by all that's holy on earth, I looked into her eyes," he told the now-spellbound audience.[6]

Rhine was disarmed but not convinced by Conan Doyle. The man was patently sincere and his beliefs appeared to have made him supremely happy. Yet his lecture had been closer to a revival meeting than a scientific demonstration. Perhaps it was unrealistic to fault him on those grounds; after all, Conan Doyle had announced that spiritualism was a new religion for the human race. When Rhine left the lecture, he had to admit that even if there was a glimmer of truth in the gospel according to Conan Doyle it was of "transcendental importance," and unscientific to ignore it.[7]

The meeting itself had little effect on Rhine's thinking, but something said there was to lead him in the direction to which he would be committed for the rest of his life. Conan Doyle had mentioned Sir Oliver Lodge as a friend and fellow spiritualist. Until now Rhine had known Lodge only as a great scientist. He had read of

Lodge's work while studying chemistry and physics, and knew that the Englishman's investigations involved lightning, electrolysis, electromagnetic waves, and wireless telegraphy. In 1900 Lodge had been appointed first principal of Britain's Birmingham University, and his honors included being president of the mathematical section of the British Association and president of the Physical Society at the turn of the century. Here indeed was a scientist of deserved repute. But no one in Rhine's chemistry and physics classes had ever mentioned that Lodge was also a leading spiritualist.

On Rhine's next trip to the university library he checked out Lodge's *The Survival of Man*, published in 1909—and it confirmed all Conan Doyle had said about him. Lodge had been convinced of survival after death through investigating a Boston medium, Leonore Piper, in 1889. No other medium before or since has faced more experienced investigators and been judged genuine. Later, during World War I, Lodge believed he made contact with his dead son, Raymond, this time through a British medium of unsullied reputation, Gladys Osborne Leonard.

"That book, *The Survival of Man*, by Lodge was to be very important to me," said Rhine. "In it, he mentioned Frederic Myers and told about the setting up of the Society for Psychical Research in England in 1882. I still have enormous respect for Lodge [some fifty years after reading the book], even though I don't follow everything or agree with everything he wrote. But after reading Lodge I was on a better level. Lodge was a master scientist and so were many others engaged in psychical research. I appreciated Frederic Myers in his way, but he was a little too emotional. It would be hard to find better people than Henry and Eleanor Sidgwick. And I think very highly of Edmund Gurney." All of these, Oliver Lodge included, were early and active members of the Society for Psychical Research.[8]

Lodge had dedicated his book *The Survival of Man* to "The Founders of the Society for Psychical Research: The Truest and Most Patient Workers in an Unpopular Region of Science That I Have Ever Known," and stated that

... the aim of the Society is to approach these various problems without prejudice or prepossession of any kind, and in the same spirit of exact and unimpassioned inquiry which has enabled Science to solve so many problems, once not less obscure nor less hotly debated. The founders of this Society fully recognize the exceptional difficulties which surround this branch of research; but they nevertheless hope that by patient and systematic effort some results of permanent value may be attained.[9]

After reading Lodge's book, Rhine discovered that bulletins of the Society for Psychical Research (SPR) were also in the university library, and he began to read of the most recent work—telepathy experiments and accounts of spontaneous telepathy and clairvoyance reported by the public. The informants were investigated and interviewed by SPR researchers who revealed themselves to be intelligent, well-informed, cautious, and persistent. In time, Rhine learned that these psychical researchers were among the leading thinkers in the country. Their work was a labor of love—most of them were unpaid. And it was obvious from their writings that they were neither religious fanatics, bereaved people still in shock, nor eccentrics trying to prove their eccentricities or hallucinations to be the way of this world and the next. In fact many spiritualists, Conan Doyle among them, attacked the SPR for its hard line. Rhine rejected Conan Doyle's permissive true-believer approach and approved of Lodge's proclaimed cold-blooded scientific scrutiny of facts—but even Lodge was not cold-blooded or scientific enough in psychical research for Rhine's full endorsement.

What cannot be emphasized too strongly is that although Conan Doyle and Lodge were spiritualists, Rhine never became one. Spiritualism involved a religious commitment and a faith. Rhine had neither. His investigations into what might be called a religious realm as well as the mysteries of the mind were scientific and not undertaken to confirm or sustain religious beliefs. His intent and his practice was to put everything to the test.

Rhine was now on the alert for anything that might lead to an understanding of man's nature. "It was in the sense of following a hope of discovering some illumination—just what, I did not know—that I turned eagerly toward this realm of mysterious happenings, real or imaginary," he explained.[10] But it wasn't only in the reports by psychical researchers that Rhine encountered mysteries.

One of his science professors surprised the class with an account of a vivid and detailed dream that had come true. When he was a youngster, he said, his family was awakened late one night by a neighbor who told them his wife had just had a terrifying dream in which her brother had fatally shot himself. The brother lived only nine miles away, but this was in the days before telephones, and his wife wanted to reassure herself that her brother was safe. Could the neighbor borrow a buggy to make sure? The professor's family said of course he could. When the neighbors arrived at the brother's home, they discovered that the nightmare was true in every detail. The brother had shot himself to death, the gun lay exactly where the sister had seen it in her clairvoyant dream. Other details exactly paralleled the dream. That tragic event of his childhood had made a deep impression on the science professor, a man with an international reputation. But he had never been able to explain it. What most surprised Rhine was that his professor had lived with the mystery for years but had not attempted to satisfy his own curiosity by at least making some investigation.[11]

"We could not explain the story either—but still we did not do anything about it," wrote Rhine. "I know now that the reason was that, after all, we did not fundamentally believe it. We did not know *how* we disbelieved it, since we did not doubt the professor's truthfulness. But one simply could not believe a story like that."[12]

Rhine, like his professor, couldn't forget it either. How did dreams that came true fit in with Watson's mechanistic man?

Watson the behaviorist was not troubled by such evidence. He could dismiss it as coincidence, faulty memory, or malobservation; he could give any number of plausible explanations. But he could not dismiss the view of his strongest opponent, a fellow psychologist, Dr. William McDougall, head of Harvard's psychology department. If Watson was the coming man in psychology, McDougall had already arrived. He espoused a "hormic" theory, which took a teleological or purposive view of life and mind, diametrically opposed to Watson's theory.[13]

Rhine came to consider McDougall as "unquestionably the leading champion of purposive psychology, which holds that the mind is not only an actual system, but that in its goal-seeking or striving character it causes people to behave as they do. . . . To behaviorists mind was a fiction."[14]

Not only Watson, but all of Rhine's University of Chicago teachers saw nothing in life but physical processes. "They were afraid of vitalists, who think life is more than a physical system, much as the psychologists were scared of dualists, who think the mind is more than brain physics," said Rhine.[15]

McDougall was a double threat: He was both vitalist and dualist.

Rhine said, "The logical thing was to take a serious look at the question. We did not begin with any preconceived beliefs, although we were rather leaning toward the mechanistic side in our own way of thinking. But nonetheless, it did not seem to account for everything."[16] While Lodge had put Rhine on the right track, McDougall was to become his guide and inspiration.

McDougall was forty-nine when he accepted the invitation to head the department of philosophy and psychology at Harvard in 1921. He made no secret of his extracurricular activity in psychical research.

Not unexpectedly, he met opposition and sometimes hostility

from the behaviorists—teachers and students—at Harvard. Fortunately, McDougall relished a fight, especially against odds. When he began to urge the study of psychical research as a university study, he expected the opposition would accuse him of trying to drag them back to the Dark Ages. He was not surprised.

The fact that behaviorism was almost an article of faith among many scientists only increased McDougall's suspicion that it was vulnerable, explaining that, "Whenever I have found a theory widely accepted in the scientific world, especially when it has acquired something of the nature of a popular dogma among scientists, I have found myself repelled into skepticism."[17]

McDougall, a heavyset man with a resonant voice, had an electric personality that could shock as well as illuminate. In profile he resembled a Roman emperor, and sometimes behaved like one, confident in his intelligence and with the poise of a man raised in a wealthy and cultured family. He had led a varied and adventurous career. The son of a Scottish chemical manufacturer, McDougall had been born in 1871 across the border in the English town of Chadderton, but rarely stayed put for long. At Cambridge University he earned a first-class degree in biology, then—heartbroken by his mother's death from cancer—he decided to be a doctor. He graduated as a physician from St. Thomas's Hospital in London, but before you could call him "doctor" he was back at Cambridge studying psychology—inspired by reading William James's *Principles of Psychology*, published a few years before in 1890.

He outdid his own reputation for doing the unexpected shortly after becoming a psychologist, by sailing to Borneo in 1899, when he was twenty-eight. There, at some risk, he gave mental tests to headhunters. He kept his head and returned to lecture, not at Cambridge, but at Oxford. Students crowded into his lectures to watch him demonstrate hypnosis—a novelty at the turn of the century. Some colleagues damned his displays of hypnosis as "unprofessional," and the religious fraternity branded them as works of the devil.

World War I gave him a chance to face even tougher opposition. After joining the French Army as an ambulance driver, he was drafted into the Royal Army Medical Corps as commander of a British shell-shock unit. There he demonstrated compassion and understanding. His great interest in the mysteries of the mind and the discoveries of the early hypnotists and psychoanalysts (he had been psychoanalyzed by his friend Carl Jung) had led to his interest in psychic research as early as 1901, when he joined the Society for Psychical Research. He became its president in 1920. A year later he accepted what he proudly and debatably called "the premier post in America," as chairman of Harvard's psychology department.[18]

As a recognized authority on hypnosis, he had contributed an article on the subject for the 1910 (eleventh) edition of the *Encyclopaedia Brittanica*. His 1909 *An Introduction to Social Psychology* had become a standard textbook destined to go through more than twenty editions. He was a prolific writer: In 1912 alone, the year he was elected Fellow of the Royal Society, he published *Psychology* and *Body and Mind*.

Rhine read *Body and Mind* ten years later. He already knew of McDougall as the most effective of Watson's opponents—and now he could understand why. McDougall was obviously a highly intelligent man of wide experience and original ideas. In *Body and Mind*, McDougall suggested that psychical research played a key role in attempting to understand man's nature. He also made a case for the mind being separate from the body, implying that survival of the mind after death was at least conceivable. These were daring suggestions. For the first time Rhine began to consider seriously what was to become his life's work. "It was with the definite purpose of undertaking investigation into possible unknown capacities of the mind, the so-called psychic powers, that I first got in touch with Professor McDougall," explained Rhine, who wrote to McDougall at Harvard in 1922, enthusiastically praising the book and expressing a keen interest in psychic research.

McDougall responded with an encouraging letter. After that, writes Rhine of himself and his wife, Louisa,

... our imaginations were caught up by the possibilities of useful work in the borderline science of psychic research. ... Dissatisfied with the orthodox religious belief which had at one time impelled me toward the ministry and dissatisfied, except as a last resort, with a materialistic philosophy, I was obviously ready to investigate any challenging fact that might hold possibilities of new insight into human personality and its relation to the universe.[19]

Rhine was prepared to abandon his studies in plant chemistry and switch to psychical research if he could obtain a job or scholarship to support himself while doing so. With this in mind he wrote to three men on June 27, 1923, asking for their help and advice.

His first letter went to the president of the ASPR in New York. He replied that workers with Rhine's educational background were needed, but he could not offer him any financial support. Rhine's second letter was to Dr. William McDougall, who replied that the only available fellowship for psychical research at Harvard was already held by Gardner Murphy. Although McDougall believed there was some money for psychical research at Stanford University, he did not think it was available. Rhine received an even more discouraging reply from Professor Joseph Jastrow of the psychology department at the University of Wisconsin. Jastrow characterized psychical research as "largely concerned with the elucidation of error, partly with the explanation of obscure phenomena," and added that "positions are few and often the critical attitude is the very obstacle."[20]

Those three replies made Rhine "fully aware that psychic research offered no monetary return. The fact that it was an unpopular field was very clear, and even Dr. Jastrow's emphasis on the critical attitude with which it was often met could have been a deterrent. All that, however, did not count against the importance of the topic for humanity as well as for himself," recalled Dr. Louisa Rhine. "As in the past, he assumed that such considerations as the financial would take care of themselves incidentally, once the major objective was undertaken."[21]

After Rhine left the University of Chicago in 1923 to work for a year as an instructor in plant physiology at the Boyce Thompson Institute for Plant Research in Yonkers, New York, he continued to study for his Ph.D. degree. Then he moved to Morgantown to teach plant physiology at West Virginia University. Louisa joined the staff, too, teaching Latin. She had been awarded her Ph.D. by the University of Chicago in 1923. Rhine got his doctorate from the same University in 1925. He had missed three years of study by being in the Marines, but made up one year in Chicago.

Psychic research still engrossed Rhine, and while he worked in West Virginia he began a frequent and fateful correspondence with J. Malcolm Bird. This enigmatic research officer for the American Society for Psychical Research was already embroiled—and would involve Rhine—in one of the strangest and most puzzling mediumistic performances in the history of psychic research.

3

LESSONS
IN DECEPTION
1925–1926

If Rhine had not yet committed himself to psychic research, he was on the brink. He knew that it might prove a dead end, and was reminded that great scientists had been ridiculed by their colleagues for dabbling, as the skeptics saw it, in this half brother to alchemy, witchcraft, and fortune-telling. There was a lot to ridicule. The antics of many "mediums" and not a few researchers were the stuff of comedy, if not farce. Some of the brightest men involved in psychic research revealed incredible blind spots. Nobel-prizewinning physiologist Charles Richet had mistaken a woman spitting out chewed paper for a miracle; Arthur Conan Doyle was duped so often by phony mediums that he seemed congenitally unable to face the fact of deception. An account of the deceivers and their dupes could fill a thick book.

But there were singular exceptions. Most of the founders of the Society for Psychical Research were more than a match for frauds, conjurers, or hysterics who claimed to be mediums.

Rhine studied the reports of the pioneer psychical researchers and was particularly impressed by the work of Eleanor Sidgwick. Together with Oliver Lodge and the American psychologist William James, she had taken a leading role in testing perhaps the most famous mental medium of all time, Boston's Leonore Piper. Working with her husband, Henry Sidgwick, professor of philosophy at Trinity College, Cambridge, and a founder and first president of the SPR; her brother A. J. Balfour, Britain's prime minister from 1902 to 1905; and Nobel-prizewinning physicist Lord Rayleigh, Mrs. Sidgwick had built up a reputation as a detached and objective expert on all phases of psychic research.

It was that resourceful group, centered around Cambridge's

Trinity College at the end of the nineteenth century and well into the twentieth, which helped to map the strange new territory dotted with dazzling possibilities, as well as booby traps. It is virtually certain that even they fell into some traps, but they never claimed infallibility nor minimized the dangers.

Rhine admitted his great debt to these pioneers:

We were far from being the first investigators to attack the problem of whether or not extrasensory perception is a fact. An enormous amount of work was available for preliminary inspection, work that was of value in suggesting points of attack and methods of operation and, in a negative way, in warning us of the pitfalls into which some of the researchers prior to our own had fallen.[1]

Knowing to some extent what he was up against, Rhine took every opportunity to learn the ropes. Encouraged by Professor McDougall's assurance that psychic research was a valid scientific pursuit, Rhine corresponded with the research officer of the American Society for Psychical Research in New York City, James Malcolm Bird, a tall, skinny man with an unusually long neck and a dry, offbeat sense of humor.

Bird had taught mathematics at Cooper Union and Columbia. Between 1920 and 1921 he had been associate editor of *Scientific American*, then a popular science journal, and secretary of the committee that judged the journal's essay contest on Einstein's theory of relativity and gravitation. He reviewed books on psychic research for the journal, and this led to his escalating interest in the subject that took him to séance rooms in the United States and Europe. He met Sir Arthur Conan Doyle on a transatlantic crossing on the liner *Olympic* during the spring of 1923, and the world's leading spiritualist praised Bird as "rapidly acquiring so much actual psychic experience that if he should criticize our movement he is a critic whom we will be obliged to listen to with respect."[2]

Spiritualists, it must be remembered, believed in the independent mind or spirit of man and in its survival after death; psychical researchers were generally—while using varying degrees of scientific rigor—not yet convinced. To complicate matters, some spiritualists worked as psychical researchers to confirm their beliefs and in the hope of converting unbelievers.

What category Bird fits into is something of a mystery. In 1925, as research officer of the ASPR, he was an encouraging correspondent. Rhine explained that he had a working knowledge of German, Spanish, and scientific French, and Bird accepted his offer to read foreign journals and translate any interesting articles on psychic matters. In exchange, Bird gave Rhine free membership in the ASPR. With the ten dollars saved, Rhine bought books, including the two-volume classic by Frederic Myers, *Human Personality and Its Survival of Bodily Death*, published posthumously in 1903.

But the thirty-year-old Rhine was not content to study the subject secondhand. He heard that a Dr. Zimmerman who lived nearby claimed to have remarkable psychic powers. Rhine took Louisa with him and introduced himself as a student of such abilities. They were invited to see for themselves. What Rhine and Louisa saw was a small table that rocked when Dr. Zimmerman rested his fingers on it. Then he scribbled some writing that he declared was directed by an unseen power. After the demonstrations, Dr. Zimmerman told Rhine that a Reverend Goddard in La Grange, Illinois, was able to bring back the spirits of the dead so that they could be seen in apparently solid form—what mediums called materializations.

Rhine walked away from his first investigation not entirely disappointed. He judged Dr. Zimmerman to be a fake who probably hoped to make money from his shaking table and shaky writing. But Rhine welcomed the experience: He had to learn to spot deception. And he wrote to Bird: "I think it has been profitable for us to get the experience with Z. He is a type I needed to meet."[3]

He hoped to investigate the Reverend Goddard sometime, but never got the chance. Instead he tested a medical doctor who lived nearby in Morgantown, West Virginia—a Dr. Stonestreet, who called himself a medium. If anything, this man was less impressive than Zimmerman, and in his letter to Bird, Rhine called the self-styled medium "a bluff," concluding: "The puzzle consists in how he can kid himself and his intimates. 'Dr.' certainly does not carry much weight in these circles, since I have had my experiences with *Dr.* Zimmerman and *Dr.* Stonestreet."[4]

Meanwhile Bird kept Rhine on tiptoe with interest in Mina Crandon, the Canadian-born wife of a socially prominent Boston surgeon, Dr. Le Roi Goddard Crandon. He was a onetime instructor of surgery at Harvard, noted for a surgical stitch he had invented. Through the spring of 1926, Bird gave Rhine a blow-by-blow account of the extraordinary—a euphemism if there ever was one—woman, now internationally famous through her astonishing and apparently limitless psychic powers.

Mina Crandon, given the pseudonym of Margery to protect her identity, a futile effort, was and still is an enigma. There is no consensus even of what she looked like, though she was photographed as often as a movie star and in much more intimate detail.

There is almost complete agreement that she was charming,

vivacious, and seductive. Margery (her name from now on), the fair-haired, blue-eyed mother of a son by a previous marriage, had been encouraged to develop psychic powers by Crandon, her second husband, after he attended a lecture by Sir Oliver Lodge. Crandon persuaded Margery to join hands with a few friends as they sat around a small table. After a few abortive attempts, the table trembled. By a process of elimination, Margery was pinpointed as the cause of the tremble. From then on, it was said, her powers proliferated—dozens of "spirits" spoke through her, until eventually a husky voice identified itself as her own dead brother, Walter Stinson. He had been crushed to death in a freak railroad accident. Walter announced himself as the spirit in charge, and from then on his was the voice to contend with as he badgered, bullied, and blasphemed before some of the greatest names of the day (as well as lawyers, clergymen, physicians, and Harvard professors), who came to Margery's séances.

Sir Arthur Conan Doyle heard of her through the psychic grapevine and advised Malcolm Bird to check her out. Bird, then associate editor of the *Scientific American*, was on the lookout for psychics who would contend for the prize money his magazine offered—$2,500 for a genuine psychic photograph, $2,500 for "a visible psychic manifestation."

To judge the claimants, a committee of experts was chosen ranging from those familiar with the tricks of the mind, to the world's foremost illusionist, escape artist, and bête noire of fake mediums, Harry Houdini. The other members were Professor William McDougall; Hereward Carrington, a British-born psychic researcher; Dr. Daniel Frost Comstock, a former member of the physics department at M.I.T.; and the chairman, Dr. Walter Franklin Prince, who was then chief research officer of the American Society for Psychical Research. Bird became secretary of this committee.

Margery had a fiercely loyal body of supporters, including the most influential members of the ASPR, to attest to her ability not only to bring her dead brother Walter back to life as a disembodied voice with a wild sense of fun, but to produce or "give birth" to his forearm from the direction of her vagina. There are photographs to illustrate this incredible event. The primitive arm with hand attached obligingly cooperated in an attempt to prove its identity. It left thumbprints in soft wax for experts to study and compare with a faint print found on Walter's razor after his death—too smudged, unfortunately, for positive identification.

According to witnesses, forty-four disembodied spirit voices spoke through Margery. Her brother Walter—the liveliest spirit of them all—played music, rang bells, stopped clocks, and threw objects around the room while Margery was restrained by wires in a cabinet that resembled a phone kiosk; an arrangement organized by Dr. Crandon to demonstrate that Margery could not be responsible for the activities, because they all took place beyond her reach. And while these physical effects were happening, said witnesses, Walter kept up a raucous running commentary, showed a quick wit and a penchant for profanity.

Walter's picture of the next world was certainly more inviting than the bright lights, hymns, and harp Muzak of common expectation. At least he seemed to be having fun there. Asked by a group of clergymen what hell was like—they seemed to assume he was there—Walter quipped, it's "now completely up to date: We burn oil." And when a preacher asked him if he felt nearer to Jesus, Walter replied, "I feel his influence more." Then he commented on the question: "That was quite intelligent for a minister, wasn't it? Usually they ask if I have afternoon tea with him."[5]

Before Rhine heard of Margery through Bird's enthusiastic letters, she had been investigated for more than two years by one group or another. The *Scientific American* committee, after witnessing Margery in her own home dozens of times, could not agree about her.

Malcolm Bird remained one of her most ardent and energetic supporters. In fact, he had been dismissed from his editorial job at the *Scientific American* and from his position as secretary of the investigating committee because his ardor compromised his impartiality.

Bounced by the *Scientific American*, Bird landed on his feet. The leaders of the ASPR, at that time more spiritualists than psychic researchers, were as enthusiastic as Bird about Margery. Bird accepted their offer to him to share the job of Dr. Walter Franklin Prince, the society research officer. Infuriated, Prince resigned and helped to form an independent, new Boston Society for Psychic Research. Professor McDougall followed. They both thought the ASPR was going to the dogs, as it was now overwhelmingly in support of Margery's mediumship and packed with people of a credulous and religious, rather than a scientific, bent.

Rhine, languishing in the backwaters of West Virginia, was fed his information by Bird, and the message was that Margery was a wonder woman. Bird characterized McDougall and Prince as unscrupulous men who were slandering the Boston charmer. Prince, he implied, was bitter and biased because Bird had taken his job. Why would the great McDougall slander Margery Crandon, Rhine wondered? But not for long. "McDougall credits Dr. and Mrs. Crandon with a deep-laid scheme to show the gullibility of scientists in the presence of alleged psychic phenomena," Bird confided in a letter of April 13, 1926. "After they have carried on for a few years and fooled everybody they can fool [according to McDougall's theory], the idea is that they [the Crandons] will expose themselves and 'blow the lid off of scientific psychic phenomena.' "

Bird ended his letter to Rhine by assuring him that McDougall's suspicions were ridiculous. "To you who have not met them [the Crandons] this probably does not sound quite so silly as it does to me who have."

Rhine was eager to find out for himself. He had read psychic literature extensively and had come across no one to match Margery's apparent ability.

His colleagues at the University of West Virginia predicted Rhine would become a successful botanist, but he was sure they were wrong. His heart wasn't in his work. He began to make plans for a new career.

He told Louisa what he wanted to do—to go to Harvard and study psychology and philosophy under McDougall. Rhine concluded that psychology was the most useful discipline from which to approach psychic research, and with McDougall as his teacher he would have the added benefit of the great man's advice. And while in Boston, Rhine could investigate Margery.[6]

Bird was enthusiastic when Rhine told him of his intentions, especially because he hoped to place Rhine as a spy in the enemy camp. He suggested that Rhine cultivate McDougall and Prince, in the guise of an innocent seeker after truth, encourage them to talk freely—and then report back.

That was a tough request. Rhine had great respect for McDougall, who more than anyone had encouraged him to become a psychic researcher. Now he was being asked to deceive the man, head of Harvard's psychology department, in the interests of science.

"I think you will agree with me that any suggestions of underhandedness in these proposals is a mere matter of fighting fire with fire," Bird tried to reassure Rhine in a June 2, 1926, letter. "If they are going to conduct a whispering campaign against Margery, we have got to adopt whispering detective methods to find out just what they are doing."

Rhine displayed a mixture of caution and cooperation when he replied to Bird's spy-for-me letter a few days later: "Whatever happens you may depend upon our service except in such rare cases as it would not be decent to 'blab.' I think I may be able to help in this case; that is, I am hoping that I shall be able to keep my skirts free."

Late in June Rhine quit his job at the University of West Virginia and with Louisa left for Massachusetts.

MARGERY
THE ENIGMA
1926

Malcolm Bird had been as good as his word. "Whenever you're in Boston," he had told the Rhines, "I'll arrange a sitting with Margery." It was all set for July 1, 1926. The Crandons had invited them to dinner before the séance, which would give Rhine a brief opportunity to get to know the couple before they went up to the darkened séance room and Margery entered the trance state. If she was as gifted as Bird said, then Rhine and Louisa were in for a singular experience.

So it was in a mood of high expectation that the Rhines arrived at 10 Lime Street, the Crandons' home in Boston's fashionable Beacon Hill district. The house gave directly on to the sidewalk. Rhine knocked and waited: The man who was to become the world's leading psychical researcher was about to meet the world's most spectacular and controversial psychic.

A Japanese butler opened the door and moments later Margery appeared, smiling a greeting. She struck Rhine immediately as "a beautiful and seductive woman."[1] There was a gleam in her blue eyes and a natural vivacity in her manner. Rhine sensed nothing uncanny or mysterious about her.[2]

The six other guests were mostly members of the American Society for Psychical Research (ASPR). Margery treated them affectionately like old friends. Dr. Crandon, somewhat dour and introspective at first, soon thawed into a genial, articulate host, leading the lively and good-humored dinner conversation. He had the assured, take-charge manner one might expect of a former successful surgeon. He now worked as a doctor for an insurance company. Crandon's appearance was unexceptional. He dressed conservatively, had crew-cut hair, rimless glasses, and a modest mustache. He had been twice married and twice divorced before marrying Margery. His father was one of the founders of the Ethical Culture movement, and Crandon had been raised in an affluent home where controversial ideas were welcomed and discussed.

For the Rhines' benefit, Crandon told how Margery's brother would return from the dead that night and make his presence known, not only by talking, laughing, and whistling, but through performing various feats. He would demonstrate that he was not a hypnotic impersonation or a secondary personality, but a distinct and separate spirit. Crandon laughed when he recalled Margery's critics, who had accused her of being a magician, electrician, radio-sharp, ventriloquist, and even a concealer of a trained serpent. Tonight, he said, the sitters must judge for themselves.

Margery described her early life on a small farm in Ontario, Canada. Her brother, Walter Stinson, had worked on the railroad and was killed some years ago after being crushed between an engine and tender. When Margery left Canada, she had worked in Boston as a church secretary. She had been married once before, and her son, John, by that marriage now lived with her. His bedroom, in fact, was directly under the fourth-floor séance room. But there was no need to worry on the boy's behalf, she said—he was used to the noises he heard overhead.

Crandon explained that Margery would not attempt to repeat her peak performance when she had been photographed "giving birth" to Walter's hand, a hand that moved as if living, and left prints in wax. But he promised the sitters a night to remember.

He emphasized that for much of the séance, Margery would be tied up with picture wire to restrict her movements in such a way that it would be obvious she could not be responsible for the subsequent physical activity.

Rhine was impatient for the séance to begin. He was hardly conscious of what he ate or drank anyway—since his bout with measles he could barely taste anything that wasn't burnt, or showered with salt or sugar. And now he was eager to see Margery the medium, and not Margery the smiling hostess. Rhine was more than ready to climb the stairs when Crandon led the way to the heavily curtained fourth-floor room reserved solely for séances.

It was bare except for a circle of chairs, what looked like a portable phone kiosk, a table holding a chemical balance, an upright glass U-tube, and a few objects in a basket. There was also a megaphone (through which Walter was expected to speak).

Margery had gone ahead to change in an adjoining room, where two of the women among the group searched her. But that didn't take long. When she joined the others in the séance room, the searchers announced that she was wearing only a dressing gown, underclothes, and slippers. They had found no hidden objects.

Margery then took her place, sitting in the glass-paneled, plywood cabinet, facing the open side. Her chair was attached to the floor by screws. Crandon tied picture wire around her wrists and ankles, threaded the wire through holes in the wooden sides of the cabinet, and secured the loose ends to tie bolts outside the cabinet. Finally he circled her neck with a leather collar attached by wire to the back of the cabinet. Rhine accepted his invitation to check that Margery was securely tied. She was.

Moments after Crandon doused the lights, Margery began to take slow, labored breaths. The sound, common in trance mediums, has been compared with the tide on a quiet night. It also has a macabre, nightmare quality. There was a long silence of at least a minute, as if Margery had fainted. Then out of the silence came a husky voice. It was Walter, said the voice, back from the dead.

Walter was cocky and confident. He whistled and wise-cracked and answered straight questions in a flip, irreverent way. He sometimes sounded like a child trying to shock, especially when he recited the Lord's Prayer in German—followed by "Go to hell!" in English.

One of Walter's tasks, announced by Dr. Crandon, was to make the heavier of two pans in a chemical balance—the one with weight on it—rise, and the pan with no weight on it drop. Crandon revealed that this "miracle" had occurred by briefly shining his flashlight. Walter also rang a bell enclosed in a box and apparently out of reach of anyone in the room, levitated a basket which had a luminous band around it so that all the sitters saw it mysteriously rise and hover overhead. And he kept up a running, risqué commentary.

Louisa Rhine, several feet away from Margery, listened to the manly voice in the darkness. Everything seemed to be happening just as Dr. Crandon had predicted during dinner. J.B. sat next to Margery, so he could see and hear more of the action.

Dr. Crandon introduced a simple but ingenious piece of equipment constructed to demonstrate to skeptics that Margery was not masquerading as her dead brother's spirit, that she did not use her own disguised voice to sound like him. The equipment when engaged required Margery to use simultaneously her upper and lower lips and her tongue. While she was thus preoccupied in maintaining the position of two luminous corks floating on columns of water, one in each arm of a glass U-tube, Walter would whistle tunes on request or keep up virtually nonstop chatter. Dr. Crandon pointed out to his attentive audience that Walter took particular pride in the precise pronunciation of difficult words. The implication was obvious: If Margery moved her lips or tongue to imitate Walter's voice, then the luminous corks would visibly change positions.[3]

So, Dr. Crandon explained, if Walter continued to talk and whistle in the darkness while the luminous floats—plainly visible to all the sitters—remained steady at different levels, it would demonstrate that Walter's and Margery's voices were independent.

He then released Margery's head from the restraining leather collar to allow her to lean forward to blow into what he called the voice-cut-out machine. He shone his flashlight to show this had been done, then switched it off.

The luminous floats stayed about twenty inches apart while Walter whistled and chattered. After about two minutes Crandon turned on the room's electric light, which suddenly dazzled the visitors, some of whom conceded that he had proved his point. Rhine was not among those who effusively congratulated Margery and thanked Walter for his wonderful work.

Nor was Louisa. She watched Rhine glance at the voice-cut-out machine, then at the chemical balance. Dr. Crandon seemed upset by that, and moments later J.B. made an excuse for having to leave in a hurry. Louisa was puzzled about their quick exit until they were out in the street and the front door closed behind them. Then J.B. explained why he had not stayed to talk or try to arrange for another sitting. Obviously angry and disappointed, he said that the whole séance was a fraud from start to "triumphant" finish. Louisa was bewildered. She had observed nothing to make her suspect the Crandons. She admitted that being some distance from Margery, she might have missed a great deal. Rhine agreed that he had been in the best position to know what was really going on, because he sat next to Margery, with Dr. Crandon on her other side. Having read extensively in the psychic research literature how fake mediums deceive, he had been specially on the alert. And when he explained in detail what he had seen and heard, Louisa, too, was convinced that he was right; the evening had been a sham.[4]

Now Rhine realized why Dr. McDougall and Dr. Prince had broken away from the ASPR, based in New York City, to form a rival research organization in Boston. Their "slandering" of Margery, as Bird characterized it, was nothing but telling the truth.

Almost from the moment he had stepped into the séance room, Rhine had been suspicious. The atmosphere was wildly inappropriate. If the Crandons really believed they were in contact with a spirit entity—and a brother, at that—Rhine would have expected them to treat Walter's appearance seriously, even with reverence. Instead, the Crandons behaved as if they were hosts of a bizarre party game thought up by a conjurer with a twisted mind.

The most damning piece of evidence, detailed by Rhine in his subsequent report, "One Evening's Observation on the Margery

Mediumship," was this: There was a megaphone which Walter was supposed to use to project his voice. Rhine saw the silhouette of Margery's foot clearly visible against a luminous plaque, "kicking the megaphone over within reach of her hand." Margery had insisted on a play of up to four inches in the picture wire "for comfort," that allowed her to move her hands inside the cabinet and, with her slender wrists, work the wire farther up her arm to give her enough play to fake some of the physical phenomena. All objects used were placed within reach of her right hand when it was inside the cabinet; Rhine noticed Margery was right-handed. When objects fell to the floor at her feet, but out of reach of her hands, she had to have them picked up by a sitter. Yet Walter was supposed to be handling the objects with his "teleplasmic terminal" or "psychic energy."

Rhine also observed that Crandon had freed Margery's hands from the wire restraint before the bell rang in a box and also before the heavier pan of the chemical balance was raised. Why did she need free hands if Walter was doing the ringing and lifting?

Dr. Crandon insisted that he had to sit next to Margery for her protection, "and to add his power to hers." It seemed clear to Rhine that this "protection" and "power" was a cover used by the Crandons to deceive.

After the séance Rhine had noticed that the chemical balance Walter had purported to raise supernaturally had a small set screw which turned easily with the fingernail. Crandon had discouraged any further inspection with a brusque comment that Rhine might damage it.

As for the voice-cut-out device, Rhine had surreptitiously inspected it and found that the "glass mouthpiece was easily removed from the rubber tubing." So it would have been possible for Margery under cover of darkness to "hold her thumb over the end of the tubing. . . . Also we do not know that there is not a place where the tubing can be bent back sharply and so closed effectively."

The basket fell to the floor when Rhine had asked Walter to chatter while holding it aloft. This indicated to Rhine that Margery had been gripping the handle of the basket in her teeth, and had lifted it by throwing her head back. Rhine believed she lost her grip and dropped the basket when—as the secret voice of Walter—she tried to speak.

Rhine also noted that all Walter's tricks had been done in the dark. Crandon shone his flashlight only when the trick was a *fait accompli*—never during the action.

With the exception of his seeing the shadow of Margery's foot kick the megaphone, all Rhine's observations might be explained away individually. But taken together, they created a convincing picture of fraud.

That night Rhine wrote up the main points in what he developed into a detailed and damning report entitled "One Evening's Observation on the Margery Mediumship."[5] After more than two weeks, Rhine's anger had not abated. On July 16 he sent off a blistering letter to Bird, remarking that a man would have had to be blind to avoid seeing fraud. I quote this letter at some length to give a flavor of his style and thinking. It also covers most of the material in Rhine's report.

We were disgusted to find that at the bottom of all this controversy and investigation lay such a simple system of trickery as we witnessed at the séance. We are amateurs, and we do not possess any skill or training in trickery, and we were looking for true psychic productions, but in spite of our greenness and our deep interest, we could not help but see the falseness of it all.

Rhine would not even concede that Margery *might* occasionally produce genuine phenomena because

... the whole atmosphere was bad. Crandon engineered the play, seldom giving "Walter" a chance to appear to be in charge; he did not behave as a man would who knew he could communicate with his wife's brother, or anyone; he broke the rules he made himself. ... I cannot think intelligent people like the Crandons would have allowed a true mediumship to have degenerated into the wholesale fraud we were witness to.

Having seen Margery faking the phenomena on his first visit, Rhine could not understand how the ASPR was still taking her seriously.

"My interest in the advancement of the science leads me to regret deeply the part which the Society played in this," he continued in his letter to Bird.

There is no doubt in my mind that you are nearly if not entirely disillusioned on this case. You must *be! I do not understand why you did not discuss it frankly with me in West Virginia. I do not understand how it will be for your ultimate good, to say nothing of your conscience, to cater to the absurd defense, whatever the impelling factors may be. Surely you will go down with the case sometime if you continue. As for my part I am done with it. I do not wish my name to even appear in the* Journal *again until it shows a change of attitude on this dirty business, nor shall I want any connections whatever with the Society if it is to be only a cloak for a rogue. I feel sure too that you will really not blame me in this.*

Now, Mr. Bird, you may not like the frankness of this letter but you will have to grant that it is "on the square"; I question strongly whether your representations of the Margery case to me can properly be described as either frank or "square." I should not be here in Boston if they had been. But that is a small matter perhaps and I am more interested at the present in seeing if there is any hope of getting the Society to save itself from the greatest scandal in the whole history of mediumship.

Rhine sent a similar letter to the ASPR's board of trustees on July 15, 1926, expressing his disappointment:

I resigned my position at West Virginia University, pretty largely on the strength of my interest in Psychical Research, in order to change to Abnormal Psychology and Philosophy.
I came here hoping to study this case because of the stand the ASPR had taken on it. And so when I found this poor bunch of tricks at the back of all these investigations and publications, it was a tremendous jolt. . . . Ordinarily one evening's fraudulent performance does not entirely disprove a mediumship, that is true, but the Crandons unwittingly exposed themselves to us in their general conversation. . . . What has your own committee found? Why do you not publish their report? I understand it too, like that of all the other investigating bodies, is negative. Surely, the Journal has not degenerated into a Crandon publication. . . . I have no other interest than the truth that we are all presumably after.

The counterattack came soon afterward from Daniel Day Walton, a ranking member of the ASPR. He had attended the same Margery sitting as the Rhines, as an "official observer," and saw only miracles. Rhine replied in a friendly and patient style on August 5, 1926:

I cannot take the fine fatherly manner in which you have written me much amiss. I have a pleasant recollection of our meeting at the N.Y. Section [of the ASPR] back in 1924 which the letter I received did nothing to obliterate. . . .

Rhine admitted to Walton that he had learned his lesson: never to investigate a case without first looking at both sides, positive and negative. He had entered the Margery séance room in a rosy glow from Bird's propaganda. And Rhine refuted Walton's point that he [Rhine] was mistaken because none of the other experienced sitters had seen Margery do anything fraudulent.
Rhine continued in his letter of August 5,

Good Lord! Mr. Walton, thousands saw nothing wrong with Henry Slade to ONE who did. [Slade was a phony psychic who pretended that spirits wrote messages in chalk on the inside surfaces of slates he held together.] He deceived experienced investigators for years until he was caught faking it. Was the one wrong because the thousands failed to see? Of course not. Numbers of years of investigation mean nothing, unless they have developed powers of critical observation and judgment.

I believe Bird and DeWyckoff are emotionally involved with this woman to such an extent that their word on anything Crandon does is utterly unreliable. Others may be too. I sincerely hope, Mr. Walton, that you are not one of the considerable number who have allowed their affections for this lovely woman to charm them into blindness toward her deceptions.

I do not wish to rob you of your beliefs, your personal faith in anybody or anything, but Mr. Walton, as a member of the Board that controls a Journal which hundreds depend upon for the truth about these things, you ought certainly to go over this case most critically.

J.B. was most disillusioned with the ASPR for degenerating from an organization devoted to open-minded research to a fan club for a fraud. The ASPR could hardly dispute Rhine's most damning evidence—after all, he was there. But instead, a representative of their board of trustees launched a broadside at Rhine himself, attacking a minor piece of his suggestive evidence. "Your whole procedure in this matter is unscientific and superficial," wrote T. H. Pierson on October 8.

Many men, having great experience in psychic matters and having attended numbers of sittings, are unable to declare the Margery mediumship fraudulent. Do you think that you are competent, with the slight experience that you admit that you have had, to definitely determine in one sitting the Margery mediumship to be fraudulent, when you base your judgment on such unscientific explanation as "by some fixture attached, probably"? [Rhine's explanation for the "paranormal" movement of the chemical scales.]

Pierson ignored the fact that Rhine had seen Margery cheating.

Do you really believe that, if the Society does not take "this opportunity [publication of Rhine's report] to repudiate the Crandons it will be a certain indication that you are lost as a scientific Society?" I doubt if I have ever known such monumental conceit in my life.

Rhine never met Bird or Margery again and, until it was reorganized in 1941 and returned to a scientific approach, had nothing more to do with the ASPR.

But attacks on Rhine by Margery supporters had not ended. When Sir Arthur Conan Doyle read Rhine's exposé he responded like an enraged father. Too far away to challenge Rhine to a duel, he paid for a black-bordered advertisement in a Boston newspaper, which read:

J. B. RHINE IS A MONUMENTAL ASS!

Fifty years later Rhine could still quote verbatim that angry advertisement.[6]

Evidence uncovered by others supported Rhine's view that the Crandons were frauds. A photograph of "supernatural" material or "ectoplasm" emerging from orifices in Margery's body was magnified many times and identified by experts as a sheep's lung tissue sewn together with a surgical stitch invented by Dr. Crandon. A thumbprint that Margery claimed was produced by her brother Walter —after his death—was found to be her dentist's. Margery had energetic flirtations, if not affairs, with several investigators, which casts doubt on their impartiality. Rhine himself witnessed Margery warmly kissing men at the séance he attended. Dr. Crandon bankrolled one investigator and was a generous host to several others, all of whom marveled at Margery's powers.*

The most damning tangible evidence against Margery still available shows a photograph of her ostensibly in a trance. A small table is in midair. But it is obviously not held there supernaturally by Walter's primitive, materialized arm. A hairy male arm, unquestionably belonging to a confederate, can be seen emerging from a curtain— and that is what's "levitating" the table.

J. Malcolm Bird eventually admitted that he had suspected Margery even while he was lauding her to Rhine. Bird's excuse for his duplicity was that he had decided to build up a secret dossier against Margery and dared not reveal his true opinion prematurely because critical investigators were automatically barred from Margery's séances.

Dr. Walter Franklin Prince, chairman of the *Scientific American* committee and research director of the Boston Society for Psychic Research, seriously considered the speculation that Margery had undergone an operation that made it painless for her to secrete sizable objects in her vagina, objects possibly made from animal tissues resembling human flesh.

---

*Dr. L. R. Crandon's spirited defense of his wife's mediumship and scorn for her critics is published in *The Case For and Against Psychical Belief*, Clark University, 1927, pages 65–109.

In Margery's defense, it was argued that since Dr. Crandon no longer worked at a hospital he could not easily obtain animal tissues from vivisectionists. But, in fact, he'd have no trouble, according to Hudson Hoagland, McDougall's assistant, who attended several of Margery's séances. Crandon may even have had suppliers at the morgue. One horrified sitter felt with a shudder that the "ectoplasmic" hand with which Margery touched her probably came from a dead woman or child.

Almost to the end Margery Crandon was boosted and tested by the ASPR. In 1938 she challenged Rhine to test her again—but balked at the strict laboratory conditions he wanted to impose. She obviously preferred the less stringent, if not sloppy, ASPR atmosphere.[7]

Dr. Crandon died on December 27, 1939. He had been ill for a long time after a fall down the stairs. Margery continued to give sittings, and it was reported that Crandon had joined Walter as a spirit communicator.

Two years later, Margery was dying from acute alcoholism. Nandor Fodor, a psychoanalyst and psychical researcher, thought now might be the last chance to solve the Margery mystery. He went to her deathbed, hoping for a confession, and she laughed at him. "Why don't you guess?" she taunted. "You'll all be guessing for the rest of your lives."[8]

Her chuckles echo through the pages of the Margery chronicle. She had laughed at McDougall, too, when he held up a length of carpet thread and challenged her to deny that it was the thread, not her dead brother's spirit, that moved a piece of furniture.

Revered as a saint by some, reputed a whore by others, Margery died in her sleep on November 1, 1941. She was fifty-four.

One frequent visitor to Margery's séances has escaped the scrutiny of investigators—John Crandon, her son by a first marriage. As a child and teenager, John slept immediately underneath the séance room and often heard noises overhead. Though curious, he never went up to see for himself because he was forbidden to enter that room during a séance and he knew better than to disobey his mother or stepfather. One night during a séance he heard a tremendous crash overhead. Next morning John opened the séance-room door and faced "the most fantastic thing I ever saw. The plywood cabinet (in which Margery often sat) had smashed into little pieces."[9] No one explained to John how it had happened and he couldn't understand how such damage could result from what sounded like just one crash. The thought of it still astonished him when he recalled it fifty years later.

He heard his mother dismiss critics as "people who had decided she was phony to keep their reputation with contemporaries."

Naturally, his mother and stepfather puzzled John Crandon,

because whatever happened in that fourth-floor séance room was hidden from him. He grew up to be a surgeon, thanks to the support of his stepfather, and to believe "there's a bit of the psychopath in everyone." Dr. Le Roi Crandon, he realizes, was more eccentric than most. But looking back, he remembers that he was also "a great bene-factor and a good father. I have never thought about the possibility of his being a scoundrel. He was a very serious man who believed in God and an afterlife. But he told me if anyone asked me what religion I belonged to, I should tell them I was a freethinker."

John Crandon is convinced that his stepfather was the driving force behind the séances and that John's vivacious, lighthearted mother, who liked to go to plays and enjoy herself generally, would never have given the sittings without her husband's encourage-ment, if not pressure. Although this leaves the unanswered question—why did she continue after his death?

Cheating took place in the later years, John concedes: "I can't go along with the thumbprints said to be Walter's and the materi-alized hands. I don't know that the voice of Walter wasn't Dr. Crandon's instead of my mother's. I did hear from an old patient of my step-father's that when young, Dr. Crandon had studied ventriloquism." Ventriloquism loses most of its effect in a dark room—but might give the person with that ability confidence that he can convincingly project a voice that sounds like someone else's.

When pressed, John Crandon says he believes "that some of the stuff was genuine, particularly in the early years." But he can't really explain his mother and stepfather, their methods and their motives, and what went on in that dark room over his head.[10]

Marian Nester generally agrees with him. Now director of education for the American Society for Psychical Research (back in the hands of scientists and not controlled by spiritualists), as a teen-ager she attended dozens of Margery's séances. And she refutes those who denied that Margery's trances were genuine. "That's hard to believe when you were there," she says.

Her father, Dr. Mark Richardson, and Dr. Le Roi Crandon were friends. Both worked as doctors for the same insurance com-pany. Two of Dr. Richardson's sons had died young, and through Margery, with Walter's help as go-between, Dr. Richardson believed that he was in touch with his dead sons. He made numerous ex-periments to test Margery's powers and never lost faith in her as a psychic.

Marian Nester told me, "My parents were so deeply into it that I never doubted it, and they were evenings of great interest because Walter was so stimulating. I feel the things Walter did were not explained away by fraud, and I don't think even the Rhines have really put their fingers on actual methods of fraud in all cases. The whole story hasn't been told. It was so complex psychologically and psychically that maybe people didn't know enough to explain it or cope with it. I still don't think it's possible to brush it off as fraud."

Although Marian Nester considers Rhine was premature in rushing into print after one sitting, she thinks "his work is invaluable. He's beyond doubt a great, great man. Nobody could fault Rhine."[11]

Another witness, but one who fully supports Rhine's conclusions, is Hudson Hoagland, today an eminent scientist. In Margery's heyday he was a graduate student and assistant to McDougall in Harvard's psychology department. He had been told by friends that the Crandon marriage was very unstable: Crandon had divorced two wives and Margery was afraid she'd be the third to go. So, went the rumor, Margery got Crandon involved in her séances to hold onto him. She also wanted to put her son through medical school. "I think the motivating factor was to keep Crandon under control," says Hoagland, who characterized him as "a nasty bastard, rotten to the core. I never liked him and he was not liked by the medical people in the community."[12]

Hoagland believes the time was ripe for Margery, just after World War I when the spiritualists were proclaiming the possibility of talking with the dead. He sees Margery as an ingenious woman who used her dead brother as a communicant and "was quite witty in the way she handled it."

At one séance, Hoagland caught Crandon faking something that would have been marvelous if genuine. "Crandon tried to cover it up by saying that when he was a Harvard student in a class given by the great William James, the frog nerve-muscle preparation had gone sour and didn't work, so that James twitched it with his finger to make it work." And Crandon tried to persuade Hoagland that his cheating had the same honorable intent—to demonstrate a truth with a little trickery. Hoagland didn't buy it. But what was Crandon's motive? Hoagland believed it was the urge to be thought a martyr. "He had thousands who praised him, thought he was wonderful, likened him to Galileo making great discoveries. In his writing," says Hoagland, "Crandon likened us skeptics at Harvard to the Inquisition that tried Galileo. I'm sure he knew he was a fake, but he was being praised by all these sycophants."

Of the scores who investigated Margery Crandon, Hoagland appears to have been the only one to obtain what amounts to a confession. "I asked her what her motive was," says Hoagland. "She knew I knew she was a fraud. And she looked at me in this cute way and said: 'Why did Mary Baker Eddy [fake]?' What she meant was: One gets prominent, one gets praise, one gets famous by this sort of mystical hocus-pocus. And those were her motives."[13]

I asked Rhine to sum up the Margery affair, and he said wryly,

"Have you got a nose for bad eggs?" But he was not unwilling to pursue the subject. "It's a messy case. More the sort of thing a muckraker would get hold of. The kind of thing that some good people, good in their field, let's say, will get into—and what a mess they can make where the normal constraints no longer apply, no longer help them.

"Margery was a beautiful woman, she was a seductive woman, and she had great fun in life. And if she took this way of holding her husband, whom other women had been unable to hold for more than a year or two—it's an interesting story. From the point of view of the literary imagination, it makes an interesting plot. The story could have great appeal if it didn't lead to the gutter. The poor woman ended up a drunk in a degenerate state in New York, in a cheap hotel, as I recall.

"The story is full of life in all its qualities. McDougall and Walter Franklin Prince were interested in it, and clergymen gathered there to see what access they could get to the spirit world along more modern lines than their own. It has a touch of the pathetic because they were all the time being hoodwinked in a way that turns out to be not highly clever, rather taking advantage of the feeling that 'Oh, people of Lime Street wouldn't do that!'

"When you get back to the kind of man that Crandon was, it just makes you smile when people argue that 'Oh, people wouldn't do that! Status means something, and heredity and all that sort of thing mean something!' Actually, the stories about Crandon indicate that he seems rather to fit the psychopathic personality type whose passions and ambitions led him into things, including a morbid interest in spiritualism and an involvement with nurses that got him relieved from the Boston Hospital."[14]

Rhine's explanation for Margery's behavior is that she pretended to have supernormal powers to hold onto a wealthy and socially well connected husband obsessed with the thought of spirit communication. When Crandon "gradually found out that she was deceiving him, he had begun to enjoy the notoriety it gave him, the groups of admiring society it brought to his home to hear him lecture and to be entertained, the interest and fame aroused in this country and Europe, etc."[15]

Margery Crandon deserves a chapter to herself in textbooks on abnormal behavior, and a spot in *Ripley's Believe It or Not*, if only because of her effect on others—not just uneducated, inexperienced hayseeds, but on lawyers, doctors, clergymen, and scientists. It is fairly clear now that she used her feet with the dexterity of a Japanese juggler and probably packed her vagina with the "ectoplasmic" hand that emerged from her body.

The evidence points to Rhine being right, or almost entirely so. But it is still possible that Margery, at least to start with, had some psychic ability.

Reviewing *Margery*, a biography by Thomas R. Tietze, William G. Roll, project director of the Psychical Research Foundation and an expert on poltergeists, marvelously recaptures the atmosphere of the Margery mediumship in one sentence: "If you can imagine a James Bond mystery with characters from *Pickwick Papers* in a setting of about equal parts of Wonderland and Watergate, you will have an idea of Margery."[16]

Add a dash of pity, a heavy touch of the macabre, and the possibility that Margery was originally a genuine medium who went wildly astray, and you have 'it—almost. Not unexpectedly, the ASPR rejected the Rhines' account of the Margery séance which was published the following year, 1927, in the *Journal of Abnormal and Social Psychology*. In this report, Rhine states that his reason for making it public was "not primarily to attack the Crandons, but to help distinguish sharply between such fraudulent activity and the genuine basis of psychic research which continues to hold our respect and engage our interest."[17]

5

Harvard
1926–1927

Shortly after the seance with Margery Crandon, Rhine called on Dr. William McDougall, while Louisa waited on a bench on Boston Common. But Rhine's timing couldn't have been worse. McDougall and his family were packed and just about to leave for a trip around the world. McDougall had either mislaid or had never received Rhine's letter announcing the date and time of his arrival.

Rhine recalled their first meeting: "There were two taxicabs outside his house in Cambridge, one filled with baggage and the other for the family. I spoke with the great man while he stood there for an embarrassingly long time. I knew how he must be feeling, but he wouldn't leave until I got certain things clear so that I wouldn't blunder into a closed alley. I don't think there are many people in the world who would have been so patient. He wrote a word or two introducing me to a man in the philosophy department at Harvard, a man who didn't know the field of psychical research. As it turned out, the man was a bit odd. When I went to see him, his quarters were an indication of a very disorganized man: He evaded any effort on my part to pin him down about the Hodgson scholarship. He didn't understand how I could go out of my field of biology and botany into psychical research. Eventually, I heard from people at Harvard that soon after that he took his own life, jumping overboard on his way to Britain. He was a philosophy man. He had been given the responsibility, which no one else wanted, forced on him I guess, to take care of the Hodgson fund."

McDougall wrote of the brief hail and farewell in his foreword to Rhine's first book, *Extra-Sensory Perception:*

Dr. Rhine arrived on my doorstep at Cambridge, Mass., one morning in June 1926, at the moment when I had completed the bestowal of my family and worldly possessions into two taxicabs.* ... When Dr. J. B.

**It was more probably early July.*

Rhine burnt his boats, gave up his career in biology and came over to psychology and psychical research, it was with the full consent, endorsement, and parallel action of his wife—a unique and remarkable event in the history of the subject. For the Rhines were not monied amateurs. [As were many of the original British researchers.] They were working scientists without worldly resources other than their earnings. When the facts became known to me I was filled with admiration and misgivings. Their action seemed magnificently rash. ... Nor was the action prompted by some overwhelming emotional personal interest, such as desire to make contact with some lost loved one. The motivation was, as far as I could and still can judge [in 1934, eight years later], the desire to work in the field that seemed to contain most promise of discoveries conducive to human welfare.

The man Rhine had been sent to spy on wished him well and left for his journey around the world.

After his first brief meeting with Dr. McDougall, Rhine hurried back to the Boston Common park bench where Louisa was waiting to hear the news. It was good and bad: McDougall was everything and more than Rhine expected—Bird had completely misrepresented the man—but he would be gone for months. Louisa was naturally disappointed, but the two of them were quickly involved with other concerns and caught up in the excitement of a new town and the start of a new life.

Rhine learned from the Margery affair that a good investigator trusts no one, regardless of social or professional eminence, and that frauds lurk among the watching and the watched. This early, traumatic lesson changed his trusting nature, and in time some critics half seriously labeled him paranoid. It was not paranoia. He had cause. In fact, any attitude other than suspicion would have been suspicious. Psychic research was a swamp and no one had yet learned to walk on water.

Rhine's exposé of Margery and his uncompromising attitude freed him from any connection with the American Society for Psychical Research and put him in close touch with two of the most reputable and experienced men in psychic research, Dr. McDougall and Dr. Walter Franklin Prince. Both were impressed by Rhine's integrity and intelligence and with his speed and confidence in detecting séance-room fraud.

. But, before solving mysteries of the mind, Rhine had a more mundane problem—to find a room closer to the Harvard campus. He settled for 65 Mt. Vernon Street, where he agreed to stoke the furnace and Louisa to clean the bathrooms in return for a rent-free room. Their savings were enough to take care of all other necessities.

Rhine hurried through his chores in his new home, then set

off to monitor lectures on psychology and philosophy. McDougall's writings had persuaded him that psychology was the discipline through which psychic research was best pursued. Psychology, after all, was the science of mind and behavior (unless you were a behaviorist and ruled out mind). And philosophy—the search for truth through logical reasoning—should be a helpful path to the same goal.

Sitting in a room where the great philosopher-psychologist William James had taught, Rhine felt as if he was breathing pure oxygen. James had done more than anyone in America to make psychic research worthy of men of intellect. He had in fact inspired McDougall to become not only a psychologist, but a psychical researcher—and through McDougall, Rhine. James had crossed the Charles River to Boston to test the famous medium Leonore Piper, whom he judged to be "in possession of a power as yet unexplained."[1] And still unexplained. James had also helped found the American Society for Psychical Research in 1884, just two years after the British organization started, and he became president of the British society from 1894 to 1895.

After his twenty-five years of psychic research, he believed that "veridical phantasms, haunted houses, trances with supernormal faculty . . . are natural phenomena which ought, just like other natural events, to be followed up with scientific curiosity."[2] Just before his death in 1910, James went on record "for the presence, in the midst of humbug, of really supernormal knowledge that cannot be traced to the ordinary sources of information—the senses, namely of the automatist."[3] He concluded: "Hardly, as yet, has the surface of the facts called 'psychic' begun to be scratched for scientific purposes. It is through following these facts, I am persuaded that the greatest scientific conquests of the coming generation will be achieved."[4] Some fifteen years later, when Rhine first read those words, he reacted as if James had been writing directly to him. And their implicit challenge had been irresistible.

James stressed the enormous difficulties, inclined at times to believe

. . . that the Creator has eternally intended this department of nature to remain baffling, to prompt our curiosities and hopes and suspicions all in equal measure, so that, although ghosts and clairvoyances, and raps and messages from spirits, are always seeming to exist and can never be fully explained away, they also can never be susceptible of full corroboration.[5]

The difficulties, of course, were part of the lure. To overcome them, Rhine wanted all the good advice he could get. McDougall was on the move and out of reach, but Dr. Walter Franklin Prince wasn't.

Only a year previously Prince had helped found the breakaway Boston Society for Psychic Research (BSPR).

When the rooming-house furnace was ablaze, all bathrooms clean, and Rhine was free of lectures, he and Louisa set out to meet Prince, walking across the bridge to Boston, heading for 346 Beacon Street, headquarters of the BSPR. Margery Crandon, largely and ironically responsible for its existence, lived only a stone's throw away. The Rhines had heard of Prince through Bird's distortions. And if he had prevailed, Prince and Rhine would have been antagonists. Instead they were to become close friends.

Rhine couldn't have found a more helpful guide to steer him through the swampy territory. A clergyman and fellow psychical researcher who knew Prince well wrote that "perhaps no man ever lived who possessed such exact and encyclopaedic knowledge of the whole literature and phenomena of Psychic Research, or who knew the history of so many mediums."[6] And although this opinion was written after Prince's death, as an affectionate tribute to his memory, the facts support it.

Prince was sixty-two when Rhine first met him in the summer of 1926, and Rhine exactly half his age. Prince had a lively, sparkling Dickensian personality that made most men pale by contrast. He had an urge to teach, stronger if anything than his interest in observation and research. He told the Rhines that he hoped to find a few younger people whom he could train and introduce to the field to carry on the work after him. Rhine became one of the first recruits, and he resolved never to fall below what he soon discovered were Prince's own high standards.

Had Rhine's interest in psychic research been halfhearted, Bird, the Crandons, those in control of the ASPR, would surely have steered him back to teaching botany, to more orthodox areas of psychology, or even into forestry, away from all the frauds and fools. Instead, he told Prince that his recent experiences in psychic research had been a salutary lesson. He wanted to learn how to spot deception in its many physical, psychological, and pathological guises. They discussed Margery and Bird like two men sharing memories of the same nightmare. Prince, McDougall, and Rhine had all investigated Margery. They had all seen through her. And this shared encounter with duplicity had sharpened their skepticism. But they all also believed that genuine psychics might exist.

Prince, with a Ph.D. in psychology from Yale, had worked as a pastor for Protestant churches in Maine, Connecticut, Pittsburgh, California, and New York. His wide range of experiences made him sound as if he'd lived several lifetimes. It is unlikely Prince would have become so intricately involved in psychic research had not a mentally disturbed eighteen-year-old woman named Theodosia wandered into his All Saints Church in Pittsburgh in 1910 and sought his help. The three tense, traumatic years that followed earned for Prince a respected place in the history of abnormal psychology—for, after trial and error, he adopted his own method to cure Theodosia of multiple personalities that threatened to destroy her mind.

Prince and his wife took Theodosia into their home and adopted her. He kept a day-to-day record of his treatment of Theodosia, which essentially consisted of putting her into a light hypnotic trance and then conversing with her five personalities. He was uniquely equipped for this arduous task, being ready to devote his time to it and having researched the subject for his Ph.D. thesis, entitled "Multiple Personality." By positive suggestion and encouragement, he strengthened Theodosia's basic personality and persuaded the intruding personalities into submission and eventual dissolution. Prince used a pseudonym to protect her identity when he published the diary of his therapeutic triumph: *The Doris Case of Multiple Personality.* It is the most detailed and complete account of multiple personality on record, a classic in the field and a testament to Prince's knowledge, patience, and compassion.[7]

Theodosia sometimes appeared to be able to read Prince's mind and to know of events which she had no normal means of knowing. Prince made notes of such occasions and of the tests he undertook to ensure he wasn't hallucinating or being tricked. He published the material in a 1926 book entitled *The Psychic in the House.* In it he proclaimed his conviction that psychic phenomena had been persuasively demonstrated in his own home. He became so engrossed in the subject that he abandoned his church work in 1917 to join the ASPR as investigator and eventually principal research officer. Then came his abrupt, angry break with ASPR, the start of his Boston-based work, and his first meeting with the Rhines.

He was pleased to tell them that Boston was not only the home of Margery the fraud, but of two other women considered genuine and remarkable psychics, Leonore Piper and Minnie Soule. They had been tested for years and no one had discovered the slightest hint of deceit. Unike Margery, they were mental—not physical— mediums, limiting their work to spoken or written messages that seemed to have a supernormal source. A widower named Thomas, a fifty-one-year-old deputy superintendent of Detroit schools, believed that he was in contact with his recently deceased wife through Mrs. Soule, said Prince. Thomas was so impressed that he was thinking of devoting much of his life to seeking evidence that his wife had survived death. Would the Rhines be interested in having sittings with Mrs. Soule? It involved taking a stenographic record of everything she said while in a trance. Prince offered to pay them ten dollars a week for such work.

Louisa immediately took a crash course in shorthand. The sittings began before Louisa had completed her lessons, so for a while she used her own brand of shorthand. The Rhines' comparative youth proved an advantage: Mrs. Soule lived halfway up a steep hill, finally reached by climbing forty-six steps. For the purpose of the experiment, Louisa sat taking verbatim notes in an adjoining room, never talking and deliberately hidden from Mrs. Soule, so that if the medium said anything significant about her, Louisa would not have helped by her appearance, facial expressions, tone of voice, or inadvertent remarks.

Rhine sat in the room with Mrs. Soule, and his task was to question the entranced medium. Neither of the Rhines was enlightened by what Mrs. Soule said during those weekly sessions over a period of several months. The medium spoke in a stream-of-consciousness fashion, without revealing anything that struck them as remarkable evidence of a supernormal power or source. But Prince was pleased with their work and the mass of transcribed material they gave him to study, and paid them, in all, some two hundred dollars.[8]

At this stage of his training, Rhine got more help from magician Harry Houdini than from Mrs. Soule. If Margery's only virtue was bringing together Prince, Houdini, and Rhine, it should earn her a spot on some honor roll. Because Prince and Houdini had suffered together on the *Scientific American* committee investigating Margery, watching others fall for her wiles, it made them friends in adversity and friendly antagonists in the continuing debate between psychical researchers and the leading skeptics.

Harry Houdini, magician and escape king, was dedicated to the public exposure of phony mediums. He claimed he had never met a genuine one. But privately he longed to communicate with the dead. He had adored his mother, now dead several years, and had vivid recurring dreams that she had returned. He would wake suddenly from such dreams, waking his wife, too, as he cried out in the empty darkness, "Mama, are you here?"[9] His complete skepticism was reserved for the public. His method of investigation differed from Rhine's in this fundamental respect: Houdini's reputation depended on his exposing mediums as fraudulent. There is convincing evidence that to "prove" a medium was a cheat, he himself cheated. Rhine, on the other hand, was commited to a/rigorous, open-minded investigation, prepared to accept a positive or negative outcome.

When Houdini's stage show, in which he demonstrated the tricks of phony mediums, reached Boston, Prince took Rhine backstage. Rhine liked Houdini at once because of his natural, outgoing manner, and listened to him with respect. While he held Rhine's attention, Houdini surreptitiously slipped a foot out of his shoe—he didn't wear socks—and using his toes, pinched Rhine's leg. As Rhine rubbed his leg, Houdini pointed out that in darkened séance rooms self-styled mediums used their toes as he had done, and claimed the pinches were greetings from departed spirits. When Rhine got home, he discovered that Houdini had pinched him black and blue.[10]

Rhine teetered between elation and gloom at the prospect of working in a field in which everyone and everything was suspect. His fellow students at Harvard were indifferent to, or actively scorned, psychic research. He once sat next to psychology student Anthony Westerhof for an unforgettable lecture by Alfred North Whitehead on the metaphysics of science. Whitehead's views were so exciting that they began to talk about it as they walked out together and, lost in conversation, "came to" outside Rhine's home. He invited Westerhof in to meet Louisa and to continue to talk. Westerhof, like Rhine, was from a country background and a bit at a loss in the city. But when Rhine spoke of his interest in psychic research, Westerhof made it plain the subject left him cold. Nevertheless they became friends. "Rhine was an energetic, lively, questing man," Westerhof recalls. "He was on the lookout for lonesome people he could befriend and make into allies. I think he was a lonely man himself. I was terribly lonely at Harvard. I had come from a little denominational school and Harvard was an intellectual shock, thrilling but strenuous, too. I did enjoy having somebody to talk to. We talked mostly about course content." Westerhof found Rhine a sympathetic listener.[11]

But the only Harvard classmate willing to talk with Rhine about psychic research was a graduate student of psychology and onetime McDougall assistant, the ebullient Hudson Hoagland, then at the start of a distinguished scientific career. Hoagland attended about seven Margery séances with a group from Harvard and for a short time had been on the council of the BSPR. Briefly he had been taken in and had even contemplated writing his Ph.D. thesis on Margery's mediumship, had it proved genuine. Hoagland realized that Rhine had shown by his own exposure of Margery that he was neither gullible nor unprepared for the phonies who flourished in the field. Why, he was even learning from the great Houdini how to spot the tricksters. But, as a student of human behavior, Hoagland was amazed that Rhine did not share his total disenchantment. And he lost no opportunity to stress how hazardous, if not foolhardy, it would be to make a career out of a search for psychic phenomena. Hoagland's derisive comments once developed into an argument in which Rhine stated emphatically that he intended to devote his life to such a quest.

"But it's such a terrible gamble," said Hoagland. "It's like digging for gold in your backyard. It is possible to find gold there, but it wouldn't be worth a man's life to do it!"

"Well," Rhine replied doggedly, "it is mine!"

"He seemed," said Hoagland, in retrospect, "like a pregnant woman who is determined to have the child despite anyone or anything."[12]

By late fall of 1926 Rhine heard that McDougall had returned from his world trip and was preparing a speech he was to give at a public symposium at Clark University, Worcester, Massachusetts. Leading advocates and opponents of psychic research and some who held the middle ground were to air their views at this first university-sponsored public meeting on the subject between November 29 and December 11, 1926. Houdini died a month before the symposium began, but his widow sent a chapter from his book *A Magician Among the Spirits* to be included in a published account of the affair. Speakers at the two-week-long symposium included Walter Franklin Prince; Columbia University psychology instructor Gardner Murphy, who commuted to Harvard to do psychical research; and Dr. Le Roi Crandon, Margery's husband, still energetically promoting her mediumship. Oliver Lodge sent a manuscript and Arthur Conan Doyle wrote a letter.

Rhine was specially interested in what McDougall said. The Harvard psychologist stressed that because psychic research dealt with the most complex of subjects—human beings—such a field should not be left to casual amateurs, the bereaved seeking comfort, or to dilettantes searching for new excitement. In his attempt to summarize observations into a general statement, McDougall continued, the psychical researcher must be extraordinarily cautious, take many precautions, and anticipate that all kinds of unknown phenomena will get in the way of clear results. Even when subjecting his observations to statistical analysis, said McDougall, the psychical researcher cannot assume, as do scientists in other fields, that the results are safe from different interpretations.[13] For thousands of years philosophers had been asking the question: "Does mind transcend matter?" said McDougall, and those who reached a conclusion were almost equally divided between "yes" and "no." He maintained this was also the essential question asked by psychic research, and in his opinion there was only one place where it could be studied in a sustained and scientific manner—a university.[14]

Neither Harvard nor Clark University responded to McDougall's appeal. Harvard doubtless thought enough is enough: It had tolerated his experiments with rats to see if the almost discredited Lamarckian theory of inherited acquired characteristics had any truth to it, and also had somewhat daringly allowed him to reintroduce hypnosis in his classes. Furthermore, Margery had given psychic research an aura of the disreputable, and too many Harvard professors and students had already been involved with the shady lady.

Clark University, apparently, decided that hosting the symposium on psychic research was its good deed for the decade.

Yet, McDougall was not disappointed. He was already negotiating with Duke University in North Carolina. Its president, Dr. W. P. Few, an English professor who was not afraid to say "ain't" on occasion, wanted McDougall to head and staff a newly created psychology department. He knew of McDougall's interest in psychic research, which he shared. The talk was that Duke hoped to become the Harvard of the South. How better, then, than to snare Harvard's distinguished Professor McDougall? It was an offer McDougall found impossible to refuse, as he would eventually be allowed, even encouraged, to introduce the first psychical research laboratory in an American university.

Rhine's euphoria at the news was diminished somewhat by McDougall, who explained that he had first to staff the psychology department at Duke with psychology instructors and organize a course of undergraduate and graduate studies. Only then could he put his mind to introducing a department of psychic research.

Meantime, Rhine had to live. His year at Harvard and the money he had saved from his work as a botany instructor were running neck and neck in a race to exhaustion.

He worked during the summer of 1927, selling aluminum pots and pans from door to door in and around Doylestown, Ohio. Rhine was exceptionally persuasive and persistent. In a few weeks he became a super salesman.

His evenings were spent reading a manuscript sent to him by John F. Thomas. He was the deputy superintendent of schools in Detroit and fellow member of the BSPR who believed Minnie Soule—the Boston medium the Rhines had investigated—had put him in touch with his dead wife. The Rhines exchanged several letters with him and judged that the evidence he had already obtained through Mrs. Soule, though not spectacular, was promising. Thomas told them he intended to go to Duke as soon as McDougall had settled in there and planned to turn his growing evidence for survival into a Ph.D. thesis. He knew of no other university in America where such a thesis would be accepted.

By November 1927 the Rhines had great news to share with their guide and friend Walter Franklin Prince. They were going to Duke with Thomas for six months to study and criticize the information he had been collecting from mediums. Thomas had agreed to pay them two thousand dollars for their help. "It was at once a chance to study under Professor McDougall," Rhine wrote to Prince, "and an opportunity to continue learning something of psychic phenomena."[15]

With Louisa at his side, Rhine drove their ninety-five-dollar "lizzie" from Ohio toward North Carolina. Rhine stopped in New York City to talk with several psychical researchers recommended to him by McDougall and Prince. Most of all he wanted advice from Gardner Murphy.

Murphy and Rhine had a lot in common, apart from psychic research. They were the same age, both had been deeply religious—Rhine had intended to be a minister of the gospel, Murphy had planned to be a missionary—but lost their religious faith in college. Both studied at Harvard and counted Walter Franklin Prince and William McDougall as mentors. Both married college-educated women who actively shared their interests and made major contributions: Dr. Louisa Rhine to psychic research, Dr. Lois Murphy to child psychology.

Gardner Murphy was born in Chillicothe, Ohio, on July 8, 1895. His father, Edgar Gardner Murphy, was an Episcopalian clergyman. His Vassar-educated mother, Maud King Murphy, had been a teacher before her marriage. Gardner Murphy grew up in Concord, Massachusetts, in an atmosphere where unpopular views were given a fair, even enthusiastic hearing. Psychical research was often discussed in the Murphy home, sparked by the investigations of William James and Richard Hodgson. For a time Murphy's grandfather, George A. King, worked as attorney for the famous psychic Leonore Piper. And it was in his grandfather's library that the young Gardner Murphy discovered Sir William Barrett's book *Psychical Research*. After that the subject never failed to fascinate him and he was to spend much of his time and money in investigating, and backing others in their investigation of the psychic world.

He studied at Yale and then at Harvard where, in 1917, he abandoned his plans to be a missionary: "I found myself in this year at Harvard thinking through with genuine desperation, headaches and insomnia, the question of religious values and meanings and whether they could be made to coincide with the monistic, or if you like, materialistic world view which Keller had made so absolutely convincing. [A. G. Keller taught Murphy Anthropology A-1 at Yale.] I decided, after much writhing, at 2:00 one March morning in 1917, that I would have to give up my religious faith. My knowledge of psychical research, however, was at this time considerable, and I made up my mind that I would pursue psychical research for its own intrinsic interest and for the very considerable possibility that it might ultimately reverse my decision regarding religion."[16]

After earning his M.A. the same year, 1917, Murphy interrupted his academic studies to join the Yale Mobile Hospital Unit for service with the American army in France during World War 1. On one leave he traveled to England to join the Society for Psychical Research in London, where the secretary gave him a reading list which he found invaluable. He became specially interested in accounts of miraculous healings at Lourdes, of the spontaneous cases reported by the SPR from 1882 onwards, and of the detailed tests made with mediums. The subject absorbed him for several hours a day.

After obtaining his Ph.D. from Columbia, Gardner Murphy was awarded the ten-thousand-dollar Harvard scholarship in memory of Richard Hodgson, an early psychical researcher, "to encourage the investigation and study of mental or physical phenomena, the origin or expression of which appears to be independent of the ordinary sensory channels."[17] At Harvard, between 1922 and 1925, Murphy conducted controlled telepathy experiments, the results of which kept his interest alive.

Already in the 1920s he was respected by psychologists and psychical researchers. Murphy was to become a psychologist of international repute, president of the American Psychological Association, as well as one of the rare psychical researchers to be president of both the American and the British Society for Psychical Research.*

Rhine and Murphy had never met before—despite both being at Harvard simultaneously—because Murphy had been a man on the run, shuttling weekly between Columbia, where he taught psychology, and Harvard, where he conducted the telepathy experiments and stimulated young investigators. Now Rhine wanted his advice.

Murphy's wife, Dr. Lois Murphy, also a psychologist, opened the door of her apartment near the Columbia campus to find Rhine standing outside just about to ring the bell again. He introduced himself, explained he was en route to Durham and wanted a few words with Gardner Murphy. She didn't invite Rhine in because her husband was bedridden with flu. Rhine gave her the impression of being a very serious man, with the earnest, concerned demeanor of a Scandinavian. Acting as go-between, Lois Murphy conveyed several questions and answers while Rhine waited at the door.

His final question was: "Does Dr. Murphy really take telepathy seriously? Because I'm considering making a commitment to spend my life at it." He was assured that Murphy was deeply and permanently committed to psychic research and expected to devote a good part of his life to it, too.[18]

It was the reassurance Rhine needed. He headed south in his car, Louisa at his side, with renewed enthusiasm that was not even dampened by two flat tires.

---

*Influenced by the vision of potentialities in scientific psychic research gained at his visit to the SPR in London, Murphy invested much of his time in developing scientific standards at the ASPR; he inspired and contributed financially to the support of young investigators and attracted outstanding scientists from Yale, Princeton, and other universities to the board of trustees of this Society.

LADY WONDER
1927–1928

A roughly painted sign by the roadside intrigued the Rhines as they approached Richmond, Virginia, on their journey to Duke. It advertised a mind-reading horse. This seemed too good to miss. They headed in the direction indicated, but a detour took them several miles out of their way. As it was getting late, they decided to spend the night in Richmond and postpone their visit to the horse.

Reading a newspaper that same evening, Rhine noted that this was the night Jack Dempsey and Gene Tunney were to fight for the heavyweight boxing title, and he came across an article about the mind-reading horse he had just missed seeing. She was named Lady Wonder—sometimes called just Lady—and had become a local celebrity. Her talents, said the article, encompassed correctly predicting the future, as well as reading minds. The paper had printed Lady Wonder's prediction when the two men previously battled for the title. She had named Tunney the winner. He was. Furthermore, the horse had been right again when she predicted that Jack Dempsey would beat James Sharkey in their recent fight.

The horse's owner, Mrs. Claudia Fonda, was listed in the local phone directory. Rhine called her and explained he was conducting a scientific study of telepathic and other unexplained phenomena in association with Duke University. Could her horse really read minds? Yes, she said. Would she allow him and colleagues to test Lady Wonder's abilities? Again, yes. She would cooperate fully and looked forward to seeing him.

Tunney won the fight again that night, as the horse had predicted.

Shortly after arriving at Duke, Rhine mentioned Lady Wonder, "the mind-reading horse," to McDougall and showed him the newspaper account of her accurate predictions. John F. Thomas, also there to begin his thesis about his attempt to make contact with his dead wife, joined in the discussion. It seemed foolhardy to contemplate questioning a horse—Rhine's critics would surely ridicule him—but he knew of an impressive enough brief history of the scientific testing of animals for psychic ability. It was probably spurred by the folklore that abounded with stories of animals that saw or sensed apparitions, displayed fear before earthquakes or other disasters occurred, and traveled great distances over unknown territory to find their way home. Owners often claimed their pets had a "sixth sense," and there were numerous factual accounts of pets that seemed—by agitated or mournful behavior—to sense when their owners were in danger or had died in distant places.

Rhine had read of the investigations of the famous Elberfeld horses in Germany from 1891 on into the twentieth century. A leading Swiss psychologist at the University of Geneva, Professor Edouard Claparede, was among those who tested and enthusiastically endorsed them. He concluded that "these horses are the most sensational event which has ever appeared in the field of animal psychology—perhaps, indeed, in the whole realm of psychology."[1] What had he been so excited about? The eleven Elberfeld horses—Clever, Hans, Muhamed, and Zarif among them—appeared to engage in intelligent conversations by indicating with their muzzles letters on alphabet blocks. They also were said to solve math problems. To add ten and five, for example, a horse pawed once with his left hoof and five times with his right.

Investigators with horse sense assumed they were being tricked by the horses' trainer; and a Berlin psychologist, Oskar Pfungt, believed he knew how. He offered to demonstrate to his friends the modus operandi of the clever horses. Having gathered a group of his friends in his laboratory, Pfungt told them to pretend that he was a horse and to ask him questions, the answers to which they suspected he wouldn't normally know, but which could be answered by rapping a number of times on a table.

Pfungt then rapped out the right answers to twenty-three of twenty-five questions. He explained that his friends unconsciously helped him by leaning forward while he was rapping on the table, and by relaxing or leaning back slightly when he reached the correct numbers. He suggested that this was the way the Elberfeld horses worked.[2]

But was it? One horse, Hanschen, was reportedly blind. Others, again according to report, answered correctly questions that were called in on telephones attached to the horses' ears. And it didn't explain how the horses, when left alone, responded to questions chalked on boards. Although, of course, humans obviously had to be around—even if partially hidden—to observe the horses' answers, and might then have made the giveaway movements.

Rhine believed that there had been few thorough tests of psychic ability in animals, because investigators were generally so convinced telepathy in animals was nonsense that their tests were superficial and consequently inconclusive. One exception had been Vladimir Bechterew (1857–1927), the Rhine of Russia, founder and director of the Institute for Brain Research in Petrograd (now Leningrad).

Bechterew was a rarity, respected equally by behaviorists and psychical researchers. A rival of Ivan Pavlov, who was famed for experiments in which he made dogs salivate at the sound of a bell after they had been conditioned to expect food when a bell rang, Bechterew claimed his own method of conditioning was superior. Behaviorist John Watson agreed and adopted Bechterew's technique for secondary negative reinforcement. It involved pairing a neutral sound like a bell with an electric shock to the foot or hand, until eventually the sound alone caused withdrawal of the foot or hand.[3] Today the method is used to cure people of pernicious habits.

Bechterew was not reluctant to experiment in many areas regarded as occult. Meeting Vladimir Durow, who trained dogs for circus performances and claimed they could read his mind, Bechterew neither scoffed nor took the man's word for it. He agreed to test them.

Rhine noted that Bechterew had used screens made of different materials to hide himself and his colleagues from the dogs, and sometimes went into another room out of sight of the dogs before giving them silent commands—simply thinking what he wanted the dogs to do. Once Bechterew thought up a task for a dog, but told no one else. He gave a silent command for the dog to jump up on one of the chairs, climb onto a table, stretch himself and scratch at a painting hanging on the wall. And the dog carried out the "telepathic" command perfectly. Bechterew believed his experiments, made in 1920, demonstrated that the thoughts of the persons involved in the experiments had directly influenced the behavior of the dogs.

Had the dogs demonstrated telepathy? Rhine's favorable but cautious conclusion was that "there seemed to be no physical obstruction capable of interfering with the transmission of the thought, and no physical means of transmission discovered. This, if correct, is the situation called telepathy."[4] Note the "seemed" and the "if correct."

Although Rhine studied accounts of such investigations more thoroughly after his experiments with Lady Wonder, both he and McDougall already knew they involved taking precautions to prevent the animals from getting physical cues from their owners, trainers, or the experimenters.

McDougall would soon be preoccupied with staffing and running the psychology department at Duke. Although he couldn't spend the whole week with the Rhines, he could spare two days. John F. Thomas agreed to postpone his own research work for a day to join in the investigation, and arranged to meet them at the Fonda farm. In an exuberant mood, Rhine wrote to Prince on November 23, 1927: "I am glad to have come here and I expect it to be one of the great years in my life." Although he had known McDougall only a few weeks, he judged him

... one of the greatest minds I have ever met, either in life or literature. He is verily the Dean of Psychology, as you are of Psychic Research. How fortunate Louie and I have been in our contacts! We ought to amount to something eventually by the very force of the contacts we have made, the dynamic personalities that are contributing to our education.

On a sparkling December morning, McDougall and the Rhines drove north together. Louisa sat in the backseat listening to the men recapitulating their plan to test Lady Wonder by gradually separating her from Mrs. Fonda. "This was in 1927—in the days before Women's Lib," Mrs. Rhine told me with a smile, to explain her less active part in the conversation.[5] But she had made herself familiar with the reports by psychologists who had been "bewitched" by clever animals, fooled by their trainers, or had actually witnessed remarkable psychic powers. Her task on this investigation was to write a full account of everything that happened.

Just outside Richmond, Rhine turned off the highway to Petersburg Pike in Chesterfield and soon saw a sign reading:

LADY
WONDER HORSE
WILL SPELL AND SUBTRACT
MULTIPLY DIVIDE
TELLS TIME
ANSWERS QUESTIONS

Children were charged fifty cents for three questions; adults, a dollar.

Claudia Fonda, a small, slightly harassed-looking woman, had a way with animals. She told the visitors that she had previously trained and exhibited a horse, but that it had been much less gifted than Lady Wonder. She had also trained a dog named Pudgy to play the chimes: "The Bells of Saint Mary's" was its *pièce de résistance*. But Lady Wonder's abilities dwarfed the others'. Mrs. Fonda had discovered the horse's talent shortly after her family bought it for a workhorse when a few months old. "I'd just *think* I should go feed Lady, head for the door, and see her galloping from the fields before I could call," she said.

Then Mrs. Fonda began to teach the horse to spell and do math by using wooden alphabet and number blocks. "I'd tell her a letter or a number and show her the right block. I taught her to nudge a few blocks together to spell words. Pretty soon Lady was spelling words I hadn't taught her."[6]

How did Mrs. Fonda account for Lady Wonder's talents? Unusual intelligence, she said, and the ability to read her mind.

Rhine and McDougall chose to test the horse in a tent near her barn, while Louisa looked on and recorded details of the experiments. It was still cold when they started on December 3, 1927, but the Rhines were used to rugged farm life. McDougall didn't complain and Thomas was equally stoical.

At first, Mrs. Fonda was given a completely free hand. She stood near Lady Wonder, both of them facing a table on which were two rows of children's alphabet blocks, lettered on one side. Lady Wonder's task was to answer questions by nosing the blocks. For later tests there were a set of plates numbered from zero to nine, and ten index cards, on each of which was an unusual design not easy to describe.

Mrs. Fonda was so active that it was quite impossible for Rhine to tell if she was signaling the animal: She spoke to the horse continually, used the whip to urge her to work, and sometimes grabbed the halter and pulled her back to make a fresh start after a mistake. Rhine watched the movements of the whip, Mrs. Fonda's head and arm movements, the tensing of her muscles; he listened to her words, her breathing, in case she held her breath as a signal, and for any throat sounds that might serve as cues.

He failed to detect any signals, but so much was going on it was hardly surprising.

Under these loose conditions, McDougall and Rhine wrote words on a pad and showed them to Mrs. Fonda. Each time, she said to Lady Wonder, "Spell the word." And although the Rhines had lived on farms and were familiar with the ability of horses to respond to slight signals, they were astonished to see Lady Wonder show almost human behavior as she correctly spelled out the following: bed, kid, Mesopotamia, Carolina, Hindustan.

Mrs. Fonda then asked Lady Wonder: "What is this gentleman's name?"

Lady (nosing the blocks): Rhine.
Fonda: "What have I in my hand?"
Lady: Whip.

Fonda: "What has Dr. McDougall on his head?"

Lady: Hat.

When she asked Lady: "What makes you so bad?" the horse replied: Fun.

In over fifty trials under these very free conditions Lady was right 94.4 percent of the time.

For the second phase Mrs. Fonda had to remain silent and still and, to prevent her from using her eyes to signal Lady, she was required to turn her back on the horse. Sometimes an eighteen-inch screen was held beside the horse's head so that at most she could see Mrs. Fonda's feet. Lady still made a high percentage of correct responses.

Then Mrs. Fonda was blindfolded and gradually moved away from Lady until, eventually, she was outside the tent. Lady soon noticed her disappearance and became unmanageable. Still, the horse scored above chance in her few answers when Mrs. Fonda wasn't in the tent

The horse's total in the second phase was 83 right out of 106 trials; or 78.3 percent correct.

For the third and final phase of the tests Rhine and McDougall attempted to eliminate Mrs. Fonda as a possible source of conscious or unconscious signaling. During this phase she was never told of the block or card the men had selected for Lady Wonder to indicate. Sometimes Mrs. Fonda was outside the tent and blindfolded with a double thickness of woolen scarf from her forehead to the tip of her nose, but mostly she was allowed to stay inside to control the horse.

In the final series Rhine, who alone knew the target, shaded his eyes with his hat and leaned motionless against a post, to avoid unconsciously signaling the horse or Claudia Fonda. If he wrote down the questions, he shielded the pencil from Mrs. Fonda's view, knowing that some people can read what is being written by following the movements of the pencil.[7]

The chance average would have been two out of fifteen correct. Lady got seven out of fifteen. All told, in the third phase, Lady got 44.9 percent right.

The Rhines wrote in their subsequent report,

One striking feature of the horse's behavior has not been mentioned, namely, her sleepy appearance when working well. Her head drooped, eyes nearly closed, nostrils relaxed, and she seemed quite inattentive. She moved no more than was necessary to touch the required block and often touched a nearer one in the next row. This passivity could be so deepened (by monotonous command, for instance) as to render her apparently motionless and almost asleep. Occasionally she would fall so deeply into this lethargy while working, that she simply remained motionless for a time. She could be awakened by a sharp command or a touch of the whip and become quickly a normal colt again.

The Rhines noted that during successful telepathy tests, humans also have been reported to be in a passive state, dreamy or at least not alert.

After six days of testing, Rhine had only one explanation for Lady Wonder's performance—telepathy. "Nothing was discovered that failed to accord with it, and no other hypothesis seems tenable in view of the results. However, we are still devoted to the end of more and better evidence and are interested at this stage in obtaining, not so much credence, as assistance in securing more evidence."[8]

The Rhines made a surprise visit to Lady Wonder on April 11, 1928, and although Mrs. Fonda was ill and distinctly nervous, she agreed to cooperate in more tests. It was disappointing. The horse didn't even reach chance results and never got an answer right unless Mrs. Fonda, too, knew the answer. The Rhines made a final visit to Lady Wonder on December 3, 1928, a year from their first arrival. They tested her for six days. Now it was quite obvious to them that Lady Wonder was responding to Mrs. Fonda's signals, especially her use of the whip.

They reported:

We were forced to conclude that the telepathic ability we earlier found the horse to possess has been now almost if not entirely lost and that Lady has become merely a trained animal conditioned to a system of signals made up of indicative body movements, voice inflexions, whip movements.[9]

Rhine and McDougall both concluded that no trickery took place during the first week-long investigation. Naturally Rhine was disappointed to find that during the final tests the horse was obviously responding to physical cues, but he believed she had been taught to do this between his first and last visit. He wrote to Prince to tell of his chagrin:

The horse has lost its telepathic sensitivity, apparently.... I can direct it myself, even when the owner is absent, by whip and movements; but I cannot direct it telepathically, as I did before. Very embarrassing indeed; it is like the case at the University of Groningen, by Brugmans. Their subject too lost his power.[10]

Dr. Harold O. Gulliksen, a University of Chicago psychologist, suggested it was not that Lady Wonder's telepathic powers—which he doubted—had failed on Rhine's last visit, but that Rhine's powers of observation had increased. He believed Rhine and McDougall had been fooled on the earlier visits. Other critics, especially magicians, agreed with Gulliksen.[11]

Yet Lady Wonder's later spectacular history during which she seems to have regained her remarkable powers, confirms Rhine's views, not his critics'.

Rhine never lost his interest in the possible psychic abilities of animals, and never turned down the opportunity to investigate those brought to his attention.

After the interlude with Lady Wonder, the Rhines resumed their work with John F. Thomas. He had helped them test the horse and was now anxious for them to suggest a scientific method to confirm his belief that he was in contact with the spirit of his dead wife.

COMMUNICATIONS
WITH THE DEAD?
1927–1928

John F. Thomas, a member of the Boston Society for Psychic Research and former school superintendent, was mourning his wife, Ethel, who had died the year before, in 1926. They had been very close. Almost from the start, when he began going to mediums, he got results which suggested he was in touch with her. That was the mainspring of his interest in the work, and kept him going back. He went to Minnie Soule, for example, for 149 sittings in five months, and he sent a secretary as proxy for 217 sittings with the same medium. He had records of everything said or written by the sensitives, as he called them, intending to evaluate the material. Many comments by different mediums, especially by the well-known Gladys Osborne Leonard in England, were about intimate, personal, family matters. He found these persuasive proof that his dead wife had been the source of the information—because he believed that only he and his wife knew of such events and private conversations.

 The Rhines, called in to help and advise him, were less convinced because they thought he had not taken a sufficiently scientific approach.[1]

 Furthermore, in writing up reports of the séances for a Ph.D. thesis approved by McDougall, Thomas wanted to stress material that the Rhines considered less than compelling evidence of survival. So they clashed. Thomas regarded their attitude as cold-blooded, even cowardly. The Rhines understood his commitment and tendency to bias because of his emotional involvement, and they repeatedly tried to encourage him to take a more objective attitude. They urged Thomas to let the facts and statistical analysis of the facts speak for themselves. Even so, as time went on, they were both favorably impressed with the growing evidence he collected.

Writing to his confidant and sounding board, Walter Franklin Prince, in the fall of 1927, Rhine said he considered part of the Thomas material to be genuinely evidential and favored the hypothesis of spirit communication to explain it. He judged Thomas to have become a good sitter who, after two years of research with mediums, was experiencing "the impatience" Dr. Hyslop* expressed with "the unregenerate, the unconvinced." Rhine's only objection was that Thomas did not understand scientific method.

Yet despite the arguments with Thomas to try to turn him into a scientist, or at least teach him to appreciate scientific method, the Rhines enjoyed their work with him immensely, and J.B. declared:

We are just now organizing our thoughts on the question of what we require for proof of the supernormal, how many reasonable hypotheses there seem to be for supernormal production of information, and how we may discover then which of these is the correct one—a sort of amateurish plan of campaign, it might be called.[2]

At this stage Rhine either believed that Mrs. Soule and several other mediums Thomas consulted were in league as part of an elaborate spy system, or that Thomas was getting some of his information from supernormal sources. He doubted that the mediums were a group of spies, exchanging information about Thomas and his wife, though it couldn't be absolutely ruled out. That left the question of whether the material came from spirits of the dead or through the mediums' own psychic abilities. Rhine considered it more likely to be coming from spirits—likely, not certain.

By the spring of 1928 Rhine was no less enthusiastic, but having read more of the literature about mediums, problems came into sharp focus. He shared his thoughts with Prince: "What a pity it is that psychic research must be cut up by so many schisms, have to deal not only with many sorts of queerness in mediumship itself, but with hardly fewer sorts of unreliability in investigators. Verily, verily, it is not a field to choose in which to be popular, or in which to find a quiet life. Though its lure is irresistible."[3]

Thomas, in a large measure, eventually adopted the Rhines' suggestions. He evaluated the information supplied by mediums as correct, incorrect, inconclusive, no recollection, or not verifiable.[4] When their time was up, the Rhines accepted Thomas's offer of an additional two thousand dollars to keep working with him for another six months.

Dr. James Hervey Hyslop (1854–1920), a leading American educator and psychical researcher, believed he had communicated with the dead.

In the spring of 1928, while still working with Thomas, the Rhines had their first personal encounter with the inexplicable. Prince had sent them the latest bulletin of the *BSPR*, called "Evidence of Things Not Seen: An Account of Psychical Experiences." The author was a Mrs. Sally Keene, and she seemed to be a remarkable new medium. Rhine was free for a few days from his work on the Thomas material and decided to try some psychometry tests on Mrs. Keene. For this, the medium holds an object and tells of her impressions concerning its history and events in the lives of people associated with the object. Rhine considered Prince's work in psychometry "his most impressive contributions to psychic research," especially with Señora Maria Reyes de Zierold of Mexico. Because of Prince's expertise, Rhine hoped he would help to persuade Mrs. Keene to collaborate in psychometry tests. But she declined, apparently overawed by Rhine's connection with Duke University.

One day, during the ultimately disappointing exchange of letters with Mrs. Keene, the Rhines returned to their room and saw a journal lying on middle of the floor. It was the bulletin of the *BSPR*, "Evidence of Things Not Seen," in which Sally Keene recounted her psychic experiences.

The Rhines were mystified, certain they had not left the journal on the floor. "I know of no practical joker in the city capable of the trick," Rhine wrote to Prince. "And I doubt if he could have performed it undetected. It has therefore impressed Louie and me."[5]

No practical joker ever confessed. Rhine concluded that if it hadn't been a practical joker or his landlady, then an unseen agent or spirit was responsible. It remains a mystery.

It wasn't until five years later, in 1933, that Thomas submitted his report and analysis of the mediumistic records, entitled "An Evaluative Study of the Mental Content of Certain Trance Phenomena,"* for which he was awarded a Ph.D. His was the first doctorate given by an American university for work in psychic research. An expanded version was published by the *BSPR* in 1937, retitled "Beyond Normal Cognition."

Among the twenty-two sensitives Dr. Thomas had used for his experiment were Minnie Soule, Gladys Osborne Leonard, and Eileen Garrett. He concluded:

There is no doubt that the records give a clear and faithful picture of the personality of E.L.T. [his wife]. It makes no difference whether I

---

*The first doctoral dissertation on psychic research was by Albert Coste, of the University of Montpellier, France, in 1893, titled "Les phenomenes psychiques occultes." The second was by Carl Jung in 1902.

*am the sitter, or my son, in experiments with mediums who didn't
know our names; or whether secretaries are conducting experiments
alone with mediums who did not know for whom the sittings were
being held. The same person is described in each case and correct traits of mind and character are given and appropriately
emphasized.*[6]

Dr. Thomas acknowledged the Rhines' help in the preface to
his book: "Dr. J. B. Rhine, for intelligent direction and support
throughout the six year period. . . . Dr. Louisa E. Rhine, for continuing
discerning interest in the records." And he wrote in the introduction:
"To checkmate any personal bias in connection with the receipt and
study of the records, I associated myself early in the project with Dr.
J.B. Rhine, of Duke University, and his wife, Dr. Louisa Rhine, both of
whom trained in biology at the University of Chicago."

The book was not the end of Thomas's search. He continued
to visit mediums believing that through them he was in touch with his
dead wife. He still took detailed notes of those sittings, perhaps
intending to publish a second book, one that might convince even the
Rhines. It was never finished: Thomas died in an automobile accident
in 1940.

Shortly after Thomas's death, an objective account of his work
was given by parapsychologist Laura Abbott Dale in the *JASPR* for
January 1941. Mrs. Dale pointed out that of those verifiable comments
by mediums relating to Thomas's dead wife, 92.3 percent proved
correct. It was unlikely the mediums obtained this accurate information from normal sources because Thomas took several precautions
to prevent such leakage. For one thing, the identities of the sitters at
the various séances were kept secret from the mediums. Might coincidence explain the results? Apparently not. Statisticians examined
the Thomas material, reported Mrs. Dale, and concluded that chance
could not account for the accuracy of the mediums.[7]

Although Rhine had agreed with Thomas that chance alone
could not explain the information he obtained from mediums, the
parapsychologist did not conclude that the investigation had demonstrated spirit survival. He was impressed but not convinced. While
working with Thomas, Rhine spotted a flaw. He did not think the
mediums were frauds, and in many cases they did seem to be in
communication with Thomas's dead wife. But all the evidence they
supplied, Rhine realized, could have been obtained through telepathy
(reading the sitter's thoughts), or through retrocognition—an extra-
sensory ability to know of past events. And try as he did, Rhine could
not find a way to eliminate those alternative explanations.

8

RATS
1928–1930

While McDougall abetted Rhine in psychical research, that "no-man's-land between the lunatic fringe on the one hand and the academically orthodox on the other,"[1] Rhine helped McDougall in an experiment regarded by the scientific establishment as an attempt to turn back the clock. McDougall had been at it for ten years and would persist for several more. He wanted to see if there was any validity in the Lamarckian theory. As a vitalist, McDougall believed it probable that living organisms are goal-seeking and striving toward perfection. To this end—this attempt at perfection—he thought it possible that the characteristics acquired by an animal during its life might be passed on to its offspring. At least one man, Jean Lamarck (1744–1829), a French naturalist, thought so.

Darwin's theories of evolution and natural selection had all but drowned Lamarck's, and the current school of behaviorists were holding the Frenchman's theory under for the third time, with cries of: "Man is merely a machine. He can be fully explained in chemical and physical terms."* McDougall plunged in to the rescue—and he was in for a long swim. He was the only scientist of note to take on both schools, Darwinian and behaviorist, whose theories were mutually supportive. His impetus was not only an urge to give vitalism a shot in the arm, but a fight against odds, which he relished.

Eventually, McDougall bred forty-nine generations of rats over sixteen years in what many scientists regarded as a lost cause. Yet during that time, surprisingly, he obtained positive results. And Rhine replicated those results, indicating, as it appeared, that a rat's acquired characteristics were inherited by its offspring, just as Lamarck suspected.

This was a direct challenge to the establishment position and,

---

*Although Darwin embraced part of Lamarck's hypothesis, later Darwinians rejected it in toto.

if not a blow, an irritant to Darwinians and behaviorists. But, of course, the experimental results of one scientist and his assistant needed independent confirmation.

Because of his thorough grounding in genetics at the University of Chicago, Rhine was able to help McDougall with the rat breeding. And he soon found someone to share his load. His Harvard friend Anthony Westerhof wanted a place to study for his master's degree in psychology. Rhine recommended Duke with enthusiasm— and soon the two of them were up to their elbows in rats. Westerhof recalls: "Dr. McDougall was training white rats to avoid light and take a dark gangway to get out of a tank of water. The rats were given an electric shock when they took the lighted route. McDougall's aim was to discover if the offspring of the rats trained to escape swiftly from a tank of water would inherit the ability to make a fast escape by a difficult route."[2]

Rhine proved to be more careful than McDougall, who was inclined to be absentminded in his use of an overhead switch and one on the tank itself. Sometimes McDougall changed the switch on the lighted side of the tank and forgot to change the switch on the shock side, something even an alert experimenter might do. This led to errors. Rhine substituted two toggle switches, side by side, which made it virtually impossible to forget to change the switches at the same time. Westerhof tried to replicate the positive McDougall and Rhine results. He failed. McDougall's explanation was that Westerhof put his rats through their paces at the same time every day, while Rhine and he had tested them at irregular times.[3]

"McDougall's rat strains had the same original heredity," Louisa Rhine told me in a 1979 interview. "He simply divided the original stock and kept one part as experimental, the other part as control. He did not mix the two over succeeding generations. Whether the greater skill his experimental rats came to show confirmed Lamarck's theory is a possibility, but not one established beyond doubt by this work. Like many pioneer projects, it needed improvement and confirmation."[4]

The Lamarckian theory still remains to be demonstrated beyond doubt.

Though Westerhof was proud to work with a maverick like McDougall, he balked at assisting Rhine in his attempts to discover if there was such a thing as perception other than through the senses. Westerhof's disdain for such research escalated as Rhine's obsession with the work caused him to use any students he could corner as guinea pigs.

Had Rhine stuck to shocking rats, Westerhof might have shown more approval. Instead, he was one of the first of a long line of critics to challenge him.

9

HYPNOSIS
1930

Rhine was like a hunter searching for a quarry reported to have left tracks in the sand, those tracks long since buried by the ocean. He wasn't sure it existed, and if it did, when or how it might appear; and if it did surface, how to trap it; and if he did grab it, how to prevent its escape. Would it have been easier to bottle imagination and sell it to a customer from Missouri? It must have seemed so. But Rhine knew many of the spectacular difficulties before he began his enchanted voyage. It was not only the evasive, mysterious nature of the quarry that was the problem. There was also the devastating effect the search had on many of the hunters. It had converted scientists noted for their care and objectivity into credulous idiots. Others who retained their critical faculties and believed they had solved the mystery after a lifetime of research and exploration confessed, finally, that they were not sure. Certainty had slipped into probability, and probability into possibility.

For the next fifteen years Rhine lost the active participation of Louisa on the journey. Their first child, Robert, had been born in 1927. Three daughters followed, the last in 1933. Louisa chose to devote most of her time to raising the children, though she supported Rhine's work no less enthusiastically.

McDougall matched her fervor. Though preoccupied with running a department, lecturing to graduate students, and continuing his Lamarckian experiment, McDougall by no means stood back and let Rhine blaze a lonely trail. He gave much of his spare time to psychical research, too.

He was, after all, seeing his dream realized. He had spelled out Rhine's mission when he said: "If Mind in any manner and degree transcends the physical world and its laws, surely it may somehow be possible to obtain direct evidence of the fact by methods of science, by observation of phenomena and by reasoning from them?" He pointed out that belief in telepathy "is held by all intelligent Christians;

for it is implied in the practice of prayer and communion." And as for his own convictions, McDougall believed that the evidence for telepathy was strong, that a case had been made for clairvoyance, and that there was a very weighty "mass of evidence indicating personality does not always at death wholly cease to be a source of influence on the living." McDougall stated that apparitions were part of the evidence for such influence. He had expressed these provocative views at the Clark University symposium in 1926, knowing that they were shared by a small minority of fellow scientists. But McDougall held that the majority was often wrong, and he had only to refer to the history of science to prove his point.

Now, four years after the symposium, he had the green light to investigate the psychic world, in a university setting and with Rhine as his eager instrument. At this stage, if McDougall was mostly the armchair detective, Rhine was the bloodhound.

The first question they faced was this: Where should Rhine pick up the trail? Rhine answered that after reading of an experiment in the 1880s by a Frenchman named Richet.

Dr. Charles Richet (1850–1935), a Nobel prizewinning physiologist, one of the handful of world-famous scientists who found psychic research of compelling interest, had used hypnosis effectively for some of his clairvoyance experiments.

Hypnosis has a long and little-known past, forgotten by one age only to be rediscovered by the next. Much of it still remains mysterious. But its therapeutic use by physicians through the ages is undisputed. The pioneer hypnotists of the modern school—of which Anton Mesmer (1734–1815), an Austrian physician, is the father, and the Marquis de Puysegur (1751-1825), his most renowned student—discovered signs of clairvoyance in hypnotized patients. While in a trance, these patients diagnosed their own illnesses, suggested effective remedies, and even accurately forecast when cures would occur. This "led the early hypnotists to search more and more into the realm of the marvelous. . . . It was contended that some of the hypnotized subjects . . . were able to read the thoughts of others, to find lost objects, and even to predict the future."[1]

Another Frenchman who began "searching in the realm of the marvelous" was Pierre Janet (1859–1947), a psychiatrist who pioneered the scientific treatment of neurosis and hysteria. He frequently used hypnosis to help him understand his patients and to diagnose their illnesses. Sigmund Freud's early work owes much to Janet. But it was Janet's excursion into psychic research that interested parapsychologists, Rhine especially. It happened by chance. As a twenty-six-year-old professor, Janet taught philosophy at a school in Le Havre. Wanting to write a thesis on hallucinations, he asked a local physican if he knew of any patients who hallucinated. No, the physician didn't. But he began to talk about unusual aspects of the mind and mentioned a woman who could be put in a hypnotic trance even though she was out of sight and hearing of the hypnotist. This intrigued Janet, and he persuaded the woman—known simply as Leonie to protect her identity—to let him test her. The experiments lasted from September 24 to October 14, 1885; at the end of the three weeks, Janet proved to himself not only that he had hypnotized Leonie from a distance, but that in a hypnotic trance she carried out to the letter instructions he gave by mental suggestion. Janet was cautious. He reported the experiments without stating outright that he had demonstrated the reality of telepathy—but in fact, to carry out his mental suggestions, obviously Leonie must have read his mind.

An account of Janet's experiments with Leonie was read at the *Société de psychologie physiologique* in Paris on November 30, 1885. It created what newspapers call "a sensation"; scientists call it "considerable interest." A few months later leading psychical researchers arrived at Le Havre to carry out their own tests with Leonie; among them Frederic Myers and Henry Sidgwick from the British Society for Psychical Research, and Charles Richet. Their results confirmed Janet's findings. However, Janet backed away, saying that he was being misquoted. He added that not enough precautions had been taken in testing Leonie, and consequently the conclusions drawn by others were questionable.[2]

Leonie remains an enigma, as does so much in parapsychology.

Richet's later clairvoyance experiments with Leonie especially influenced Rhine. In 1888 the French physiologist hypnotized the woman and asked her to identify playing cards he had hidden in opaque envelopes. Her best score was twelve right out of fifteen guesses, and Richet estimated the odds against her getting it by chance were one quintillion to one. Not impossible, but extremely unlikely. These odds were based on the theory of probability, thought up some three hundred years ago by the French mathematician Pierre de Fermat to oblige a gambler who wanted to know the odds in making a certain bet. Rhine would follow Richet's lead and make use of the mathematics of probability in his work.*

Richet failed when he later attempted to demonstrate the hypnotized Leonie's clairvoyant ability before a group at Cambridge University in England. But Rhine was impressed by the simplicity of the experiments and, if they proved positive, the awesome implications. All you needed was a pack of hidden cards to show if man's mind could transcend matter and defy the laws of space accepted by the scientific establishment.

Janet's experiments in telepathy naturally required at least

A gambler also started Rhine testing for mind over matter (psychokinesis).

two people, as it was a mind-to-mind affair. To test for clairvoyance, only one person was needed. An experimenter could even test himself by trying to identify concealed objective targets, such as the suits in a pack of playing cards. Then, after hundreds—or better, thousands—of trials, he would total the hits. By submitting this result to probability mathematics, the experimenter knew how close to or far from chance his calls had been.

Acknowledging his debt to Richet, Rhine used cards numbered from zero to nine rather than playing cards. By chance alone, people should guess an average of one out of ten. A score well above that average, especially if it could be sustained, would mean something other than chance was at work. It was up to Rhine to ensure that the something was not cheating or miscalculation.

So Rhine began exploratory work in clairvoyance. To escape being asked by him to guess the identity of the hidden cards, one had to be fast on his or her feet, or very slippery. And he encouraged his psychology students to make similar tests on themselves and friends.

Rhine took his work with him. He tested his family and his neighbors. At parties he was rarely without his cards and it's unlikely he missed many chances to challenge the guests to a guessing game. He'd mark the scores on anything at hand—the back of an envelope or a laundry list.

To stimulate interest he took a friendly though challenging approach, like an impresario cajoling an opera singer to hit a high note neither is sure is there. And he was cautious during these tests "without looking like a watchdog."[3]

He spent the summer of 1930—his vacations were always working vacations—visiting children's camps near his home, masquerading, as far as the kids were concerned, as a new diversion. He told the youngsters gathered expectantly with pads and pencils that he was holding a guessing contest, using ten cards he had marked from zero to nine. The results were not impressive.[4]

Rhine resumed work at Duke in the fall. His evidence now pointed to the grim likelihood that one horse in Virginia had been a whiz at telepathy* but had since lost her touch; and that his tests with humans of all ages had failed to demonstrate unequivocally that there was such a thing as extrasensory power.

Was he downhearted? No. He was euphoric, buoyed by the thought that almost certainly no psychology department in any other university in the world would have allowed him to pursue ESP research. And McDougall was actively encouraging him with financial assistance from both the department budget and the university

---

*"The greatest thing since radio," he wrote to Lady Wonder's owner, Claudia Fonda, according to author Milbourne Christopher in ESP, Seers & Psychics.

research fund. It wasn't a fortune, but it would keep him going in a modest way. And he had been given no deadline.

His colleagues, Helge Lundholm and Karl Zener, although mainstream psychologists, seemed caught up in the excitment generated by Rhine's drive and enthusiasm and willingness to try anything, no matter how outlandish and especially since their department head was interested. Here were two very bright, experienced psychologists offering their assistance, and Rhine admitted that "the suggestions of my colleagues, Lundholm and Zener, could not, I think, have fallen on more eager ears anywhere on the inhabited globe. The encouragement of their offers to cooperate was the only thing needed to overcome the diffidence I felt in introducing these unconventional problems into university laboratories."[5] Zener and Lundholm made different suggestions at about the same time, and Rhine decided to try both.

Zener proposed attempting to replicate a 1928 experiment by a British psychical researcher, Ina Jephson. She had tested 240 people at one time, asking them to identify playing cards in sealed envelopes. When those people took the hidden cards home with them, clairvoyance was apparently demonstrated. When they were later asked to make their guesses with the experimenter in attendance, the scores dropped to chance. It appeared that when the opportunity to cheat occurred, people cheated; although there could be other explanations for failure.

The idea of mass testing appealed to Rhine. Perhaps out of their combined psychology classes a psychic star would emerge.

He wanted to use targets that could be evaluated more certainly than the numbered cards, for some people had lucky and unlucky numbers and might call them too frequently or avoid them altogether and so cloud results. Zener, an expert in perception, gladly agreed to think up simple symbols that were clearly distinct from one another. Rhine finally settled for the five cards still in use: a cross or plus, circle, square, star, and wavy lines. As a friendly gesture, Rhine called them Zener cards, until Zener became embarrassed by the association. Now they're known as ESP cards. By using these in packs of twenty-five, with five symbols in each, the experimenters had a simple way of testing. By chance alone, a subject should guess an average of five right out of twenty-five.

Lundholm suggested giving hypnosis another try. In altered states of consciousness, especially hypnosis, the extrasensory world had seemed more accessible to many of the early psychical researchers. Rhine agreed, but didn't know how to hypnotize. No problem; Lundholm and McDougall would teach him. Rhine was an apt pupil. He not only used hypnosis for ESP experiments, but taught it in his psychology classes and used it therapeutically.

"The history of parapsychology is interwoven with the history of mesmerism and hypnosis," Rhine told me in an October 30, 1978, interview. "McDougall was very good at and interested in hypnosis and so was Lundholm. . . . Go back to the history of hypnosis and you discover some of the British and other European explorers in the field spent years on a subject sometimes. They would give hundreds of sessions—men like Bernheim.* We never spent very long with it; we didn't have the time.

"I gave a course in hypnosis at Duke to train and teach a few selected people. One was a young man with a business friend who had migraine in the usual recurrent way. And this man pleaded with my student to use his newly acquired skill. And he hypnotized him. He reported to me six weeks after—and the man still had no recurrence of migraine, which was an unusually long time [for him to be free of migraine].

"I got into this sort of thing myself, more or less accidentally. I was once working with a secretary whose help I needed very much and she told me she was just coming into her menstrual period and wouldn't be able to work for the next few days. I asked her if she would like to be helped on that and she eagerly responded. And we got something then which almost pulled me out of my enthusiasm for parapsychology—at least for a time—because she responded so beautifully [to the hypnotic suggestion] and escaped her period of pain so completely that she begged me to do this for her regularly. Well, I wasn't headed for that, much as I sympathized."

Anthony Westerhof was increasingly critical of Rhine's work and methods—to him Rhine was overzealous and excessive in grabbing at anyone as a possible subject for an experiment. He especially damned what he saw as Rhine's misuse of hypnosis.

"Rhine was overdramatizing the effects and getting students he was hypnotizing greatly excited by what they thought of as this marvelous new 'miracle.' He was very much a disciple of the notion that courses ought to be interesting and exciting, whatever else they were. Some students thought Rhine was Jesus Christ. Others regarded him as a phony. This opinion of phoniness was more common among graduate students.

"Although McDougall was interested in hypnosis, it was in a much more dignified way than Rhine. Some students were said to have raved on a bus about Rhine bringing out several personalities and so on; that is, he purposely made things very dramatic. [Echoes of the criticism of McDougall's handling of hypnosis in his younger days

*Hippolyte Bernheim (1840–1919). Sigmund Freud learned hypnosis from him and from Jean Martin Charcot. Bernheim's Suggestive Therapeutics: A Treatise on the Nature and Uses of Hypnotism (1888) is a classic.

in England.] McDougall simply presented the methods and didn't encourage anybody to try it. In spite of that, students took over hypnosis on their own and did such things as hypnotizing other people in the dormitory. There was one case in which a student's family had been wiped out in an automobile accident, and under hypnosis he got to weeping profusely. And the students couldn't stop him. They got McDougall up in the middle of the night. He told them there was nothing to do but let him become so fatigued that he'd fall asleep. Those early days were pretty interesting."[6]

Especially for Rhine. He had seen the power of hypnosis for himself. The ability to stop pain seemed almost miraculous. He anticipated that it might also be the key to an ESP breakthrough—so Lundholm hypnotized volunteers to test them for telepathy. For one series of tests students were given a posthypnotic suggestion that they would reveal the number or letter of the alphabet Rhine or Lundholm had in mind. Another experiment required the student in a post-hypnotic state to place his finger in the center of a circle that was divided into slices, like a pie. He was then asked to move his finger into the segment mentally selected by the experimenter.

Results of these tests, though only just above what would be expected by chance, encouraged Rhine to keep at it.

The Westerhof-Rhine friendship had gone from cool to cold. The big freeze came when Westerhof was presenting a dissertation for his master's degree and had to defend it before a committee—and Rhine was among those he would have to face.

"Rhine was on my dissertation committee and called me one day," Westerhof recollects. "He'd learned I'd expressed skepticism to various people about the soundness of his ESP experiments and he told me, if I remember correctly, that I was unfair and behaving as if insane and had a serious persecution complex. His attitude certainly was threatening."[7]

McDougall chaired the dissertation committee and looked on with benign amusement as Westerhof and Rhine battled in a low-key but aggressive exchange. Westerhof said he had no faith in Rhine's experiments. Rhine vigorously defended them and made it clear that he considered Westerhof a wet blanket with a closed mind.

Finally, when the time came to vote on Westerhof's work, Rhine abstained. Nevertheless, Westerhof passed.

Afterward, Westerhof recalls, "Rhine talked to me with tears in his voice about the good days when we were friends."[8] But their friendship was never rekindled. It was unlikely Rhine would find much time for someone who scorned his work, and remained scornful.

Rhine's good days, in fact, were just ahead.

10

BREAKTHROUGH
1931

Duke had become the first university to bring miracles into the laboratory for long-term study: miracles, because they seemed to defy the laws of time and space. The embryonic science of parapsychology* was coming to life, and the search had begun in earnest for the elusive, ephemeral and quite possibly nonexistent extrasensory powers and perceptions. But why associate the enterprise with psychology? Because, explained Rhine, psychic phenomena appeared to demonstrate personal and purposive characteristics.[1]

At first just four men were actively involved—William McDougall with his two former students, Karl Zener and Helge Lundholm; and J. B. Rhine. All except Rhine were trained psychologists. But he had studied psychology for a year at Harvard and was to continue those studies at Duke. Now they were a team, exploring for the hidden energies of the mind. Many of their colleagues thought the team would be more usefully employed in hunting for a unicorn— until the unicorn metamorphosized in the guise of a student named Linzmayer.

Adam J. Linzmayer didn't give a damn about psychology. In the spring of 1931, the dog days of the Depression, he was an economics undergraduate just managing to stay at Duke by working during the vacations. He took psychology as an elective, and although he respected —even admired—McDougall and Rhine, he sometimes cut their classes by getting a friend to call his name at roll call. He felt justified because he was on a secret mission for the president—Franklin Roosevelt— and needed free time to work at it. An anonymous visiting professor had recruited Linzmayer and a handful of other students—all of whom remained anonymous—to form a secret Think Tank. Their objective was to come up with ideas to beat the Depression. Linzmayer

---

*McDougall and Rhine adapted the German word parapsychologie and called their experimental approach to psychic research "parapsychology."

attended the hush-hush meetings faithfully and eagerly, proud to be called upon to help his country. Suddenly the meetings were disbanded. The visiting professor, he was told, had become seriously ill. The man never returned and that was the last Linzmayer heard of the secret Think Tank.

For a while Linzmayer wandered about the Duke campus like a charging knight thrown from his horse. He was unable to have even the satisfaction of talking things over with former members of the select group—he didn't know their names.

Now he had no reason to skip psychology classes. He attended them, but without enthusiasm. And when Professor McDougall interrupted one lecture in the large amphitheater to hand out cards wrapped and sealed in foil to each student, Linzmayer casually listened to the instructions and carried them out listlessly. It was a guessing game. McDougall explained that there was one of five symbols written on the hidden card and students were requested to write on the outside which symbol they thought it to be and also to sign their names. Linzmayer obeyed, almost without thinking. But at subsequent lectures, when more hidden cards were handed out, he tried a little harder, used a little thought.

Was he becoming paranoid? He noticed that when he answered his name at roll call, both McDougall and Rhine stared at him. Had they discovered that at previous lectures someone else had answered his name? He was uneasy when Rhine called him aside one day.

Rhine explained that of the hundreds of students asked to guess the symbols on the hidden cards, Linzmayer's three right out of five were the best results. Would he be willing to do more experiments of this nature? Linzmayer already allied himself with those who saw Rhine as Jesus rather than jackass, and when Rhine explained the ultimate purpose of these tests, the economics student agreed to cooperate. Once again he was being asked to help in a worthwhile cause—and this could have even more impact than ending the Depression.[2]

However, results of the next few tests were disappointing, and Rhine suggested a different tack. Had Linzmayer ever been hypnotized? No. Would he be willing? Yes. Rhine assured him that it was harmless, but that early psychical researchers reported remarkable results with some of their subjects.

Unfortunately, Linzmayer was difficult to hypnotize. When he turned up at the parapsychology lab on the evening of May 21, 1931, he resisted Rhine's attempts to put him into a trance. He fought Rhine's suggestions as if—although consciously he wanted to cooperate—his unconscious rebelled. The most Rhine achieved was putting Linzmayer into a light trance.

Disappointed, Rhine left Linzmayer on the couch and walked over to the window. Rather than dismiss Linzmayer and record the evening as wasted effort, Rhine began to run a test. He first checked that the pack of cards he held face down were out of Linzmayer's line of vision. To make certain, he shielded them with his free hand. He glanced at the top one. "What is it?" he asked. Linzmayer guessed correctly. "And this?" Right again. Linzmayer made nine guesses in a row and every guess was right.

Rhine was elated. The odds against accurately calling nine ESP cards in sequence are about two million to one. Rhine asked Linzmayer to return the next day. Again he called nine times in succession without a mistake. The odds against twice making those calls by chance are astronomical, and when he was told, Linzmayer shared Rhine's excitement. On that second day, Rhine resumed testing until Linzmayer had called a total of 300 cards. He got 119 right—almost double chance expectation. No one at Duke had come close to that score in months of testing.

Trying to work out what conditions gave best results, Linzmayer concluded that they occurred when he looked out of the window of the lab.

Linzmayer took exams during the next ten days and had no time to spare for Rhine, who was naturally eager to continue testing. He had found his exceptional ESP scorer at last—but almost at the end of the academic year. Linzmayer, short of money and with a summer job lined up, was anxious to go to it without delay. The only opportunity for Rhine and Linzmayer to get together again was on the last day. Knowing how much it meant to Rhine, Linzmayer told a friend to wait for him—they were going to drive home together—and agreed to give Rhine every spare moment of that last day.

So, on the last morning, June 3, Linzmayer arrived at the laboratory on the top floor of the Duke Medical Building. He remembered he made his best scores by looking out of the window. He gazed across the treetops; Rhine turned the cards. Results were good, but not outstanding. Rhine thought boredom might be eroding Linzmayer's ESP and decided to fight monotony with scenery, by driving the young man through a nearby forest. Rhine planned to stop at intervals of several miles, but he was so keen to test Linzmayer as much as possible that he made the first stop in the old Essex about a mile early. He left the engine running to drown out his voice should he unconsciously whisper the answers, put a large notebook across Linzmayer's knees as a makeshift table, and took a pack of ESP cards from his pocket.

Linzmayer prepared for the test by leaning back in his seat beside Rhine and looking up at the roof. There were no mirrors or shiny surfaces to reflect the cards. But, as an added precaution, Linzmayer closed his eyes and kept them closed throughout the test.

Rhine cut the pack, drew off the top card with his left hand, tipped it toward himself just enough to glimpse the symbol as he shielded it with his right hand, then put it face down on the notebook. Linzmayer felt the pressure as Rhine put down the card. About two seconds later, without touching it, he said, "Circle."

"Right," said Rhine, laying it as the first on the "right" pile.

He put the next card down. "Plus," Linzmayer said. "Right," said Rhine. "Waves." "Right." "Waves." "Right." "Star." "Right."

Linzmayer called fifteen cards in succession without a single mistake. Amazed, Rhine stopped for a while.

"No conceivable deviation from probability, no 'streak of luck' which either of us had ever heard of could parallel such a sequence of unbroken hits," said Rhine later. "We both knew that the thing Linzmayer had just done was virtually impossible by all the rules in the book of chance, but he had done it."[3]

Of the next ten cards, Linzmayer got four wrong, so that his total score was twenty-one correct calls out of twenty-five.

"We both knew," wrote Rhine, "that we were on the threshold of proof for the existence of extrasensory perception which would be able to satisfy even the most skeptical."[4]

Rhine conceded that the testing had not been under strict controls, and was at best exploratory, but "with all the skepticism I can muster . . . I still do not see how any sensory cues could have revealed to Linzmayer the symbols of those twenty-one cards he called correctly."[5]

Linzmayer was almost as exuberant as Rhine, but he was also anxious to leave for his long journey home. Rhine said he wanted to try more tests. Linzmayer protested, but Rhine persisted in driving on through the forest, stopping occasionally for more tests.

Admitting to himself that he was being "heartless" and "ruthless" in overriding Linzmayer's urge to quit, Rhine pressed him to stay longer than he had promised, to see if being hurried and pressured to work against his will would affect his scores.* It clearly did. In six hundred previous trials he had averaged ten right calls for each twenty-five cards. Pressured and rushed for nine hundred further trials, he got chance or just below—four or five cards right for each twenty-five calls.[6]

Rhine and Linzmayer were the only witnesses to that remarkable occasion of high ESP scores that justify calling Linzmayer an ESP

---

*Rhine had a definite point in mind when he pushed Linzmayer to exhaustion—to see if ESP works like other mental abilities in connection with or response to physiological conditions.

genius. Rhine judged Linzmayer to be unshakably honest. He even tested him under sodium amytal and gave him a chance to cheat—but Linzmayer didn't take it. Linzmayer characterizes Rhine as "an absolutely honest and objective scientist. I would say that without qualification. I think he is without doubt possibly the finest man I've ever known. I admire him completely." Linzmayer did not deny that cheating occurred at times. "I have seen students admit to fooling Dr. Rhine, and he immediately said: 'Let them go!' That was all. I can remember one student in particular. Dr. Rhine threw his rule on the table and said: 'I'll test no more with you!' I asked Dr. Rhine: 'What happened?' and he said: 'I just knew he was trying to cheat!' "[7]

More than forty years later Linzmayer recalls that car ride in the old Essex through the North Carolina countryside: "I remember how angry I was with myself that I was in one of these moods where I let what had gone before affect me. We had a run. And then I started reasoning, 'It can't be a plus [sign] again.' And that was my first miss. I found that the way to score successfully was not to attempt to use my judgment on what happened before. The first figure that came into my mind: I found that was the best way to do it. One of the things I admired very much about Dr. Rhine was how he was very thorough in any testing he did. He leaned over backwards not to help, almost. I feel sure he was anxious to have the results be good, but I also feel he was so much a scientist he didn't want to encourage anything unfairly."[8]

Parapsychology's golden era was just beginning. Rhine was satisfied that he had seen ESP at work. But *how* did it work? And would it manifest itself again? Linzmayer had to return home to New Jersey for the summer. Perhaps Rhine could get him back in the fall. Perhaps? Rhine would surely get him back.

11

UPTON SINCLAIR AND ALBERT EINSTEIN 1930–1932

While Rhine tested children in the North Carolina summer camps during July and August 1930, McDougall tested the wife of novelist Upton Sinclair in their Pasadena, California, home. Sinclair's second wife, Mary Craig, had what appeared to be psychic experiences from childhood, at times apparently reading her mother's mind, anticipating her wishes, and even sharing a dream—of looking for a needle in the bed. Once, in late November 1916, she told Sinclair that she felt their mutual friend, novelist Jack London, was in great mental distress. Two days later, they learned that he had died on November 22—and soon after heard that he had killed himself with a morphine overdose.[1]

Determined to put her apparent powers to a foolproof test, Mrs. Sinclair not only tore her husband away from his writing on social injustice to conduct telepathy experiments with her, but dictated the methods. One was to lie in semidarkness on a couch in her study, while Sinclair sat some thirty feet away in the adjoining room, with the door closed. Sinclair thought of an object, sketched it with a pencil, then called out, "All right." Mrs. Sinclair closed her eyes and achieved a state of concentration through relaxing—a practice she had adopted for several years in efforts to perceive by extrasensory means. When an image came to her repeatedly, she opened her eyes, sat up, and sketched it. They then compared sketches.

At times her written descriptions were so accurate that only astonishing luck, collusion, or ESP could explain them. In an early experiment with her brother-in-law Robert L. Irwin, he had drawn a table fork. Her written description was: "See a table fork nothing else." Exactly right, yet he was in Pasadena at the time and she in her Long Beach home thirty miles away. After Sinclair had drawn a cow with its tongue sticking out, Mary Craig wrote: "Muley cow with tongue hanging out." It's true, his drawing did look like a strange breed of half mule, half cow.

Sinclair contracted to have these experiments published as a book, to be called *Mental Radio*, and asked McDougall to write an introduction. McDougall agreed. He hoped the book would arouse others to undertake similar experiments; regarded Sinclair as a fearless, honest man and the greatest American alive; and not least of all he was impressed with the book. His verdict, in the introduction, was that "the degree of success and the conditions of the experiment were such that we can reject them as conclusive evidence of some mode of communication not at present explicable in accepted scientific terms only by assuming that Mr. and Mrs. Sinclair either are grossly stupid, incompetent and careless persons or have deliberately entered upon a conspiracy to deceive the public in a most reprehensible fashion."

McDougall wanted to test Mrs. Sinclair for himself, but she was reluctant. In contrast to her gregarious, outgoing husband, she was a hypersensitive, private person, and she was also going through menopause. Although she felt that her psychic abilities depended on solitude and complete relaxation, because of her respect for McDougall and her urge to know the truth about herself, she eventually agreed to cooperate with him. So McDougall took a trip to the West Coast and asked her to try to identify cards in sealed envelopes. Her results were above chance, though not as striking as in the previous sketching tests with her husband. Unwilling to abandon a promising subject, McDougall proposed that Rhine should continue the testing the following summer, and the Sinclairs said he would be welcome.

But Rhine was preceded by another visitor—Albert Einstein. He called on the Sinclairs early in 1931.

How Sinclair persuaded Einstein to write a preface for *Mental Radio*, in which he plugged the book, even today baffles scientists antagonistic to ESP, some suggesting that he must have done it under the "old pals" act. After all, if true, telepathy would put Einstein's space-time theory in jeopardy. As we shall learn later, Einstein had an ambivalent atttitude toward Rhine's work. Einstein did not endorse telepathy in the preface—but he accepted it as an open question.

Einstein wrote of his confidence in Upton Sinclair's honesty, reliability, and powers of observation. He did not consider it possible that Sinclair was trying to deceive the public in *Mental Radio*, but, at the same time, he admitted the results of the Sinclairs' telepathy experiments baffled him. Einstein speculated that if [as he clearly hoped and believed] telepathy did not explain the phenomenon, perhaps some unconscious hypnotic influence between the couple was involved. If that was true, Einstein concluded, it should still be of great psychological interest. And he enthusiastically recommended those interested in psychology to read Sinclair's book.

Was Einstein suggesting that the Sinclairs had unconsciously put themselves in hypnotic trances, during which time they shared the same thoughts? This would be just another way of describing telepathy.

His friendly attitude toward Sinclair is understandable. Both were driven men with a childlike purity of vision that baffled and antagonized the worldly wise; both were humanists and socialists who believed fervently in the brotherhood of man and in social justice.

As for proving his own intuitively held beliefs to be true, Einstein said:

If you want me to prove what I believe, I can't. You know them to be true but you could spend a whole lifetime without being able to prove them. The mind can proceed only so far upon what it knows and can prove. There comes a point where the mind takes a higher plane of knowledge but can never prove how it got there. All great discoveries have involved such a leap.[2]

These could be the words of a psychic or medium. They fit in with his response to people who tried to get him to take a stand for or against God. When cornered by the Jewish philosopher Martin Buber, Einstein answered: "What we [physicists] strive for is just to draw His lines after Him,"[3] which sounds like an attempt at celestial or transcendental telepathy—to read and interpret the mind of God.

Sinclair believed that his houseguest Roman Ostoja might convert Einstein to a belief in the extrasensory world. Ostoja was able to put himself into a cataleptic trance during which he could lie horizontally, supported only by chairs at his head and feet. He didn't sag even when a 150-pound rock was placed on his abdomen, and showed no sign of injury or even discomfort when someone swung a sledgehammer and smashed the rock. Sinclair was so intrigued by this lean, muscular, dark-eyed man that he treated him as a member of the family, and invited friends and relatives to attend séances at which Ostoja demonstrated his powers. One evening, while Ostoja was in a trance, his knees and ankles held by sitters, a thirty-four-pound table rose four feet in the air and then moved slowly sideways for eight feet. Sinclair had been one of the eyewitnesses. If only Ostoja repeated this performance before Einstein, thought Sinclair, the world could no longer scoff.

The great scientist agreed to attend a séance at Sinclair's home, and brought with him a doctor friend, Professor Richard Chase Tolman of the California Institute of Technology, and Helen Dukas, Einstein's secretary. She recalls that momentous occasion: "Sinclair addressed us before the séance and said we shouldn't be afraid if suddenly the piano starts to play and flowers come from above. I was frightened to death. It was a really scary atmosphere. And, oh my gosh, suddenly the doorbell rang and I nearly jumped out of my skin. I was sitting outside the circle and I went to the door—and it was just a harmless telegram. And the medium went into catalepsy and made mumbling noises. And then . . . nothing happened."[4] Sinclair was naturally very disappointed and blamed the failure on 'hostile forces.' He said that because they were not believing in it that there was a counter-influence."[5] Walter Franklin Prince tested Ostoja and judged him to be a fraud. He explained to Sinclair that the man was obviously a clever magician as well as a con artist. Sinclair eventually broke off with Ostoja, transferring his interests to a medium named Arthur Ford.

A third party (probably Sinclair) told Rhine that during this visit to the United States, Einstein said how much he empathized with Rhine, who was being bombarded by critics. If anyone had suffered from critics, it was Einstein. Typical was Captain Thomas Jefferson Jackson See, a U.S. Navy mathematical astronomer who denounced Einstein as an impostor and plagiarist whose "fundamental postulates are crazy vagaries, disgraceful in a scientific age and repudiated by reputable French and German scholars."[6]

A few months after Einstein left the Sinclairs, Rhine prepared to join them. His summer, as always, would be a working vacation. He was in a buoyant mood after his successful work with Linzmayer. First he led a group of researchers away from the sweltering Durham city heat to a mountaintop laboratory at Cragsmoor in New York State. The building was reputed to be haunted.

Then Rhine set off for California to meet the man he admired enormously. Since boyhood, Rhine had hero-worshiped Sinclair, who claimed that when he died, "Social Justice" would be found written on his heart.[7] And that was no braggart's boast. Few in America had done as much to help the poor and put-upon. Through his efforts in exposing the nauseating conditions in Chicago meat-packing plants, both the lives of the workers and the purity of the meat were improved. His 1906 book, *The Jungle*, graphically revealing the filthy conditions, moved the government to pass the first pure-food laws. When his 1927 novel, *Oil*, showing the corruption and bribery in the oil industry was banned in Boston, ostensibly for its explicit sex scenes, Sinclair went to Boston and sold the book in the streets. The following year, at his wife's insistence, Sinclair began to test her for telepathy, and the outstanding results brought Rhine into the picture. But when he arrived on the West Coast and tried to give Sinclair his estimated time of arrival, Rhine couldn't reach him. Sinclair's phone number was unlisted and the operator refused to divulge it. Although Rhine was expected, Sinclair didn't know when, and he was caught by surprise.

"He was huddled under a big Mexican sombrero, weeding the garden," Rhine recalls. "He looked up at me and I smiled. I can see his eyes dancing around. 'What are you doing here? How did you get in?' and so forth. But in a moment I had identified myself and he was warm and friendly—as he always was. McDougall thought he was the greatest man in America and was amazed at the grasp of his mind. He must have been a tremendous and speedy reader. And he had an imagination that was huge compared to his size. He was a slightly built man. You got to know him quickly because he had no blinds and no locks on his doors. He would be guarded at his front door—but he'd leave the gate open. That's symbolic. He was the kind of man you felt you wouldn't need to pry to get to know him."[8]

Rhine and Sinclair hit it off and, after this first meeting, they corresponded regularly, sometimes as often as twice a week.

Sinclair kept Rhine up to date with the psychics he encountered in California, genuine and fake, and the séances to which he invited Charlie Chaplin and Theodore Dreiser. He was Rhine's eyes and ears on the West Coast.

Sinclair was eager to learn of the latest ESP news from the greatest living authority, while Rhine was proud to have such a loyal and lively correspondent.

But at his first meeting with the Sinclairs, Rhine was disappointed. Mrs. Sinclair said she was too ill to submit to Rhine's card tests. This was like telling him he mustn't breathe. However, she almost made up for it by describing his research as the most important work in the world and willingly answering his questions. One was: What led you to take such a serious interest in telepathy?

Mrs. Sinclair recalled their conversation in her autobiography:

I told him at some length of my search for God and for a purpose in the universe, and I knew that the place to find Him was in the mind. Rhine remarked that this had been his own motivation. Upton told at length of his interest in the subject of psychic research, dating from his youth, and how long he waited for a chance to witness some proof of the reality of such phenomena. At last it had come about by accident—he had discovered it in his own home![9]

Mrs. Sinclair characterized Rhine as:

.. a consecrated man not interested in personal fame. What he wants is understanding, and the power to give it to others. This has made a close bond of friendship between him and my husband, who shares this attitude toward both understanding and fame.[10]

Some say she was wrong about both men—that, in fact, they were supreme egoists for whom fame was partly the name of the game. Sinclair was so set on winning the Nobel Prize that he paid his former secretary, Ernest S. Greene, to canvass for 770 signatories from 55 countries to support his candidacy—among those responding favorably were Albert Einstein, William McDougall, Bertrand Russell, George Bernard Shaw, Sir Arthur Pinero, Siegfried Sassoon, and Romain Rolland. He never got the prize.[11] Sinclair certainly out-egoed Rhine—and the closest J.B. got to the Nobel Prize was a letter by Carl Jung suggesting he deserved it.*

What Sinclair's friendship meant to Rhine can be judged from the start of a letter he sent to the novelist on August 29, 1932: "Little did I suppose that back twenty years ago or more, when my father read 'you' to us from the *Physical Culture Magazine* (I think you translated 'Damaged Goods,' didn't you?) that some day that author would send me one of his books.† Believe me, it was one of the proudest moments of my life and it will be almost as great an event to my old father as it was to me."

Much as Rhine wanted to stay with the Sinclairs, in the hope that Mrs. Sinclair would submit to his card tests, he had an appointment with Linzmayer at Duke in a few weeks.

In a September 9, 1953, letter to Carleton Smith, founder and president of the National Arts Foundation, Jung wrote: "A prize should be given to people who successfully suppress the outburst of political madness, or of panic (Churchill!), or who produce great ideas enlarging the mental and spiritual horizon of man. Great discoveries concerning the origin of man . . . or the nature of the psyche (for instance J. B. Rhine for his extrasensory perception experiments) should be rewarded."

†*Probably* Mountain City, *a novel that was partly a* roman à clef.

12

THE HUMAN
GUINEA PIG
1931–1933

Reluctant to lose touch with Linzmayer, his first consistently high scorer, Rhine had lured him back to Duke in the fall of 1931 with a small grant to cover expenses for a week and what may have seemed like a promise of immortality. Using the ESP cards, Rhine tested him for clairvoyance. Results were so-so. Had he lost the sense of adventure? Was it too much like work? Rhine wondered. Or was it because Linzmayer had a reputation to uphold and the strain inhibited ESP? Rhine tried to enliven the tests with challenges and changes of setting. They had worked before.

In all, Rhine tested Linzmayer for clairvoyance 945 times. By chance he should have guessed 189 right. He guessed 246, an average of 6.5 out of 25; well above chance, but a dramatic drop from his 9.9 average earlier in the year. At least Linzmayer was still capable of demonstrating clairvoyance. Rhine hoped to test him again in the spring.

Throughout the winter of 1931, 24 people made 800 card calls. Their average was 6.5 out of 25, just high enough to keep ESP alive, but few individuals seemed able to sustain high scores. Rhine speculated that this inability was the inevitable result of boredom—that to maintain enthusiasm at such a routine task was impossible. ESP appeared to be an unconscious faculty and because of that, no one could be trained to improve. He compared it with the ability to write poetry, pointing out that the same obstacles to writing poetry—initial self-doubts, self-consciousness, strangeness, distracting environment —also inhibited ESP. Unfortunately, removing those obstacles did not automatically guarantee the production of either poetry or ESP.

In March of 1932 he again persuaded Linzmayer to return from New Jersey to Duke. His average clairvoyant score had improved slightly since his last visit, from 6.5 to 6.8.

To say that Rhine resorted to secrecy in his work is probably an exaggeration, but the atmosphere at Duke persuaded him to soft-pedal anything like hypnosis, still then easily misunderstood by parents. Duke was a conservative, even straitlaced university with aspirations. The decorous behavior of the divinity students on campus in an atmosphere already dampened by the Depression tended to highlight anything that seemed frivolous or foolhardy. It was remarkable that such a university would shortly house and sponsor the first parapsychology lab.

Rhine feared that bad publicity could kill his research before it got off the ground. Rumor had already distorted his use of hypnosis into a magic cure for migraine and period pains. A busload of Duke students listened avidly to other tall tales of one man giving birth to seven personalities and another able to see without using his eyes— after Rhine had entranced both men. So when Rhine decided to test a drug on a volunteer—Linzmayer—to see if it affected ESP, he made sure there were no witnesses.

Rhine arranged to be alone in the lab on the afternoon that Adam Linzmayer arrived to take sodium amytal—a narcotic drug, which Rhine assured him was harmless and not habit-forming. Linzmayer first demonstrated ESP in his normal condition by sustaining his recent correct guessing at an average of 6.8 cards out of 25. Rhine then gave him the first dose of sodium amytal, and both men waited for it to take effect. Nothing happened. Half an hour later Rhine repeated the dose. And waited. Again nothing happened. Linzmayer, who had "playfully resisted" as if he was too powerful to be put under, really seemed immune to the drug. Rhine risked one more dose. That did it. Linzmayer behaved as though moderately drunk. "His tongue was thick and his speech somewhat incoherent. He was talkative and frank and had trouble in walking straight."[1] And in that state he scored an average of five right calls out of twenty-five; exactly chance.

Testing became more and more difficult, as Linzmayer began to slump in his chair and grew less and less capable of sitting up straight. Finally he staggered to the couch used for hypnosis sessions, lay down, and fell asleep. The three doses of sodium amytal had combined to knock him out. Rhine had what looked like a drunk on his hands.

He thought to call for help, then realized that would be fatal. One witness and the story would be spread through the dormitories that Rhine was drugging students. And he didn't want to have to explain Linzmayer's condition to anyone, even to scotch rumors, because he was reluctant to be forced to disclose "my research prematurely to campus curiosity."

Shaking Linzmayer and shouting at him had as much effect as if he had been a dummy. Rhine resorted to hammering on the soles of his feet until Linzmayer opened his eyes and then, with Rhine's help, stood upright. The two men slowly shuffled across the room like exhausted marathon dancers. Rhine checked to see if the corridor was empty before helping Linzmayer into the elevator that took them to the rear exit. The coast was clear. They continued their shuffle to Rhine's car, where Linzmayer slumped in the backseat. He was asleep again before Rhine got the car started.

Hoping fresh air would revive Linzmayer, Rhine drove him through the countryside for about an hour with all windows open. It didn't work. So Rhine headed for his home, where he hurriedly made coffee, brought it back to the car, shook Linzmayer awake, and persuaded him to swallow two cups full. Rhine took the cup and jug back to his house. When he returned to the car, Linzmayer had dropped off to sleep again.

By now it was late evening and Rhine had the cover of darkness. He used it to smuggle Linzmayer into his dormitory while the other resident students were at supper. Again he had to shake him awake and then support him as the two of them shuffled slowly to the bathroom, where Rhine left Linzmayer under a cold shower murmuring sleepily that he'd be okay.

Rhine was enormously relieved to see Linzmayer the next day—wan, but otherwise showing no signs of his ordeal. Linzmayer, for his part, was pleased to hear he had made another important contribution to research. The experiment, said Rhine, had clearly indicated that the narcotic drug eliminated Linzmayer's ESP, without destroying his sensory perception. Thinking about the aftermath of the experiment, Rhine realized that in their efforts for science the two of them had given a good imitation of a scene from a Charlie Chaplin comedy.[2]

Linzmayer returned to Duke in the spring of 1933, and in 2,000 trials his average dropped to 5.9, maintaining its downward drift to not much above chance. Rhine speculated that he was partly to blame for this decline through pressuring Linzmayer to work when he was anxious to leave.[3]

13

THE GOLDEN ERA
1932–1934

The search for a second Linzmayer obsessed Rhine during the summer and fall of 1932.

The results from one high scorer could be dismissed as a freak performance. If ESP existed and was part of man's nature, then others must have it, too. So the need to find another above-chance scorer was urgent, if ESP wasn't to take its place in the history of pseudo-sciences alongside phrenology, numerology, astrology, and reading the future from the entrails of slaughtered animals. Demonstrating it in one man would convince nobody worth convincing.

Rhine, now thirty-seven, responded expectantly to every squeaking door, ringing phone, and unfamiliar footstep in the corridor in his search for the next ESP star. He tested eighty students, but not one gave a hint that he or she was a second Linzmayer. Instead they called so close to chance that they confirmed the theory of probability. Eighteen of them did slightly better or worse than chance, and he retained them for further testing.

As a psychology instructor Rhine had surprised and amused his sophomore class by telling them he was learning psychology along with them, having recently switched from botany. One of his students, Joseph Gaither Pratt, who, like Rhine, had abandoned plans to become a minister, had been particularly impressed with Rhine's frankness and striking personality. Pratt lost touch with Rhine after that course, until his senior year when, to his delight, Rhine was his instructor in logic. Again, Rhine confessed he was only teaching the subject because he wanted to learn it himself. But it was obvious to Pratt that Rhine's main interest was in the ESP tests he was giving whenever he found the opportunity.

Although Pratt doubted the existence of ESP, he thought it was a subject worth scientific study. So when Rhine offered him a job as his research assistant in ESP, Pratt accepted. Pratt needed the money to support himself during a semester of graduate work in psychology, but he also relished the idea of working with Rhine whose enthusiasm and drive seemed almost superhuman. Pratt's first task was to find willing Duke students and then to give them ESP tests.

Starting in January 1932, he worked with about a dozen students, none of whom displayed ESP. Anxious to succeed, though believing he was employed in a lost cause, Pratt tested himself for hour after hour, day after day. His results were no better than those of the others he had tested, and naturally reinforced his doubt in the existence of ESP.[1]

Although Rhine had rejected orthodox religion, he had no qualms about recruiting divinity students as guinea pigs or researchers. With this in mind, he gave a talk to an assembly of them in the spring of 1932, outlining his motives, methods, breakthrough with Linzmayer, and subsequent repeated failure with others. One of the students waited behind afterward.

He was diffident and shy, but he immediately held Rhine's attention. His name, he said, was Hubert Pearce, and he knew for a fact that psychic powers existed. "How is that?" Rhine asked. Because, said the student, both he and his mother had such powers. As a boy in Arkansas, Pearce had seen his mother rest her hands lightly on one end of a heavy oak table and ask several men in the room to try to prevent it from rising. They put all their weight on the table and strained to keep it down. She warned them it would break if they didn't let go. But they held on and as Pearce watched, enthralled and scared, the table buckled, then split across the middle. Pearce told Rhine he thought he had a similar uncanny power—and was afraid of it.

Such claims were no news to Rhine, but they invariably failed to check out. However, Pearce's nervous, hesitant manner enhanced his credibility. And Rhine was ready to grasp at almost any straw. The problem was that Pearce didn't want to be tested. Rhine assured him that there was nothing to fear and that by working with him, Pearce had a chance to confirm some of the mind-over-matter miracles reported in the Bible. What could be more fitting than a divinity student demonstrating the true nature of man, his spiritual or transcendental gifts, and in a doubting world adding scientific validity to biblical teachings? As usual, Rhine's twin gifts of patience and persistence worked. Having reassured Pearce that his fears were unfounded, Rhine handed him over to his assistant, Gaither Pratt.

To put him at ease, Pearce was first tested with the ESP cards in his dormitory and then in the Duke psychology lab. Pratt gave him fifty chances to demonstrate clairvoyance—with the card symbols hidden from both men. The results were dismal, indicating that Pearce had imagined or wildly exaggerated his powers. But Pratt kept at it and

Pearce's average scores began to climb. He went from chance expectation of five right out of twenty-five, to six, to seven, to eight, and finally
to nine. His average hovered around nine for hundreds, then thousands
of trials.

Pearce had not yet matched Linzmayer's most spectacular
calls—nine right out of twenty-five, three times consecutively, and
fifteen correct calls in succession—but his high sustained average
was unmatched. Gradually, greater precautions were introduced to
prevent Pearce from accidentally or deliberately cheating. At times
screens were used to hide the cards from him. When Pearce was
allowed to handle the cards, Rhine supplied a new pack for each run,
to guard against the possibility that Pearce had marked the backs or
could manipulate them to his advantage by some cardsharper's or
conjurer's trick.

Visitors had a sharp but temporary depressing effect on
Pearce's clairvoyant powers. With Dr. Karl Zener present, Pearce's
average score dropped from 11.5 to 5, then climbed back up to 9.9. Dr.
Thomas caused the average to drop from 10.3 to 5.2, then he saw it
climb to 15. When McDougall came to watch, Pearce's average fell from
11.3 to 6.5, but soon rose to 9.3. Lundholm saw it seesaw from 9.8 to 7,
then reach 9.7. A local magician known as Wallace the Magician
arrived on a day when Pearce had tonsillitis and his average was a
comparatively low 7.5. The magician's presence apparently lowered it
even more, to 5, but he stayed for 125 more calls when Pearce raised his
average back to 7.5.

Rhine found a way to introduce observers without their
presence reducing Pearce's score. If the visitor was ostensibly acting as
a coexperimenter or had a job to do, there was no dip in Pearce's
scoring.

For two years of frequent testing, Hubert Pearce sustained his
score and even increased his average to 10 right out of 25 by the time he
graduated as a minister. Pearce could score high or low on request,
getting 9 right out of 25 when asked to call high, and 1 out of 25 when
told to aim low. And once, with Rhine testing, Pearce outdid anyone
ever tested at Duke before or since.

Invariably the last to leave his laboratory, Rhine was there late
one afternoon when Pearce stopped by briefly, in a hurry to keep an
appointment. Recalling the experiment with the reluctant Linzmayer
tested under pressure—when he, too, was anxious to leave—Rhine
wanted to see if a similar pressure would depress Pearce's score.
Pearce remained standing and kept his topcoat on. However, to humor
Rhine, he called a few cards from a pack Rhine had in his hands. He
was unusually wrong—five times in succession. Ignoring Pearce's
pleas that he had to leave, Rhine joked that the dismal score must be an

indication of how anxious Pearce was to get out of there, and challenged him to try five more calls. Pearce was right for three out of five. Sensing that the challenge had done the trick, Rhine light-heartedly stepped up the challenge, saying: "I bet you a hundred dollars you can't get this one." Pearce got it right. Rhine returned the card to the pack and cut. He offered another hundred dollars. Pearce guessed right again. He got 10 right out of 10; 15 out of 15; 20 out of 20. He had now surpassed Linzmayer. In all, Pearce called 25 right out of 25—an extraordinary feat in parapsychological history. Had he done it by luck alone, Pearce would have beaten odds of 298, 023, 223, 876, 953, 125 to 1. And had Rhine been serious about the betting, he owed Pearce $2,500.

Pearce did not share Rhine's elation. If anything, he seemed more subdued than usual, saying flatly: "You'll never get me to do that again." Puzzled, Rhine asked him why not, because it had seemed an effortless feat. "I don't know," Pearce replied, "but you'll never get me to do it again." And he was right.[2]

Rhine speculated that Pearce sensed subconsciously that the effort had in fact been tremendous and so was reluctant to repeat the ordeal. Unfortunately, Pearce could not elaborate; he just knew he would never reach such heights again. Perhaps if Rhine had questioned Pearce under hypnosis or the influence of a truth drug, he might have revealed the mystery. But Rhine never attempted such probing, fearing that introspection might harm ESP capacity.

What would he have done had there been no Hubert Pearce to renew the possibility of ESP's existence? He and Louisa had agreed that if ESP had proved illusory—or too elusive to be demonstrated—they would resume their earlier plans and either return to botany or to a more outdoor life in forestry.

Pearce was a watershed in Rhine's career. Pearce's test results, together with those of Linzmayer, convinced Rhine that he was moving in the right direction.

Nothing of Pearce's ESP work has been more discussed or questioned than his distance experiments at Duke in 1933, which seemed at first sight to have eliminated any possibility of cheating.

This was the plan they followed. Pearce called at Pratt's research office, where the two synchronized their watches. Then Pearce left for his cubicle on the far side of the library building. By looking from his window Pratt could see Pearce leave the building, cross the narrow campus, and enter the library. Pratt sat at a card table, shuffled a pack of twenty-five ESP cards, cut them, and put the pack face down on the table. He then took one card at a time from the pack, from top to bottom, and placed it still face down onto a book in the center of the table. He left each card there for one minute.

During that time Pearce, sitting in his cubicle a hundred yards away, was to record the symbol that came to mind.

Pratt looked at the symbols only at the end of the experiment, when he recorded the card order which Pearce had tried to match.

Both men made duplicate copies of their records to compare results should they meet later that day. They sealed their original records in an envelope, writing the date and their signatures on the outside, and handed these envelopes directly to Rhine.[3]

Pratt reports that

The scores on the twelve runs which we did at a hundred yards were: 3, 8, 5, 9, 10, 12, 12, 12, 12, 13, 13, 12. These scores add up to a total of 119 hits where 60 is the most likely chance number. You may still choose the chance explanation if you insist, but you would have less than 1 chance in 100,000,000,000 of being right! Since it is not reasonable to invoke the chance explanation against such heavy odds, we are bound to find some other interpretation. The conditions appear to leave ESP as the only possibility.[4]

Pratt moved to Dr. Rhine's laboratory, while Pearce stayed in the same spot in the library; the distance between them now increased to about 250 yards. In forty-four runs of twenty-five cards for each run, Pearce's score swung wildly from as low as zero to as high as thirteen, but his overall average was a million to one against a chance explanation.

McDougall warned Rhine that the results were so remarkable that skeptical scientists—that is, most of them—would believe Pratt and Pearce were in collusion rather than accept that they had demonstrated ESP. So after giving Pearce a few months to rest, Pratt tested him again, with Rhine as a witness. Pearce's scores then were twelve, three, ten, eleven, ten, ten. Chance would have given an average of five.

Rhine called these distance experiments the Pearce-Pratt Series. Taken as a whole, Pearce's results should have put ESP into the realm of accepted scientific fact, or at least among the tenable theories—because the odds of his getting them by luck are 1 in 10,000,000,000,000,000,000,000. All that had to be ruled out was conscious or unconscious cheating by Pearce, Pratt, or Rhine, separately or together.

Campus rumors had Pratt and Pearce in collusion. A divinity student—now a minister—cheat? Yes, said the critics, he needed the twenty-five cents an hour he was making, especially during the Depression, and Pratt wanted to keep his job at fifty cents an hour.

They had a good thing going. After all, if Pearce had lost his "power," they'd both have been out of the money. Others suggested that Pearce cheated unconsciously, to advance the holy cause of religion—or to do Rhine a favor. But Rhine had been a witness to many of the tests, alone with Pearce or teaming up with Pratt. Rhine was in it too, said the campus skeptics. It's his baby.

These were not vague rumors, hard to pin down. Rhine heard them directly from Sara Ownbey, a graduate psychology student who thought Pearce was fooling Rhine.

Somehow Pearce is cheating, she told Rhine. Rhine described all the precautions taken to prevent cheating—from screens to new packs of cards, and constant vigilance. She was not convinced. Finally, Rhine suggested that she take a pack of ESP cards to see if she could get cues from the backs or edges. A few days later, Miss Ownbey admitted that not only had she been unable to obtain cues from the cards, but that in testing herself she had achieved remarkable positive results, getting as high as fifteen right calls out of twenty-five.Tested by others, her average scores remained high, ranging between eight and eleven. Despite her own success, she continued to suspect others of cheating and warned Rhine against some of her friends who were being tested.

Pearce's being a divinity student did not lull Rhine into a false sense of security. He noted that when Pearce was doing well, he rarely looked at the backs of the cards; when asked to look away from the cards, his scores remained high. Pearce also did well at "down through" tests, when without anyone touching the pack after it had been cut, he named the symbols on all the cards from top to bottom. How he could have cheated on those occasions without having advance access to the cards—or without being in cahoots with the experimenter—challenged the imagination.

Rhine even called on the services of the local magician, Wallace Lee, to see if he could spot any flaws in the procedure or catch Pearce in the act. He was also asked to use his magician's know-how to attempt to match or surpass Pearce's scores under the same conditions. Lee failed to find any trickery in Pearce's work—and his own score was at a chance level. But although Pearce's cheating seems improbable, it was not impossible.

Fortunately, other students began to show signs of ESP. T. Coleman Cooper made thousands of tests and averaged 8; May Frances Turner averaged close to 9; George Zirkle's average was about 8.5 and he once equaled Pearce's record of 25 successive hits. Most of these high scorers were graduate students in the psychology department. When Zirkle married Sara Ownbey, another high scorer (the one who had been so suspicious of Pearce) ranging between 8 and 11, both their scores dropped. Rhine didn't blame this on their married state but on their "very natural shift of interest."[5]

Pearce, a sensitive, highly strung young man, lost his consistent high-scoring ability after his girl friend sent him a "Dear John" letter. This confirmed Rhine's belief that ESP is elusive and ephemeral. It required relaxed concentration, self-confidence, and freedom from distraction.

To the charge that his subjects had succumbed to the temptation of filthy lucre, Rhine responded:

The few times I have seriously offered a money reward to subjects for good scoring have not been successful. The subjects themselves protest that such rewards interfere. I doubt if this would be true for every subject, but the students who were working in our laboratory had, on the whole, sufficient motivation, and money would have been a distraction.

He goes on to point out in *New Frontiers of the Mind* that

Some of them, although they needed the money badly, would not accept the hourly wage which subjects were offered as a routine to justify our demanding so much of their time. [As much as eight hours nonstop.] Their interest in the work itself or their friendship for the experimenter, which I acknowledge most gratefully, furnished the main motivation both for most of the assistant experimenters and for the subjects themselves.

Rhine shared his excitement with Prince, writing:

I now have one man [Hubert Pearce] who can get dependably twice the chance prediction in long series and in several hundred trials has gotten 1.5 times the chance prediction by calling rightdown through a cut and untouched pack of 25 cards. It is interesting to know that he is the son of a non-professional medium, is a young minister and comes from a psychic family. I find that the narcotic drug, sodium amytal, inhibits this clairvoyant perception and I want to try next fall the stimulant drug, caffeine. . . . All of our subjects whom we have pushed to the point of strain have lost this capacity for extrasensory perception. One man I have been able to push (19%) down below chance prediction through a series of 500 trials by pressing him against his desire. Another I have been able to run down to 40% of chance prediction (that is 60% below) by urging him to go as slow as he could. I have no improvement from hypnotic suggestion but I feel that I have not yet had the proper conditions for a test.[6]

Rhine's candor is disarming. He frankly admitted that his early experiments were far from watertight and that he had mislaid records of almost 500 calls. They were mostly the results of tests made with a neighbor and his wife. As Rhine recalled, she was usually above chance, he mostly below, so that their overall results would not alter the beyond chance value of the 90,000 test results by half a point. Rhine even conceded that further test results might turn up between the pages of a book he had been reading, had used as a temporary filing cabinet, and then forgotten. But he insisted that they would be inconsequential in the final analysis.[7]

The denigrating picture of himself as the cautious scientist who lapses—however briefly—into the role of absentminded professor has this to be said for it: He appears to be a man one can trust to reveal the facts, even when they show him in a questionable light.

When Rhine and McDougall reviewed the total results, they could hardly believe them. Pearce alone, in 10,300 trials under guarded conditions, had an overall average of 9.1 calls out of 25, when 5 out of 25 would be expected by chance. He had demonstrated clairvoyance to exist. Was it time to tell the world? Rhine asked Walter Franklin Prince for his advice. Prince agreed that the results were almost too good to be true, even "alarming."

"You say the results are somewhat alarming: I feel the same way about them," Rhine wrote to Prince on February 13, 1934.

I can hardly accept them myself. But one cannot go back on such simple observation as the performance of his own wife and children and friends. In fact, it seems to be such a commonplace procedure, and yet at the same time such a significant one, that I am not going to be surprised if we find that the whole business of supernormality has been carefully concealed from us by our cut-and-dried concept of normality. I find myself, however, struggling to take the whole thing as calmly as possible and to go on just repeating and varying and repeating some more. It would take more courage than I have to publish these things now. I will let them stew for awhile and then let them age for a longer while before I approach the point of publication.

He found the courage a few months later.

Rhine wrote in the preface to his book about the ESP experiments that he made sure "ten times over" in testing and retesting at every reasonable point of doubt, and had by the time of publication conducted almost one hundred thousand individual tests.

His motive in publishing was to give the results wider exposure. He was prepared for incredulity, even hostility from reactionaries, having already encountered their dogmatic attitude that ESP simply wasn't possible and consequently experiments in the field were redundant. But Rhine believed a scientific attitude of cautious inquiry and facing facts was replacing the reactionary response to the new and unfamiliar. In his preface he also told how he had been spurred in his ten-year quest to learn of man's powers and his place in nature, after reading of telepathy experiments by Oliver Lodge, a young British physics professor. Rhine characterized his own work as a modest step in the exploration of the unrecognized boundaries of the human personality. But he was not merely a researcher: He hoped that his efforts ultimately might have practical value. If man could be shown in a new light, for instance, it might point toward a better philosophy of life and living.[8]

Although Rhine's *Extra-Sensory Perception*—or versions of it—was probably read by millions worldwide, only a handful of men and women joined him in his continuing quest. Yet, under his firm leadership, during which Rhine showed an unswerving devotion to scientific method, this small group earned for itself recognition as scientists engaged in a legitimate branch of science. J. B. Rhine's name soon became irrevocably linked with parapsychology: To many he was, and remained for fifty years, THE parapsychologist. By that time several other universities in the United States and abroad had launched their own parapsychology laboratories and more researchers were getting positive results. But neither Rhine nor anyone else was ever able to match the phenomenal results he'd achieved in his pioneer years. Why?

He believed the extraordinary pioneering atmosphere, the spirit of fun, and exceptional teamwork partly explained his unique success. He had never known anything like it before or since. It was like a wonderful game in which they were all on the same side and all eager to win. Then the critics got at them, questioned their experimental precautions, challenged their methods, and disputed their results. Tension and contention replaced the buoyant atmosphere of the early 1930s, which never returned.[9]

Soon after *Extra-Sensory Perception* was published and reviewed in the summer of 1934, Rhine wrote to a friend:

The results already published are being received by other workers, scientists, critics, etc. I am very pleased indeed with the wide acceptance of the work. "Epoch-making" seems to be a favorite word. ... The N.Y. Herald-Tribune ran an editorial on May 29, reviewing the predictions by a group of scientists at Chicago for the next century. The writer ended by saying that his prediction of the greatest advances of science as seen in 2034 would be along the line of our work here.

Rhine could not conceal his exuberance when he added:

It seems to be true, as many have said, that the world is somewhat ready for the truth about mind and its larger meaning in the universe. It will be thrilling to be a part in the system of discovery that reveals it!

"What impressed his readers [of *Extra-Sensory Perception*] most, I think, was the seeming ease with which he achieved his miraculous results," wrote Dr. R. A. McConnell.

In three years he found eight college students, who, in more than 60,000 card guesses made under a wide variety of conditions, achieved an average number of successes more than fifty percent greater than the expected chance average. In many instances near-perfect scores were reported with the use of card decks in which the probability of a chance success was one in five.

Admittedly, all of Rhine's subjects showed a "decline effect,"* but for the most part this occurred only after a period of many months. To those who understood statistics it sounded as though, if one wanted to walk on water every day at four o'clock, all one needed was a deck of cards and a willingness to try.[10]

Rhine's conclusion was unequivocal: His experiments had demonstrated the existence of extrasensory perception. He would never change his mind about that.

Of these golden, pioneer days, Dr. Louisa Rhine recalls: "It was exciting. If you want something badly enough and think you're about to get it—you're excited."[11]

And looking back, Dr. R. A. McConnell, a research professor of biophysics, writes:

Perhaps there was something in Rhine's personality akin to the "charisma" of great leaders in politics or religion. Having myself worked very hard to produce rigorously controlled but rather modest evidence for psychic phenomena, I must confess that the history of the research of that period has me in a little of the same awe and disbelief that I feel toward the Italian Renaissance.[12]

Rhine believed his experience as a successful salesman in his college days had helped: "The task of the salesman, in the best sense

---

*A drop in average scores to nearer the chance level, or below.

of that word, is to inspire interest and enthusiasm and create confidence."[13] He vainly longed to recapture the excitement of the 1930s, when it seemed like a glorious contest, or a climb to the summit of a mountain never conquered before. "What would I not give if we could have kept it like that; or renewed it," Rhine wrote. "But, of course, human beings simply cannot go on living on the peaks they scale. And the reception waiting for us from a naturally skeptical world helped us quickly enough to pull ourselves off the heights of enthusiasm."[14]

14

TRANCE MEDIUM EILEEN GARRETT 1934–1936

Rhine was wary of mediums: His first three encounters had been with frauds. And although the fourth, Minnie Soule, had given the widower Thomas reason to believe he had been reunited through her with his dead wife, Rhine's own meetings with Mrs. Soule had been less than overwhelming. But reports of another medium, Eileen Garrett, restored his interest—especially as McDougall had vouched for her integrity and remarkable talents. She was a vital, intense forty-one-year-old Irish woman, unique among mediums in her almost desperate urge for self-investigation. She wanted to know if the voices that spoke through her when she was in a trance were real or imaginary personalities. McDougall had frequently seen her in London, England, after World War I, when he belonged to the British Society for Psychical Research. Between 1924 and 1928 she went through the equivalent of a university course for mediums, putting herself in the hands of Hewat McKenzie, founder of the British College of Psychic Science.

Eileen Garrett became his most remarkable student, and in time even those who treated the supernatural as a matter of course spoke of her feats with awe, as if recounting biblical miracles.

When she went into a deep trance, she lost her Anglo-Irish lilt and spoke in two distinctly masculine voices. One called himself Uvani and said that his purpose was to prove the survival of the human personality after bodily death. Uvani was formal and spoke in an ornate manner. The other introduced himself as Abdul Latif. He was hearty and outgoing and advised sitters how to lead happy, productive lives. Latif revealed that he had been born in Baghdad in 1162 and died in the same town sixty-seven years later. He claimed to have been a great Muslim physician. Many other trance personalities spoke through Mrs. Garrett, but Uvani and Latif were permanent visitors. It was their true identity that she sought to discover throughout her life. She longed to know if they were figments of her imagination brought to life through her trance; split-off parts of her personality; or what they claimed to be, spirits of the dead.[1]

Despite her eagerness to be tested and her complete cooperation with researchers—she made no stipulations; they could do exactly as they liked—documentation of her psychic manifestations was disappointingly scanty. Few controlled experiments occurred, and none of the kind Rhine would have enforced. So that, if Rhine could test her, his would be the first careful assessment of her abilities.

Meanwhile, he had to be satisfied with secondhand accounts. In the fall of 1931 Eileen Garrett had crossed the Atlantic to New York, where she demonstrated her trance mediumship for a few months under the auspices of the ASPR before traveling on to California. There, Dr. Anita Muhl, a psychiatrist, persuaded her to cooperate in telepathic experiments that had the elements of a party game and were meant to appeal to Mrs. Garrett's gregarious nature. She was asked to attempt to describe Dr. Muhl's friends and their homes in distant foreign lands. All of the people, of course, were strangers to Mrs. Garrett, and she had never seen their homes.

The most ambitious of the experiments involved Mrs. Garrett sitting in a San Diego home, attempting telepathic contact with a Dr. D. Svensen in Iceland, over four thousand miles away. He was chief of the division of mental health in Reykjavik, Iceland. Eileen Garrett had never met him nor been to Iceland.

While Dr. Muhl watched and a secretary waited to take a verbatim record, Mrs. Garrett put herself into a trance. As if in a dream, she found herself, she said, approaching a house near the sea along a path bordered with flowers. She passed through the walls of the house—like a ghost—as the man she sensed to be Dr. Svensen descended the stairs, and she heard him say, "This will be a successful experiment."

The doctor had a bandage around his head, she remarked in a drowsy voice, then repeated what she had heard him say, "Make my apologies to the experimenters at your end. I have had an accident and cannot work as well as I had hoped." She predicted that Dr. Svensen would reach for a book about Einstein and relativity, which next moment she "saw" him do. He read a few words from this book, and Mrs. Garrett repeated the gist of them.

A day after the experiment a cable arrived from the Icelandic doctor in which he mentioned his head injury, and in a follow-up letter he described his room and his physical activity during the telepathy test, which matched Eileen Garrett's account.

She had, in fact, demonstrated more than telepathy—hearing

his voice required clairaudience, anticipating the book he would read showed precognition, seeing the objects in his room was clairvoyance. The disappointing denouement is that all the original records of the experiment have vanished—the verbatim notes, the Icelandic doctor's cable and letter. Dr. Muhl and Eileen Garrett are dead, and Dr. Svensen, to my knowledge, had never publicly confirmed Mrs. Garrett's extrasensory powers. Mrs. Garrett explains in her autobiography that "the records which were at the time made and given to Hereward Carrington [a psychic researcher] for examination were lost sight of. At the time of his death [1958], they had apparently disappeared."[2]

News travels fast—even by normal channels—in psychic research circles.

At first Rhine heard only that Mrs. Garrett had described the happenings in a house in Iceland, some four thousand miles away. It reminded him of the test King Croesus of Lydia was purported to have imposed on various oracles in his search for one who could truly predict the outcome of a war. When Rhine learned the details of what Eileen Garrett had accomplished and was reassured by McDougall of her honesty, he was more than eager to investigate her. He got the chance when Mrs. Garrett made another journey to the U.S. in 1934. She knew of Rhine's work and respected McDougall as a friend and scientist. In accepting Rhine's invitation to be a guinea pig for three weeks in the spring, Mrs. Garrett said she was prepared to work up to six hours a day. She would impose no conditions, and would undertake any tests he suggested. She attempted to demystify her special talents—trance mediumship, clairvoyance, and psychometry—by saying that they were as natural to her as eating or sleeping.[3]

It would be hard to say who was the more excited, Rhine or Garrett, when arrangements had been made for the tests at Duke.

Rhine regarded Mrs. Garrett's imminent visit as a momentous occasion, as it promised to be "the first systematic examination of a recognized medium."[4] Anxious not to botch it, he asked Prince for advice, but Prince was suffering from "a strange nightmare of nerves" and his only practical suggestion was to have at least two witnesses and to hire a stenographer to record *everything* said during the tests.[5] This Rhine did.

Mrs. Garrett arrived on April 1 and renewed her warm friendship with McDougall. She recalled later that he was "intensely interested in communication through feeling, and these problems deeply concerned him. ... I well remember that when I once held the youngest baby of Dr. Rhine [Rosemary], McDougall would ask me questions about the empathy engendered between myself and the infant."[6]

Rhine put Mrs. Garrett through card-calling tests, which she found dull and unstimulating. And, says Rhine, "it was only after several days' work that she rose to an average per day that became significant of the actual clairvoyant capacity. As a whole her clairvoyant work was significant, but not as good as many of the best Duke students. But her telepathy results were on a par with the best."[7]

Then Rhine set himself the task of discovering whether Mrs. Garrett or Uvani possessed the psychic abilities. To do this he used ESP cards to test her normal waking state for both telepathy and clairvoyance. Then she went into a trance, Uvani announced his appearance, and Rhine tested Uvani.

In response to questions, Uvani denied that he had either clairvoyant or telepathic powers. He said that during the tests, he used Mrs. Garrett as an instrument. This puzzled Rhine. If, as he was willing to presume, Uvani had left his senses on the sands of Arabia when he died centuries ago and was now, as he claimed, a spirit, how did he operate without utilizing some extrasensory means?

Rhine's tests showed that "the Uvani personality . . . averaged close to the results obtained by Mrs. Garrett in her waking state. The most remarkable point is that he, too, showed the high telepathic and the low clairvoyant capacity which she did." Rhine concluded that the "gifts are the gifts of the medium, whatever Uvani himself may be."[8]

Excluding the results of the last week of testing, when Mrs. Garrett was ill enough to require medical attention, but kept going, her averages were about 10.1 for telepathy in the waking or normal state, 9.1 in trance. During 8,000 trials for clairvoyance she averaged 5.7 awake, 5.6 in trance. Critics are justified in saying that Rhine should have included—even emphasized—the results while Mrs. Garrett was ill. Or, if he expected, as is likely, that the results would be poor during her illness, should have called off the tests until she had recovered.

To his own satisfaction he discovered that Eileen Garrett had extrasensory powers above the average. And why would her telepathic powers exceed her clairvoyant powers? Perhaps because telepathy required the involvement of other minds—and she found that more stimulating.

Consequently, Gaither Pratt devised an ingenious test that would both appeal to her imagination and challenge her powers in a controlled situation. The controls were not perfect—if perfect controls exist—but not far from it. She accepted the challenge and returned to Duke in 1935. The test was this: What could she tell about a person by holding an object belonging to him—that object being the only contact between them?

Psychometry, as this is called, was one of Mrs. Garrett's self-proclaimed gifts.

Rhine chose twelve from among the men and women who volunteered to be subjects for the experiment in psychometry. Pratt asked them to bring a personal object belonging to a dead person with whom they had been associated. They were instructed not to utter a word once they were in the experiment room. "Sit and think of deceased ones who were close to you and from whom you would like—if possible—to have information of their present existence," Pratt told them. "Try to put skepticism aside for the time and enter into the spirit of the experiment. This sympathetic, expectant attitude may produce better results, if only because it places you in a position comparable to that of the telepathic agent [with Eileen Garrett the receiver]."

The volunteers waited in room M445 on the fourth floor of the medical building at Duke. A secretary led the first subject to the experiment room, starkly empty but for a chair and an electric fan, and took the personal object from him, to carry to Dr. Pratt in the next room. The sitter was now alone, the only sound in the room a noisy fan intended to drown out any words spoken by Eileen Garrett in the adjoining room, the heavy door to which was closed.

Eileen Garrett was already going into a trance as the secretary entered the room through a corridor and handed the personal object to the waiting Pratt. Then the secretary left for room M445, where she would wait to bring the next subject to the experiment room.

Following Prince's advice, as in the Rhine experiment with Garrett and Uvani, a stenographer was ready to record every word uttered at the séance.

Mrs. Garrett appeared to be dozing off as she sat in a comfortable chair, her eyes out of focus, her breathing shallow. Then she threw her head back and her eyes rolled upward. She took short gulps of breath and moaned softly. Pratt noticed that although her eyes were now closed, the lids flickered continuously as if she was dreaming. Moments later she crossed her arms over her breast and began to sway back and forth. "It is I, Uvani," she said in a deep male voice. "I give you greetings, friends. Peace be with you."

"Thank you, Uvani," Pratt replied, as if to a friendly visitor. "I have here an object, Uvani, which I hope will be able to help you in making contact."

And the unique experiment began.[9]

One frequent criticism of the medium-sitter relationship is that the sitter is liable to help the medium out by prompting, jumping to conclusions on flimsy evidence and, through the will to believe, interpreting vague messages as watertight evidence for survival or ESP.

Pratt avoided the danger of sitters giving too much away by not letting them give *anything* away. Eileen Garrett neither saw nor heard the twelve volunteers who appeared, one at a time, in the next room. They neither saw nor heard her. And to prevent the sitters from bias in favor of messages meant for them, they weren't informed which ones did refer to them.

After Mrs. Garrett's flowery trance messages via Uvani had been transcribed from the secretary's shorthand notes, Pratt paraphrased them into simple discrete statements and shuffled them around in random order, to which only he had the key. He had them typed in that order. Each of the twelve sitters then received this complete list of statements with no clues as to which referred to him or her. They were asked to rate all the statements, true, false, or don't know.

Pratt explained: "In this way we attempted to eliminate the possibility that a particular sitter might have accepted too many of the medium's statements as correct because of the knowledge that the medium intended them to apply. The method also avoided errors of the opposite kind: if a skeptical sitter had known which was his own record, he might have rejected statements even though they were true."[10]

The results were a triumph for Mrs. Garrett and reassured Pratt that he had designed a productive experiment. He estimated that the odds against her providing the information by chance were 1,700,000 to 1. And he naturally concluded that she was able to get information by extrasensory means.

The often specific information she gave, the language of which Pratt simplified, included: "There is a strange little box in your room of German or Saxon make. . . . There is a toy dog in your room. It is grotesque. Given to you by a lady. . . . You have a brother deceased. He died very young. His name was Robert or Rupert. . . . There is a man, deceased, who was connected with you. His name was Greely. He was connected with education."[11]

Both Rhine and Pratt thought the results had clearly demonstrated Eileen Garrett's exceptional ability, although Rhine still preferred his own less theatrical methods. He concluded that "the simple routine test for telepathy and clairvoyance showed with greater economy of energy and much more clarity her capacities for extrasensory perception."[12] He was right, but the Pratt experiment and Rhine's own attempts to "unmask" Uvani had been—literally—more entracing.

No other medium was again tested so exhaustively by Rhine or Pratt. But one thing they did not settle was the question of communication with the dead. Were Uvani and Abdul Latif discarnate spirits or subliminal aspects of Eileen Garrett's personality? Rhine was not able to tell. All the information she had provided while in a trance might have been obtained by telepathy or clairvoyance. Rhine knew of no test that would establish for sure that Eileen Garrett's informants were the spirits of the dead. That would have to wait.

He did acknowledge that those 1934 and 1935 experiments were a turning point in parapsychology as a science. For the first time, tests in a university laboratory had confirmed a psychic's extra-sensory abilities.

She and Rhine never lost touch, and in 1952, she launched and ran the Parapsychology Foundation in New York City. It became one of the most active centers of parapsychological research and of pub-lications, as well as a sponsor of international conferences. In the early fifties she gave Rhine a research grant of twenty-five thousand dollars a year for several years.[13]

Other investigators attempted to discover the true identity of Mrs. Garrett's voices. None got any closer to the answer than had Rhine. Jungian psychologist Dr. Ira Progoff tape-recorded many hours of her trance messages and concluded: "In the depths of all of us, we have untold wisdom."[14]

15

THE STAB
IN THE BACK
1934

Exactly one day after Rhine began his important experiment with Eileen Garrett at Duke, his three colleagues—Lundholm, Zener, and Adams—wrote a letter to McDougall, the department head, aimed at crippling—if not destroying—Rhine's career.

The three pyschologists had reason to resent Rhine's rapid promotion in the department. He was, after all, a biologist largely self-taught in psychology, with the exception of his year at Harvard. He seemed to have been given star treatment and to be acting like a Pied Piper in luring graduate students away from orthodox psychological studies. Irritated into attack when a graduate psychology student spoke of psychic research with evangelic zeal and Rhine as the savior, Rhine's colleagues put their psychology to use and wrote to McDougall on April 9, 1934:

It seems to us that grave dangers have arisen possibly threatening the integrity of the group. We have distinct evidence to the effect that there is a feeling among [graduate students] that progress in psychology at Duke is conditioned by active interest in psychical research.

They went on to inform McDougall, then vacationing in England, that some pro-Rhine students were aggressively trying to convert fellow students to psychic research and stifling rational discussion on other branches of psychology. They claimed that their own research work was in jeopardy because the graduate students they needed to help them were being browbeaten or brainwashed into Rhine's camp. And, in their opinion,

. . . one of the most intelligent students seems to have completely lost

his emotional balance over the subject. . . . He is quoted by another graduate student to have stated in a discussion that, "I regard Dr. Rhine as the most intelligent, most widely read, and greatest psychologist in the world, the Galileo of our age."

Although Rhine's three colleagues didn't suggest treating him like Galileo, they implored McDougall to tell them what to do about the situation, hoping for a radical change without anyone involved being injured,

. . . Yet we are confident that mere admonition will not suffice. We write to you because the future success and happiness of our individual work and the continuance of the present department as a center of psychological research and a center particularly of hormic interest [a not-too-subtle touch this, as it was close to McDougall's heart] is severely endangered by the present situation."

McDougall must have finished the letter with a sigh. How much easier to deal with fake mediums than frustrated scientists. He was as dedicated as Rhine to psychic research—and he admired Rhine. But he was also trying to build a psychology department. Should he clip Rhine's wings and try to cool his ardor? Or was his ardor largely responsible for his success?

When Rhine heard of the letter to McDougall, he was shattered. But he took time to think over his reply and to strike the right note. His letter to his three bitter colleagues and indirectly to McDougall was intended to save the situation without surrender.

This is the letter he wrote to Drs. Lundholm, Zener, and Adams, dated July 8, 1934:

Gentlemen:

Some days ago in talking to Dr. Zener I stumbled upon the fact of your letter to Dr. McDougall, and I expressed to Dr. Zener in frank terms my views of the matter as I then saw it. He is at liberty to repeat this, so far as I am concerned.

Later, in a moment of larger perspective, I realized that men of your position and culture must indeed have been violently alarmed, or else unendurably irritated, to have taken the action you seem to have done, especially to have done it in the secretive and circuitous way you selected. From this larger view, it is plain to me that, whether or not you were justified in your action, I can only regard the situation with profound sorrow and regret, and would welcome any possible remedy for it, short of downright frustration of my major life interests. I am moved in this interest in great part by the shame and sorrow, which, on reflection, I feel, that you should have felt

*impelled, rightfully or wrongfully, to force the painful fact of depart-
ment dissension upon the peace of mind of our absent leader; and by
the hurt I have experienced, learning that three of my friends and
colleagues conspired to strike—whether without malicious design or
in total ignorance of likely consequence, I do not know—at the most
valued confidence and friendship I have ever enjoyed. That I, my
actions, or my fortunes should have engendered, however unwittingly,
this unhappy result, is enough to warrant this concern of mine, and
to move me to ask your cooperation in the interests of mutual
satisfaction and general departmental good feeling.*

*It is enough for me to say that I do not want to contribute
further to such disagreeable relations as now exist, and would more
than welcome the approach of anyone with friendly suggestions,
advice, or claims of injustice. In my judgment, the more direct the
approach, the better the resultant understanding.*

*My own aims, as well as, doubtless, your own, lie so far
beyond the present scene that, when properly viewed, the immediate
troubles seemed dwarfed. If they can be settled now, I am sure their
significance will dwindle in retrospect. I assure you of my honest and
earnest desire to meet you, without regard to difficult points of right
and wrong.*

*It is probably not necessary to say that this is not supine
surrender of pride, and no Quixotic gesture of magnanimity. It is,
practically, the wisest course I know to take, with the understanding I
have. Nevertheless, I do what I do wholeheartedly.*

Rhine indicated he was sending a copy of the letter to Dr.
McDougall. On the face of it, the letter is remarkably restrained. The
covering letters to McDougall more vividly expressed his feeling of
being stabbed in the back. McDougall displayed a very even hand in
his effort to lower the temperature that summer of 1934—a summer in
which Rhine's first book (*Extra-Sensory Perception*) was published, a
leading medium was successfully tested, and Walter Franklin Prince
died. The department head responded from across the ocean:

*I regret that this disagreement should come just now to mar the
enjoyment of your publication as well as threaten the harmony of our
department. I really think you are taking the whole thing too tragically,
and do not look at it sufficiently from the point of view of our three
colleagues. We have to recognize that a priori the dangers they are
anxious to avoid, namely, an unbalanced and excessive interest in
P.R. [psychical research] on the part of some students [is bad for the
department]. I also feel that they, seeing, as they believe, signs of the
materialization of that danger, were quite right and within their
rights, in giving expression (a very temperate statement) of their*

anxiety to me. It's true I would have liked them to broach the subject with you and discuss it perfectly frankly. But whether they should do that was a nice question.

The difference between you and them is just one of the inherent difficulties of bringing P.R. into a university, which I hoped we at Duke might successfully avoid. It would be a great pity to have to admit failure. I really don't think you have any serious grievance against them, and beg that you will give them credit for the best of motives. Why impute other motives, even if the imputation is plausible and may well have a grain of truth?

I don't know whether you have seen a copy of the letter written to me, but I should be glad for you to see it, although it was not meant for your eyes.

Many thanks for all the other news and congratulations on the reception of your book and especially on the cash consequence.

The outcome of the uneven battle was mixed victory and defeat. The other three members of the psychology department now resumed their own work in mainstream psychology and all but ignored Rhine's efforts. Yet with some magnanimity, Rhine wrote on August 10, 1937:

In the early stages of the Duke experiments, when help was most needed, it came unsparingly and generously not alone from my wife, Dr. Louisa Rhine, but from my colleagues, Professor William McDougall, Dr. Helge Lundholm, and Dr. Karl E. Zener.[1]

McDougall and the university president, Dr. William Preston Few, continued to support Rhine wholeheartedly.

His colleagues were not the only opposition Rhine faced at this time.

After the first flush of enthusiastic praise for Rhine's *Extra-Sensory Perception*, other critics got to work. They questioned the honesty of both experimenters and subjects. They questioned Rhine's use of mathematics. Does the math Rhine uses really explain the good results? Are we sure Rhine applies math and the law of probability correctly? They raised the question of nonrandom shuffling of cards, sensory leakage in the experimental room, errors in recording the results of the experiments, unconscious (involuntary) whispering that may have given away the symbols on the target cards—and incompetent experimenters. Some asked whether these results were just the tip of the iceberg. Had a large number of nonsignificant results inadvertently or deliberately been excluded from the published account?

Prominent among Rhine's critics were Dr. Harold O. Gulliksen of the University of Chicago, Dr. Chester E. Kellogg of McGill University, Dr. John L. Kennedy of Stanford University, Dr. Vernon W. Lemmon of Washington University, Dr. Robert Thouless of Cambridge University (later won over), Dr. Raymond R. Willoughby of Brown University, and Dr. Dael L. Wolfle of the University of Chicago.

Rhine replied to some of his critics:

A few persons may be willing to believe that every one of the investigators in the Duke experiments has been so incompetent all these years as persistently to make errors in the same direction, thus accounting for the high scores reported. Actually one English critic went so far as to write us that for him this explanation was preferable to the theory of clairvoyance. [Another critic,] also an Englishman . . . believes that my assistants, subjects and colleagues have all been "pulling my leg," practicing a systematic and consummate deception. Such an event would not be entirely without precedent. There is a rumor about a chemist who was seeking to transmute mercury into gold and who had an assistant more sympathetic than reliable. This assistant dropped traces of gold into the solution in order to encourage his chief, presumably believing that the gold ought theoretically to be there anyhow! . . . Best known of all is the German geologist whose students prankishly buried fossils for him to "discover," arranged in line with his own theory, finally even helped him to dig up one bearing his own initials.

I could put up a strong defense, I believe, for the generally fine character of the group of men and women with whom I have worked. The "leg-pulling" conspiracy would have to include members of my own family and persons who are now staff members of college institutions; in all, a score of persons, some of whom did not know one another. But again the easiest reply is reference to the findings of researchers in other places.[2]

Eventually experts—including Dr. R. A. Fisher, the dean of British statisticians—conceded that Rhine's mathematics were valid. And Duke mathematician Dr. Joseph Albert Greenwood confirmed the theory of probability. He conducted a massive matching test of five hundred thousand ESP cards, which were dealt mechanically. The result demonstrated that when any possibility of ESP was eliminated, one would get by chance an average of five cards right out of twenty-five called.

Would most scientists now accept ESP as a demonstrated fact? No, they would not.

16

LIFE AFTER DEATH
AND
MIND OVER MATTER
1934

Walter Franklin Prince was dying in the summer of 1934, but he had made a gallant effort to finish editing Rhine's first book, *Extra-Sensory Perception*, and see it through the press. In one of his last letters to Rhine, he let him know that a couple of years before,

. . . an influential person asked me who was competent to succeed me in case of death, as research officer for the Boston Society for Psychic Research. I replied that in my judgment the best fitted young man in America of whom I had any knowledge was yourself, although of course I added that it was not to be expected that you with a secure academic position would be willing in fact to undertake the work.

Rhine replied that Duke University would be prepared to affiliate with Prince's organization to ensure its survival. In fact, the Boston Society for Psychic Research amalgamated with the American Society for Psychical Research in 1941, after the deaths of Prince and McDougall. The breakaway society thus returned to the mother when, after the Margery fiasco, she showed signs of mending her ways.

Prince died on August 7, 1934, soon after hearing of the enthusiastic responses to *Extra-Sensory Perception*. He had been Rhine's first true guide in psychic research, a good, lively friend and energetically loyal supporter. Prince was "a scientist," wrote author Fulton Oursler, "because he wanted facts, but he was also a poet because he sought the truth."[1] The death of such a staunch friend and the opposition of all three colleagues weighed on Rhine, but nothing kept him down for long.

Because of his successful experiments with Eileen Garrett, her friend—Frances Payne Bolton, a wealthy congresswoman from Ohio—was ready to finance him in survival research. She wanted to know if there was life after death and if the living could communicate with the dead. Rhine's carefully considered reply to Mrs. Bolton shows that he would not mislead her to get much-needed financial support. The research to prove survival would be difficult, he explained, and he did not intend to attempt it until he had investigated more thoroughly both mind over matter (psychokinesis) and clairvoyance.

In writing to Mrs. Bolton that summer of 1934 Rhine spelled out his achievements, goals, and the looming problems. He suggested that if the mind did survive bodily death, then it existed either in a sort of limbo, unable to affect our world of matter and energy, or that it did in fact influence matter. If the latter were true, it might explain the ability of discarnate minds to communicate through mediums. Rhine told her that he had massive evidence that the living mind directly influences matter, and that he would continue to "pile up mountains of proof of psycho-kinesis" over the next year to challenge the doubters. He intended also to apply himself vigorously and devotedly to continued testing for clairvoyance and "mental forcing," or perhaps "parapsychic intrusion," which he described as "the ability of a mind to intrude of its own· volition into the mental life of another." He realized that many would be impatient with his caution and "lengthy over-proving of each little point," but he wanted never to have to retreat, before eventually tackling "the great Mt. Everest of problems" that most interested Mrs. Bolton: how to find evidence that the mind survives the body. He hoped to organize an institute for parapsychology* to undertake this program, he said, but didn't want her to think this was a fund-raising letter. "When I begin to 'fish' for financial aid for that, I will do so openly and frankly."

Money was not Rhine's biggest worry, nor was the loss of support from his three colleagues. It was the failure of Hubert Pearce to maintain his high scores. "If we could recover Pearce's ability now it would be of the greatest possible importance," he continued in his letter to Mrs. Bolton.

This falling-off of our major subject is most upsetting, even though it is of some value in throwing light on the nature of the phenomena. We must turn this apparent misfortune to as good account as we can and find others. We have about thirty subjects under test at the present time in our search for new candidates.

---

*The Institute for Parapsychology came into being thirty years later, in 1963, with the financial aid of Mrs. Bolton and several others.

Rhine believed that completely mechanizing dice throwing would diminish or kill criticism that experimenters or subjects had physically affected the results. Then if the average scores were above chance after hundreds or thousands of trials, psychokinesis could be advanced as a likely cause, after eliminating other possibilities, such as biased dice. Hubert Pearce had promised to make a dice-throwing machine for Rhine. But what had happened to Pearce, in Rhine's view the greatest living proof of ESP? When last heard from several weeks before, he was heading for Arkansas, fresh out of divinity school.

17

FRIENDS
AND CHAMPIONS
1934

After weeks of silence from Pearce, a letter arrived from him in early November, announcing that "Pearce's Electric Crap Shooter," as he jauntily called it, was on the way. Rhine was relieved to hear that the source of his most striking evidence for ESP was alive and well and not lost in the mountain fastnesses of Arkansas. A Methodist minister providing a crap-shooting machine to demonstrate the existence of a transcendental mind might seem incongruous, even ludicrous, but Pearce's family owned a metal works where the machine was constructed, and Rhine, after all, had chosen to explore the extrasensory through the methods of physical science and of mathematics.

Pearce had a tale of woe to tell. He believed that when the narrow-minded church authorities heard he had been involved in parapsychological experiments, they gave him a dilapidated church way up in the mountains that no one else wanted. It was the next step to banishment. His attempts to clean up the church building, placate the authorities, and minister to his flock explained why he had not done any self-imposed ESP experiments nor written to Rhine in weeks.

In his breezy reply of November 13, Rhine said the machine had arrived, looked clever, promised to be everything he was looking for, and "I am sure we will have lots of fun in any case." He envied Pearce his life in the mountains "and if you don't make a good job of the church I will come up and take it myself, when I get tired of things here." Rhine reminded Pearce that the young man had hoped for a challenging job and now he had one. But Rhine was obviously not merely trying to cheer up the harassed minister. He wanted his most productive and promising subject to continue working with him. "If you ever feel as if you can hit the old stride again," wrote Rhine, "we will move the Ozark Mountains to get you here, or if it is necessary we will go out there."

Rhine was not able to get Pearce's machine to work because there were a few screws loose. He soon had those in place, but it still needed more attention. He put it aside for a while and challenged his seven-year-old son, Robert, to a hand-thrown game of dice, with a marshmallow as a prize for the winner. Robert enjoyed games with his father—he knew they were more than games, in fact, and that made them especially exciting. Rhine himself usually threw above chance, but Robert often beat him. This time Robert won again with an average of five to Rhine's four and a half—both of them a shade above chance.

By early December Rhine wrote to tell Pearce that he had the electric crap shooter working and to repeat how eager he was to do more tests with the young minister. He hoped Pearce was "running the old devil out of those mountains at a furious pace." He concluded, "There is a place open for you whenever you want to come back, be it for a month or a ten-year period." Rhine mentioned a visit to Duke by Dr. Gardner Murphy and how much Murphy had wanted to question Pearce about his method of working at ESP.[1]

Pearce's reply a few days later was promising. He was not ready to quit chasing the devil; however,he had been testing himself with the ESP cards and results were above chance. He wanted Rhine to know that he would have devoted more time to it, "but taking over a church that is all shot and reorganizing it and putting it on its feet, and getting everything ready for Christmas is quite a job." He offered to do more work after January. He regretted missing Murphy, but said he'd answer his questions by mail.[2]

Perhaps realizing he was pressing Pearce too hard, Rhine wrote: "I think it is better that you look upon this [ESP] as your recreation and take your church as your main task."

If he couldn't work with Pearce, there was always Rhine's own son, Robert, ready and willing.

Robert remembers going from his home on Nation Avenue up to the parapsychology lab "sort of stuck away in the third-floor attic quarters of the physics building. I used to go up there to watch the white rats in little cages." He did card tests there, too, and was rewarded with candy. He recalls his father leaving for work shortly after eight to walk to the west campus, about three miles away. As a result of growing up on a farm and his experience in the marines, Rhine enjoyed physical activity. "If time permitted, he'd walk home for lunch and then back again. If the weather was bad, my mother would drive him. He was almost always absorbed in his work. To me at that time he was a father and that's the way all fathers were. On

Saturday, if he didn't go to the lab, he had a little study and he would go in there and close the door and sometimes he'd put on Beethoven or Bach or Brahms or the opera on Saturday afternoon. But he'd be in there with his books and papers and we [Robert and sister Sally, two years his junior] learned it was OK to come in and out of the house, but 'don't bring a whole tribe of your friends stomping down the hall because Dad's working.'

"Ever since I can remember, Dad would ask Mother to burn the toast a little bit so he knew he was eating it and he'd always put seasoning on what he was eating so that he could taste it. He'd refer to the fact that his sense of taste and smell didn't exist or that it was very, very poor. Once, when he wasn't paying attention, he poured milk on his grapefruit. He used to drive an old Buick and because he was color-blind, my job was to be in the front seat not only to read the road signs, but to read the traffic lights, because then there was no consistent system with red always on the top and green on the bottom.

"He had a good mechanical ability but he didn't use it much. He knew how the furnace worked with the electric motor. If something broke in the house, my mother would have to get after him a bit and say: 'Wait a minute. Go to the office five minutes later. Could you fix this door latch?' And he'd say: 'Yeah, yeah. I'll get to that maybe this afternoon if I can finish in time.' A little later I realized what was happening and learned to work with the tools and then I might be the one who put the buckle on the screen door. But for a university-oriented professor, a research man in a nonmechanical field, he had a pretty good awareness of mechanical things."[3]

Rhine tried to hypnotize Robert a few times without success, but over the years the boy saw his father hypnotize several volunteers.

Before the end of 1934 Rhine heard from Charles Ozanne who was to become a financial backer. Ozanne had retired from teaching history and philosophy at Harvard and Radcliffe. Like Mrs. Bolton, he was especially interested in survival research. He told Rhine of sittings with the Boston medium Minnie Soule, the same medium Thomas had started out with in his efforts to contact his deceased wife, and whom the Rhines had tested for Walter Franklin Prince. Ozanne wrote to Rhine:

A good many years ago—in 1913 and subsequently—I had a series of sittings with the medium through whom Dr. Hyslop [a leading psychic researcher] got his best results, the woman he calls Mrs. Chenoweth [pseudonym for Mrs. Soule], then living in a suburb of Boston. When I first met her, she said many things about me that seems clearly to indicate some form of perception different from what people ordi-

narily know. There was a large amount that was so profoundly true to the inner spirit of the situation and personality that I was convinced then, and still am confident now, that there were real communications to me from those of mine that were no longer living.

At the end of the same year, 1934, Rhine changed an acquaintance into a friend and champion. He was Dr. Gardner Murphy, a Columbia University professor of psychology whose passion equaled Rhine's in his pursuit of the outer fringes of knowledge. He and his wife, Dr. Lois Murphy, also a psychologist, made a lightning visit to Duke and afterward, on December 7, he wrote to Rhine:

I can't tell you how profoundly grateful I am for the opportunity to share in this most extraordinary quest, and to know such an extraordinary person. You know that I speak simply and honestly; so that I can say without any indirectness that it has been an intense satisfaction to talk with so great a man and to glimpse some of his vistas of scientific worlds to conquer.

Rhine replied by return:

I think the chief benefit of your visit to the work as a whole is the recognition from outside from someone of your position and reputation that the work is worth doing. . . . It is perhaps an advantage, at least to me, that we are somewhat different in our objectives. I feel on my part that your influence will be a somewhat steadying one, and this is always needed, and it is possible that my own intensity and persistence may be of some value.

And he followed up with:

Your first letter giving me the impressions of your visit here is one that I shall treasure very highly.
It leaves me with a combined feeling of humbleness, that you should feel as you did, and of inspiration to accomplish still more work that will meet with the stamp of approval of men like yourself. . . . The haunted house trip is off for the holidays, but when I do get to New York it will be a pleasure to call on you and Mrs. Murphy.

Eight years before, in 1926, Rhine had stood in the doorway of Murphy's apartment with the question, "Is it worth devoting one's life to the work?" From now on, he'd never doubt it, although he would endure many moments of disappointment and despair.

18

QUESTIONS
AND ANSWERS
1934–1936

Had Rhine reported a gold mine in his backyard, or a sure cure for old age, the response could not have been more immediate or urgent. When news of his experiments reached the public in 1934 through his first book, *Extra-Sensory Perception*, the world wanted to question, enlighten, or use him. He heard from those who had seen the fakirs' "miracles," witnessed the shamans' shaking tents, witch doctors' voodoo powers, and the spirit made flesh in dimly lit rooms—and they all wanted to share their esoteric knowledge with Rhine and convert him to their beliefs. The deluded and the disreputable turned up at Duke in person—self-proclaimed psychics who demanded to be put to the test or to receive without testing the Duke lab stamp of approval. It was clear that many of these wanted a passport to fame or a more lucrative life.

Rhine replied to the deluge of mail helped by volunteer assistants. He tried to console visitors with glazed or feverish eyes who were convinced they were being telepathically bombarded with the malevolent thoughts of others. There was no persuasive evidence, said Rhine, that such terror tactics were possible. If his assurance and steady gaze failed to convince them, he suggested they should see a doctor. Others who described trips to distant planets, frequent conversations with William Shakespeare, and the ability to see all in the palm of the hand were told that they might be gifted with imagination but were not necessarily psychic. Some cursed Rhine for his reluctance to endorse their special sensitivity.

One woman visitor boasted to Rhine that she had

... acquired disciplines that would make my experiments seem trifling. Twenty percent above chance? A hundred percent right is her

124

average! Of course, there is always a theoretical background. "The lotus has opened" or she has been initiated by a special contact with an oriental priest into mysteries beyond my comprehension. Over and over I go through my standard routine explanation . . . "Whether you use the 'oldest of the sciences' or the pyramids or Yoga or the lines of the palm matters not in the least, if you can produce good, clear-cut results that permit of only one interpretation, that of perception without sensory means. If you cannot, you are outside our field of study. Until you prove your powers objectively, we haven't much in common or at least we do not know that we have." At that point I look anxiously at my watch or at the door or at the mail from other inquirers which I have not yet been able to read. Sometimes that worked. Not always. . .

Yet I must not leave the impression that we are unsympathetic to these people. All we are unsympathetic to is the way they are floundering about without a line, a method, to pull them ashore. In my judgment they represent intelligent humanity of a prescientific era. Many of them are fine, aspiring souls trying to find a better explanation of man and a better code of action for his conduct. The fact that I have the instrument of scientific method to use and am that much more fortunate makes me want to find them such truth as there may be, though they may be all too ready to accept it even uncritically.[1]

Rhine was most interested in letters from informed and critical fellow researchers, many in Britain, responding to his book and to the reports that he was now throwing dice to test for psychokinesis, or mind over matter.

Other correspondents mistook Duke for a psychic supermarket where you could hire sensitives to find lost watches or mislaid wills, or a coven for scientifically approved fortune-tellers. Most of the mail—which was carefully filed—told of the writers' dreams that came true in almost every detail, ghosts they had seen, objects that moved when no one touched them. Good ideas were also filed away for the time when there might be a larger staff to handle them.

Rhine was in his office when a casual visitor, who looked about nineteen, introduced himself as a gambler. He claimed that when throwing dice, he could control his own results with willpower and he could depress the scores of his opponents by subjecting them to mental stress. Rhine challenged him to demonstrate this power. He accepted the challenge and was slightly successful. Rhine couldn't recall the name of the young gambler, but in a letter to Prince admitted that the visitor had stimulated him into undertaking a long series of dice throws. Results showed there was something to the young man's claim of mind influencing matter, or psychokinesis, as it came to be called.[2]

News of Rhine's psychokinesis experiments crossed the Atlantic, where English psychologist W. Whatley Carington persuaded thirty-seven volunteers to test themselves and send him the results. Carington was one of the first psychologists to use Jung's word-association test on mediums to see if the responses of mediums and their "spirit guides" to the same set of words were similar. He concluded from these tests that the "spirit guides" were the mediums' secondary personalities and not separate entities. He had also pioneered the use of the lie detector.[3] The results of his psychokinesis tests were confused. There was only one high scorer out of the thirty-seven, and Carington didn't trust him. Consequently he wrote to Rhine imploring him to guard against fraud. He stressed that skeptics were liable to dismiss all positive results as fraudulent unless reports of the experiments demonstrated—not merely asserted—that fraud could not have occurred.[4]

Rhine welcomed well-informed and well-intentioned critics like Carington and invited him to continue with his frank advice and warnings as "a good blast of criticism . . . helps me to straighten my research in the future." Rhine had recently been attacked by a council member of the British SPR for doing research with subjects who were not witnessed and who recorded their own results. Defending himself to Carington, Rhine emphasized that at this stage he "was not trying to *prove* the existence of ESP." He was seeking to discover its "much needed principles, relations and laws." Even so, he assured Carington, "do not think for a moment that I have been *trusting* people."[5]

Another Englishman, Professor E. R. Dodds of Birmingham, a veteran psychic researcher, felt Rhine should have given more elaborate descriptions of both conditions and precautions for each separate experiment. Rhine partially agreed. Dodds also said Rhine should have indicated if he always kept the cards locked up between experiments. Rhine agreed. Had he always kept them locked up between experiments? Well, he didn't think it necessary for the long-distance work, when there were screens between cards and subject and when the subject guessed down through a pack (the pack was cut, then placed face down on a table and the subject guessed the order of all twenty-five symbols without a card being touched).

"We were working with the more customary academic atmosphere," Rhine replied to Dodds,

. . . with our own students and assistants, and with only the usual desire to please, which every psychologist may count on with all his subjects. I grant that I have taken the matter of trustworthiness

somewhat less concernedly than I would have if I were dealing with a group of mediums. . . . I feel it is important to publish all of the results to permit evaluation of the anti-coincidence value, but I think we can meet some of the conditions on such points as honesty of the assistants if we have this point later covered by an adequate group of data. For instance, as you know, I include large blocks of unwitnessed data for what they are worth, because I consider the question of good faith of the subject who produced them are settled by a series in which he was adequately witnessed. . . . But to be quite honest, I do wish I had been more explicit, as for instance in the example you cite on page 74. "We" there actually meant only "myself." Pratt was not present.

I read with great interest and satisfaction your review of Dr. [Carl] Jung's book. This reminds me of a good letter I had from him recently, expressing a strong interest in this work. [See Appendix A for some of the Rhine-Jung correspondence.] He was, I find, investigating mediums when I was scarcely out of the cradle.[6]

Precautions and more precautions was the theme of the letters coming in from Britain. Dr. Robert H. Thouless of Glasgow University, author of *Straight and Crooked Thinking*, thought that "the skeptic is right in refusing to regard as critical any series of experiments in which the same pack of cards is used in successive tests if the subject can see the backs of the cards used and has been told in checking what was on the face of each card." This, of course, would not apply to the distant experiments or occasions when there was a screen separating the subject from the cards.[7]

Meanwhile, in England, psychic researcher H. F. Saltmarsh had joined forces with G. N. M. Tyrrell for an ingenious ESP experiment. Before World War I, Tyrrell had journeyed to Mexico for the Marconi Company and introduced wireless to the Western Hemisphere. After 1923 he devoted himself to psychical research. He is the author of *The Personality of Man*, and became president of the Society for Psychical Research in 1945.

To test for ESP, Tyrrell built a "light machine"—five light bulbs in light-sealed boxes. The lights were lit randomly. The subject lifted the lid of the box in which he thought the light was on. Hits and misses were recorded automatically. The machine was adjusted to rule out telepathy. Results, the two men told Rhine, seemed to indicate clairvoyance and precognition at work.

Rhine was delighted with the light machine experiments and wrote to Saltmarsh:

They constitute the most comprehensive confirmation of our work here, and you appreciate what that means to me. . . . I feel as if the work now no longer needs to depend upon either my own honesty or my own efficiency, and it's a great relief, even though I was thoroughly sure of the main ground before I published. Our own experiments here now have totaled several hundred thousand.[8]

The following day Rhine congratulated Tyrrell:

Your work with Mr. Saltmarsh was the first work of its kind to be reported to me from abroad after the publication of my own experiments. I am inclined to think of telepathy and clairvoyance as basically closely related, and to think of them as not completely restricted by time and space relations as are the sensory modes of cognition. This would make retrocognition and precognition, along with cognition of distant objects, subordinate phases of clairvoyance in general—or, as I would like to think of them, as extrasensory perception unlimited by the usual space-time connections.[9]

To those eager to know if his researches had found evidence for life after death, Rhine replied: "What we have so far found in the ESP research would be at least favorable to the *possibility* of survival of personality after death."

Eileen Garrett's friend Frances Bolton wanted Rhine to continue survival research. She invited him and McDougall to Washington, D.C., in February 1935 and agreed to support the parapsychology laboratory for five years at $10,000 a year. Part of the money was to raise Rhine's salary from $3,500 to $5,000 a year. By this time he had to support a household of six, including three daughters and a son. He had not had a raise in salary at Duke for six years, though his family had doubled and he had been promoted to assistant professor.

He had to deal with these down-to-earth issues, but the mail refused to let Rhine stay down for long. A letter came from Salem, Massachusetts, reporting that "a very honorable lady, member of the Methodist Church and not known as a 'Medium,' has been answering questions for me by the use of the table which tips once for 'no' and three times for 'yes.' I do not question the honesty of the lady, in fact I know she is not CONSCIOUS of moving the table, but I wish to find out if the answers are not subconsciously and unconsciously relayed to the hands from her own mind."

In all probability, the reply was—in all probability.

A planned trip to a "haunted house" with McDougall had to be called off because they couldn't be in six places at once. However, Hubert Pearce was planning an investigation on Rhine's behalf. He wrote from Searcy, Arkansas, about two young women in the hill country whose strange powers had converted even educated skeptics.

The women were said to blindfold a person, spin him around a few times until he lost his sense of direction. Then someone else took an article and hid it. The women put their hands on the blindfolded person for a few moments until he felt an urge to move—and he always moved straight to the hidden article and brought it back. Pearce intended to check the women out, to test them with ESP cards, and report the results to Rhine.

Because the long-distance Pearce-Pratt series had been so successful at Duke, Rhine wanted to replicate the experiment at a much greater distance, with Pratt as the experimenter at his home in North Carolina and Pearce trying to call the cards from his home, hundreds of miles away. Rhine offered to pay Pearce fifty dollars a month to spend a couple of hours in the early mornings at this task. Pearce was still having a little trouble persuading the local church authorities that a man who had some knowledge of psychology and parapsychology was not the devil's advocate. But he agreed to Rhine's suggestion—if there was no hurry to start. First of all, though, he wanted a sketch of Pratt's room, with an indication of exactly where the ESP cards would be placed during the experiment. Pearce felt that visualizing where the cards were would improve his scores. He found time for this experiment in the spring of 1936, but it only confirmed the decline effect. His scores were not far off chance.

Rhine never lost touch with the ESP stars of the early thirties. Linzmayer, the first high scorer, wrote to tell of his tragic dream that came true. He dreamed about a young woman he knew casually. In the dream she died after giving birth; he noted how she looked in her coffin and the clothes she wore. At the time he had the dream the young woman was in fact unmarried. But shortly after the dream he heard that she was pregnant and had married the expectant father. The dream had been so vivid that Linzmayer described it in some detail to a college friend. And then real life began to imitate the dream. Although the woman survived the birth of her child, she died a few months later. Her husband told Linzmayer that she had died from complications directly attributed to the birth. Linzmayer and his college friend went to the funeral and saw the woman in her coffin. She had the same dress and smile Linzmayer had noted in his dream. Linzmayer's dream confirmed the thrust of many other letters to Rhine that precognition did occur, and often during altered states of consciousness. Linzmayer's account was of special value because, before the event occurred, he confided his dream to a witness, which gave added weight to its authenticity.[10]

Critics sometimes asked Rhine why people with ESP didn't clean up at Las Vegas. Linzmayer did. He went three times and came away the winner of a thousand dollars or so each time. Rhine could cite him as evidence for psychic powers in and out of the lab.[11]

Experiments in the lab continued to take precedence over everything else; after all, they were the keystone of his work. But Rhine found time to squeeze in trips to investigate a blindfolded boy with "magic powers." He wasn't the last "magician" to peek under his blindfold. Rhine also took field trips to test psychics with glowing testimonials, who invariably lost their sparkle when Rhine confronted them—though he admitted that failing his tests did not automatically mark a person as lacking psychic powers.

These days Rhine never publicly exposed people he caught cheating: He had wasted too much time and energy tangling with Margery's misguided ASPR supporters to go that route again. Instead, he simply avoided any future contact with those he'd unmasked, and alerted his fellow psychic researchers, keeping it in the family, so to speak.

19

EDGAR CAYCE—
THE SLEEPING PROPHET
1935–1936

Although the main thrust of Rhine's work consisted of controlled experiments with ESP cards and dice, few if any likely leads in the outside world were ignored. By 1935 any wonder man or woman, strange sight or sound, faith healer or mind reader, was likely to be brought to his attention by a growing list of informants throughout the country. Having neither staff nor funds to vet every "psychic" reported to him, at times Rhine asked his informants to investigate for him in their home territory, to weed out obvious frauds, publicity seekers, or the deluded.

  Rhine spotted Dr. Lucien Warner as a potentially good informant when the Pasadena, California, psychologist wrote to him on January 4, 1935, and revealed an extensive training and a natural curiosity. Warner had experimented with both rats and dogs. His attempt to produce a super breed of German shepherds had half succeeded—the dogs had better brains but worse looks. Rhine replied to Warner that the breeding experiment would greatly interest McDougall, an avid audience for any work on eugenics. Rhine was struck by Warner's wide-ranging experience—premed studies in North China, psychological and genetic research in Switzerland, and now as a research associate in the zoology department at Pomona College. "You are much more of a scientific man than I," Rhine replied to Warner. For some time Rhine had wondered what was being done with the $250,000 endowment for psychic research at Stanford University. Professor Coover's telepathy experiments were apparently the sole use that had been made of the small fortune. Did Coover now realize his results had indicated ESP to exist and not the reverse, as he had mistakenly concluded? Was the rest of the endowment going to waste? Could Warner question Coover on these points on Rhine's behalf? Rhine also suggested that Warner read Upton Sinclair's *Mental Radio*, then try to test Mrs. Sinclair with the ESP cards. Quite an assignment! Rhine also tried to arouse Warner's interest in McDougall's Lamarckian experiment, writing: "It is an experiment that needs someone who will have the courage to repeat it."[1]

Warner spoke with Coover and found him cautious and noncommittal. But the following February, Warner and his wife spent an engrossing evening with an anything-but-noncommittal business-man, David Kahn, who raved about the psychic powers of his friend Edgar Cayce. Since 1901, said Kahn, Edgar Cayce had been curing the sick. He did this by putting himself into a light trance, during which—although he had no medical training—he diagnosed the illnesses of distant strangers and suggested reportedly effective treatments. He never remembered what he said while in the trance, but a stenog-rapher recorded Cayce's words and these were mailed to people who had asked for medical help. News of his ability to diagnose illnesses by clairvoyance and to make prophecies was reported in newspapers and magazines, and he had become known, even abroad, as The Sleeping Prophet of Virginia Beach.*

The patient was told the time and date of his appointment—not to attend a doctor's office, but to remain in his own home. At the appointed time Cayce relaxed on a couch in his home, having put himself into a trance. A secretary read to him the name, age, and location of the patient, who might be anywhere in the world. After a few moments Cayce would murmur: "Yes, we have the body." It was as if the patient had been transported a few hundred or even thousand miles into the room. Then Cayce gave a detailed diagnosis and suggested treatment to restore mental and physical health. Every-thing he said, as recorded by a stenographer, was then sent to the patient.

Cayce's remedies were usually simple but unorthodox; often they were almost-forgotten folk remedies. Nobody is reported to have died from Cayce's "cures," but thousands of grateful letters testify to his success. Some are from doctors. Few if any of the testimonials could survive a court of inquiry by the AMA or convince a skeptic armed with more rational explanations, such as that many of the patients had psychosomatic illnesses or would have been cured without any treatments. But to the thousands who believed they had

---

*In 1943 the demand for Cayce's medical "readings" resulted in a two-year waiting list. He died in 1945, having given 14,249 readings to 5,772 people. Today the readings are filed at the spacious, modern headquarters of the Association for Research and Enlightenment, Inc. (A.R.E.) in Virginia Beach, Virginia. Students and writers are welcome to examine them.

benefited from Cayce's remedies, he was a marvel and his abilities miraculous.[2]

And so it seemed to Rhine's emissary, Dr. Warner, as he listened to David Kahn. Warner wondered if Cayce could call the ESP cards and score above average. Score above average? He'd get every one right, Kahn assured him. There would be no mistakes. When Warner relayed his conversation with Kahn, Rhine was enthusiastic. Yes, Rhine agreed, let's test Cayce, but at his own specialty—medical diagnosis. One of Rhine's daughters was ill. He'd ask Cayce to help her. On April 6, 1936, Rhine sent Cayce this day letter:

Please give physical reading Tuesday Elizabeth Ellen Rhine National Avenue no number outside city limits Durham. Refer Lucien Warner. Thank you. Will join organization later. Have been much interested in Dr. Warner's inquiries into your work. He is much impressed. Appreciate your cooperation with him. All information welcome.

Warner assured Cayce that three-year-old Elizabeth Ellen would be at her home at 10:40 A.M. on the day arranged.

In Virginia Beach at 10:40 A.M. on Tuesday, April 7, 1936, Edgar Cayce went into a trance, and his secretary, Gladys Davis, wrote what he said—a diagnosis of Elizabeth Ellen's illness and a suggested treatment. Cayce had not been told, but following a case of flu she had developed pneumonia. She had recovered from that, only to suffer from emphysema. At least that was the orthodox medical opinion.

The entranced Cayce said:

As we find, the basic disturbance would require the deeper activity into the entity's experience. But we find that help, aid, may be brought for the body. While the first apparent physical cause arose from infectious disturbance throughout the gastrointestinal tract, there has been left in the present a disturbance that makes for inco-ordinations through the activities of the body; through those actions of the lymph in its inability to function through the lacteal area, the caecum and those extensions in same to the ileum plexus. . . .[3]

A covering letter suggested that a Wet Cell Appliance be used for up to six weeks. The cost would be twenty-eight dollars, including chemical solutions. Instructions on how to use the appliance were included.

A follow-up letter from Cayce's son, Hugh Lynn, explained that remarkable results had been obtained with the appliance, and that he would be glad to supply one at no cost if Rhine would test it and report the results. "We sincerely seek a clearer, deeper under-standing of all types of psychic phenomena, and believe that the only real test lies in results," Hugh Lynn concluded.

Because Edgar Cayce was concerned that Rhine should under-stand his motives, he wrote to him:

In compliance with your wire, we undertook the information this morning (April 7) ... a copy of which you no doubt have in hand by now. Through the years I have never made any claims for such information; I do not comprehend it. And my only excuse for being engaged in a work of this nature is the testimony from so many who have been helped. I know what it has meant in my own immediate family, and I'm hoping and trusting that the information through these sources will prove just as helpful to you as it has to me personally. I appreciate your interest, and assure you that it is our sincere desire to be of help whenever and wherever possible. We realize that we have nothing to sell, and that we can claim nothing; for we do not know beforehand ... ever ... what to expect. But let's hope for the best."[4]

Rhine was disappointed with the Cayce reading. "So far as any medical judgment or my own common sense goes, it was entirely wrong," he told Lucien Warner.

There have been no intestinal symptoms, no incoordination of which we have any evidence. So much for the reading itself. ... I have looked over some of the jargon that he has sent me. It has a very familiar sound and comes from a lot of different centers, mainly New York and southern California. Many of them claim, of course, to have some practical benefit. The Freudians claim that, too, but God knows. ... There will doubtless be some remarkable hits, because the chances are fairly small against failure in some of these matters. That is, given the knowledge which every member has to furnish, and the knowledge furnished on the application regarding the past, which lets it be fairly well known what his age, sex, nationality, etc., are; given also some general impression about seasonal effects and the probability of, let us say, pneumonia at one time of year, infantile paralysis at another, etc. ... In any ultimate analysis it would not be possible to strike an evaluation that would convince the hard-boiled world we have to meet, and as a matter of fact, to answer our doubts. Therefore, at the very best there would have to be a high number of very striking cases. There is bound to be a certain number of hits, even, let us say, a diagnosis of pinworms or tuberculosis, if he is working daily at this sort of thing and has been at it for years. What are the chances that

such a hit will happen by chance alone under the circumstances? . . .
I will make a polite and friendly little letter in reply to Cayce's
to cover the case for any continued study which you might wish to
make and to preserve in any case friendly relations with him. . . . But
the whole thing is as near to the ridiculous as anything I know of, even
though if I had time to try everything I should certainly give it a try
just to be open-minded. . . . There are, in my judgment, about a dozen
cases over the country that are much more promising than this. He
[Cayce] may, however, be the best thing you see on your horizon, and
you are the judge as to that. . . . For that matter, a chap like Arthur
Ford offers a better prima facie *case than Cayce, although I should*
certainly watch him carefully. Still, they are both in the same general
class, and Ford is right there in New York City. You can locate him
with the aid of any spiritualist.[5]

Arthur Ford (1897–1971) was the psychic in whom Upton
Sinclair had shown an early interest. Rhine wanted to test him, but
they never got together.
    Rhine explained to Hugh Lynn Cayce that

. . . the diagnosis was, so far as all symptoms go, entirely incorrect. . . .
You will understand, of course, that since I am myself making studies
of parapsychical phenomena, that I am fully prepared philosophi-
cally to understand failure in such cases, even if I did not know that
you yourselves disclaim any certainty of perfection in your work. . . . I
have had so many failures in this work that they only make me hunt
further for the successes which we do, under the right conditions,
frequently obtain.[6]

Cayce's son, Hugh Lynn, urged Rhine to continue the investigation, writing what seemed like an irresistible invitation to check the
Cayce record. Hugh Lynn explained that he had devoted just three or
four years to a constant study of the work,

. . . while the readings as given by my father have a history of some
thirty-five years. I have myself observed and checked case after
case in which the analysis is positively correct. . . . We have over
fifteen thousand copies of these psychic readings on various in-
dividuals and subjects in our files. Thousands of these cases are
complete with reports on very favorable results. Complete reports,
including physicians' parallel examinations, X rays, etc., showing
correct analyses and remarkable results number more than a thou-
sand. My father continues to give two or three of these readings each
day for individuals in all parts of the country. In many of these,

*definite and specific examples of unusual powers of clairvoyance are
appearing frequently.*[7]

Hugh Lynn gave Rhine an open invitation to Virginia Beach to
see the Cayce files, discuss the work, and offer suggestions.

Rhine did not go to Virginia Beach, although Cayce's failure to
pass Rhine's one test is unlikely to be the reason he dropped the
investigation. He never completely lost interest in the Sleeping Prophet
of Virginia Beach. And it is probable that had Cayce turned up at
Duke, Rhine would have put him through tests in and out of trance.

Cayce's prophecies—including the reappearance of the island
of Atlantis and Cayce's own reincarnation in 2100 A.D.—must have
reassured Rhine that he had made the right decision to leave the man
to other researchers, and the illnesses of himself and his family in the
hands of trained physicians.

20

A MENTAL PATIENT
AND
DREAM TELEPATHY
1936

Rhine spent the early months of 1936 trying to get a woman released from a mental institution. She was said to be psychically gifted and he wanted to test her—but first he had to free her from the institution. To protect her identity she was known as Mrs. H. No less a psychical researcher than Dr. Alexis Carrel—a Nobelist—recommended the woman, but warned Rhine to go slow, implying that any high-powered investigation might upset her. He suggested that to begin with, an assistant work with the woman.

Rhine next heard from clergyman and psychical researcher Dr. Elwood Worcester that Mrs. H. was being released under his guidance for a visit to Boston. "A great deal will depend on her behavior on that trip and her success in working as he reports it to me," Rhine explained in a letter to Carrel on February 13.

I am delighted to know you intend seriously to look up your notes on your work with Mrs. H. with a view to bringing them to publication. The Journal of Abnormal and Social Psychology *has published four articles from me on my work and I am quite sure would be much more open to publication from you than they have been to me. . . . They published my work on Mrs. Garrett, I think largely on the basis of its having been carried out in two personality states—in trance and in the normal state.*

The investigation of the "mentally disturbed" Mrs. H. took on the aspects of an Alfred Hitchcock thriller, according to Rhine's letter to Professor Hornell Hart of Hartford Theological Seminary:

Dr. Elwood Worcester* has been engineering the arrangements with Mrs. H. and has secured her release temporarily for experimental purposes. He assures me that arrangements are easily possible for Mrs. H. to come down to Duke University. If, therefore, arrangements could be made for a study of her, let us say in a private home or an office or a laboratory somewhere in Hartford, there would be, I feel sure, no difficulties with Dr. B. . . . Dr. Worcester maintains that there never was anything fundamentally wrong with Mrs. H. and that she was the victim of her husband's designs for remarriage, which were facilitated by her psychical activities. Taking advantage of these, with which he had no sympathy, he was able to commit her and secure a divorce. Of course, I am relying on Dr. Worcester's judgment. He has had a great deal of experience with mental disorder, however, and perhaps should be able to judge. Within recent weeks Dr. Worcester has had Mrs. H. in Boston where she gave a number of experimental sittings. He speaks encouragingly of her capacities.

Rhine suggested that two of Professor Hart's more mature and responsible students who were interested in the subject should study Mrs. H. "sympathetically but cautiously."[1]

Rhine's plan was frustrated by Mrs. H.'s ex-husband, who cut off her contact with the outside world. The man's motive, Worcester thought, was to prevent her from meeting normal, intelligent people because through them she might get free—and complicate her former spouse's life. It was the first potential subject Rhine lost to a mental institution, though he knew many of his critics thought that's where he belonged.

Worcester had another true story to tell Rhine, again with overtones of an Alfred Hitchcock movie. His neighbor Theodosia, adopted daughter of the late Walter Franklin Prince, had dreamed that she saw a yellow truck with no lettering on it pass her home in Hingham and go up the winding road a few hundred yards beyond, to the bungalow of neighbors who were, in fact, away at the time. In the dream she saw two men get out of the truck and load it with all the furniture from house. The dream had been so vivid that next morning she went to the neighbors' house and, looking through the window, was astonished to see all the furniture gone, including the bathtub.

By the nature of his job, a policeman is almost immune to surprise. But Hingham's chief of police was hard-pressed not to lose his

---

*Dr. Worcester, an Episcopal clergyman, founded the Emmanuel movement to use medicine and psychotherapy with religious and spiritual guidance in a combined effort to help people with physical, mental, or nervous problems. He was a friend and colleague of the late Dr. Walter Franklin Prince.

sangfroid when Theodosia reported a crime she had seen committed in a dream. She quickly explained that she had checked on her dream and confirmed that part of it was a fact—the house in the dream which she recognized in real life had indeed been stripped. The police chief double-checked and found she was right. He was in for an even bigger surprise. When he asked Theodosia if she would be able to identify the two thieves in her dream, she gave an unmistakable description of two of neighboring Cohasset's leading citizens.

Nevertheless, he ordered two detectives to tail the men. They were eventually seen getting into a yellow truck without lettering that had been parked near an isolated house. After the men drove off, the detectives searched the house. It looked like a furniture warehouse. They waited for the truck to return, saw it crammed with furniture, and arrested the two men on suspicion. At the trial, Theodosia identified the men as her dream robbers. Two other men were arrested as gang members who had been helping to strip unoccupied houses in the area. The four men were sentenced to a total of fifty-four years in prison.

It was one of the best examples of dream telepathy Worcester had ever encountered, especially as Hingham's police chief confirmed Theodosia's bizarre but vital role. To Rhine it was fascinating, but almost too good to be true, and because it was impossible to rule out normal explanations for Theodosia's sleuthing, he withheld his verdict. He became more convinced when telepathy happened closer to home—at home, in fact.

Louisa tells of coincidences of thought between her and daughter Betsy (the third of her four children) and wondered if it could mean telepathic communication, both in dreams and while awake. She describes one episode in her book *Hidden Channels of the Mind*:

One night I was awakened from a nightmarish dream by a loud cry from my three-year-old daughter sleeping in an adjoining room. The dream had left me trembling and covered with perspiration, for in it I was being pursued up the road to the house by some looming indescribable creature and I was making a last desperate rush to get inside the door before it overtook me, when my daughter's cry brought me back to reality.

"I'm scared, Mama, I'm scared," she sobbed.

"But why? What scared you?"

She hestitated and said finally, "I guess it was a bear."

In this instance, fear was the outstanding item: hers seemed like a contagion of my own. The nameless creature, the "bear," only an invention to explain the fear, a rationalization.[2]

And, again, Louisa Rhine writes:

I am quite certain from my own experience, for instance, that in the 1930s, if I had not been "married to ESP" I would never have considered it more than an odd coincidence that one of my small children [again Betsy] seemed so often to voice my unspoken thoughts. Only after repeated observation of coincidence between her remarks and my own thoughts and because as a family we were then becoming ESP-conscious, did I finally keep a diary recording these incidents.

In time it became quite evident from this record that one of the four children had telepathic tendencies.[3]

21

HOLLYWOOD
1936–1937

California, the state of excitement, again beckoned Rhine in the sun-drenched summer of 1936. Upton Sinclair, Rhine's West Coast informant, had lost confidence in Roman Ostoja, who had levitated a table while the novelist looked on but failed to raise even a leg during the séance Einstein attended. It was now clear to Sinclair that he had been taken in by a professional magician whose bag of tricks included being buried for hours in an airtight coffin. Ostoja's claims to psychic powers and to being a genuine Polish count did not survive investigation. But this was not a fallow period for mediums, and when one failed or was found out, another made an entrance. After his break with Ostoja, Sinclair concentrated on Arthur Ford, who read messages in sealed envelopes—or so it seemed. Sinclair wanted Rhine to test Ford.

But Ford had flown when Rhine arrived. Fortunately Rhine did not have to depend exclusively on Sinclair to find West Coast wizards. His journey had been sparked by extravagant newspaper accounts of a boy who could outfence the world's greatest fencing masters. He did this, said the reports, while heavily blindfolded with adhesive tape. How? He was reportedly guided by the spirit of an ancient Persian named Napeji. A fencing instructor attested to his supernatural prowess as a fencer; Persian scholars endorsed the authenticity of the Persian spirit. Dozens of physicians were stated to believe in the boy's supernatural ability. Hamlin Garland (1860–1940), a Pulitzer-prizewinning author and enthusiastic amateur psychical researcher, proclaimed the boy to be the greatest living medium.

Rhine spoke with some of the Persian scholars who had endorsed the genuine character of the Persian spirit. Then he asked Dr. Reynolds, who was in charge of the boy, to let him see the youngster in action. There was no doubt the boy fenced remarkably well. Rhine's next request demonstrated the difference between an amateur and professional investigator: He asked Dr. Reynolds and his associates to blindfold him exactly as they had the boy. They did this to their satisfaction, which was the beginning of the end. Rhine told them that he had no difficulty in peeking beneath the blindfold. Nobody else, apparently, had thought to try the blindfold out for himself.

The boy was persuaded that the masquerade was over and disappeared from the psychic scene.

"It looked pretty striking because of the endorsements by Persian scholars and by prominent medical men," Rhine explained in a letter to Eileen Garrett. "Unfortunately, the Persian side of the case was found to be grossly exaggerated, the fencing master probably wanted advertisement."[1]

If Rhine had wanted to emulate Houdini he could have spent his life exposing psychics—there were enough to go around, especially in the film capital of the world, where fact and fantasy danced a perpetual fandango.

Psychic phenomena were taken for granted among some writers and stars. Mediums were treated like telephone operators, waiting to connect long-distance calls to the next world if the price was right. Or they were expected to predict the future in detail as though they'd already seen it at a Hollywood preview. Any psychic worth her salt could call up Rudolph Valentino from the grave for a chat and maybe a few acting tips. As for the living stars, if they didn't have their personal medium or fortune-teller, they hadn't really made it.

Actor Lionel Barrymore lived opposite Heaven, the name members of a psychic-religious group gave their Beverly Hills home. When traveling with one of his teenage disciples, their leader—a fat, pink-cheeked man in his thirties who claimed extraordinary psychic powers—registered at hotels as "Jesus the Christ" and "The Virgin Mary." Then he modestly added—"No publicity."

"Jesus" tripled his followers in one day when, said court testimony, he "soared around," throwing ten thousand dollars in big and small bills to his disciples scrambling for the cash on the carpet. Barrymore made an irate phone call to the Beverly Hills police department because the frenzied bill collectors disturbed his sleep. Where "Jesus" was soaring to wasn't clear, but he landed in prison with a three-year sentence, found guilty of transporting a teenage girl across state lines for nonspiritual purposes. Rhine just missed meeting him, although "Jesus" would have made a natural subject, being, as he said, in constant contact with spirits of the dead.

Upton Sinclair steered Rhine away from discussing the local prominent doctor who believed he was on a secret assignment to take a rocket trip to the moon, to talking instead of trance medium Arthur Ford's recent feat—reading a message in a sealed envelope. There were so many tricky ways of doing this that Rhine didn't take Sinclair's word for it. He agreed, however, to invite Ford to Duke to see if he could read the hidden symbols there.

Sinclair took Rhine for an unexpected visit to Charlie Chaplin in his movie studio. The comedian said that Sinclair had converted him to socialism, and recommended to Rhine an Eastern film showing natives carrying out religious ceremonies involving self-torture. Rhine wrote away for it, on behalf of the psychology department. Later Rhine called on local mystics and mountebanks on the off-chance that a genuine psychic might lurk behind a phony front. He found none. He must have felt, at times, as out of place as McDougall among the Borneo headhunters. From then on any of his staff showing an interest in astrology, numerology, palmistry, Rosicrucian literature, religious cults, black magic, occult and ancient wisdoms from the four corners of the globe, were treated by Rhine as if they were trading in pornography.

Rhine was rarely given credit for steering clear of what William James bluntly called "the lunatic fringe" and refusing to be involved in their pursuits. He didn't denounce them because he regarded denunciation without investigation as unscientific. But to many, if not most, orthodox scientists, Rhine was beyond the pale for working in an area inhabited by dubious characters reporting implausible if not impossible events.

Compared with his British counterpart, Harry Price, Rhine was establishment. Englishman Harry Price was famed, if not notorious, for his investigation of ghosts in Borley Rectory, Britain's most publicized haunted house. While Rhine checked out the gypsy tearooms and the fencing youngster's blindfold in the summer of '36, Price was climbing to the top of Germany's Bracken Mountain on an enterprise that would have taken Barnum's breath away. When Price reached the summit, he and C. E. M. Joad, a distinguished London University professor of philosophy, drew a "magic circle" on the ground. The circle was a sticky mixture of bats' blood, church-bell scrapings, soot, and honey. As forty-two photographers and seventy-three reporters stepped on one another's feet, jostling for a closeup, Price led a young woman and a goat into the magic circle. Exactly at midnight he signaled the young woman to begin a Latin incantation. Price aimed to put a legend to the test. According to this legend, said to have been started with Faust, if the magic formula was obeyed exactly, the goat would turn into a youth of surpassing beauty.

What did happen inspired a succinct story-in-a-nutshell headline in the British *Sunday Dispatch*—"SAME OLD GOAT!" But the goat

surely was Price, for bringing parapsychology into even more disrepute. Shaken out of his habitual hyperbole, George Bernard Shaw
characterized the mountaintop hijinks as a rather unusual means of
seeking amusement.[2]

The Swiss psychologist Carl Jung wrote to Harry Price, appalled that Price, a man of science, would lend himself to superstition.
Jung took psychic research seriously and endorsed Rhine's more
sober approach to mystery. Rhine himself was wary of all Harry
Price's work, before and after the trip to the mountain, regarding him
as a showman.

22

THE
VANISHING WOMAN
1936–1937

While Rhine was in California, he was the cause of an uproar in a psychology class in New York. One of the students at Hunter College mentioned Rhine's experiments and Bernard Riess, an assistant professor of psychology, responded with the scholarly equivalent of a Bronx cheer. Other students protested that Rhine was a careful scientist. To still the noise that followed, Riess said that he would give Rhine a chance to condemn himself. He'd invite him to lecture at Hunter College. When it was known that Riess intended to invite Rhine, the psychology department went into shock. One colleague, with whom Riess often had political arguments, bluntly ordered: "Don't!" That was all Riess wanted to hear. He sent the invitation by the next mail.[1]

Fresh from his trip to the wacky West, Rhine looked forward to a return to the rational. However, the tumult that greeted his talk at Hunter College was not unlike the reception "Jesus" got when he ran out of dollar bills.

Riess himself was as damning as any of his students. "Your work lacks a scientific hypothesis," he told Rhine. "It involves a belief in the supernatural or the transcendental. And if you can't prove ESP is a physical emanation, then your work is unscientific. Furthermore, all of your experiments don't seem to add up to very much." The skeptics cheered.

Accustomed to these charges, Rhine had his answer ready: "If you're such a hot experimentalist, why don't you do an experiment yourself? There's nothing like that to convince you. Set up your own conditions and your own safeguards."[2]

Rhine had appeared at Hunter College on a Friday. Riess had the weekend to think over the suggestion. When he took his next psychology class on Monday, a student asked first thing, "Are you going to accept Rhine's challenge?"

Riess asked if anyone in the class considered herself "psychic" or knew of anyone with that talent. Of the dozens of students, only one raised her hand. She had a friend who was psychic—maybe she'd take part in an experiment with Riess. If she was willing, Riess said that he'd try to disprove Rhine by setting up the most favorable conditions to elicit ESP and then not getting it. After a great deal of persuasion, the "psychic" woman agreed to talk with Riess over the phone. He told her how he wanted to test her. She wished to remain anonymous. He agreed. In fact that was part of his plan, to avoid the charge that in order to fake results, the two of them had cheated or collaborated.

At the moment he only knew her first name, her address, and phone number. He later discovered that she lived in White Plains, a quarter of a mile away from his Scarsdale home, was twenty-six, lived at home, and was "sick of it." Ill health had compelled her to leave a women's college where she was a music major. From their brief conversations, Riess judged her to be an intelligent, frustrated young woman whose only diversion was visits to concerts. To Riess she was always to remain just a voice at the other end of the phone. And in his report of the unique experiments, published in the *Journal of Parapsychology*, Riess doesn't even give away her first name, referring to her throughout as Miss S.[3]

Miss S. agreed to be waiting at the phone just before 9 P.M. on December 27, 1936, when Riess said he'd call. They would then synchronize their watches and from nine onward, at one-minute intervals, Riess would test her ESP, using the ESP cards and mimeographed record sheets Rhine had sent.

It was almost nine o'clock. Riess phoned Miss S. He sat at his desk and shuffled the deck of twenty-five ESP cards. It was nine. He turned the top card face up, looked at it, and recorded the symbol on his record sheet. Miss S. had a minute to write down her impression before he looked at the next card. When he had gone through the pack, he reshuffled it, gave her a ten-minute break, and went through the deck again. That was it. He phoned her again, wished her good night and asked her to mail him her record sheet.

Riess tested Miss S. like this at irregular intervals for four months, until April 1937, when she said she was too ill to continue. He hoped they could get together again when she recovered.

Then he began to calculate her scores by comparing her records with his. She had made 1,850 calls. Riess expected her to average 5 out of 25 and prove his contention that ESP was a myth. Instead, he found that Miss S. had made the highest scores in ESP history, an astronomical average of 18.24 hits out of 25. Nobody before or since has come anywhere near that. She had one perfect score of 25 out of 25, 3 of 24, 1 of 23, and 3 of 22. Either Miss S. had psychic powers second to none, she had tricked Dr. Riess, or he had left something out of his report.

Skeptical critics, of course, inclined to the latter views. Psychology professor C. E. M. Hansel of the University College of Swansea, University of Wales, suggested that the young woman broke into Riess's home, defied or circumvented his formidable housekeeper and altered the results.[4] Some even doubted that Miss S. existed.

Miss S. told Riess she was fit enough to resume testing on July 18, 1937. She said she'd just recovered from a nervous breakdown. Riess later learned from her physician that he'd been treating her for a hyperthyroid condition. The two illnesses, of course, are not mutually exclusive.

Although Miss S. felt she was doing as well as in the earlier tests, her scoring for 250 card calls averaged 5.3 out of 25, barely above chance. After the 250 trials she refused to go on. Riess called her home at the end of August, and was told that she had left for the Midwest. He never heard from her again. Later he learned that the family had moved and the father was dead.

Riess confirmed the rarity of high scorers when, soon after completing his work with Miss S., he tested sixty-seven college girls and none scored above chance. In his report about Miss S., Riess admitted that it was only suggestive—that for it to have been mathematically more persuasive, he should either have shuffled the deck of cards after each guess, or have taken one card at a time from a series of twenty-five decks of ESP cards.

The secret of Miss S.'s identity and the truth about her powers probably rest with the Hunter College friend who recommended her. Dr. Riess is as baffled as everyone else, except that he doesn't doubt that there was such a woman. She had, after all, changed him from skeptic to inclined-to-believe.

To parapsychologists, Riess's feat was both fabulous and frustrating. How much Rhine would have given for a chance to test Miss S.! But at least through suggesting such a test he had converted Riess to his side. And Riess was soon to prove a valuable ally.

23

DR. GARDNER MURPHY
AND THE *JOURNAL*
OF PARAPSYCHOLOGY
1936–1937

Had Rhine searched worldwide for someone to share his quest for the nature of man, he might not have come across a better friend or colleague than Dr. Gardner Murphy. If anyone inherited the mantle of William James it was Murphy, a shy, selfless, generous man with, wrote Aldous Huxley, "an excellent, fertile and open mind."[1]

An attack of encephalitic influenza in 1925 had left Murphy virtually blind and a semi-invalid. Two years later his sight was restored by following the unorthodox advice of Dr. Frank Marlow, who made a careful study of muscle imbalance and corrected it. Nine years later he was almost miraculously restored to health by a man regarded as a quack, Dr. W. H. Hay. His treatment was a radical detoxification and diet program emphasizing vitamins and foods containing high vitamin C and avoiding foods leaving acid residues. As a result, Murphy explains, "such experiences with 'deviations' and heterodoxy were enormously and profoundly significant in their interaction with my belief that psychical research could be essentially sound although damned from the housetops by all sound and sturdy intellects of the era."[2]

His health greatly improved in 1934, Murphy's interest in psychical research was revitalized after reading Rhine's *Extra-Sensory Perception*. He went to see Rhine at Duke, had a whirlwind tour of the laboratory, and was hooked.

Murphy wondered if he could replicate Rhine's remarkable results, and was willing to spend his own money to finance such a project.* If Rhine agreed, Murphy would pay Gaither Pratt to experiment at Columbia for two years. The last thing Rhine wanted was for Duke to remain an isolated outpost for psi research. (Psi includes both extrasensory perception and psychokinesis.) He and Pratt gladly accepted Murphy's offer. It was something of a miracle that Murphy was able to sponsor ESP experiments at Columbia, a behaviorist stronghold if there ever was one. Because of his active interest in ESP, Murphy—an assistant professor of psychology—was regarded by colleagues at Columbia as a good man gone wrong. They tolerated his extracurricular activities as they might any brilliant man's harmless eccentricities. Fortunately, Murphy had fine-tuned antennae and sensed how far he could go without arousing squawks or orders to quit from the psychology department. His low-key manner and penchant for understatement helped keep criticism good-humored and allowed him to encourage psi research uninterruptedly.

In almost every way Rhine and Murphy complemented each other, with Murphy the catalyst and critic and Rhine the experimenter, the man in the hot seat. Murphy described himself as "a midwife for research,"[3] contributing to the birth and development of promising investigators. And it isn't difficult to extend the metaphor to place Rhine as the father of the problem child. His sometimes unjustified enthusiasm over a blazing comet of an ESP performer was tempered by Murphy's skepticism and caution. Rhine would be careful in his methodology, but at times drew overoptimistic conclusions. Murphy, in his wife's words, was "very, very demanding and on the whole skeptical rather than being able to easily accept results. I think Gardner was more critical than anyone."[4]

Which explains Rhine's overture to Murphy in a letter written May 14, 1936.

I feel sure that a great deal of the future research in parapsychology in America, if not in the world, will depend upon how well you and I manage things, how well we understand each other, and all that. I have been speculating for nearly two years as to how well and how closely we could cooperate, trying to get as objective a picture of it as I could. I have asked a few others, including Lois, who know us both, but cannot get much help from them. I am certainly game to try at a closer arrangement. I believe we could make a go of it if we both, as would be the case, were determined to do so.

Dr. Gardner Murphy generously funded psi research from the royalties on his books, among them the ground-breaking survey Experimental Social Psychology, *1931, coauthored with his wife, Dr. Lois Murphy.*

The two men never worked closely together at Duke, but they visited one another and frequently corresponded. They were in a sense partners, united against an almost solid wall of doubting psychologists. And when Rhine persuaded McDougall that the only way they'd get their work into print and before the world was to publish a journal themselves, Rhine asked Murphy to help edit it.

"We have constantly disagreed on problems of publication and this is likely to continue," Murphy replied frankly, and proceeded to diagnose Rhine's weak spots.

I don't want to run any risk whatever of spoiling a splendid friendship with you. Probably fifty percent of what you and McD. feel should be published I will have to oppose or ask to have rewritten. I think at times your enthusiasm causes your critical standards to fall perilously low. Is there any merit in the tiresome casting of negative votes; isn't tension fairly sure to arise?

We might avoid this by using a device used by the London SPR: say once every issue that responsibility for both "facts and reasoning" rests entirely with each author. When it comes to loose and unwitnessed experiments, where do we come out on this basis? Isn't the standard of the journal as a whole set by the standards of the authors admitted to its pages? On the other hand, you and I are much too busy with research problems to give time to long correspondence about the rewriting of articles. . . . But you see the difficulties looming. Let's face them fairly.

You have an extraordinary habit of putting important news into a cryptic sentence. If Margaret can do sealed pack work, it's an epoch-making event, from my viewpoint, in terms of where we are going. In fact, if she can, I'd probably want her here next year not only as experimenter but primarily as subject. Will give all my available time to studying this. Please tell me what she did, conditions, method of preparing procedure, number of cards called, actual grouping of calls, total number of such attempts and the scores.

Apparently Margaret's powers soon suffered the inevitable decline.

Rhine pressed ahead for his plans for a journal, with Murphy to play some major role. To Gaither Pratt, still working with Murphy, he wrote:

I am very anxious to hear from Dr. Murphy on the matter of the publication. I am strongly in favor of starting off our Journal with a large paper from you, perhaps long enough to take up the whole number. I have more hope at the moment of getting the matter of funds straightened out, but I do not want to go too fast without knowing just what Murphy's views are.[5]

The same day, November 2, 1936, Rhine appealed to Mrs. Crunden, a money source to whom he had been introduced by the ever helpful Eileen Garrett:

In a recent conversation with Professor McDougall I went into the matter of the founding of a journal, its great importance to the establishment of parapsychology upon a dignified basis, its assurance of permanence in interest and standing, and . . . I know, after ten years of acquaintance with him, that if we get it financed he will edit it. He was founder of one of the most outstanding if not the most dignified journal of psychology today; namely, the British Journal of Psychology.

Rhine said there would be no problem getting contributors of the stature of Dr. Pierre Janet and the Nobel-prizewinning Dr. Alexis Carrel, but that he would be on guard

. . . against too many fingers in the pie. It has been our research program that has created the need for the Journal. It seems likely that for some years we had better keep the thing fairly closely under our control. . . . Of course we are not going to become in the least excited. We shall keep the most conservative tone to the Journal, but the journalists, magazine and book writers are going to "go wild" over the stuff they dig out of our perfectly scientific journal. . . . If everything goes well, as I anticipate, it will be the best known scientific journal that has ever come off the press. But now you will think I am becoming hypermanic and I must restrain myself. . . . If therefore you are the person whose interests, sympathies, and understanding of the importance of this work lead you to make provision for its establishment and to ensure its successful continuance, I believe I can promise you, speaking for the growing group of us who are vitally interested in this field, the deepest gratitude and every assurance that your generosity will not only be recognized but will bear good fruit.

The first issue of *The Journal of Parapsychology* appeared in March 1937, and despite Harvard antagonist Professor Edwin Boring's caustic question to Rhine: "How are you going to keep it filled?"[6] the journal has appeared without fail for over forty years.

Though Gardner Murphy didn't spend his sabbatical year working with Rhine at Duke, he did coedit the journal during its fledgling years. McDougall, as Rhine predicted, accepted the editorship once the journal became a fact.

True to his intent, Rhine kept the journal under his control. It is unlikely anything was published in it without his approval. McDougall had less than two years to live and much of the editing after that fell to Gardner Murphy. To Rhine's good fortune this outstanding psychologist, a man of exceptional talent and influence, had joined him as an ally and friend at a critical time. Rhine would soon be facing the biggest fight of his life against great odds and would need every friend he could get.*

---

*Concerning the relationship of Gardner Murphy and J. B. Rhine, Louisa Rhine wrote to me on December 21, 1981: "Both were careful, critical thinkers. J.B. was not one to be carried away by sudden enthusiasms. Instead, he was a careful, persistent type, every inch the experimentalist. Murphy's main benefit to J.B. was that he was in a way a brother-in-arms, but not down in the trenches and taking the flak. J.B., from his front-line position, had to be both critical and practical, while Murphy's suggestions often were inapplicable."

24

RHINE, JUNG, FREUD "I SEEK THAT WHICH IS IMPOSSIBLE" 1937

Of those who made common cause with Rhine, none gave him greater pride or pleasure than the noted Swiss psychiatrist Carl Jung. He was involved with the extrasensory when Rhine was a child, and had concluded it to be a fact, based on his own vivid personal experiences and extensive investigations. Rhine and Jung met only once—in New York in 1937—but they corresponded over the years.

Psychic research as an experimental science gained its first big momentum in the late nineteenth century, when the hypnotic state was seen to have much in common with the self-induced trances of mediums; and researchers believed that through hypnosis they were able to tap a reservoir of psychic power. At the same time, Sigmund Freud and Jung thought that by using hypnosis they could reach the depths of their patients' minds and bring hidden traumatic memories to light, where the power to harm was diminished or destroyed. Freud later dropped hypnosis, encouraging his patients instead to talk freely, persuaded that the "forgotten," disturbing thoughts would eventually surface, where they could be faced and effectively defused.

During this psychoanalysis Freud's colleagues, Jung among them, came across what appeared to be examples of telepathy. Initially, Freud resisted any aspect of the occult like a man fighting a drug habit. At different times he gave such conflicting statements about psychic phenomena that those both for and against quote him to support their views. Yet the record shows strong evidence that Freud, like his temporary disciple Jung, became a believer.

It would have been odd, had Jung ever doubted. His mother's

family saw visions, fell into trances, and uttered prophecies. His mother had been required by her clergyman father to sit behind him while he was composing his sermons to ward off distracting spirits.[1] Like Rhine, Jung's active interest in ESP started after he read of experiments by the pioneer investigators, several of whom founded the British Society for Psychical Research in 1882. Their reports on telekinesis, hypnosis, clairvoyance, and prophetic dreams spurred him to give a talk on psychical research to his fraternity at Basel University when he was twenty-two. He concluded that the soul existed and was intelligent and immortal.

Two years later, in 1899, he heard that his fifteen-year-old girl cousin, Helene Preiswerk, was a medium and held séances in her home a few miles from his. He asked her, in the interests of science, to give the séances in his home, as he wanted to make a serious study of her trance communications. She agreed. A few days before the first séance there was an explosion in Jung's home like a gun going off. Jung rushed in from the garden to calm his mother and a servant. The noise had come from the sideboard. He unlocked it and discovered that a bread knife had shattered into four parts; but strangely, there were no marks on the bread next to the knife nor on the inside of the basket.

Less than a week later a ninety-year-old table split from the rim to beyond the center, again sounding like an explosion. Jung hurried in from the next room. He could find no explanation for the split. There was no central heating that might have caused a sudden temperature change. The only explanation came from the teenage cousin after she began her séances in Jung's home. She said that on the days of the explosions, she had vividly thought of the projected séances. Jung was inclined to believe this was the answer, especially when he found she could produce raps in furniture and in the walls without touching them.

Jung attended Helene's séances for two years, until he caught her throwing objects supposed to be moved supernormally. His conclusion was that mediums are often hysterics who are likely to cheat when their supernormal powers fail. He put Helene in that category. Jung polished his notes of the séances into a dissertation for his medical degree, which he delivered before the faculty of medicine at the University of Zurich in 1902. His caution is evident in the title: "On the Psychology and Pathology of So-Called Occult Phenomena."

As a young psychiatrist in charge of the hypnotism clinic at Burgholzi mental hospital in Zurich, Jung read of Freud's psychoanalytical theories. He wrote enthusiastically to Freud, approving of his ideas and methods. Both men were soon exchanging warm, confiding letters, discussing their patients and their successful use of psychoanalysis. Jung quickly became Freud's heir apparent.

They began their almost weekly correspondence in the spring of 1906. The following year, on November 2, Jung wrote to say that he had been elected an honorary member of the American Society for Psychical Research, adding: "I have been dabbling in spookery again. Here too your brilliant discoveries are confirmed. What do you think about this whole field of research?"

If Freud replied to the question, his letter has not been unearthed. But when the two men met in 1909 and Jung again brought up the subject, Freud responded with "Bosh!" and "Sheer nonsense!" Jung persisted, writing to Freud of a case he was analyzing in which "first-rate spiritualistic phenomena occur." Freud advised his "dear son" to "keep a cool head, for it is better not to understand something than make such sacrifices to understanding."[2] But, just two years later, Freud began to capitulate. After hearing accounts by his friend, psychoanalyst Sandor Ferenczi, of successful telepathy experiments he had made with a psychic and of telepathic experiences with patients, Freud wrote to Jung on June 15, 1911: "In matters of occultism I have become humble, since the great lesson Ferenczi's experiences gave me. I promise to believe anything that can be made to look reasonable. I shall not do so gladly, that you know. But my hubris has been shattered."[3]

He teetered between belief and doubt, admitting that the subject of occultism perplexed him to distraction. Then, after making tests with Ferenczi and his own daughter, Anna, Freud wrote to his biographer, Ernest Jones, in 1926: "When anyone adduces my fall into sin, just answer him calmly that conversion to telepathy is my private affair like my Jewishness, my passion for smoking and many other things."[4]

Freud had become a covert parapsychologist who tried to conceal his interest from all but a few friends: Psychoanalysis, after all, had enough opposition without being linked with the occult. Jung, after breaking with Freud, plunged deeper and wider than the master into the occult ocean where, like some modern Ulysses, he heard disembodied voices, sensed himself possessed by spirits, and came dangerously close to losing his reason in his urge to explore the mind's psychic depths. He emerged from this awesome experience sane but badly shaken. Despite his youthful fervor in discussing the paranormal, maturity brought caution: "I have suffered enough from incomprehension and from the isolation one falls into when one says things that people do not understand."[5] Some listeners responded to Jung's accounts of his psychic adventures as if he were a lunatic, so— like Freud—he too grew secretive, although there were times when he lowered his guard.

Jung was in his outspoken mood at the start of the century when he psychoanalyzed William McDougall. Because the two men had a mutual fascination with psychic research, they freely discussed their own experiences in the field. Rhine eventually benefited from McDougall's memories of these talks. Jung was a rich source of often painfully acquired information about the little-known powers of the human mind.

The Swiss psychiatrist traveled to America in the summer of 1937 to deliver the Terry lectures, "Psychology and Religion," at Yale. En route he stopped in New York City for a luncheon given for him and Rhine by their mutual publisher, William Sloane. There, Jung, a lively and commanding presence, jokingly boasted that he got into the parapsychological field long before Rhine (in fact, when Rhine was two) and gave his enthralled audience—mostly book editors—a wide-ranging account of his experience. [6]

Rhine had started a correspondence with Jung as early as 1934, trying to draw him out on the subject of parapsychology.

Jung replied that he had learned to keep quiet about his psychic experiences as "others concluded you were either crazy or insincere." On the contrary, Rhine regarded Jung as "beyond comparison, the most distinguished living psychologist."[7] Rhine eventually broke Jung's resistance. He told Rhine about the splitting tabletop. Rhine acknowledged that it was very unusual but could have a normal explanation. However, the shattered knife baffled Rhine, and he admitted that

... when I read in the psychiatrist's letter that an old, steel-bladed bread knife also went to pieces about the same time, accompanied by a similar loud explosive report, I was frankly puzzled. I have a photograph of the knife, which shows the blade clearly broken into four sections.* The phenomenon still appears unexplainable to me in terms of anything known at present. The psychiatrist himself regards these happenings as cases of PK [psychokinesis], in some way connected with the medium, though he does not pretend to know how the effects were produced. [8]

In corresponding with others, Jung applauded Rhine's experimental work, which confirmed his own personal experiences. Despite his fear of ridicule, Jung left no room for doubt that he believed in the reality of the extrasensory world. He and Rhine generally agreed on many aspects of psi, including the sensitive subject of repeatability. Jung thought that the repeatable experiment is desirable to strengthen the position of parapsychological studies with

---

*Jung had sent Rhine a photo of the shattered knife and given him permission to display it at Duke.

the scientific community, but that "the experimental method would not be generally applicable since most of the events are spontaneous and irregular." To which Rhine added that not enough was known about psi to do a repeatable experiment. That would have to wait for the future.[9]

Jung implied in a letter to a third party that Rhine deserved the Nobel Prize. Rhine returned the compliment. In reviewing *The Interpretation of Nature and the Psyche*,* coauthored by Jung and W. Pauli, Rhine remarked that Pauli was a Nobel Prize physicist, and added "Scientists of the mind, of course, do not receive such honors as are given scientists of matter."[10]

Had Jung been on Rhine's staff, he would have been discouraged from his excursions into the study of astrology, I-Ching, yoga, unidentified flying objects, and alchemy. Nevertheless, Rhine wrote that in Jung,

his extreme tolerance and breadth of approach is indicated by his exploratory experiment with the borderland claims of astrology. The sheer courage of such an excursion by a man of science of the Western World and his willingness to publish his findings (generally speaking, negative) with unreserved forthrightness, makes his action one of the boldest performances on the pages of scientific history.[11]

Praising Jung for a pursuit he would have forbidden to his staff—or at the very least, would have discouraged—was not hypocrisy on Rhine's part. He had mapped out the parapsychological territory he wanted to explore, and made it emphatically clear where the border was. The more esoteric areas he left to others. With Jung there seemed to be no borders. And Rhine could admire his daring without wanting to join him. Jung, after all, indicated his goal when he carved over the fireplace of his home at Bolligen the words: *"Quaero quod impossibile"*—I seek that which is impossible. He acknowledged that Rhine was on a similar quest "because parapsychology is one of the most difficult problems ever put to the human mind."[12]

To Rhine's regret, there were few Jungs in the world. He and Rhine and a few other scientists were like a handful of swimmers in a rough sea of skepticism.

---

*Pantheon Books, 1955.

25

THE OPPOSITION
1936–1938

It seemed to Rhine that for every supporter like Jung and convert like Riess, the Hunter College psychologist, he gained a dozen denigrators who damned him in print or other public places. Scientists he had respected and admired stooped to Machiavellian trickery and duplicity to stop or sabotage his work. They lost their scientific detachment in their efforts, not to discover the facts, but to make him fall on his face.

Even the influential chairman of Harvard's psychology department, Professor Edwin G. Boring, joined the all's-fair-in-love,-war,-and-ESP brigade. In the fall of 1936 Boring invited Rhine to talk to the faculty at an informal dinner. Rhine went and gave a talk about his ESP experiments. Boring responded in a letter to Rhine a few days later to the effect that he was baffled and incredulous.

Distrust and disbelief were so great, in fact, that according to a sympathetic-to-Rhine insider among the Harvard psychologists, a trap was being set for Rhine, with the dinner talk as the first step. This informant told Rhine that there was a plan to invite him to Harvard to demonstrate his methodology. His work would be secretly monitored, and presto!—Rhine would be revealed as a fraud or dupe. Forewarned, Rhine declined any further invitations from Harvard.

The waves of enthusiasm that buoyed him after his first book, *Extra-Sensory Perception*, was published in 1934, had turned, gained force and were sweeping back to demolish him. He could hardly pick up a journal without seeing his work savaged. And the attacks were not all irrational. Some were astute, carefully reasoned—and demanded a response.

Psychology professor Chester Kellogg of McGill University launched a slashing attack in the *Scientific Monthly* in October 1937:

Since Dr. Rhine's reports have led to investigations in many other institutions it might seem unnecessary to prick the bubble as the truth eventually will out and the craze subside. But meanwhile the public is being misled, the energies of young men and women in their most vital years of professional training are being diverted into a side issue and funds expended that might instead support research into problems of real importance for human welfare. This has gone so far that a new Journal of Parapsychology *has been founded.*[1]

That was just one of several anti-Rhine blasts by psychologists.

Rhine wrote a despairing letter to Upton Sinclair on November 29:

After reading reviews, editorials and so forth, in Social Frontiers, New Republic, *and* The Nation *after the publication of my second book,* New Frontiers of the Mind, *I am beginning to wonder whether there is such a thing as a genuine liberal or whether there are not just persons who have a liberal streak touching upon one issue, with perhaps compensating conservatism on other issues. You are yourself about the only good exception to this that I can think of. I am developing a strong magnetic pull for brickbats, it appears. At the same time I am trying to develop an adequate philosophy, trying to tell myself, for instance, that this is the struggle which any idea must go through and that the unscrupulous tactics of some of the critics give me a better advantage when I am able to reply. But the fact is, I would rather be allowed to go on calmly at work and let the critics alone!*

The critics, however, planned a showdown. Rhine was invited to present his case for ESP at the annual meeting of the American Psychological Association in 1938, the first time ESP would be on the agenda. He realized he would have to face his critics en masse in what promised to be a fight for survival. Dr. Harold O. Gulliksen of the University of Chicago agreed to be an opposition speaker at that meeting. His doubts had been spelled out in the January 4, 1938, issue of *The American Journal for Sociology.* In an article headed "Extra-Sensory Perception: What Is It?" Gulliksen gave a brief, telling account of the weaknesses he found in Rhine's work, the opening blows in a fight that is still raging:

E. H. Wright, an English professor at Columbia, compares Rhine's work to that of Copernicus, and states: "We may even be on the brink of marvel." Harry Scherman, writing for the Book-of-the-Month Club, *compares Rhine to Darwin. Waldemar Kaempffert, the scientific editor of the* New York Times, *says: "This amounts almost to potential omniscience." Kaempffert also states that psychological journals have "critically considered Rhine's work and on the whole pronounced it good." ... The immediate practical result of Rhine's experiments has been a wave of popular interest in the Duke University work.*

Gulliksen considered Rhine's work under four heads:

1. The amount of independent verification. Kellogg* reported that eight laboratories had confirmed and six had failed to confirm Rhine's findings.

2. Rhine's experimental methods. Kellogg complained that as described in Rhine's books they were too vague.

Rhine's response was that he had never been asked for additional details of an ESP experiment, but he would be ready to supply them on request. Rhine admitted that he had been asked for additional statistical data, but that this had in no way changed the conclusion of the original report.[2]

3. Direct contradictions found in Rhine's writings. Kellogg pointed out that at one time Rhine wrote that techniques for eliciting ESP are difficult, but elsewhere stated they're simple. (Here, I believe, Kellogg misunderstood: Rhine was describing ESP itself as a complex and difficult field, not his methods for trying to elicit it.)

4. Discrepancy between Rhine's data and his speculations. Kellogg thought that Rhine's failure to find telepathic powers in the last tests of the horse Lady Wonder could be explained by Rhine's enhanced powers of observation during the last experiments. And Kellogg suggested that Rhine could have been fooled in the earlier tests when his powers of observation may have been less acute. (This would also have to apply to the other observers.)

Kellogg generously granted that

... the fact that all these observations are true does not prevent Rhine's conclusion about the existence of extra-sensory perception from also being true. However, it should be borne in mind that Rhine's work has been under scientific scrutiny only a short time. ... Several rather serious oversights have been discovered in that time. Who knows what errors will be discovered in the future? In the light of all the facts, it seems premature for Rhine to assert, "No one—not even a psychologist—can reasonably doubt that ESP is a mental process."[3]

Professor Chester Kellogg of Canada's McGill University.

In a few months Rhine would have a chance to answer Gulliksen and the massing opposition at the annual meeting of the American Psychological Association. That meeting, Rhine felt, could make or break him.

26

IN THE LION'S DEN
1938

Overwhelmingly, scientists of all stripes joined the negative camp, indifferent or hostile to ESP. Rhine's three fellow psychologists at Duke—Adams, Lundholm, and Zener—would gladly have seen him disappear. Privately, they ridiculed or slandered him—and there are graduate students then, professors of psychology today, who still support that attitude. Prince was dead and McDougall was dying. But Rhine was never completely alone. Now his strongest, most informed supporter was Gardner Murphy.

Rhine had learned to expect mainstream scientists to use unscrupulous means to drive parapsychology underground or back to where they thought it belonged, in the realm of pseudoscience and superstition.

Columbia's James McKeen Cattell, dean of American psychology, secretly visited Duke's President Few to try to stop Rhine's work. Says Rhine: "If Dr. Few had behaved the way most university presidents do—most presidents are half politicians—he would have stopped it."[1] Few was made of sterner stuff and believed Rhine's efforts were worthwhile. So Cattell's sabotage attempt failed.*

But that wasn't the last. Famed scientist Irving Langmuir, awarded the Nobel Prize for chemistry in 1932, devoted most of one day attempting to prove to Rhine that ESP was a myth and Rhine's methodology ridiculously inept and inadequate. What had aroused Langmuir was the behavior of a nephew at M.I.T. who read Rhine's first book, *Extra-Sensory Perception*, and immediately plunged into his own ESP experiments, which gave positive results. In vain Langmuir tried to ridicule the nephew into quitting, then predicted that if

---

*James McKeen Cattell (1860–1944), president of the American Association for the Advancement of Science in 1924, was awarded the annual gold medal of the Society of Arts and Sciences in 1930, the Legion of Honor in 1937.

162

he persisted in the tests he would eventually and inevitably get chance results. After telling Rhine of the foolish nephew, Langmuir concentrated on the foolish Rhine. First he gave Rhine a long list of definitions of science and of nonscience. Then he described one of Rhine's experiments and said that every single approach he had defined as "nonscientific" was manifest in that experiment.

"True," Rhine replied to Langmuir. "*If* I had done the experiment the way you've described it, I'd agree with you that it was nonscientific. But you haven't read my account. I didn't do it the way you've described."[2] By this time Rhine was used to vehement critics who were only vaguely familiar with the details of his work. However, Langmuir was right about one thing: The nephew who persisted with the ESP experiment eventually got chance results, as Langmuir had predicted. Rhine could have made the same prediction. He was now well aware of the decline effect in scoring, even among his best subject. He never knew it to fail.

When opposed by individual scientists, even of the caliber of Langmuir, Rhine gave as good as he got, or better. He welcomed the chance to air the issue, straighten out his critics when they were wrong, and listen to their advice when he was wrong or stymied.

The upcoming massive opposition he faced was a different matter. For the first time in its history, the American Psychological Association had included parapsychology on the agenda during the annual meeting scheduled for the fall of 1938. The chairman of the meeting, Dr. John L. Kennedy of Stanford University, had been quoted as saying he was ready to drive the last nail in the coffin for ESP. Rhine, invited to defend his work, looked forward to that with mixed feelings. Although he would have a chance to state his case, it was evident the opposition would be out in force to try to slaughter him.

A run-through in the spring gave a hint of things to come. At a meeting of the APA's eastern branch, held in Manhattan during the first week of April 1938, which Rhine did not attend, three speakers attacked and none defended him—other than a few among the two hundred there, who murmured protests in favor of fair play.

Psychologist Hyman Rogosin of New York City opened for the opposition, saying, "The science of probability is extremely controversial; moreover, science does not use probability to prove the existence of something which is otherwise undemonstrated." He characterized Rhine as being under the influence of McDougall, who once belonged to a "dubious" society for psychical research. And he claimed that both Rhine and McDougall believed in discredited Lamarckism. This wasn't true. They were both interested in testing his theory, without "believing" in it.

Dr. Frederick Hausen Lund of Temple University said he had tested 596 students with the ESP cards out of sight and reach, and not one had scored above chance.

The critics aroused "thunderous" applause, according to *Time* magazine. But the third speaker, Dr. Steuart Henderson Britt of George Washington University, raised laughter as well. First he gave a demonstration of reading the ESP cards that put him up with the psychic marvels—he called twenty-four right out of twenty-five. Then he explained his secret. The designs on the cards were so heavily printed that in the right light, they could be seen from the backs. He also showed that the symbols could be felt from the backs of the cards.

Those acts would be tough for Rhine to follow in the fall. The *Time* magazine report of the meeting, headlined "Battle of the Rhine," stated that "Rhine admirers have compared him to Abraham Lincoln, and others Sigmund Freud and Charles Darwin rolled into one."[3] But the whoops and war cries of his opponents made Rhine appear more like General Custer. True, Rhine had not had a chance to defend himself at the Manhattan massacre. But it seemed from the *Time* account that had Rhine been a criminal, his attorney would have advised him to take the Fifth and decline to testify on his own behalf.

An apprehensive Rhine faced the "enemy" at the annual convention of the American Psychological Association in Columbus, Ohio, on September 6, 1938. The chairman, Dr. John L. Kennedy, had been quoted as the psychologist eager to drive the last nail in the coffin for ESP. It was clear that many of his colleagues would be eager pallbearers.

Several hundred psychologists packed the chemistry lecture lab to continue the second round of the battle of the Rhine. Fred McKinney, a psychology professor from the University of Missouri, watched Rhine with astonishment. He'd never seen a man pace up and down so nervously. When Rhine turned on a faucet and let water pour on his wrist, McKinney guessed it was to stop from fainting under the strain. Dr. B. F. Skinner, later to be a famous behaviorist, was amused to see Rhine draw a glass of water that came out almost solid rust.[4] He was like a man before a firing squad. One psychologist thought Rhine was going to have a heart attack.

Dr. Steuart Henderson Britt, who had raised chuckles and applause at the recent New York APA meeting, vividly recalled the Columbus meeting after forty years. "Rhine was facing a skeptical and, I have to say it seemed to me, a hostile audience, who were probably thinking 'nobody's going to believe him.'

"Anyway, when he stood up to talk, Rhine said: 'I'm feeling very faint' and he turned on one of these faucets and ran water over his wrist because, he said, 'I feel I'm going to faint.' And I'd never seen a man do that. I was a skeptic, but I really felt great sympathy for this poor man. It was like Daniel in the lion's den. And here he is facing this audience. He's just nervous. I'd never seen him before, but he impressed me then as a very sensitive type of man. When it was question period I stood up to ask what were not meant to be insulting questions but were meant to be piercing questions about techniques and specifics of design and the controls. And they were not satisfactory answers.

"My 'attack' was not in any sense intended to say 'this phenomenon does not exist or cannot exist'; my 'attack' was to question the methods and the controls that had been used. My question was: 'Have there been adequate controls to demonstrate this phenomenon exists?' And of all the things they raised that time I could never see any evidence of a positive side, because all the experiments were done so sloppily. When I stood up to ask Rhine a question, my wife tugged at my sleeve as if to say, Don't! Oh please don't get up to attack him! He looked like a man who was about to faint.

"After that meeting I was more skeptical," says Britt; but acknowledges, "There's one thing Rhine certainly did. He got the three letters, ESP, into the language of the world."[5]

Curiously, when asked to recall how many psychologists attended that meeting, estimates from those who were there range from forty to one thousand. The low estimate, generally, is from psychologists unfavorable to ESP; the high figure is from the supporters. Rhine's own journal reported some six hundred. That was not the only discrepancy in remembering the same event. Rhine himself has quite a different recollection of his emotional state at that meeting—nowhere near fainting, not even close to a heart attack. "I probably wanted to see if I had cold water or warm water," was Rhine's explanation for running water over his wrist. "I wanted to drink it. As a matter of fact, anybody who wouldn't have been nervous in that situation, I would say, almost, it would be hard to believe.

"I wouldn't have missed it for anything, so it wasn't fear. But I was tense, no doubt. I had helped lots of students to overcome that state and I'd usually say, 'If you can make a joke of it . . . if you can get them to laugh with you, then you're safe.' And one of the things I did was to say, 'You psychologists probably won't know what I mean when I say, "My tongue does cleave to the roof of my mouth." I never knew what that meant before.'

"All of them laughed heartily and I knew they were with me from then on. I estimated there were six hundred there. They were crowded in. If they noticed at all, they would have noticed how much more they applauded me than they did the 'enemy'! There wasn't any doubt from the signs from the audience that they were with us in the respect that they wanted us to have these things investigated."[6]

Rhine responded to criticism of the faulty ESP cards by saying they were manufactured to be used in shuffling machines and behind screens, that heavier cards without defects were subsequently made for unscreened work. He said that a warning was printed in the first number of the *Journal of Parapsychology* to appear after the ESP cards were in circulation. Readers were advised to use screens in all serious experiments.

"Our plan has been to try to catch what looks like ESP and, gradually improving the safeguards as we go, bring the phenomenon, if possible, up to the point where there can be no question about the interpretation of the results," he told the crowd. "It is apparently necessary in most instances to use this procedure instead of that of plunging at once into the most developed and elaborate conditions and then searching for good ESP subjects under those already-perfected conditions. We must, then, try to keep these general types of methods in mind and improve them both. Toward this end, your help and criticism is very much needed and very much appreciated."

Gulliksen, whose recently published criticism seemed almost irrefutable, now conceded his satisfaction with the safeguards for Rhine's ESP work. "The methods of the ESP research were frankly and openly discussed in a symposium before the American Psychological Association," wrote Rhine and associates.[7]

The published record of this symposium shows that no significant weakness in the methodology as presented by those engaged in the research was pointed out by the large body of assembled psychologists, or by those presenting critical papers on the program. No serious criticism at all was offered against the methods of evaluation. Gulliksen, who led the criticism on safeguards against sensory cues, expressed agreement as to the adequacy of the main provisions taken—opaque envelopes, opaque screens, and distance.

Hypotheses of recording errors and deck-cutting errors were suggested by Kennedy, but it was made plain by [Gardner] Murphy that the precautions proposed against recording errors were already in use, that significant work with independent recorders had already been done, and the recording errors even to the extent reported by Kennedy could not account for the results. Like every other branch of psychological research (or research in general), the ESP test procedures have undergone considerable development and improvement, but in their present form . . . it is not easy to find any comparable research more excessive in its precautions, more careful in

its handling of records, and at the same time attempting to cope in a
crucial manner with a more elaborate range of counter-hypotheses.[8]

Psychologists attacked and parapsychologists defended. Dr.
Bernard F. Riess was called upon as a recent convert to describe and
defend his remarkably successful experiment. He admitted one small
mistake. "I hear Dr. Murphy found one error [in recording the score of
hits by Riess's subject] and I owe him ten dollars for finding that one,"
said Riess. "But with that error eliminated, the only other error that
may have crept in is a possibility of deception, and the only person
who could have done the deceiving is myself, since the subject at no
time knew how well she was doing nor had any idea of the cards
which were being turned by myself in my room, a quarter of a mile
away from where she was working. Outside of that there can be no
criticism of the method used. I had the deck of cards at my desk,
shuffled them at the stated time, turned them over one by one,
making a record of each card. I had my desk piled with examination
papers and half the time I don't think I was conscious of any serious
concentration on my part. I kept the records locked up in my desk and
sometimes it was a week before I turned up the scores and found the
number of high scores she was making."[9]

Riess left the meeting "angry at Steuart Britt, because Britt felt
the only conclusion he could come to was that I had faked the data.
He got up from the floor—and said it in the discussion. I don't know
whether he used the word [faked], but that was his implication. We
had known each other before. In those days the APA wasn't so big that
you didn't know people. We became quite friendly after that."[10]

In fact, Britt says he was not the only one there who suspected
that Riess's great scorer existed only in his imagination.[11]

Forty years later Riess still declined to reveal her identity,
even though he believed she was dead. "At the time of the daughter's
disappearance both parents were much distressed and made me
promise to let nobody know their names and addresses," Riess told
me in 1978. "This information unfortunately cannot be made available. I don't have any permission to release names. There is a certain
restriction in this due to the fact of confidentiality," concluded Riess,
now an industrial psychologist.[12]

Rhine returned to Duke, feeling not that the enemy had been
routed, but at least they had been kept at bay and in one or two areas
had even retreated to look for stronger positions.

Even so, parapsychology seemed bedeviled by the flawed
experiment. Riess's had seemed ideal: conducted by an intelligent
skeptic, the experimenter physically isolated at all times from his
subject, with sufficient runs to be significant, yet—there were no

independent witnesses. And even the existence of his subject was doubted.

Was it true, as William James had speculated, that "the Creator has eternally intended this department of nature to remain *baffling*, to prompt our curiosities and hopes and suspicions all in equal measure, so that although ghosts and clairvoyances, and raps and messages from spirits are always seeming to exist and can never be fully explained away, they also can never be susceptible of full corroboration." But, he went on, "it is hard to believe that the Creator has really put any big array of phenomena into the world merely to defy and mock our scientific tendencies; so my deeper belief is that we psychical researchers have been too precipitate with our hopes, and that we must expect to mark progress not by quarter-centuries, but by half-centuries or whole centuries."[13]

However, Riess was eventually converted by his own experiment and other evidence into a believer in ESP. He became coeditor with Gardner Murphy of the *Journal of Parapsychology* for several years.

27

HIDDEN EVIDENCE
1940–1946

It took a world war for Rhine to contemplate giving up his work at the parapsychology lab, and even then he intended to direct it by remote control, from the fighting front if necessary. Soon after Pearl Harbor, although he was forty-seven with four children, Rhine felt an irresistible tug to reenlist in the Marines. He had everything planned. His son, Robert, was well taken care of, spending his turbulent teenage years living and working on a farm owned by a family friend, learning to love country life as much as his parents did. Louisa would continue to look after their three young daughters, Sally, Betsy, and Rosemary.

Rhine chose Betty Humphrey to run the lab during his absence. She had a bachelor's degree from Earlham College, Indiana, and in two years as research assistant had done "magnificent work."[1] He arranged to mail her instructions and expected her to keep him up to date on everything that was going on. Mrs. Dorothy Pope and others were told to continue publishing the *Journal of Parapsychology*.

So, one morning in early 1942, Rhine shook hands with his staff and said he was off to rejoin his regiment. They all idolized Rhine, and regarded him as a great man. His departure was dramatic and emotional. They could expect him back when the war was won, he said, which—judging by his confidence—seemed only a day or two away. Rhine embraced his wife and daughters, and a small, tearful crowd waved him good-bye.

Rhine returned a few hours later. He had been rejected on medical grounds. His hearing had deteriorated since the previous world war and he was no longer able to fast-talk his way past the doctors. It was quite a letdown. To compound his disappointment, he soon found himself the only man at the lab, as all his male assistants, including Gaither Pratt, left for war work or military assignments. The parapsychology lab consisted of Rhine and Humphrey; the staff of the parapsychology journal, Rhine and Pope.

As a mountaineer, Rhine would have found footholds in a hill of sheet glass. He now thought up a useful occupation for a lab staff of one. For several years, records of PK experiments had piled up and been kept in a basement safe. Here was the opportunity to study them, to see if they might reveal any as yet hidden secret. Rhine set Humphrey the task of reexamining all the results of those experiments. Most particularly, Rhine wanted to know if she would discover a "decline effect" in PK records. ESP subjects invariably scored higher at the start of tests, giving support to the saying "beginners' luck." One explanation for such an effect is that people try harder when they first start out on a task. The falling off in ability is paralleled in memory, learning, and sense perception.

Rhine followed Humphrey's analysis like a man watching his horse lead the field. Her final results showed that there was a typical decline curve in PK experiments that appeared when dice were thrown by hand, cup, or machine. To Rhine, the most important aspect of this discovery was that no one could have faked those curves, because at the time the tests were undertaken, from 1934 on, no experimenter or subject knew that anyone would later examine the records for that hidden evidence.

With some justification Rhine believed that, as evidence for PK, it was a complete confirmation of the original work. He compared this evidence dredged up from the basement safe to fossils in the strata of the earth. And this material could lead to only one conclusion—that the mind of man could, however slightly, direct rolling dice. PK, in other words, was a fact.

"There must, therefore, be an energy convertible to physical action, a mental energy," Rhine concluded.

The discovery is the fifth great step toward the objective of solving the problem of man's relation to the physical world. In the first of those steps the conclusion was reached that mind-to-mind interaction occurs without a known physical medium. The second, dealing with the ESP of objects, showed that the mind could enter into active cognitive relation with matter without the use of any known sensorimechanical means. The third step found this mental capacity able to transcend space, and the fourth the time dimension as well. Now in this fifth advance, the extra-physical system of the mind comes back at the physical object and exerts a very slight and erratic, but still a significant, influence on moving cubes, one strong enough to alter their fall to an extent discoverable only by the delicate methods of statistics, but reliable enough to allow for a large accumulation of confirmatory data by independent investigation.[2]

Rhine invited independent investigators to check the PK records Humphrey had been through. None accepted, although Gaither Pratt, who could hardly be described as independent, later checked and confirmed Humphrey's findings.

For Rhine those records (the early ones were scribbled on the backs of laundry lists and used envelopes), were solid gold. "I can conceive of no stronger evidence for psi* today after thirty years have passed," wrote Rhine in *The Handbook of Parapsychology*, 1977.[3]

Rhine's work was immeasurably helped by a home that was run for his convenience, and a wife who fully shared his interest in ESP. His youngest daughter, Rosemary, witnessed only one quarrel between J.B. and Louisa—a sharp word from Louisa, raised eyebrows from Rhine, and that was it. Children, of course, do not see everything. Rhine had been disturbed by his own parents' frequent quarrels and determined that his children should be protected from scenes of marital discord. So that when J.B. and Louisa did have a difference of opinion, they settled it away from the children.[4] But generally, home life was smooth: The Rhines had a lifelong love affair with each other and their work.

The girls adored their father and cherished exciting and unexpected Sundays with him. Most of the day they lazed around the house, perhaps listening to opera over the radio while J.B. worked in his study—often on a new book. Then, sometime in the afternoon he emerged, and the fun would begin. Everyone would pile into the car, and they drove for a few miles, then got out to explore unknown territory—sometimes following a river or a rocky hill. Rhine would stride ahead, with Louisa and the girls hurrying to keep up. Once he found a forest spring, stooped to cool his face, called them all over, and gave them what he called "an elephant bath," splashing them all, to their delight. When it grew dark they built a fire, then sat around the flames as Rhine played tunes on his ocarina. Those were the spring and summer Sundays of the war years.[5]

As if to make up for the absence of the other researchers, Betty Humphrey launched into several research projects that advanced the slow but accumulating knowledge of ESP. One was to see if personality affected ESP scores. She invited volunteers to draw anything they chose on a blank sheet of paper, then judged their personality from the drawing. If it completely covered the paper with

---

*Cambridge University doctor of psychology, Dr. Robert H. Thouless, accepted the suggestion of his collaborator Dr. B. P. Wiesner to use the Greek letter psi to apply to both ESP and PK. Psi was, like the algebraic x, noncommittal and could be used until the true nature of the phenomena was discovered. Rhine agreed to the use of psi and it has been generally used since 1943.

uninhibited, bold lines, she rated the person as expansive, or extrovert. If the drawing was timid, covered only a small part of the paper with faint lines, she rated the person as contracted, or introvert. Results of her tests showed that the extroverts were more likely to be clairvoyant. In time she was to test mental patients for ESP before and after shock treatment, and found no significant difference.

Foiled in his attempt to rejoin the Marines, and feeling he was not doing enough for his country, Rhine was elated when the Army asked for his help. In a series of hush-hush meetings he told them that PK was not strong enough to divert enemy planes nor telepathy effective enough to read enemy minds. The Army suspected as much, but wanted to know if hypnosis could be used as a war weapon. Rhine believed it might be used by our own forces to great effect. He told the Army representatives of a former Syrian student who had been intrigued by the apparent ability of fakirs to torture themselves without suffering pain. The student, too, wanted to be able to resist pain, and persuaded Rhine to teach him self-hypnosis. Shortly after, the young man was in an auto accident and taken to a hospital. He recovered consciousness on the operating table as the surgeon was about to give him a local anesthetic before suturing a head wound. The student asked the surgeon not to administer the anesthetic, but to allow him a few moments to prepare himself. Rhine had a letter from the surgeon to the effect that the young man, apparently in a self-induced hypnotic trance, showed no sign of pain while the wound was stitched—without anesthetic.[6] What a boon this could be to wounded soldiers, Rhine suggested, though he knew many doctors scoffed at hypnosis and even doubted there was such a thing.

No, the Army was not interested in a substitute for morphine, hoping to use hypnosis for a more deadly purpose: Could a non-aggressive man under hypnosis be made to kill?

Rhine used to go into Humphrey's office and tell her, "If you overhear anything, don't say a word. It's highly secret." Rhine undertook several hypnosis experiments for the Army, but there were no corpses around and the whole thing came to naught.[7] It is still an open question whether a hypnotized subject can be made to act against his normal bent.

Ironically, the war gave Rhine respite from the almost nonstop barrage of justified and unjustified criticism he had suffered from his scientific colleagues. Dorothy Pope and Gaither Pratt found that between 1935 and 1936 there had been five critical articles about Rhine's work, forty-two between 1937 and 1938, twelve between 1939 and 1940, and, surprisingly, none between 1940 and 1941.

Perhaps he had blunted much of the attack with his 1940

book, *Extra-Sensory Perception After Sixty Years,** which contained a summary and analysis of all psi experimental results at Duke. Of the seven leading critics of ESP, only three accepted Rhine's invitation to air their views in the book. Of these, only one remained adamantly critical. With a real war then just around the corner—and already ablaze in Europe—Rhine's hostile critics appeared to be offering him a truce.

But although he may have taken the steam out of his scientific opponents, it did not mean they endorsed his work. Scientific journals still declined to publish his experiments. Having failed to carry scientists with him, he took an almost foolhardy risk: He went public. Rhine cooperated in a Zenith radio show from Chicago in which listeners were invited to test their ESP, and he wrote articles and gave interviews for popular magazines. His name became a house-hold word, and not a complimentary one in scientific households. Some of the Duke faculty scorned Rhine for what they saw as an attempt to put his findings to a popular vote. Others saw him jeopardizing his scientific credibility by self-promoting activities. But most of these critics were judging by show, not substance: Few of them had bothered to read a word of Rhine's reports in the *Journal of Parapsychology*. By going public he was at least able to get some of his work across. He described the Zenith radio experiments as "instructive. Much better intentioned than conducted."[8] They also resulted in a massive increase in mail from people who wanted to share their ESP experiences with him.

Upton Sinclair heartily supported Rhine's public appearances and wrote to tell him so. Sinclair's were not the only supportive letters from California. British author Aldous Huxley wrote on December 30, 1942:

To me, the great interest and importance of your work is that it will finally compel those who suffer from "voluntary ignorance" to reconsider the anecdotal evidence and to accept a good deal of it as valid—with fascinating consequences for religion and philosophy. . . . Under suitable conditions, the mental activities of individuals and groups release forces sufficiently powerful, if not to move mountains, certainly to cure serious lesions and even perhaps to multiply food. (The "miracles" of the nineteenth-century Cure d'Ars in this matter are borne out by a lot of testimony.)[9]

While he received a letter from Huxley every few years, Rhine

---

Written with Pratt, Smith, Stuart, and Greenwood. Published by Bruce Humphries, Boston.

could expect an almost weekly letter from Sinclair, discussing war strategy, advising working progress, or expressing disappointment that medium Arthur Ford had ducked out of arrangements to be tested at Duke. In fact, Rhine had planned to test Ford in secret and off the Duke campus. He knew of Ford's unsavory reputation, and as he explained to Sinclair:

The stories of drunkenness, homosexuality, wife desertion and the like that seems to have been associated with his name, may, of course, have nothing to do with his mediumistic capacities, but they would make it difficult to have him around the University.[10]

In the summer of 1943 Sinclair sent Rhine four hundred manuscript pages of his *Presidential Agent*, one of his novels in the Lanny Budd series in which Lanny appeared as Sinclair's alter ego. A medium appeared in the novel, and Sinclair wanted to know if it was a convincing portrait. Rhine thought she was almost too good to be true, though he had not given up hope that such a marvel existed. In fact, Sinclair's account had determined Rhine to cast his net wider in an attempt to find a medium to match her. Rhine planned to spend the spring of 1945 on such a search, but was bedridden with meningitis. It put him out of action for three weeks, and he made a slow recovery.

In July he sat up in bed reading Sinclair's latest book, *Dragon Harvest*. He finished it at three in the morning and that day wrote to tell the author he was "a literary giant."[11]

With peace in 1945, Rhine looked forward to the return of the young men who had left him for the war. None had been casualties, though Professor McDougall's son Kenneth had been killed in France.

Letters continued to arrive for Rhine from people relating their psi experiences. Would his lab experiments show psi to follow the same patterns observed in spontaneous cases? It was evident that a parapsychological Einstein was urgently needed to examine the psi evidence, of which the decline effect formed a small part, and to formulate a theory. Until then the bulk of the scientific world could be expected to show indifference or hostility. The fact that psi was such an ephemeral phenomenon, its tantalizing will-o'-the-wisp nature and its shadowlike quality placing it just within grasp but always out of reach, and especially because of its almost lawless nature, prompted Aldous Huxley to write on December 16, 1946: "I admire you for not going mad under the strain of devising scientific experiments in a field where there is no really satisfactory hypothesis!"

28

SPONTANEOUS ESP
1946–1948

With his staff back from the war and eager to experiment, Rhine had to raise money to pay their salaries and to buy equipment. The lab had been operating on a shoestring for years, and many good ideas had to be set aside for lack of financing. In the summer of 1946 Rhine went to New York City to broadcast a talk on "The Relation Between Psychology and Religion"; publisher William Randolph Hearst ordered his Sunday magazine to produce a two-page article on the broadcast. But Rhine had to seek funding from lesser lights than Hearst. The following summer he spoke to a group of Wall Street bankers and their wives. Rhine listened to a lot of big talk and received about one thousand dollars, which prompted him to confide in Upton Sinclair: "From my brief contacts with people of wealth, I get the impression that they have not discovered the real value of money or its place in a well rounded philosophy of life."[1] One can almost hear Sinclair echoing his heartfelt agreement.

By 1948 Louisa felt free to rejoin Rhine as an active researcher. The youngsters were now able to care for themselves. Robert was twenty; Sally, eighteen; Betsy, fourteen; and Rosemary, thirteen. Louisa was eager to do experimental work, but Rhine persuaded her to tackle something he thought more pressing. There were thousands of letters in the files from people relating personal psi experiences, a potential wealth of information. She wanted to know if those accounts, like the PK records, followed an unmistakable pattern that would parallel and therefore tend to substantiate the psi discoveries made in the lab. Rhine knew to a small extent how psi operated in the lab: Similar to other psychological processes, it was most evident at the start of an experiment, trailing off at the end. Psi was strongest in confident, outgoing people given an encouraging, friendly, gamelike atmosphere, and weakest in those who were emotionally upset or under pressure. Narcotic drugs depressed psi powers. One might expect to find it most often in those who believed psi to exist. Would the same hold true for spontaneous psi experiences? And would those experiences suggest productive new psi research projects in the laboratory?

Before Dr. Louisa Rhine began an analysis of spontaneous psi experiences, she answered outstanding letters from fearful correspondents. To those frightened people who were scared of their own ESP, thinking it marked them as freaks or as mentally deranged, she replied that it was apparent that such experiences were normal, shared by a large proportion of the population, although the exact percentage was unknown.

Having, she hoped, given some comfort, Louisa got to work on the analysis of the psi experiences. She eliminated all reports that didn't ring true—if they were obvious hoaxes, inconsistent, could easily be explained normally, or if the writer seemed mentally unbalanced. She was left with thousands that made sense and which she judged could have been psi experiences.* Whether they were true or illusory, of course, could be disputed. But she believed that similar plausible ESP experiences by many different people tend to support each other. If a thousand witnesses in various places and of varied backgrounds report that a clock stopped in the home at the moment a relative died, for example, it wouldn't be unreasonable to assume that such events happen and may be connected, even allowing for those that could be written off as coincidence, imagination, faulty memory, tall tales, or malobservation.

Louisa Rhine concluded that

... the common denominator of all ESP experiences, trivial or tragic, is that they seem to bring information, no matter how obscure, which presumably the persons, for sometimes vague, deeply personal reasons, want to know. And so, although many ESP experiences involve crises, their range is theoretically unlimited. ... We can now assume that psi occurs not only in the laboratory but spontaneously in nature.[2]

What emerged from her study was a confirmation of results that had been secured in the laboratory.† That objects could be moved by an unknown power had been experimentally demonstrated in the parapsychology laboratory by throwing dice and getting scores that could not be explained by chance. It was paralleled

Twenty-five years later she had some fifteen thousand such reports.
†*Described fully in her books:* Hidden Channels of the Mind, *William Sloane, 1961; and* ESP in Life and Lab: Tracing Hidden Channels, *Macmillan, 1967.*

outside the lab by poltergeist activity reported by many correspondents. Vivid and detailed dreams or waking premonitions that
came true or were found to have been true at the time of the
experience reinforced the positive results of experiments with ESP
cards for precognition and clairvoyance.

While his wife concentrated on reports from the outside world,
Rhine continued with almost feverish enthusiasm, starting at seven-
thirty in the morning, skipping lunch, working until after dark, and
taking work home with him to read in bed until the early hours.

Rhine's former critic, the British psychologist Dr. Robert H.
Thouless, had attended a Chicago symposium, "Feelings and Emotions," in 1948. On his way back to Britain, he stopped at Durham to
meet Rhine.

"By this time my skepticism as to the reality of ESP had been
overcome," Thouless recalls.

*This was partly as a result of the weight of confirmatory evidence
from Duke University itself and from elsewhere. Partly the influence
of my friend B. P. Wiesner, a biologist, who had, from the beginning,
been less prejudiced against the paranormal than I was, and partly to
the fact that I was beginning to get positive results myself in ESP
experiments. Unfortunately, by this time, the spectacular rates of
success reported in his book [Rhine's] were no longer found in Rhine's
laboratory, although some investigators still obtained a steady low
rate of success which remained significant evidence of the reality of
the phenomena which were being investigated. Why the first flush of
high-level success did not continue is one of the mysteries of parapsychological history. Critics of the laboratory often put forward the
explanation that this is due to the tightening of experimental conditions. This, however, cannot be the sole explanation, since some of
the spectacular successes were obtained under very rigid conditions.*

*Mrs. Rhine, with whom I discussed the question, attributed it
to the fading of the atmosphere of single-minded enthusiasm which
belonged to the early days of the laboratory. Both of these factors
may have played a part in the general decline of the rate scoring.*

*Meeting J. B. Rhine for the first time, I found him a pleasant
grey-haired man of powerful build. He was warmly welcoming as
were all his staff who showed me their experiments and allowed me
to act as an experimental subject, in which role I did not achieve any
startling rate of success.*

*In the week-end I joined a party from the laboratory who went
with Rhine for a ramble in the Duke forest. It was perhaps characteristic of him that he preferred to walk where there were no*

paths. There were few paths at that time in the region of parapsychology.[3]

This pioneering spirit of Rhine's was soon demonstrated. Although he carefully restricted his research to activities that met his rigid definition of parapsychology, he could stretch it quite reasonably to include a case of suspected diabolic possession.

29

EXORCIST
1949

The Rhines traveled to Washington, D.C., in the summer of 1949 to investigate the case of a teenage boy who appeared to have been possessed by a malevolent spirit. *The Washington Post*, on August 20, reported the results of the battle for the boy's sanity:

In what is perhaps one of the most remarkable experiences of its kind in recent religious history, a 14-year-old Mount Rainier boy has been freed by a Catholic priest of possession by the devil, it was reported yesterday. Only after twenty to thirty performances of the ancient ritual of exorcism, here and in St. Louis, was the devil finally cast out of the boy, it was said.

Millions know of this extraordinary event through the distorted novel and movie version by William Peter Blatty, titled *The Exorcist*, in which the boy becomes a girl, and the housewife mother a movie actress. And, though no lives were lost in reality, the fictional account has two violent deaths.

His exaggerated version of the event is not through lack of knowledge. He is one of the few people who has been told the identity of the boy and has corresponded with the exorcist. Blatty probably knows as much about "possession" and exorcism as anyone not personally involved.

To save the boy and the exorcist from being exploited and harassed, their identities have been closely guarded. For the record, the boy is known as Roland. The Rhines learned about him from the youngster's Lutheran minister, Reverend Luther Miles Schulze. It was to him that the boy's worried parents appealed for help, telling him that their son had been attacked by mysterious unseen forces that pulled at his bedclothes, toppled plates from tables, and plagued him and them with eerie noises.

It sounded like a poltergeist attack to Rhine, and the mysterious forces might be explained as psychokinesis, the power of the mind to move objects.

The Rhines examined the minister's bedroom, where Roland had spent one night and Reverend Schulze had witnessed things he still couldn't explain.

"How did it all start?" Rhine asked.

Reverend Schulze said that the first hint of the terror that was to follow was a scratching sound coming from the ceilings and walls of the boy's Mount Rainier home, near Washington, D.C. His parents suspected mice and called in the exterminator. He could find no signs of rodents, and all his efforts failed to silence the scratching, which, if anything, became louder. It was followed by a noise in the hall, like an invisible creature walking in squeaky shoes. At times, dishes and furniture moved inexplicably.

These noises and movements were frightening enough, but then the unseen forces seemed to focus a spiteful attack on the fourteen-year-old boy. They grabbed at his bed covers and once, when he tried to hold them, he was pulled out of bed onto the floor.

When the boy's parents came to Reverend Schulze for help, he asked them if they had any idea what might be the cause of the disturbances. They had no tangible evidence, but thought the boy's tormentor was an earthbound spirit, perhaps a relative with animosity that persisted beyond the grave. They believed in demon possession.

"At first I tried prayer," said Reverend Schulze. "I prayed with the parents and the boy in their home and with the boy in my home. And there were prayers for the boy in church. I ordered whatever it was disturbing him, in the name of the Father, Son, and Holy Spirit, to get out and let him alone." But the disturbing force was immune to both exterminator and prayer. "It did not shake my faith," said Reverend Schulze. "Sometimes prayers are not answered exactly as we ask them to be. Sometimes God just gives us the strength to see things through."[1]

Reverend Schulze advised the parents to consult a psychiatrist, thinking that Roland's troubles might be consciously or unconsciously self-inflicted. They never explained why, but the parents resisted following this advice, as if acknowledging that the boy's need of psychiatric care would be more unendurable to them than his being possessed by a malevolent spirit.

Their family physician wanted to have the boy put in a hospital for observation, but the parents again refused.

They returned to Reverend Schulze six weeks later, on February 17, 1949, even more anxious than before. The weird noises and movements now tormented the boy day and night. He was hardly ever able to sleep. At this rate, he could go out of his mind from lack of sleep alone.

The minister offered to have the boy spend a night at his home, and the parents accepted. If their son got even a little rest, they would be grateful.

It was this stage of the minister's account that specially interested Rhine. Most of the story until now had been secondhand. What follows was vividly witnessed and remembered.

Roland's father brought him to the minister's home after dinner and then left. Reverend Schulze reassured the boy: "You're going to have a good night's sleep," he said. "Nothing like that ever happens in this house."

He was in for a few surprises. His wife had agreed to spend the night in a guest room adjoining the master bedroom, where Reverend Schulze and Roland retired to twin four-poster beds. The room was clearly lit throughout the night by a street lamp. The minister is a warm, approachable man, but Roland was disinclined to talk or in any way confide in him. They said their prayers and wished each other good night. It was some time later that Reverend Schulze heard the boy's bed creaking. He noticed Roland was still awake, although it was quite late. He put out his hand and felt Roland's bed shaking "like one of those motel vibrator beds, but much faster. The boy was still. His limbs and head and body were perfectly still but the bed was shaking."

Reverend Schulze said he'd make some cocoa, and they could drink it in his study. Perhaps that would help Roland sleep. While the two of them drank cocoa, the boy displayed no signs of fear or apprehension. What struck the minister most was his lack of curiosity. He simply didn't ask any questions. Otherwise he seemed a normal, pleasant youngster, perhaps quieter than most boys his age. He mumbled his thanks for the cocoa and they returned to the bedroom.

Reverend Schulze suggested that Roland rest in a heavy armchair—there was no likelihood of that shaking, and the minister could keep his eye on it from his bed.

Soon after the boy obediently sat in it, the minister saw the chair start to move. As if under its own power, the chair went backward several inches. Schulze told Roland to lift his feet off the floor to add his full weight to the chair. The boy obeyed at once, but the heavy chair continued to move until it hit the wall.

Although Reverend Schulze said that up until this moment his dominant emotion had been curiosity, not fear, he told Rhine that what happened next amazed him. The armchair was extremely heavy, yet it moved as if in the grip of a malevolent and massive force or several strong invisible individuals that tipped it sideways in a slow motion. It moved as though the air was made of treacle. Reverend Schulze estimated that the chair took more than a minute to land on its side and deposit Roland almost gently on the floor.

"Why didn't the boy move out of the chair—he had plenty of time?" Rhine asked. He seemed to be in a trance, recalled the minister.

Later, Reverend Schulze righted the chair and sat in it himself. He noted it had a low center of gravity, and though he repeatedly tried to tip it sideways, using all his strength, he couldn't.

After the boy was tipped from the chair, the minister decided the floor was the safest place for him to rest, and arranged a goatskin for a mattress and a blanket to cover Roland, at the foot of one of the beds. Then the bewildered and shaken minister returned to his own bed.

Not long after he saw Roland sliding away from the bed.

The minister called out, "Stop that!"

The boy answered, "I'm not doing it!"

But he continued to slide across the floor until stopped by the wall.

"Where were the boy's hands?" Rhine asked.

They were above the blankets. The minister could clearly see the boy's legs outlined, too. They were stretched out straight and still, which ruled out normal propulsion with hands or feet. In fact, he told Rhine, he never had any reason to suspect Roland of deliberately causing the uncanny movements.

Reverend Schulze realized his home was no more a haven from the strange phenomena than the boy's own home, and finally persuaded the parents to send Roland to Georgetown University Hospital for tests and observation. His condition deteriorated while he was there. He began to behave wildly, and when a blood-red message was scratched on his skin—"Go to St. Louis!"—he was transferred to St. Louis Hospital. Roland had a favorite aunt in the city, and doctors thought being near her might pacify him. But more and more he began to act as if he really were possessed.

The minister recalled that one hospital report included the remark that Roland "could expectorate in a steady stream." More crudely shaped scratches suddenly covered his body. Once the word *SPITE* appeared in ragged capitals, like an angry welt, and another time there appeared what could have been a primitive image of the devil. Twentieth-century medicine had no more effect on his condition than prayer.

If Roland was possessed by a malevolent spirit, the only known cure could be as agonizing an ordeal as the possession itself. His parents knew this, but it was their last hope. They agreed to an exorcism.

A Lutheran minister, Episcopal priest, and Jesuit priests took turns putting Roland through the grueling ritual more than twenty times over thirty-five days. During the exorcism his body jerked in violent spasms, and he showed astonishing strength and agility, hurting several people who tried to restrain him. He appeared to urinate more than he drank. He also displayed the dubious talent of a sharpshooter. However quick the battle-scarred exorcist's evasive tactics, Roland repeatedly spat in his eye.

At the climax of the twenty-seven-page, fifteen-hundred-year-old ritual, when the Jesuit exorcist commanded the demon to leave, the youngster had violent tantrums, screaming, cursing, and mocking the priest's Latin phrases.

In May, after more than a month of the exhausting treatment, Roland no longer screamed and cursed, or spat at the priests, and the weird, inexplicable noises and movements of things ended. The exorcist, fasting for the ordeal, had lost fifty pounds.[2]

Rhine was interviewed by a *Washington Post* reporter and quoted as saying it was the most impressive poltergeist phenomenon that had come to his attention.[3]

William Peter Blatty read the *Washington Post* report while studying at Georgetown University; later he made contact with the Jesuit exorcist and converted the facts into chilling fiction, as a novel and movie.

The exorcist wrote to Blatty: "I can assure you of one thing; the case in which I was involved was the real thing (possession). I had no doubt about it then and I have no doubt about it now."[4]

Reverend Schulze, too, believes Roland was possessed by some supernatural force.

Rhine did not commit himself. He had not witnessed any of the phenomena and had only the word of a witness. He wondered if Reverend Schulze had unconsciously exaggerated some of the facts as the most honest and intelligent people may do at times, especially when confronted by the unexpected and the traumatic.[5] The incidents were similar to some of the anecdotal accounts Louisa Rhine was collecting, and the movements of the armchair, the boy's bed, and other objects could be attributed to an inexplicable force called psychokinesis.

"The PK branch of parapsychology, which deals with 'mind over matter,' is one to which we must turn for a possible explanation of the poltergeist," he wrote later.[6] However, he knew that to try to explain one mystery by another is not very illuminating. And in Roland's case, whose mind was doing the moving? A living or disembodied one?

When he returned home from Washington, Rhine was pleased

to see his mail had brought Upton Sinclair's latest book, *O Shepherd, Speak!* It was the tenth and last of the Lanny Budd fact-fiction series. And in it the writer gave Rhine the equivalent of the Purple Heart. He wrote:

For the past fifteen years—all the time that Lanny had been fighting Hitler and Mussolini—the patient Dr. Rhine had been working to evolve a method for the mass production and testing of psychic phenomena. . . . The consequences of believing what Dr. Rhine had proven were so devastating to the ordinarily received ideas about the mind, and indeed about all human affairs, that the average psychologist just couldn't face it, and the average college professor couldn't face the thought of what his dean would say and his prexy and his colleagues. It called for heroism, and the men who have that endowment usually choose livelier jobs than teaching in a classroom.[7]

30

DOWSING
1949

Working late one fall night in 1949, Rhine was interrupted by an excited phone call from author Kenneth Roberts. He said he had found a man who could work wonders with a willow twig shaped like a wishbone.

Roberts had seen him in action. After Maine forest fires, when Roberts's farm was parched, Henry Gross walked across the dry grass, holding a twig that suddenly pointed downward. Roberts dug there and discovered desperately needed water. Would Rhine come to Maine and test Gross right away?

Although dowsers were unable to explain their ability, Rhine believed it might be an aspect of ESP. Those who called it intuition were perhaps simply using another name for extrasensory perception. Rhine was interested, but cautious. There was always a mountain of work waiting for him. This could be another wasted effort.

Roberts sensed Rhine's caution, but persuaded him to make the journey to Maine.

Rhine arrived at Kennebunkport on November 5, 1949. He later described Gross as "a normal, healthy, friendly man of middle age who has been until recently a state game warden."[1]

Rhine wanted to start his own tests at once, although it was almost midnight, so he and Gross took flashlights out to the backyard. Roberts stayed in his kitchen. It was his task to turn the water on and off when Rhine gave him the signal—a signal Gross could not see. He was to tell Rhine when the rod indicated the water was running through the underground pipe several feet below him. The experiment was repeated again and again and again. Rhine continued his experiments early next morning, despite the steady cold rain. He sat at a table in the guest room of the barn, from which he could see the meadows below where Gross had located the water pipe. This brought water from the springhouse to the barn—a distance of about eight hundred feet. Roberts sat on the bathroom seat, from where he could reach the water faucet.

Hidden from Gross, Rhine signaled Roberts by hand when to turn the water on and off for thirty-second intervals. Gross was challenged to report when the water was running or still. By mid-morning, after at least forty such trials, Roberts suggested that Rhine join Gross in the meadows to see how the dowser worked on real veins, rather than on man-made water pipes.

We had Henry's rod pick out, at a distance of one hundred and forty-one paces, a spot where three veins came together, wrote Roberts. We paced off the distance. It was correct. At one hundred and forty-one paces two attendant workmen bored with a posthole auger. At four and a half feet, Henry assured J.B. the three veins would be found flowing into the hole.[2]

Workmen dug at the spot and reported that three veins bubbled into the hole at three feet.

Kenneth Roberts felt that Rhine's interest was in establishing whether or not Gross had extrasensory powers. Roberts, however, was convinced that dowsing was a special faculty related to water.

Gross's total score was below chance, and Rhine believed it could be explained by the dowser's unconscious resentment at "being forced into so artificial a practice of his art."[3]

According to Roberts, he was with Gross in Kennebunkport, Maine, discussing a drought in Bermuda on October 22, 1949. Gross had a map of Bermuda. He passed his divining rod over it and indicated four areas where he said fresh water would be found, although experts claimed there were no freshwater springs on the island. Drinking water normally was obtained from rainfall, the water being trapped by roofs and kept in storage tanks. Roberts told Rhine that a few months later, in April 1950, fresh water was found in three of the four areas Gross had indicated, enough for the islanders and for visiting ships.

Rhine replied:

No wonder we so-called scientific people look so funny to you. You would have to go out into the Atlantic Ocean, choose a whole island for a dowsing test, and get a bunch of big shots in on it so that it couldn't possibly be minimized. That, of course, is the way to put a test across, especially since there is supposedly no fresh water on the island; but it takes an order of confidence almost supernaturally colossal to take such a chance. If you really have struck fresh water, or unambiguous signs of the existence of fresh water, you have a story that will shake the skepticism of even a good many geologists.[4]

Geologists, apparently, are not easy to shake—especially by newspaper accounts.

Soon after Rhine's test, Dr. Gardner Murphy and other ASPR investigators arranged for twenty-seven dowsers to test their skill in Maine. They were taken to a sandy slope under which, they agreed, water could be found. They were asked to predict at what depth water would be found and the rate of flow. The actual boring showed estimates were no better than would be obtained by chance and not as good as estimates made by a water engineer who used rational inference to estimate the water depths.[5]

One of Rhine's assistants, Dr. Remi Cadoret, later eliminated the possibility that the dowser used his knowledge of the topography and microclimate of the area to detect water. Cadoret invited dowsers to detect a penny (as some dowsers claimed to be metal detectors) hidden under one of the squares on a board divided into squares. He divided a map representing the yard at his home. A penny was hidden in the yard. Dowsers were asked to indicate which square contained the hidden penny. Scores were significant but less impressive than those claimed by dowsers in the field.[6] Karlis Osis, another Rhine researcher, followed up Cadoret's work by several dowsing tests undertaken at varying distances from the spot. He reported success at all but the greatest distance.[7]

After Rhine had worked out the results of his experiments with Henry Gross, he concluded that dowsing is probably an extrasensory faculty in which clairvoyance or telepathy is involved, and is subject to the same decline effect as psi as a whole.[8]

Before long, the U.S. Army was to call on Rhine to carry out similar experiments—not to see if a man can detect hidden water by ESP, but if dogs could discover hidden mines without being given any physical clues. The Korean War had made such an experiment of urgent importance.

In 1967 Hanson Baldwin, military analyst of *The New York Times*, reported the successful use of divining rods made of coat hangers, during the Vietnam War. Marine Corps officers of the engineer units of the First and Third Marine Divisions told him that "coat-hanger dowsers" supplemented mine detectors. At Camp Pendleton, Major Nelson Hardacker, commanding officer of the 13th Engineer Battalion of the Fifth Marine Division, demonstrated the use of the coat hangers to Vietnam-bound marines. He explained their employment to detect a concealed tunnel or cache of arms, underground water, and sewage pipes. Baldwin tried it for himself and detected a hidden tunnel. Louis J. Matacia, an operations analyst at the Marine Corps schools at Quantico, Virginia, was credited with starting the coat-hanger dowsing. Baldwin quoted him as saying: "I have talked to physicists in the Defense Department and at Johns Hopkins; neither can tell me why it works. The Intelligence Department at Quantico is trying to find out why it works; they cannot find an answer at all."

J. B. Rhine, age 22, and his sister, Myrna,
on her wedding day, the day before he left to join
the Marines in World War I. (Courtesy JBR)

Pioneer psychical researchers, facing page, left to right, top row, F. W. H. Myers, William James, Frank Podmore; bottom row, Henry Sidgwick and Richard Hodgson, who is showing how "spirit photographs" are faked. More pioneers, top, from left, Edmund Gurney and Eleanor Sidgwick, and below, Oliver Lodge and William McDougall.
(Courtesy JBR)

In these extraordinary photographs taken in the 1930s, Dr. Richardson (right) holds what Margery Crandon claimed was the materialized hand of her dead brother, Walter. The "hand" looks more like a foot. Rhine's investigation of Margery revealed her to be a fraud. The foot possibly belongs to a Margery accomplice cajoled by her charm into the fraudulent event.

Karlis Osis using a maze in 1953 experiment with a cat. Could it be telepathically directed to one of the two feeding stations with equal amounts of cat food in them? (Courtesy JBR)

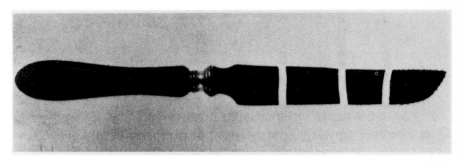

The knife that spontaneously shattered into four pieces in Carl Jung's home. Jung sent this photograph to J. B. Rhine. (Courtesy JBR)

At the Foundation for Research on the Nature of Man, at Durham, North Carolina, 1965—staff, wives, summer students, and visitors. Front row, from left, W. E. Cox, Rex Stanford, Charles Honorton, Louisa E. Rhine, J. B. Rhine, Marie Avery, Dorothy Pope, John Freeman. The Rhines' daughter Sally Feather is second from the right in the back row. (Courtesy JBR)

Joseph Banks Rhine in 1960 when he was sixty-five. (Courtesy JBR)

31

AN UNEXPECTED
SUPPORTER
1951–1953

Rhine had a personal stake in the Korean War. His twenty-two-year-old son was fighting there as a Marine captain. Although Rhine was fifty-five, given the chance, he would have joined him. Still, he had his own less deadly battles to face at home. The idolizing assistants and students of the thirties and forties were now more critical, anxious to break away from Rhine's rigid methods, and eager to research subjects he had proscribed. Had he been a professor of biology or physics, none of his students would have dreamed of trying to do his own thing. But parapsychology being comparatively new, some whose scientific training was sketchy thought they had as much right as Rhine to lay down the law. Rhine knew the route he wanted to take and was tough on those who straggled, leapfrogged or zigzagged. Keep it clear, keep it simple, don't jump to conclusions from one single experiment—these were his watchwords. The daring and the undisciplined defied him. Raised voices, slammed doors, conspiratorial whispers in corridors were not uncommon, nor was the sound of a car starting off with a shudder, never to return.

If Rhine had the money to pay for a more highly trained staff, many of his problems would not have existed. But it was not only scientists he wanted, but dedicated scientists. To Rhine the work was paramount, and he told those not prepared to work grueling hours at often monotonous tasks that they would probably be happier elsewhere. Researchers came and went. There was talk of renaming Rhine's lab "the revolving door."

But the problem of restless young Turks was less pressing to Rhine than his need for money. He was chronically short of it. There was never enough to finance important research projects or to hire well-qualified researchers. All he had was his own salary as a psychology professor, and occasional contributions from a handful of well-wishers. So he tried to tap the Rockefellers.

The chances of the Rockefeller Foundation supporting psi experiments were slim. None of the Rockefeller brothers had shown even a glimmer of interest in parapsychology. If they were to give support now, their decision would depend on the recommendation of an impartial investigator. The man they chose to evaluate Rhine's work, Dr. Wilder Penfield,* was the foremost authority on the brain.

Like many innovators, Penfield made his scientific breakthrough by chance. He pioneered a brain operation for epileptics—cauterizing scarred brain tissue. While operating in 1933, his electrode tip accidentally touched part of the patient's cortex. To Penfield's astonishment this caused the patient, in the surgeon's words, "to relive all that he had been aware of in that earlier period of time as in a moving picture 'flashback.' "[1]

Touching a part of the brain—the temporal lobe—was like turning on a tape-recording of all the patient had been conscious of at a certain point in the past—the sights, sounds, and feelings. It was an extraordinarily vivid experience for fifty-three of his patients, exactly as if they were back in time.

After marveling at the stream of consciousness from the past activated by a gentle electric current applied to the brain, Penfield turned his thoughts to telepathy. He concluded that the mind is still a mystery and the source of its energy unknown, so that no scientist could positively deny mind-to-mind communication. In other words, he regarded telepathy as an open question.

Penfield accepted the positive evidence for the validity of prayer, while admitting that he knew of no scientific way to prove or disprove it. He presumed then that telepathy between man and God occurred during prayer. From that he reasoned that if telepathy was also possible between man and man, some outside energy can reach a man's mind. And "in that case," wrote Penfield,

... *it is not unreasonable to hope that after death the mind may waken to another source of energy. ... Since every man must adopt for himself, without the help of science, his way of life and his personal religion, I have long had my own private beliefs. What a thrill it is, then, to discover that the scientist, too, can legitimately believe in the existence of the spirit!*[2]

---

*Dr. Wilder Penfield, professor of neurosurgery and director of the Montreal Neurological Institute at McGill University, 1934 to 1960. He died in 1976.

This belief in the spirit made Penfield almost a minority of one among his scientific peers, aligning himself with poets, theologists, prophets, and philosophers, and some—but by no means all— parapsychologists.

Rhine was extraordinarily lucky to have such a man judge the value of his work. And as might be expected, Penfield told the Rockefeller Foundation that Rhine's efforts were worthy of support— which amounted to forty thousand dollars over four years.

32

KARLIS OSIS
1951–1953

With the Rockefeller money assured for four years, Rhine telephoned Karlis Osis, who worked in a lumbermill in Tacoma, Washington. Osis was not a typical mill worker. He was a psychologist who had emigrated to the United States, where he quickly discovered there were few professional opportunities for a man whose Ph.D. thesis had been on extrasensory perception. Rhine heard about him and wanted him on his staff.

If there were a prize for the person who did his first ESP experiment in the most unlikely place, Osis would have been in the running: He conducted his in a displaced persons' camp in Europe. Osis was a Latvian caught up in World War II, whose homeland had been overrun by the Russians. Reading Rhine's *The Reach of the Mind* in its German translation while in the camp had spurred him to experiment. Although he realized his precautions had been inadequate, the strongly positive results sustained his interest and he planned to try more with tighter controls.

Osis believed in an extrasensory dimension to life because of a vivid personal experience.

At fifteen, he had been bedridden at home in Latvia, with tuberculosis, and given a fifty-fifty chance of survival. This was in the days before wonder drugs. His aunt, for whom he had no special affection, was dying at the other end of a large house. She had suffered a stroke and the doctor gave her at most two weeks to live. One night, at dusk, Osis's room was flooded with "light you could read by—as if the whole room was living. And I felt a tremendous wave of joy and light in myself. It was an experience I had no concept of, being a country boy. What would I know about that? I was totally amazed." And then a relative came in and told Osis his aunt had just died.[1]

What intrigued Osis most was not the bright light and his

reaction, coinciding with his aunt's death, but the paradoxical sense of tremendous joy, a feeling totally at odds with the way he had been conditioned to respond to death.

After he was freed from the displaced persons' camp, Osis read parapsychological literature at the University of Munich and, realizing how much light parapsychology could throw on human personality, chose it as the subject for his doctoral thesis in 1950.

He gladly accepted Rhine's offer to join him at Duke in 1951. Osis' Latvian accent and Rhine's faulty hearing at first caused communication problems, but it did not take Rhine long to know he had an exceptional man on his staff.

Rhine had assured Upton Sinclair that he was going to cast a wider net in his search for gifted mediums. With this in mind, he sent Osis to a spiritualist camp, on the remote chance that he would encounter one there. It was a lesson to Osis in the illegitimate methods of phony mediums. He reported to Rhine that though some of the people in the camp might have had psychic talents, he saw no evidence of it. But his trip had not been wasted. He discovered how the mediums used "spies" to supply them with information about sitters. They passed this on, often while in simulated trances, as if it came from departed spirits. Rhine was pleased Osis had seen through the chicanery, disappointed that he had not uncovered another Eileen Garrett.

Not long after, Rhine received a letter from Gerald Heard that was to send Osis off on another investigation. Heard, a friend of Aldous Huxley's, was a British writer and lecturer on religion and philosophy. He was interested in psychic research, and in his letter to Rhine he related a strange experience that testified to survival after death. He had been given a message purportedly from his dead grandmother through medium Olga Worrall. The information, according to Heard, could not have been known to anyone other than his grandmother, himself, and his brother, who lived in England. Because of this, Heard was sure that the message did indeed come from his dead grandmother. For the first time in his life he believed that survival had been decisively proved.* Rhine corresponded with Heard to get more details and found that Olga Worrall had mentioned an accident Heard had suffered as a baby. Heard knew nothing of it until Mrs. Worrall wrote to him that the accident had been revealed to her by the spirit of Heard's grandmother. Heard had then checked with his brother in England, who confirmed such an accident had occurred, news of which had been kept secret to protect a nurse who

---

*It was not decisive proof to Rhine. As Heard's brother was still living, Mrs. Worrall could have obtained the information from him telepathically.

had been the cause of it. Only the nurse, Heard's brother, and his grandmother had known of the accident.

Rhine knew that both Olga Worrall and her husband, Ambrose, had good reputations as psychic or spiritual healers, working without charge in Baltimore. He sent Osis to try to persuade Mrs. Worrall to submit to tests at Duke. Maybe she would be the psychic star for whom he was looking.

When Osis reached Baltimore he telephoned Mrs. Worrall to tell her he was in town and explained his mission. "He wanted me to work with Dr. Rhine, shuffling cards," Olga Worrall told this writer. "To me, that would have been most boring and ridiculous. I'm sure Dr. Rhine did tremendous work, but I had and still have more important things to do in the field of spiritual development and comforting people than to sit shuffling cards. Anyway, I don't like cards."[2]

Osis persuaded her and her husband to do a few simple tests while he was a guest in their Baltimore home. The tests were inconclusive, but Osis judged from all the available evidence, much of which was anecdotal, that "the Worralls had terrific spontaneous abilities which are hard to produce on demand."[3]

With mediums like Olga Worrall and Arthur Ford reluctant to cooperate with him, Rhine took a renewed interest in animals. Even with willing human volunteers in the lab, psi remained hard to manipulate. Rhine thought he might get a better handle on it with creatures that had no reputations to uphold, and no incentives to cheat or exaggerate. But his essential reason was that he wanted to know if lower species than man showed signs of psi.

At the start of his work, Rhine was joined by his daughter Sally. Of Rhine's three daughters, she was the only one to become a parapsychologist, although they all took part as subjects in experiments.*

Sally had graduated from Duke in 1951, at twenty-one, having majored in biology, with a special interest in psychology and animal behavior. She could not have arrived in the lab at a better time, or with better credentials. Everyone was involved in making a big survey of homing and migration and investigating a wide range of animal behavior. One aim was to see if anecdotes about animals that pointed to psi ability could be put to the test in the lab. Karlis Osis had already begun working with kittens, and Sally helped him.[4]

Osis began his lengthy experiments with kittens, and when he finished they had grown into cats. In one experiment to see if cats receive telepathic communications from humans, Osis put the animals

---

*Betsy became a dog breeder, Rosemary a businesswoman selling insurance.

into a maze. They emerged at a point where there were two feeding stations—both filled with equal amounts of food. Hidden from the animals, Sally Rhine Feather tried by telepathy to direct each cat either to the right or the left feeding station according to a pre-arranged random order. Osis and Dr. Esther Foster conducted a similar experiment to discover if cats used clairvoyance to reach food. Then, only one of the two feeding stations contained food, and neither the cats nor the experimenters knew which one. Osis took care that the animals could neither see nor smell the food, then recorded how often they went first to the feeding station with food.

In both experiments the animals generally scored well under good conditions, which included affectionate handling. They failed most often when distracted or poorly handled, just like humans.[5]

An unexpected finding was that opera stars are not the only prima donnas. Osis found that "One of my star subjects, a big cat called Baltins—Latvian for white—had to be the first in an experimental session. He was a big star, and when I called him he would run and jump up from the ground to my shoulder. He'd sit there and look down on the others. Then I could get positive scores with him. But if I picked up some other cat first, he [Baltins] scored poorly. It was a very delicate situation."[6]

Osis wanted to know what use cats would normally make of psi, if they had it. His experiments failed to give an answer. Then one day he noticed that Puzy, one of his star performers, was missing. A short while later he saw her coming back from the meadows, apparently after a hunting expedition. He tested her and she made a wonderful, unforgettable nine out of ten. He caught her again coming from a hunting trip and her score was similarly high. And he thought: " 'Now I know how to turn on the cat's ESP—get an artificial mouse and create a hunting situation.' But it didn't work that way."[7]

It seemed so logical that a hunting situation would be the natural trigger or release for the ESP function in cats. But after those two exceptional scores, he was never able to substantiate his theory experimentally.

The idea that animals are machines was repugnant to Osis. He made pets of the cats he worked with and got to know them well as individuals.

For another experiment, Osis was helped by his teenage daughter, Gunta. They released cats from a cage in the middle of Rhine's meadowland, about ten miles from the cats' home. Osis and his daughter hid behind hedges on the meadow's perimeter, hoping that through ESP the cats would come to them. But it never worked—the couple always had to reveal themselves or call the cats.

During one such experiment one of the stars, Princess, disappeared for good. Even when Osis and his daughter called her, the cat moved away from them. "In a strange situation, because of friendship and security, I had expected her to run to us," said Osis. "We made a great effort to find her—called all around the woods and came back the next day and searched. I was really upset."[8]

Betsy Rhine was enlisted for a similar experiment with her dog, to see if it would use ESP to turn left or right, when taken to a crossroads, in order to find her. The results were inconclusive.

Both Osis and Rhine were disappointed when they had to stop the lab experiments with animals. The rooms where the testing equipment had been built were claimed by the philosophy department, and its members successfully objected to the smell of the cat food.

33

PIGEONS AND PSI TRAILING 1951–1953

When Rhine was a boy, his father told him the story of the farmer who explained how he plowed a field studded with tree stumps. "I go around them," he said. Rhine remembered the lesson: He, too, went around obstacles. He didn't abandon animal research, but pursued it far afield, even abroad.

Newspaper reports about remarkable animals were often the catalyst that sent him and his assistants out of the lab and into the world. Whenever he read of a homing pigeon reaching its loft after an exhausting flight of hundreds of miles over unknown territory, or a lost dog returning home after a long journey over land it had never seen or smelled before, Rhine was onto it, because such ability might be psi. If a staff member or "scout" on the spot could investigate, he was recruited, but there were times when Rhine went himself. The mystery of homing pigeons even took him and Gaither Pratt on a flying trip to Europe in 1951. There they watched another scientist try to resolve the seemingly miraculous ability of pigeons to find their way home.

The dazzling feats of collision avoidance by blind bats once seemed to point to ESP, until investigation yielded the almost equally wonderful answer: radar. Rhine believed pigeons might home through extrasensory means.

Dr. Gustav Kramer of the Max Planck Institute in Wilhems-haven, Germany, had discovered that pigeons kept a steady course over long distances by responding to changes in the sun's direction. But how did they start off heading in the right direction when in a strange spot, miles from home? No one knew.

In Wilhems-haven, Rhine and Pratt watched Kramer release pigeons about ten miles from their loft and from different locations.

They all returned with apparent ease. Next, Kramer told the American parapsychologists, he planned a much more ambitious test—to release the birds from two hundred miles away. Rhine was back at Duke when he heard the results of the two-hundred-mile experiment. Many of the pigeons had reached the loft in just a few hours after that long flight over strange territory. Kramer believed they had been guided by the sun, but how they set off in the right direction still mystified him.

Pratt built a pigeon loft in his backyard to see if Duke could solve the riddle before the Max Planck Institute did. But when he started releasing the birds in the summer of 1952, many never returned. Rhine suggested they send for the expert, Dr. Kramer, before they ran out of pigeons.

Kramer broke his journey in "New York to visit scientific colleagues in his own field, ornithology," wrote Gaither Pratt.

When he explained he was here at the invitation of the Duke Parapsychology Laboratory, he got some serious words of warning and advice regarding the consequences of associating with a research center that dared even to raise the question of whether ESP might be involved in pigeon homing.... Dr. Kramer took one look at my loft [where Pratt kept the pigeons shut up most of the day] and made one suggestion: Open that prison and let the jailbirds fly free.

Pratt took Kramer's advice. Two months later, Pratt released birds 140 miles from their loft and over half of them got home.[1]

The Office of Naval Research was interested in Pratt's efforts to discover the basis of the pigeons' homing ability and financed continued investigation. Robert Van de Castle, then Pratt's research assistant, remembers, "We would go out early in the mornings and get pigeons from the loft he had at Durham and travel out to the four directions—north, south, east, west—and go back and observe how long it would take them to return."[2]

When Rhine heard from a man who claimed his pet pigeon had flown to him while he was hospitalized over a hundred miles from home, he investigated. Although it had happened some ten years before, Rhine read all the reports he could find about it and questioned witnesses.

This is what he gathered: In 1940, Hugh Brady, the twelve-year-old son of the sheriff of Summerville, West Virginia, became ill and was driven in an ambulance over the mountains to a hospital in Philippi, 120 miles from his home. One snowy night, as he lay in bed in the hospital, he heard a noise at the window. Although it was dark, he could see it was a pigeon tapping as if to ask to come in. Brady was convinced that the bird was his own pet, which must have somehow found its way to the hospital. He told the nurse it was his bird out in the snow and begged her to let it in, until he broke her resistance. She opened the window and the bird flew in. Sure enough, there was the band around its leg—AU C&W 167—identifying it as the boy's pet. Brady was allowed to keep the bird in a box beside his bed. When his parents arrived a few days later they were astonished to see the bird. They were sure it had not followed the ambulance because they had seen the bird around their home a day or two after their son had been taken to the hospital. One answer, of course, was that it might have used ESP. Rhine checked the story and it stood up. The boy, his parents, and the nurse all confirmed the facts.[3]

One of Rhine's better-informed critics, and a leading behaviorist, Harvard's Professor B. F. Skinner, was also deeply involved in pigeon behavior. Although he did not categorically deny the existence of psi—it was an area he chose not to investigate—he maintained that it had not been experimentally demonstrated.[4] His research with pigeons demonstrated his view that the nature of man and animal is mechanistic, and both can be conditioned to behave almost any way an experimenter chooses. Among his more ingenious efforts was to condition a pigeon to turn in circles like a ballet dancer, accurately aim bombs falling from an aircraft, and even simulate playing table tennis. Rhine saw Skinner's beliefs as limited and limiting. Rhine was persuaded by his laboratory experiments and the reports of spontaneous psi experiences that there was more to man and animal than mechanistic psychology would allow. As the pigeon proved one mechanistic point for Skinner, so Rhine hoped the bird would demonstrate another, extrasensory, point for him.

Today scientists know that pigeons see, hear, and smell a world that is unknown to man. The human eye has yellow pigment in the lens to screen out ultraviolet rays: This protects the retina from sunburn and possible destruction. But the pigeon having no such protection, can see both polarized and ultraviolet light. This raises as yet unanswered questions. Why has the human eye developed so that it is blind to the world seen by birds and other vertebrates? And why doesn't the ultraviolet light from the sun burn a hole in birds' eyes? Not only do pigeons have incredibly acute vision, but they can hear a tone eleven octaves below middle C—the lowest sound ever detected by an animal in laboratory tests. And they can smell and distinguish airborne odors indigenous to different areas.

Discoveries by Dr. Melvin Kreithen and Professor Thomas Eisner at Cornell led to speculation that pigeons hear and steer by infrasound (very high frequency sounds beyond human hearing) from surf, storms, and wind that travels thousands of miles.[5]

Other theorists suggest that the birds navigate by the stars at night, the sun by day, and, when skies are overcast, use the magnetic earth as a giant compass to find their way. But much of this is speculation and the ESP theory has not been disproved. How pigeons set out in the right direction is still a tantalizing puzzle, especially for parapsychologists.

While the U.S. Navy was financing Pratt to try to solve that mystery, the U.S. Army supported Rhine for a three-month trip to the California coast, where he directed a secret experiment with two German shepherds.

34

SECRET WORK FOR THE ARMY 1952–1953

Fifty-seven-year-old J. B. Rhine crouched behind a sand hill on a lonely, windswept California beach north of San Francisco, surreptitiously watching two German shepherds. He was on a secret assignment for the U.S. Army.

The dogs were being tested to see if they could locate buried land mines by ESP. Rhine's son, Robert, was still fighting in Korea, and Rhine realized that the success of the experiment might save the young man's life as well as those of scores of others.

Someone in the U.S. Army who knew of Rhine's promising experiments with animals had speculated that if dogs had ESP they might be able to use it to detect land mines buried too deeply under shallow water to be detected by their physical senses.

Subsequently, the Engineer Research and Development Laboratories, Fort Belvoir, Virginia, asked Rhine to devise and carry out an experiment to see if dogs could locate hidden objects by ESP. Dr. Luman Ney, a Stanford Research Institute chemist, was hired as an observer. Ney also helped Rhine find suitable dogs for the test: Binnie and Tessie, German shepherds. They had been intensively trained to locate underground objects by using their physical senses. Rhine's objective was to see if the dogs could discover buried objects out of range of their physical senses. Two other observers were engaged for the experiment—Wilbert W. Toole, representing the U.S. Army, and William Johns, a consultant on dog training and an expert in guide-dog training.

So, while Gaither Pratt was at Duke experimenting with homing pigeons through the summer and fall of 1952, Rhine worked with the two German shepherds.

Rhine first marked out on the beach several straight lines of tape, knotted every yard and specially marked each five-yard interval, for a total length of twenty-five yards each. He or Dr. Ney then buried small wooden boxes—simulated military Schu land mines—at intervals a few inches from the tape and four inches under the sand. They planted one box in each five-yard stretch of tape, close to the center of whichever one-yard span had been chosen (following a random order prepared earlier from random number tables).

Rhine and Ney in turn made sure the dogs and Joe Simpson, their handler, were not able to see them bury the mines. To ensure that dogs and handler were deprived of physical clues, Rhine chose a test area under shallow water. Almost constant winds blew away from the dogs and handler any possible olfactory clues. The hard-packing sand became like stone when it settled back over the buried mines, but to make sure there were no visible clues the experimenters disturbed the sand with one of the boxes over every yard-length space along the whole test area. Footprints near the test area were eliminated by raking and the whole test area smoothed by a straight-edged drag.

When Rhine did the planting, Ney made sure he, the dogs, and the handler could not see Rhine at work. Then Rhine found a spot to hide, to avoid unconsciously guiding dog or handler to the places he had hidden the mines. The dogs had been trained to sit to indicate discovery of a buried object. Their handler walked the dogs, one at a time, alongside the tape and marked the place where the dog sat with a thin white splint.

Ney made a record of where these were. When one dog had completed the experiment the white splints were removed, apparently leaving no trace on the underwater sand, and the second dog was taken over the same trail. When Ney did the planting, Rhine stayed with dog and handler to make sure they could not see where Ney had buried the mines.

The handler was asked to give the dogs praise and encouragement after each response, but Rhine told him not to attempt to guess the location of the hidden boxes nor to influence the pace or reaction of the dogs in any way.

Most of the experiments were double-blind, which means that the experimenter, who alone knew where the mines were buried, was not the one who recorded where the dogs sat; so there was no danger of his accidentally or intentionally influencing the outcome.

The results of tests with targets buried in sand underwater were as follows: For 48 trials, when Rhine planted the targets and there were two experimenters present on two of three days, the dogs got 37.5 percent hits, when they would be expected to get 20 percent by chance. For 95 trials, when Ney buried the targets and the two experimenters were present every day, the dogs got 44.2 percent hits. And for 60 trials, when Rhine planted the targets and was the only experimenter (because Ney was not available) the dogs got 31.7 percent hits. So, for a total of 203 trials, in which the dogs should by chance have gotten 20 percent hits, they got 38.9 percent hits.

Rhine admits that "the exact length of the experimental series with the dogs had not been fixed in advance. The dogs had been doing well in June, July, August, and the start of September, but when, in a three-day period, the hits per day ran at 45%, 30% and 20% in succession," Rhine decided to end the tests.[1]

Characteristically, Rhine showed his concern for animals by including in his official report:

Although the dogs had been trained by the older method of punishment with steel traps (a method which happily has been abandoned), the dog-handler relationship was obviously a close one.[2]

Rhine concluded:

A firm case probably cannot be made from these studies for the claim that the two dogs showed ESP ability. It is possible that Simpson could have given slight cues to the dogs on the strength of his own ESP ability and could even have done so quite unconsciously. This fairly obvious alternative was recognized at the time as a possibility. An alert reader today will likely wonder why, then, it was not arranged to test his own mine-locating ability. But in that day and at that stage all the participants were concentrating too much on the dogs and it might have endangered the already delicate psychology of the handler to have asked him to compete with the dogs. The ERDL was concerned only with practical results, and the Duke Laboratory wanted to find out first whether ESP could be successfully used in this way.

So, as it stands, the experiment shows only that the man-dog combination did for a time produce a very significant order of success in locating the boxes under conditions that rather strongly indicated ESP.[3]

It would cost the Army less to attempt to replicate the experiment than to train one recruit, but no such attempt has been made, unless secretly.

The one vital question that remains unanswered is, What normal sensory powers does a dog have to detect a buried object? Until that is established, attributing a dog's prowess to an extrasensory source is not convincing. Even though Dr. Ney could not explain the significant results other than by ESP, he admitted he did not know if the water control over olfactory stimuli was adequate.

Robert Morris emphasized this point when reviewing the work in 1977 in *Handbook of Parapsychology*. He agreed that Rhine's results were very strong, but points out that the dogs may have had olfactory clues, "since odors have been known to cling to such locations for quite some period of time," and that there may have been "tactile-vibrational clues, since the sand above the box may pack more densely when stepped upon than the sand at the other places."[4]

Rhine did not disagree: Although the tests were underwater, they were not unquestionably watertight. It was the indication that a man-dog combination had specially enhanced ESP powers that most intrigued Rhine and was one of the possibilities that kept his interest alive in animal experiments and investigations.

Rhine's report was secret for nineteen years, being declassified in 1971.[5]

Had the Korean War persisted beyond 1952, the Army might have sponsored similar promising experiments. Surprisingly, the war in Vietnam did not generate a renewed Army interest in animal psi. Or perhaps it did—and those experiments are still classified.

Rhine was convinced that he had experimentally demonstrated psi to be a fact, but he had to admit in a December 1952 issue of the *Journal of Parapsychology* that

... *parapsychology has definitely failed to impress the majority of American psychologists.... From the [Dr. Lucien] Warner report we now see that ... although five out of six psychologists do not recognize ESP as a likely possibility,* only a little over an average of one in six claim to have based their opinions on any acquaintance with the scientific reports! *Seventeen percent in both surveys even admitted to having reached their opinions on the basis of hearsay. But the really significant revelation, to our judgment, is the fact that approximately* 20 percent in both surveys put on the record that they reached their conclusions entirely on a priori grounds: *they had their minds already made up on the question in advance. They admitted they were not judging the case by the evidence....*

Thus far the sciences have been very successfully rescuing large areas of problems from supernaturalistic interpretation. But in over-zealously barring out anything that even suggests the supernatural, they have evidently developed a too-narrow conception of the natural, *one that equates it to the physical—the physics of space, time, and mass. There is a need now to recover certain areas of unsolved problems from the extremes to which these tendencies have carried modern scientific thought.... Those who know the evidence for psi and can foresee the eventual acceptance of it can now the better appreciate its significance in turning the materialistic tide of thought because of the very immensity of the difficulties that are still to be met.*[6]

If anyone thought Rhine was uncertain about the existence of psi, it was dispelled by his fifth book, *New World of the Mind*, 1953, William Sloane Associates, in which he wrote an unequivocal and positive: "It has now been established by scientific means that there is an extraphysical element in man." In that book Rhine dispels suspicions that he is really a Methodist minister manqué, but shows himself to be religious in the sense that Einstein was religious, or like anyone who is stirred by the wonder of life and the universe. Organized religion lost an arresting thinker in Rhine. But let him speak for himself:

Every religion provides through its doctrine what its founders and followers believe are the answers to the question of what man can do about his destiny, and how he can best live his life.

If today, then, it were possible to catch the spirit of these founders and equip ourselves with the truth-finding methods of our own day, we might, for example, be able to advance the spiritual aspects of Jesus's contributions as much as the healing side of His mission has been advanced by those same methods.

The spirit is important; medicine itself would still be where it was in the first century B.C. had it had not been that the progressive, inquiring individuals in the profession prevailed over the conservative, backward-looking membership. The same struggle goes on in every department of human affairs. The spirit, the will to find out, the driving force, comes first. But the methods, the ways by which problems are solved, are the wheels of progress in knowledge and understanding.

So far as methodology goes, the procedures of natural sciences could just as well be set to work on the question of whether there are invisible genes or intangible cosmic rays. Any effect that reaches any man, from any source, and shows any regular relationships whatever, will reveal itself by its own operation when the properly inquiring study is made by an observer qualified to interpret the results. By the very nature of the universe, especially its causal character, one cannot get an effect without a cause; and this cause is potentially discoverable through the study of its consequences and the conditions under which they occur.

If prayer is effective and if the thoughts of men do reach out to other personalities in the universe beyond the range of the senses,

*it must be through the medium of extrasensory perception. If, origi-
nating in any personal agency anywhere, celestial or mundane, there
is an effect produced upon the physical world in answer to prayer, it
would have to be a psychokinetic effect, a psi phenomenon. . . . There
is belief, of course, that a divine personal agency exists to which
prayer is directed. The cooperation of this agency itself could in all
sincerity and propriety quite well be included in the research plan. In
fact, the older world religions were supposedly founded with the aid
of miracles, that is, cooperative demonstrations by divine agencies.*

*Such small fragments as the psi inquiries have produced
must not be expected to be impressive in themselves. Rather, they
may well be only a small fringe of islands representing a continent of
spiritual reality. . . .*

*The basic issue underlying the clash of ideologies in the world
today is a theory as to the nature of man. Most thinking people know
that blind faith in dogmatic revelationist religion cannot counter the
claims and promises of communism. It is, in fact, all too plain from
the history of communism's gains that it has thrived best where
authoritarian religion has had its longest and strongest control over
the lives of the people. . . .*

*The point to be most clear about is that this acceptance of
psi's contribution of a new approach to religion would be a constructive step. . . . What are the proper questions? The starting point
should be: How sound a basis of knowledge has any given religion on
which to support any given tenet? One by one every important doctrine needs to be thoughtfully reexamined as to its foundation. Does
anyone really yet know, for example, what extrahuman help a human
being can call upon and count on in the guidance of his life? What
sound and tested teaching is there to prepare a man to face such a
final act as death? . . . If one asks these and similar questions, and
insists on frank, definite answers, an appalling situation comes to
light. It is that no one knows or pretends to know, in a way he can
prove, the answers to those or any other of the greater questions of
religion. . . .*

*Finally the truth dawns that to these central questions even
the most consecrated scholarly leadership in all the religious systems
does not have the answers that would satisfy the ordinary standards
of evidence of everyday life in the bank or the court or the market-
place, let alone in the sciences. In the face of the realization,
dogmatic religion comes to assume the shape and proportion of a
gigantic group delusion, cutting itself off deliberately from the tests
of reality by which its position could be verified and by which its
course toward greater positive knowledge could be directed. For in
this old attitude is an almost complete abandonment of realism, a*

surrender to a system of unverified fantasy that, in a single isolated individual, would be diagnosed as psychotic. . . .

These are not negative, anti-religious thoughts. . . . There is ground for hope. Religion can yet save the world, save it from misery and fear and confusion and strife, if it can save itself from becoming completely a relic of the past; if it can capture and hold leadership in the knowledge of man's place as a spiritual being in a universe that is, we now know, at least not devoid of spiritual forces. . . .

If due investigation should find no evidence of any or all of the "other worlds," heavens, summerlands, happy hunting grounds, nirvanas, and such, that have been taking men's minds off their present world through the ages, it might lead to an extremely healthy shift of human effort and attention to the problems of the present life. Life would take on a larger area for having its boundary defined. If, on the other hand, some kind of world of independent spirit agency can be discovered, as there is reason to think may be possible, its establishment would manifestly bring to religious life an incomparably greater meaning and potency. The discovery would do for religion something like what the germ theory did for medicine.

It takes a certain daring to suggest including "a divine personal agency"—known familiarly as God—into an experimental design. But even Rhine's most vehement critics never accused him of timidity.

35

SUGAR THE CAT
1953

Rhine had barely returned home from his work with dogs in California, than he set off for Oklahoma to examine a cat and question witnesses who claimed it had made an astonishing fifteen-hundred-mile journey across strange territory. If what they said was true, then this cat—named Sugar, left behind in California by a family moving to Oklahoma—had later traced them to their new home.

The cat's owner, Stacy Woods, a retired school principal, told Rhine how he had been preparing to move with his family from Anderson, California, to live on a farm in Gage, Oklahoma. They intended to take their cat, Sugar, with them, but he had other ideas. Although he never hesitated to fight even fierce dogs, he was scared of riding in cars, so when the family was all packed and ready to go, Sugar made a run for it and kept his distance. The Woodses reluctantly left the cat with friends who promised to care for him.

Over a year later, in August 1952, the Woodses were working in their barn in Oklahoma when a cat jumped through an open window and landed on Mrs. Woods's shoulder. She was so startled she left it there, purring away for a moment or two, before brushing it off.

This male cat attached himself to the family. He was the image of Sugar, with the same cream coloring and the same hip-joint deformity. He displayed a similar fighting spirit with dogs and even tackled coyotes. They were convinced that he was Sugar, who somehow had traveled fifteen hundred miles to reach them.

Back in California, the friends who had taken care of Sugar were about to set out by car to visit the Woodses and dreaded telling them the sad news of Sugar. He had stayed with them only three weeks after the Woodses had left, before disappearing.

When they arrived at the Woods's home in Oklahoma, they were astonished and delighted to see Sugar. They, too, confirmed the cat's hipbone deformity, and were convinced he was Sugar and not a look-alike imposter.

Rhine examined the cat and judged him to be a tough and healthy animal. He questioned the Woodses carefully.

When he gave a press conference shortly afterward, he faced professional skeptics. *Time* magazine, December 7, 1953, reported:

Around the semicircle of Rhine's audience there was evident disbelief. The professor, who has spent twenty-six of his fifty-eight years studying just such phenomena, shook his shock of greying hair and shrugged. "You see what a fix I'm in?" he asked. "Here you have a line of incredibility, and I'm just beyond it. That's why this work is so interesting." Then he added: "I don't know that I believe it myself."

The case of the homing California cat was much like others cited in his New World of the Mind, *just published (Sloane; $3.75). And the newsmen's reaction was typical of both lay and professional response to his work.*

Rhine was less cautious when he wrote about Sugar in the *Journal of Parapsychology*: "Such a cat would be able, if any quadruped could, to make its way over the extremely rugged terrain in the fifteen hundred miles between California and Oklahoma, provided he could find his way."[1]

Was it Sugar? Had he traveled by ESP? Rhine was too much of a scientist to give a positive yes or no. But he persuaded the Woodses to agree that when the cat died Duke would get his body. An autopsy might give clues to his prowess. But the cat escaped that final investigation. He never returned from a hunting trip.

Rhine's daughter Sally helped him to select and analyze the best fifty-four cases of psi-trailing from their world-wide collection, involving twenty-eight dogs, twenty-two cats, and four birds.*

The Rhines stressed four points in evaluating psi-trailing:

1. There must be a reliable source of information.

2. The animal must be clearly identifiable by name-tag, license number, or unusual scar, for example.

3. The general circumstances must make sense and be internally consistent.

4. The account must be supported by independent testimony from others and the animal must be available for inspection.[2]

After subjecting their fifty-four accounts to this evaluation,

---

*Psi-trailing is a form of psi in animals (anspi) with which a pet is thought to reach its owner in a distant location where it has never been before.

J.B. and Sally Rhine concluded that, although many passed their four-point criterion, irrefutable proof was still missing. Rhine could not say, as he did about ESP and PK, that psi-trailing was a fact.

The tantalizing nature of Rhine's work was that when one door closed, others opened, and when they shut, the first was found to have opened a crack, and when that closed. . . . Now you see it, now you don't. Without his statistical method he might have seemed like a child enchanted by an illusionist. The other essential difference being that Rhine was on the alert for deception. Some assistants felt he overreacted and risked overlooking psychics with unusual ability.

Contacts in Sweden had written to Rhine about Olof Jonsson as a remarkable medium who was willing to be tested. Rhine invited him to Duke—and angrily ordered him sent back to Sweden the following day.

36

JONSSON
1953

To make psychic Olof Jonsson feel at home when he arrived at Duke from Sweden, Rhine and several researchers decided to give him the nearest thing to a Scandinavian meal. So they took him to a German restaurant. Soft-spoken but assured, Jonsson appreciated their hospitality, and the group was soon transformed from suspect and interrogators to confiding friends. The parapsychologists wanted Jonsson to know he would not be dealing with gullible amateurs. One of them had a pack of cards with him and showed Jonsson card tricks phony psychics had tried to pull, of which he and his colleagues were well aware. Jonsson had wondered how experienced and knowledgeable Rhine's assistants were. He asked for the pack and did a few tricks he had witnessed in Sweden, to see if the parapsychologists would spot how they were done.

Rhine reacted as if someone had lit a firecracker under his seat. Send Jonsson back to Sweden immediately! Cancel the experiments! He would not test the man under any circumstances. Rhine scenting fraud was like a fainting victim introduced to smelling salts.

Some of the researchers tried to persuade Rhine to change his mind. Jonsson had made a long journey across the Atlantic especially for the tests. He might very well have been trying to test their ability, as he claimed. Being able to do card tricks was not positive proof that he was a fraud. What harm would there be in testing him, if they used fraud-proof methods?

To everyone's surprise, Rhine changed his mind and allowed Jonsson to stay and to be tested. The tests were positive, showing Jonsson to have psychic abilities. Normally Rhine would publish an account in the *Journal of Parapsychology*, but although he had relented and proceeded with the tests, he was still wary. Jonsson had put him on guard. Suppose the man was eventually found to be a trickster who had cleverly eluded the fraud-proof precautions? If that happened and Rhine had published the Jonsson experiments for the world to see, then the failure of the parapsychology lab to spot the fraud would be evident. With that in mind, Rhine decided not to publish an account of the successful experiments. In fact, Jonsson's name is missing from much of the parapsychological literature covering that period.[1]

However, he left a lasting impression on Karlis Osis, who tested Jonsson many times. One night when they were working late in the lab, Jonsson took a pill he said he got in Algiers, which was supposed to make him very clairvoyant. While Osis hid the ESP cards from him, Jonsson called thirteen of the symbols of a deck correctly. "Now," said Jonsson excitedly, "Dr. Rhine has never seen real ESP. Let's show him what real ESP looks like." It was almost ten at night. Osis was caught up in Jonsson's enthusiasm, but wondered "if Rhine would take it kindly if we intruded. However, Olof was so forceful that I agreed."[2]

Four of them set out by car; Osis, Jonsson, Esther Foster, and another girl headed for Rhine's farmhouse, several miles from the lab. When they reached Rhine's pasture near his home, Jonsson said, "Can we stop here? I want to see if it still works."

Osis agreed to stop and test Jonsson for telepathy. They all got out of the car and Osis gave Mrs. Foster a pack of ESP cards he had kept in his pocket and which he had earlier put in random order. He told the girl to stay behind the car with Mrs. Foster, as a witness. Then he and Jonsson walked together to a spot about thirty yards away. Osis kept the pace of the experiment by signaling Mrs. Foster with a flashlight. Each time he did so, she looked at an ESP card in the light from the car, and tried to project the thought of it to Jonsson. Osis wrote down Jonsson's calls. He got an extraordinary seventeen right out of twenty-five.

The enthusiastic quartet, feeling that they were witnesses to a remarkable event in parapsychological history, were relieved to find when they reached Rhine's home that he was willing to listen to their story. He took it very calmly, saying, "That's fine. Let's do it again."

In Rhine's presence Jonsson scored only one hit in twenty-five, remarkably below chance. It was a big letdown. Osis and Foster did many more tests with Jonsson, who achieved positive results, at times under tight conditions. The only plausible explanation they could find was that Jonsson had outstanding psychic ability. If so, then that night at the farmhouse Rhine's presence had apparently been the inhibiting factor causing Jonsson to fail.[3]

Parapsychologist W. E. Cox thought Olof Jonsson was a remarkable psychic, despite his propensity for playing tricks. "I discovered him doing something tricky, but also saw he was quite real.

He could let me hold the cards [star, waves, square, circle, cross] behind my own back. And if I'd say, 'I want to draw a star next,' he would concentrate a minute and say, 'There, draw a star.' And I would. There's no trick in that. And the other time I sealed up twenty-five cards and he named them in another room. That was absolutely incontrovertible.

"But when I told Rhine, he asked: 'Whose cards were they, Ed?' And I said, 'They were Olof Jonsson's, because this was spontaneously done and he had the cards.' And Rhine said: 'That's out for me.' And I agreed with him. That's why I never published that experiment."[4]

37

KRIPPNER'S ODYSSEY 1950–1955

Professors of psychology at the University of Wisconsin derided Rhine's pursuit of psi as a fool chasing a fantasy. One of their students, Stanley Krippner, disagreed. As a child he had awoken one morning feeling unaccountably sad for an uncle the moment the phone rang to announce his uncle's unexpected death. That childhood experience substantiated Krippner's feeling that there is something to ESP. So he discounted the professors' sneers as herd reaction to uncomfortable ideas. Psychologists, not too secure in their comparatively young profession, tended to cling to the known like shipwrecked sailors in a safe cove reluctant to explore the rest of the territory.

Krippner thought a university should be a place where unpopular, even wild, views were discussed without rancor. As a member of the Forum Committee, he had already persuaded several speakers of varying political hues to lecture on campus, among them William Buckley, Jr., Owen Lattimore, John Dos Passos, and Eleanor Roosevelt. There had been opposition to all of them, but nothing like the howl that greeted the news that J. B. Rhine had been invited. Shaken by the storm of protests, the Forum Committee asked the psychology department's acting chairman for his advice. He conceded that a Rhine lecture would be crowded because of the subject's appeal to the bereaved and emotionally unstable. But in his opinion, Rhine's talk would confuse people about the true nature of psychology. The committee had heard enough; they virtually canceled the lecture by refusing to pay the three-hundred dollar fee Rhine had requested.

Krippner was a fighter. He and others wrote to several distinguished scientists, hoping they would rally behind the free-speech-for-Rhine banner. Krippner put his greatest hope in Einstein. He knew that Einstein had recommended Upton Sinclair's book on telepathy; the great physicist had shown himself to be a liberal, open-minded man whose name alone conjured up thoughts of tolerance and fair play. His support would surely change a few minds. So Krippner wrote to Einstein at Princeton's Institute for Advanced Study, confident that if Einstein had the time and inclination to reply he would unconditionally support free speech. To Krippner's shocked dismay, Einstein replied a few days later, agreeing with the opposition. He wrote that Rhine's experiments did not seem credible. He could not understand how telepathy and clairvoyance, though of a very different nature, reportedly showed their influence statistically in the same order of magnitude. Einstein was misinformed because, far from believing telepathy and clairvoyance to be of a different nature, Rhine thought they were aspects of the same phenomenon. Einstein also noted that Rhine claimed that neither distance nor time influenced the results, which was counter to his own space-time theory. The idea of precognition, of being able to identify a card *before* it had been chosen (by a person or machine), especially struck Einstein as incredible. Yet he admitted he had not studied Rhine's experimental methods fully and therefore was not able to judge their merit. Einstein's final comments most disillusioned Krippner. The great man wrote that his scientific instinct objected irresistibly to ESP. In his opinion, an audience, after listening to Rhine, would not be able to make a rational judgment. So, wrote Einstein, he for one would not arrange such a lecture.[1]

It seems incongruous that Einstein should doubt Rhine's experiments yet admit that he had not fully studied them; that after boosting Sinclair's book on telepathy and thereby encouraging tens of thousands of readers to take telepathy seriously, he should be less than enthusiastic about Rhine's far more extensive and tightly controlled work on telepathy.

In his biography of Einstein, Ronald W. Clark tells of Einstein listening to Nobel prizewinner Dr. Alexis Carrel discuss spiritualism. Carrel is quoted as saying to Einstein, "But doctor, what would you say if you observed this phenomenon yourself?" And Einstein is reported to have replied: "I still would not believe it."[2] Einstein's secretary, Helen Dukas, confirms that the exchange between the two men may very well have taken place.[3] Krippner regretfully informed Rhine that he was unable to raise the fee for his lecture, but did not tell him of Einstein's discouraging views.

Even without Einstein's backing, Krippner persisted in his plan to bring Rhine to the campus. Three years later, in 1953, he again suggested Rhine as a speaker in a debate to support the proposition

that the existence of psychic events had been experimentally demon-
stated. This time no speaking fee would be involved. Rhine would be
lecturing to the chemical society in Chicago and was willing to talk to
the Wisconsin students on the same trips without a fee. The Forum
Committee unanimously accepted Rhine's offer.

Krippner invited the acting chairman of the psychology
department to speak in opposition to the proposition. He showed a
satirical sense of humor in declining the invitation, comparing himself to a scientifically trained atheist asked to debate with the Catholic
Bishop Fulton Sheen the proposition that immaculate conception has
been experimentally proved. He ended his letter in the same comic
vein, suggesting that after Rhine's lecture Father Divine should talk
on Recent Advances in the Art of Healing.[4]

Rhine, too, had a wry, sometimes sardonic sense of humor,
and he must have smiled to himself at the maneuverings obviously
occurring at the University of Wisconsin. He had been invited to talk
and then rejected, invited again to debate and his opponent bowed
out. It wasn't hard for him to imagine the struggle young Krippner
was having. Rhine made things easier for him by offering to talk
alone, without an opposition speaker.

Publicity for Rhine's lecture evoked a fresh rash of anti-Rhine
propaganda. Strangely, the faculty members who ridiculed him most
were all liberal-minded and intelligent. The tenor of their criticism
can be judged by the remark of a professor to his class: "If you're
interested in ESP you might as well hear about it from the horse's
mouth—and from the biggest horse's ass of them all."[5]

One of Wisconsin's famous raging snowstorms had begun
when Rhine arrived on December 8, 1953. Krippner met him at the
railroad station, surprised to find this embattled scientist "a stocky
man with deep-set eyes and a mane of silver hair," who had a gentle
manner and good humor. Rhine was delighted to hear that philosophy professor Dr. A. Garnett probably the only member of the faculty
to believe in Rhine's work, would join them for dinner.

Krippner expected the lecture to be poorly attended. The
snowstorm was at its height. Many students were preparing for
examinations and there was a popular theatrical show in a nearby
building. Yet over a thousand students crushed into the hall, well past
its official capacity. The student who had agreed to introduce Rhine
backed out. He hoped to attend medical school and needed recom-
mendations from his psychology professors. He was afraid he would
not get them if he was too closely identified with Rhine. So Krippner
introduced Rhine.

"Rhine centered his talk around the themes of how new ideas

emerge in science, why they arouse dissent, and gave suggestions as to in what way they might be judged," Krippner wrote.

In the case of parapsychology, he simply asked that the data themselves be examined as well as the methods by which the data were obtained. . . . He urged the students to question traditional ways of thinking and hold fast to their convictions once they had been formed through reason and experience.[6]

Rhine received an ovation, and a few days later wrote to Krippner:

I had a good stirring time with the chemists in Chicago, although it was not nearly so exciting as my experience in Madison. In fact, I have not had more fun in years than I had up there with you folks.[7]

Only one psychology professor had turned up to meet Rhine after the lecture and then said nothing critical to his face. However, a week later the student newspaper quoted the professor as damning Rhine for throwing away data just below or just above chance and excusing it by saying the subject was not working properly. Krippner sent off a copy of this accusation to Rhine, who fired back that the professor's statement "would be, to the scientist, the most libelous thing that could be said; it would represent an implication of scientific dishonesty." Krippner kept the fire burning by forwarding the critical professor a copy of Rhine's letter. The professor was undaunted. Later, at a public forum chaired by Krippner, the psychologist stated that no one had replicated Rhine's work. Krippner responded that Rhine's basic results had been replicated by a dozen or more investigators throughout the world.[8]

There were more pro and con comments about Rhine by Krippner and the psychology professor in the months ahead. Rhine's lecture had aroused tremendous interest in his work and was heatedly discussed in various university classes for several months.

Krippner graduated from the University of Wisconsin in 1954 and afterward spent many days with the Rhines at their farm, where he met other members of the Parapsychology Laboratory, including Karlis Osis, W. E. Cox, and J. G. Pratt, learning from them—among other things—that parapsychology was a poorly paid and poorly funded profession.[9]

Krippner was at a parapsychology laboratory staff meeting in 1955 when news of another attack on Rhine was announced.

George Price, a medical researcher, had published an article in *Science*, official journal of the American Association for the Advancement of Science, that all but called Rhine a fraud. Price suggested that experimenter fraud was "the one explanation that is simplest and most in accord with everyday experience" to account for positive ESP and PK results. Price described several ways ESP test results by Rhine and S. G. Soal, the British parapsychologist who had once been a Rhine critic, could have been fudged to produce significant results.[10] Price's views were promoted by many other skeptics as the exposé from which parapsychologists would never recover.

Rhine's response was surprisingly calm. He announced he would write to Price and explain the laboratory's procedures, hoping that would counteract Price's charge. Rhine's patience paid off. Seventeen years later, in 1972, *Science* published a letter titled "Apology to Rhine and Soal," in which Price retracted his former statement.*[11]

During Krippner's visits to Duke, Louisa discussed her rapidly growing collection of letters, many from people relating apparently prophetic dreams. J. B. had first taken a scientific interest in dreams after Walter Franklin Prince told of his own prophetic nightmare. Prince had dreamed of a train smashing into another outside a tunnel. He woke with a cry of horror, the noise waking his wife. He told her of the dream. Later he read in a newspaper that about three hours after that dream an identical train crash had occurred about seventy miles from his home.[12]

Krippner eventually became first director of the Maimonides Dream Center, in which experiments with sleeping volunteers confirmed the anecdotal accounts of precognitive dreams Louisa had received.

---

*His apology was premature, in Soal's case. Strong evidence emerged later to show that Soal had in fact either faked or fudged his results.

38

DR. REMI CADORET
AND CHRIS
THE WONDER DOG
1950s

British parapsychologist Dr. R. H. Thouless tested himself for psychokinesis and got poor results. He thought the monotony of the work was to blame, so he enlivened the proceedings by reading poetry aloud as he continued the experiment, and his results improved dramatically as long as the poetry held his interest.*

An American parapsychologist working with Rhine stepped up the diversionary tactics. In 1952, Dr. Remi Cadoret was testing himself in DT (down through) experiments, attempting to read the signs on a pack of ESP cards from top card to bottom without moving them from the pack. He tried everything he could think of to make the task fresh and spontaneous—reciting poetry aloud and to himself, reading and reciting prose, singing out loud, and whistling while he worked. His aim, he says, was to keep "my mind off the task and the goal of scoring high, with its attendant anxieties." Normally, his scoring would be expected in time to decline—but while he kept up the concurrent diverting activities the scores stayed high.

Cadoret also took part in such diverse experiments as seeing whether people who claimed to be healers could speed wound-healing in mice (they could); whether hypnotized students would outscore nonhypnotized students at ESP tests (they did); and pioneering efforts to establish whether the activity of a subject's alpha brain waves was greater when he achieved positive ESP scores (it was).†

---

*Thouless, R. H., "A report on an experiment in psychokinesis with dice and a discussion on psychological factors favoring success," Proceedings of the Society for Psychical Research (1951), No. 49, pp. 107–130.
†Cadoret, R. J., "Effects of novelty in test conditions on ESP performance,"

Yale-trained Cadoret—a physician on the way to becoming a psychiatrist—was given a glimpse of the shape of things to come immediately on his arrival at Duke to join Rhine full-time.

He recalls:

Karlis Osis got booted out the same time I got there. I think Karlis and Malcolm Turner, a statistician, had gotten some of the data on distance ESP experiments and looked into it—and that really infuriated J.B.

The conclusion of Osis and Turner was that there appeared to be a slight physical effect on psi ability over distance—a decline, refuting Rhine's belief that psi is nonphysical and not affected by time or distance. Osis admits the decline effect could be of psychological origin, with the subjects expecting their powers to decline with distance.

"All I know," continues Cadoret,

is that when I got there—and this indicates J.B.'s Machiavellian propensity—knowing very little about anything, I was put on a committee. And the committee, composed of Gaither Pratt, Louisa Rhine and me, was to decide whether Karlis should be asked to leave the lab. The charge to the committee was that Karlis was guilty of something akin to high treason. It was never spelled out, but it was just that Karlis was disenchanted with the laboratory—Karlis must go.

The committee never all met together. Gaither would meet with me while we were out working in his garden.[Cadoret laughs at the memory.] It was really quite a farce, but I imagine what J.B. did was confront Karlis with the fact that "a committee of your peers has indicated that you'd better get out of here, boy!" And that's the way he operated.

I think what really got the Rhines was that Karlis had been writing letters indicating his unhappiness to people J.B. regarded as his staunch supporters. There was another possibility. Karlis had been talking to Mr. Ozanne, who used to come up to the lab regularly, and he and Karlis were buddy-buddies. And I think Karlis would tell Ozanne how he'd like to work on survival research and that was Ozanne's big bug. And he'd probably go in and give J.B. hell for not working on survival. It was very complicated, though. Karlis was kind of railroaded out of there.[1]

The Journal of Parapsychology (1952), No. 16, pp. 192–203. Fahler J., and Cadoret, R. J., "ESP cards tests of college students with and without hypnosis," J of P (1958), No. 22, pp. 125–36. Cadoret, R. J., "An exploratory experiment: Continuous EEG recording during clairvoyant cards tests," J of P (1964), No. 28, p. 226.

Cadoret first went to the parapsychology laboratory on a part-time basis after graduating from college in 1949.

I went down in February and left in June and found it extremely interesting. I did some research with Gaither Pratt and published a paper in 1950. Then I worked in the summer of 1950 for two months—between first and second year of medical school. And I was just fascinated with the field and research in the field.

Right after I finished interning in the summer of 1955, I was going to work there. I moved to Durham and accepted a position and then I had trouble with my draft board. They wanted me in the Air Force. That's why I went to the Air Force.

So I've been there [the parapsychology lab] on a number of occasions and every time I went, there had been almost a complete turnover of the males. I talked with J.B. about it and he always had a very plausible explanation—why somebody didn't fit in, or why they preferred another field. He's very good at that type of explanation.

When I first went there were just a couple of grad students [as well as Pratt and Osis] and they were very unhappy because it was so hard to get any kind of experiment through J.B.—he was so critical.

But aside from that, there was a very good spirit. Every Sunday we used to go to J.B.'s house. He had a big house and garden and we'd play baseball, sit around and talk. And then we'd get fed. It was a delightful way to spend an afternoon. We'd go out hiking—J.B.'s a great hiker—over hills, and when it comes to a river, he takes his clothes off and swims it. Walking with him was really good. It was a very, very pleasant experience.

There's a lot of macho about him—it's a very important part of his life. He splits wood, rides a tractor and does things that the rest of the MEN of the world do.

Most of the time he spent talking parapsychology. He's one of those people who breathes it 28 hours a day.[2]

When Rhine got word that a clever dog named Chris, who lived in East Greenwich, Rhode Island, had been trained by his owner to answer questions—and that his answers seemed to indicate ESP of a high order—Rhine eagerly discussed the mutt with his staff. He picked Remi Cadoret to test the dog.

Cadoret was an inept choice—even though the results he got indicated that Chris, to some extent, lived up to his reputation. He was a poor selection—perhaps dictated by a small staff—because Cadoret had no rapport with dogs. He was inclined to ignore them rather than to pet or make a fuss over them. Karlis Osis had already discovered and reported in his experiments with cats that they achieved better results when handled affectionately. Chris, a mongrel dog, communicated with humans by pressing his paw on their arms—twice for no, three times for yes. According to witnesses he accurately predicted the results of horse races, could tell the time, and two years before it happened, forecast the date of his own death. He was one day out. By all accounts he was the Lady Wonder of the dog world.

Rosemary Goulding, a neighbor of Mr. and Mrs. George H. Woods who owned Chris, was so bowled over by the dog's talent that she signed an affidavit that read: "During the first week of December 1957, I said, 'Chris, I want you to give me the winners of the first two races at Narragansett tomorrow. Now give me the post position of the winner in the first race.' "[3]

Chris pressed her arm three times. Asked for the post position of the second race winner, he pressed nine times.

The number three horse won in the first race by 3½ lengths. In the second race, the number nine horse, a long shot, came from behind to win by a nose. "Chris hit the daily double with odds of 144 against him," said Goulding in her affidavit.

Now an affidavit is not scientific evidence, but attests, at least, to the fervor Chris aroused in those who encountered him.

The dog's vet, Dr. Martin Kaplan, backs up Goulding.

I called him Chris the wonder dog. I had a horse getting ready for a race at the Suffolk Downs in Boston. Chris was my patient. He suffered a heart condition. He would not communicate with me in any way. He would have nothing to do with me, but he was very fond of my oldest son. He'd answer his questions.

In this case it was an important race with a horse that we had raised and we were anxious for the horse to do well. My son told Chris he had a horse running and asked would he win. Chris said, "No"—by tapping. "D'you think he'll come in second?" and Chris said, "No." "Third?" Chris said, "Yes."

On this occasion he came in third.

The horse, Mike Hudson, then ran in another important race. Chris said he'd win and he did. He was voted the best New England 2-year-old—the best horse I ever owned.[4]

Says Rosemary Goulding:

It's so incredible. I can't explain it. I can only report what I saw. I majored in psychology at Brown University, which is a behaviorist school, and, at first, I was very, very skeptical.

I had a professor, C. J. Ducasse, come down to see Chris and he got Duke interested.

I had known the Woods for several weeks before someone

said, "That's the dog you were so interested in." I had read some of the published accounts about him. And then I stayed and they showed me, and I was really amazed. Later the dog would work with me by himself. He worked with some people—not everybody, though.

Chris seemed to have a sense of humor, because he was asked what he thought about cats and he spelled out "d-u-m-b." When he was asked what he thought about himself, he spelled out "s-m-a-r-t." When asked how he did this, he'd always say, "S-m-a-r-t d-o-g."*

He was a mongrel, part beagle, a quiet, affectionate dog. An ordinary dog, you wouldn't think anything of him just to look at him. He didn't fight with other dogs. The only thing he did that I thought was so dog-like was that they couldn't get him to stop chasing cars. And he'd come in and you'd say, "Did you chase cars today?" And he'd always tell the truth and say "Y-e-s." When he was asked why, he'd answer, "F-u-n." He was the cutest dog, I'm telling you.

Some people were scared of him, when he was answering questions. The reactions of people were funny. I think myself, it almost seems to me like some kind of mutation. I did hear that the Russians had trained dogs like him, but I've never read anything on it.

The Woods never made a nickel out of Chris. They gave it all to the SPCA. They didn't want anyone to think they were exploiting Chris. How they got him was that some people moved out of the neighborhood and left Chris to them. He was terrible at first, just impossible, until they discovered his ability. He would run the house and act like a crazy person. One day somebody came in with a dog that she'd trained to count up to 10 or 12. Chris was sitting there watching and Marion Woods said to Chris, just for the fun of it: "Can you do that?"

And Chris came right over and counted to 10, by pressing his paw on her arm ten times. When George came home that night Marion told him and he didn't believe it. But it went from there to all kinds of things. George acted almost like a parapsychologist himself. He tried out everything and everything he tried, Chris could do. He got a big clock and set the time to see if Chris could tell time, and he could do it immediately.[5]

Dr. Cadoret came from the parapsychology lab to test Chris, and remembers him "as just a mutt about the size of a water spaniel. The Woods had a very close relationship with this dog and as a result of these unusual things, all kinds of people would be called in, and be associated with it. It was quite a socializing event when you had half a dozen people there working with the dog."[6]

---

*Using a tapping code for letters of the alphabet.

And how did Chris do when put to the scientific test? His results were good, indicating ESP powers to an exceptional degree.

When Cadoret tested Chris he apparently had a marked effect on the results. "The dog always consistently missed the answers when I was there," he says. "The hits were consistently below so that they would be expected to happen by luck only twelve times in one thousand such tests."[7]

Cadoret's explanation for Chris making a significant negative score in his presence "would be similar to when humans are asked to perform under conditions of high stress."[8]

Rosemary Goulding points to the cause for the stress.

He didn't become friendly with Chris. We'd say to Cadoret: "Go out for a walk with Chris and talk to him on the way. Do anything you want!" But he didn't test Chris as you or I would. He was always looking to see if there was anything wrong—treating him like a suspect. I certainly had no signals. A dog that's trained for the stage can't sustain an act for more than a few minutes; Chris would work for three or four hours."[9]

Says Cadoret:

I did take the dog for walks and I did feed it. To tell you the truth there are damned few dogs in the world that I warm up to. We have two dogs and cats. I don't dislike dogs. It just takes me a while to get on with them.[10]

Which might explain why Chris went into reverse when Cadoret was around.

Rhine, however, was pleased with the overall results and accepted the report for publication. It appeared in *The Journal of Parapsychology*, Vol. 22, No. 1, March 1958.

But what never appeared was the remarkable prediction Chris was said to have made about his own death. According to Rosemary Goulding,

Chris was asked when he was going to die—after he'd had a heart attack—and he tapped out on Mr. Woods's arm that he would die in 1962, then he tapped out June and then 10.

He missed by one day. He died on June 9 of that year.[11]

Cadoret found much of his work with Rhine exciting and unpredictable. He made one trip to California "to a poltergeist and as soon as I got there the poltergeist stopped poltering. I stayed for a week, but when it became evident that the manifestations weren't likely to happen, I departed."[12]

Then there was the time spent checking up on other researchers' possible mistakes or fraudulent results.

Rhine mistrusted a lot of results and he liked to check up on them in various ways. We spent most of the summer with Esther Foster, who's dead now, and a fellow named Ken Bates, who was one of the many guys who went through his lab and left after a short time, doing little else but analyzing the records [of experiments undertaken during the 1930s but never published] every which way, to determine whether they'd been fudged or not—just from internal evidence. The results were completely inconclusive.

J.B. was very leery about giving people free rein to do anything. You always had to talk over experimental designs with him. And when it came down to it, he would say he had the right to do that because, after all, he was dishing out the money.

If you didn't do it exactly his way there was considerable unpleasantness. And in your position at the university, you had no tenure. You served entirely at his wish. There was no control over him from the administration. He got his own money. It was just a wild situation.

I decided I didn't want to stay under those conditions and I so informed Dr. Rhine. He was very nice about it, writing to different people for a position for me. He made the initial contact with the medical school in Manitoba, where I went from Duke. The chairman of the department in Manitoba was quite interested in parapsychology and I did some work there, but gradually I got into other areas of research and today [1979] I'm in psychiatry full time.

I believe ESP was probably proved to exist before Dr. Rhine. The problem with it was and is that the conditions under which it appears are just not worked out. Once they are—fine.[13]

How does Cadoret the psychiatrist rate Rhine the man?

He was definitely outstanding. His great attributes were his religious fervor and tenacity and enjoyment of a fight. He always liked a good fight and he liked nothing more than when somebody was so publicity-conscious as to put it [the challenge to a fight] in a first-rate magazine and then he'd get on his white horse and slay the dragon.[14]

39

RHINE
AND HIS STAFF
1950s

When Rhine showed his staff that in a battle of wills there would be only one winner, and they were looking at him, they must have thought they were eyeball to eyeball with Rhine the marine rather than Rhine the scientist. He would make suggestions gently, but expected them to be carried out to the letter. The stubborn, do-it-my-way-or-else side to his character was rarely if ever witnessed by any but his young staff members. Others saw him as a charming, charismatic man—which he was, as well.

Those who dared to oppose him found that Rhine was prepared to escalate a skirmish "all the way up to atomic warfare," recalls Remi Cadoret, now a professor of psychiatry.[1] Depending on where you stood, this could be Rhine's strength or fatal flaw. Yet even his detractors agree that it was Rhine's single-mindedness and perseverance that kept parapsychology afloat and on a steady course when waves of the enemy tried to sink it. Though, these same critics will add, some of Rhine's sailors were put ashore seasick, vowing never to go to sea again.

Was he irrational and unreasonable to discourage his research assistants and associates from investigating less experimentally accessible subjects like life after death, reincarnation, out-of-body experiences, and the whole range of altered states of consciousness?* Was he wrong to be affronted and curt with a young man

---

*"I don't remember anybody fighting for UFOs or astrology—we had a united front on that," wrote Dr. Karlis Osis in a note to the author in January 1981. "Most troubles came from proposed research strategies and theories of ESP or PK, rather than the outlandish topics. The rebels often were on the more conservative side than J.B. Sometimes it was the reverse, sometimes they fought for newer methods in design and statistics."

found reading on the premises a book on esoteric mysticism? Some say he put the brakes on imagination.

But he had good reasons for doing so. Rhine was convinced that he must show parapsychology to be a legitimate scientific pursuit limited to investigations that could provide clear-cut, unambiguous results.

Not all his staff were prepared to meet his demands—and he would not tolerate opposition.

Betty Humphrey worked with Rhine for fourteen years, but when she allied herself with J. Fraser Nicol, a statistician and historian, her days were numbered. Nicol had been hired from Britain. Unfortunately he and Rhine saw eye to eye on practically nothing. A quiet-spoken Scot, Nicol was accustomed to speak his mind; and at staff meetings when Rhine invited questions, Nicol rarely hesitated. The other staff members used subtler or more devious methods to express their views or pursue their pet experimental projects. Nicol lasted ten months, and when he left, Humphrey went with him. They later married.

Humphrey recalls the almost comic-opera final days. "Fraser and I fell into disrepute because we disagreed with Rhine. Fraser and I were doing an experiment and we used a big stuffed antique chair from down the hall for the subjects to be more comfortable while calling cards. Rhine fired me three times in one week and Fraser and I were trying to carry on with the experiment, which was going quite well. And Rhine was particularly mad about something that morning and said: 'Turn your key in to the secretary before noon and get out!' And I said: 'We've got a subject coming in at one o'clock. Is it all right if we keep that appointment?" So he said: 'Yes, provided you turn your key in' [to the office]. The secretary was out to lunch, so I turned my key in to the other secretary. And Rhine asked where my key was. And the secretary he thought I had given it to—now back from lunch— didn't know anything about it. So Rhine was so mad he tried to wrestle this enormous stuffed chair out through this very narrow door. I said: 'What are you doing? You said we could have this subject.' He said: 'You didn't turn in your key.' I said I did, so he had to wrestle the chair back in, looking very sheepish."[2]

Rhine offered them both traveling fellowships—he would finance their work away from the lab—but they didn't accept. He even offered to send Nicol to Australia, where he could do research some distance from Rhine. That offer wasn't taken up either.

Humphrey worked for a short-time with Dr. Nicol under the wing of Dr. Gardner Murphy at the ASPR, then quit the field. She never returned to parapsychology, moving instead into mainstream psychology. So Rhine lost "the best research assistant I ever had."[3] Nicol became an expert on the history of parapsychology, taking a special interest in the pioneer days.

Osis left two years later, having worked with Rhine for five and a half years. "The animal psi experiments were Rhine's project and passion," he said. "When I was working on them, he was friendly and supportive. He set his sights high. What he really wanted from parapsychological research was to get at the roots of ESP or psi, find out how it really works, the basic nature of man in that respect. I think animal psi was one of his disappointments. A large part of his motivation to launch the project was that one could do with animals much more than you could do with humans. In humans, psi was so elusive, so hard to manipulate in experimental situations. So he thought he would get a better handle on it by using animals. It turned out that animals were just as difficult.

"It would be wrong to say that Rhine turned down new ideas, but he certainly wanted to shine in his own place; he wouldn't be outshone by anyone else. We used to say as a joke that we had a policy: Make a big noise about a new idea, and then Rhine will probably turn it down. Now you wait for half a year or so—he will forget about you but not the idea, which will be presented as his own. We certainly always fought for our projects—but we lost often. Usually, when you put the dog on the track of the rabbit and he smells rabbit, he runs like mad. When experiments worked that well, for some reason or other Rhine used to take us out and put us on a different track. I don't know why he did so."[4]

Rhine, of course, simply believed the experiments were getting nowhere, and that the researcher could be more productively employed.

"There were quite often tensions and strong conflicts in the lab," said Osis. "But in one sense Rhine was always on the right track: He insisted on good precautions against sensory leakage. This is where he had had the most flak [in previous experiments] and he was very, very insistent on it, even to make somebody bitter who wanted to be more freewheeling."[5]

Rhine saw survival research as premature. Osis disagreed. "Rhine actively discouraged work on this. He thought the likelihood of survival after death to be merely a remote possibility," says Osis, who thought it was very well worth pursuing. So, on that very basic issue, he disagreed with Rhine. They had another source of conflict. "Rhine is an impulsive personality, despite his sticking-to-itiveness in daily work. And he had many strong opinions as a scientist, insisting on his own interpretation of our data. That was quite often the cause of our differences."[6]

Over twenty years after leaving Rhine, having devoted much of that time to survival research, first for Eileen Garrett and presently for the American Society for Psychical Research, Osis can see him perhaps more objectively, his emotions recollected in tranquillity. "I think Rhine was a very important person in parapsychology, but he was not quick enough to see his dominating role was over after the late fifties. Despite the negative and colorful side, I feel in retrospect the positive will stand out greatly, and that's how he'll be remembered. That's how I try to remember him. When you have a colorful personality and a very strong drive in a person like him, you always have a negative side, too. But without the strong drive to organize which he had, it's probably not possible to succeed in parapsychology.

"You probably encountered different kinds of ex-Duke people, and I am one who is not emotional. I think I have a pretty good understanding about Rhine. We usually all were quite emotional when we left. At one time I was bitter, but I think I graduated out of that.

"He was colorful, he cast a large shadow, and he had a lot of strengths. He was a great man. He had some trouble in regard to relations with his personnel, but he was a genius at Kissinger-type relationships—to influence people who were far away, and able to stimulate researchers in so many places to work on ESP. I think that was his genius."[7]

The secret of having a smooth long-term relationship with Rhine was never to join his staff. Parapsychologists who kept in touch with him by mail and frequently visited him at his home and lab have unclouded, almost idyllic memories of the man.

40

THE FIRE BUILDER
1953–1955

Rhine's warm, friendly, caring letters still had the power to attract people to work with him, among them an undergraduate at Syracuse University, Robert Van de Castle, who was thrilled in the early 1950s when the parapsychologist gave him an assignment.

Van de Castle's task was to determine if a lost dog had found its way home after making a journey of thousands of miles. The owners, a Syracuse family, had lost the dog in Fort Lauderdale, while vacationing in Florida. Nine months later, the SPCA in Syracuse picked up a dog covered in burrs, whose pads were almost worn away. When a local paper ran an item about him, several families turned up at the SPCA kennels, hoping he was their missing dog. He ignored them all until the Syracuse family that had lost their dog in Florida arrived. Then he leaped over a fence, greeted them ecstatically and, most significantly, bounded up onto their pickup truck to sit in the place where their dog had always traveled. He looked like an exhausted replica of their dog. But "looked like" was not good enough for Rhine. If the dog had traveled thousand of miles and found his way home, then it would be a spectacular example of psi trailing, as Rhine called such an apparent ESP ability of animals. He wanted to make sure that was the case.

What would Rhine consider adequate proof? It had already been established that the lost and the found dog were the same breed, dimensions, and color—with photographs as evidence. That was only partial proof, said Rhine. He understood the dog lost in Florida had previously suffered a broken leg; and assumed its vet would have an X ray photograph of that break. If Van de Castle could get an X ray of the same leg of the recently found dog, and it revealed an identical break in the same spot, that would be as close to proof as Rhine could expect.

Van de Castle believed he was about to make a valuable

contribution to the psi-trailing mystery when the family let him see the dog and showed photographs of the one they had lost in Florida. The two dogs looked remarkably alike. Now all Van de Castle had to do was obtain an X ray of the dog's leg. But to his great disappointment, the family refused to allow it; saying that they had been harassed by strange mail since the story of their dog had been published and balked at doing anything that might bring them renewed publicity.

So once more, the vital clue to establish the fact of psi trailing evaded the researcher. Rhine, as disappointed as Van de Castle, applauded his efforts and encouraged him to pursue ESP experiments with a three-hundred-dollar grant and "keep at it!" letters. Recently married, the young student used his wife as a subject. He asked her to guess hidden colors and hidden names, and she scored high. Although he suspected his controls were inadequate, he submitted a report of the experiment to Rhine. It was Van de Castle's very first attempt at a scientific experiment. Rhine published it in the *Journal of Parapsychology* in 1953, and Van de Castle was hooked.

Rhine's support strengthened the student's resolve to write on ESP for his master's thesis at the University of Missouri, over the protests of several teachers. He was getting a hint of the academic roadblocks Rhine had had to clear or maneuver around.

When Van de Castle began to look for a job and found that his master's thesis on ESP was not an "open sesame" to a career, Rhine came to the rescue. He had been in contact with a professor at a Florida university, a man self-described as head of a productive department involving both biological and psychological experiments. This professor had reported positive results in ESP experiments and a possible breakthrough in a cancer cure. Did he have room for a bright young man in his department? Rhine asked. He did. Could Van de Castle continue ESP research there? He could. Van de Castle was hired. His salary was low, but Rhine helped with a thousand-dollar grant to support the work.

Van de Castle soon realized that the professor was either a scoundrel or a psychopath. He had described his staff as seventeen full-time chemists and biologists, when all he had was Van de Castle, a part-time secretary, and a part-time biologist. He was engaged in shady deals with state senators, promoting a phony cure for cancer, and reporting success in ESP experiments with fake scores. This was Van de Castle's first traumatic encounter with the frauds that haunt and discredit parapsychology.

He had access to the documents revealing the rip-off professor's involvement in the bogus cancer cure. On an attorney's advice, Van de Castle made Xerox copies of those documents and took them to the college president, expecting to be thanked for exposing corruption. Instead, the president shakily telephoned the professor and urgently requested his presence. Conversation stalled until the professor arrived, and then he and the president turned on Van de Castle as if he were the criminal.

In shock, he wrote to Rhine a full account of the Florida fiasco and was immediately offered a job at Duke. To Van de Castle it seemed like going to Mecca. Until then Rhine had been a tremendously important, almost fantastic figure from afar, a man he admired extravagantly who had never failed to help and encourage him. He arrived, "enthusiastic, involved and motivated."[1]

The professor bombarded Van de Castle with letters demanding the return of the incriminating Xerox-copied evidence. Rhine advised Van de Castle to return it, saying: "Let's not make waves. We have enough problems in the field."[2] Although he saw it as capitulation, Van de Castle returned the material. He was pleased at least to know Rhine had broken off with the professor, and had ensured that reports of the man's ESP experiments were never published in parapsychological journals.

This was Van de Castle's first disillusionment with Rhine—he had expected him to denounce and fight the professor in a showdown. Rhine could have spent most of his time in crossing swords with the fraudulent and foolish who falsely claimed positive ESP results, but it would have been like asking a relay runner to stop and help put out brushfires. His first priority was always his own work. Nothing, if he could help it, was allowed to disturb that. His and Louisa Rhine's seven-day-a-week devotion to parapsychology was a fact of life to their children. Betsy, the middle daughter, had it brought home one Sunday when Professor McDougall's son Angus called and was told both her parents were working. "What?" he said, "on Sunday? Don't they know that thunder will strike them if they work on Sunday!"

Although Van de Castle had apotheosized Rhine from afar, at close quarters he resisted joining the several hero-worshipping women who surrounded Rhine and called him boss.

To Van de Castle's dismay, the friendly letter writer seemed a Jekyll and Hyde character who became, in the lab, "opinionated and authoritarian, ruling with an iron hand. Everyone was behaving in a paranoid fashion, walking around on eggshells and feeling that to hold a conversation, they had to close the door." Rhine ran the lab "by divide and conquer methods, saying to each one of us that because the work was so important and he wanted things to run smoothly we should tell him if anyone wasn't working effectively or was gossiping mischievously."[3]

Van de Castle did not help matters at the weekly meetings, when he rhapsodized over the work of other parapsychologists like

Gardner Murphy and Gertrude Schmeidler, implying their contributions were more important than Rhine's.

The famous medium Eileen Garrett provided lighter moments when she visited Duke. Van de Castle saw her as "a charismatic figure with a mischievous smile, someone you felt really had a lot of power. When she was in a room she'd dominate it."[4]

Another parapsychologist, W. E. Cox, met Eileen Garrett at Duke and "enjoyed very much hearing her reminisce about the old days. Once she put her hand on Rhine's knee and said: 'Oh, couldn't we have a wonderful romp in the Elysian fields if we were younger! Mrs. Rhine took it with equanimity, knowing the two of them were over the hill."[5]

But Van de Castle found lighter moments too rare to make life tolerable.

Rhine could be devastating in his criticisms of his staff—and his harsh words sent some of them off into different fields forever. Van de Castle decided to quit after Rhine called him to his office and blasted his work as "the biggest catastrophe" they carried out in the lab. Exasperated, Van de Castle replied: " 'This is something I've had to say to you for a long time; I really don't like the way you've treated me. You're overbearing, and I'm leaving with a feeling of relief and liberation. 'Or words to that effect."[6]

Rhine sat quietly listening to Van de Castle, waited for a few moments until Van de Castle had obviously finished, and said: "Okay, go ahead and leave, then."[7]

And that was it.

From the retrospect of twenty-five years Van de Castle saw Rhine in perspective: "He had an extraordinary talent for writing very supportive, meaningful letters. And he was a bold pioneer. Here was this man, despite all these unknowns and all these mysteries, who kept plugging away, trying to unravel them. I have great respect for his intellectual qualities. I think that his ego and that authoritarianism allowed him to keep going despite a lot of adversity and criticism, and he hung in there under fire and just kept moving forward."[8]

Some of the staff made excuses for Rhine's tough tactics. They admitted that he was very much ego-involved in whatever he tackled, but thought that was in his favor, and not a flaw. He had a lot of problems, not the least being lack of money, yet, say his boosters, he never refused to help or advise them.

Margaret Anderson and Rhea White were at Duke when Van de Castle was there and shared similar experiences. Dr. Anderson with Rhea White decided to take Van de Castle's advice and "bootleg" an experiment they wanted to do involving schoolchildren and teachers, without Rhine's approval. When Rhine went to the California

coast for three months for the secret experiments with dogs or to
England to lecture, Gaither Pratt was in charge of the lab. Then
researchers were freer to do what they wanted.

Rhine had previously discouraged Anderson's project as too
ambitious. "Do pilot experiments first," he told her. She and Rhea
White took advantage of his absence to conduct the experiment and
got good results. "And then, of course, it was great," says Rhea White.
"He wanted us to repeat it and he wrote and talked about it. This was
because it had worked. And he forgot all about the fact that he hadn't
wanted us to do it."[9]

Their tests indicated that where there was a mutual good
feeling between teacher and pupil, psi scores by the children were
above chance; where there was not, scores were below chance.
"Teacher-Pupil Attitudes and Clairvoyance Test Results," by Margaret
Anderson and Rhea White, was published in the *Journal of Parapsychology*, September 1956. Results included this dramatic comment:
"One of the scheduled teachers was unable to take part in the
experiment because a fire destroyed the high school in which she was
teaching." Dr. Gertrude Schmeidler suggests that the partial failure to
replicate this research is because

*... while Anderson in her early studies was able to create a feeling of
enthusiastic but pleasantly relaxed interest in the ESP experiment
among the teachers she recruited, we cannot be sure that other
experimenters were able to do so. The teachers' attitudes toward the
experiment were an uncontrolled variable.*[10]

Dr. Anderson was struck by Rhine's enthusiasm. She had
never seen anything like it. He was excited and encouraging in the
early days; the work was going well and they had no disagreements.

"I was with him for four years. He was a very virile man and a
very handsome man," said Dr. Anderson. "He sawed his own wood
with a chain saw and built the biggest fire I ever saw—way up to the
top of the fireplace. He had a lovely, charming home life. He had a
sense of humor. He could laugh—but I doubt if he could laugh at
himself. If he heard criticism, he handled it in such a way that it
didn't bother him. Louisa—there was the strength behind the man.

"The one big argument I had with J. B. Rhine was that I
always thought the role of the experimenter was never given enough
attention. It's almost axiomatic—if you're doing an experiment, the
experimenter is part of the act. Rhine never wanted to talk about it. I
was always told that my suggestion for an experiment to discover
'What is the role of the experimenter?' was an unworthy, stupid
idea."[11]

Rhea White "was very impressed with Rhine as a man of

integrity, with a will of iron and a mind of his own—to the point of inflexibility. He and I had a lot of conversations on the importance of the experimenter. So did Margaret Anderson. One of my major interests is that the experimenter is a catalyst making psi appear in the experimental situation. Rhine often used the analogy that you can put a rabbit in the oven, but unless you turn it on, it's not going to cook. And an experimenter is the one whose personality is the catalyst that creates the heat, that makes the rabbit cook. We would also talk of ways to interest the subject in the experiments. But here's the contradiction. He was always talking and writing about the importance of the experimenter, but when it came to other people's ideas about it, it was very hard to get through to him.

"Everybody who went to the lab would talk about the magnetism of the man, through correspondence or meeting him in person, and of his holding up all the ideals. But when it came right down to it, he seemed to go against them rather than for them—more a case of closed-mindedness than anything else.

"In Freudian terms he was the father figure, and all the sons especially who came had a hard time with him—a matter of trying to topple him off the mountain, I guess. And they would leave. They would come, they would have their own ideas—which in many cases we all thought were very good—and they'd want to carry out their own projects, and they wouldn't be allowed to. Or they had to change them more in line with what Rhine thought was right.

"If I had to use one word to characterize Rhine, it would be *single-minded*."[12]

Rhea White's characterization of Rhine, single-minded, was a quality Aldous Huxley admired in him: his dogged refusal to be deterred from his goals.

Aldous Huxley revisited the lab for a few days in October 1954, and Dr. Anderson, Rhea White, and Van de Castle took turns to have breakfast with him and discuss their work.

Rhine had persuaded Huxley to give a talk to the English department at Duke on visionary experiences.* The largest hall on the campus was packed. It was an unusually warm night for October—during the day the temperature reached ninety-seven degrees—and Huxley was dressed in winter woolens. Before the lecture Rhine suggested to Huxley that he should take off his jacket, but the writer had retained some of his English feeling that that sort of thing was not done in public. So Rhine took the chairman aside "and asked him to lead the way by taking off his own coat," Rhine recalled for Sybille Bedford, who published the account in her 1974 biography of Aldous Huxley. "And there, with that university audience (of pre-hippie days

---

It became the basis of his book Heaven and Hell.

at that) the two men marched onto the lecture platform with their jackets over their arms. It put everyone at ease immediately, and anyhow, the audience was completely captivated. Aldous was a person, as you know, whom it was easy to like spontaneously. His gentle dignity and a suggestion of frailty, that perhaps came from his vision, made one lean a little his way in a helpful attitude. . . . I myself was deeply impressed by the hold which he had upon that audience."[13]

Rhine's considerate gestures, as in the case of the Huxley jacket, endeared him to many who saw only that side of him. It was as much a part of the man as his iron will.

After his lecture at Duke, Aldous Huxley wrote to Rhine on December 12, 1954, praising the parapsychologist's scientific approach to his work, and adding:

I am appalled by the superstitious passion for marvels displayed even by intelligent and well-educated men. I am thinking of a doctor friend of ours who, through a medium, consults his defunct professors and obtains from them, naturally enough a complete confirmation of his own views about medicine and treatment! And I know of others who have just gone off, on a tip by the spirits, to look for buried treasure in Arizona—in the teeth of the statement, in every serious history of the Southwest, that the aborigines did no mining and the early Jesuits and Franciscans either none or very little. Needless to say, no appeal to facts or reason is of any avail. A large percentage of the human race . . . get so much fun out of their mental derangement that they don't want, at any cost, to be cured.[14]

Huxley did not doubt that there was an extrasensory element in man, but neither he nor Rhine could persuade most American psychologists that psi was a vivid and vital fact of life.

Van de Castle had lasted only one year with Rhine. Anderson and White both stayed for four years. All remained in parapsychology. Van de Castle is today director of the Sleep and Dreams Laboratory at the University of Virginia Medical Center, Charlottesville. White became director of information for the ASPR. Anderson works with parapsychologist Dr. R. A. McConnell at the University of Pittsburgh.

Rhine's fire-building propensity, as remarked by Dr. Anderson, suggests an obvious but compelling metaphor for the man himself. At a distance the glow and light and warmth attracted and delighted many; close to it, some of them were burned, or overcome by smoke.

If Rhine was an ordeal by fire, those who survived were better scientists for it. His lessons were painfully unforgettable.

41

REINCARNATION
AND BRIDEY MURPHY
1952–1956

Rhine was ambivalent about the use of hypnosis for psi experiments. He knew it was a promising tool, but feared there were too many unknown factors involved when hypnosis was used. Hypnosis itself was almost as mysterious and inexplicable as psi. Morey Bernstein, one of Rhine's correspondents, engaged in spectacular experiments with hypnosis. Though Rhine might have discouraged them in his own staff, he gave Bernstein his cautious support. Bernstein was at first interested in using hypnosis to diminish pain. When he had seen a man in a trance show no pain as a needle was stuck through his hand, Bernstein thought, "My God, if that's true, then the mind must be separate from the body." Doubtless many men have launched creative and productive careers on equally slender evidence.

After learning how to hypnotize, Bernstein volunteered to control the pain of his friends and neighbors. Local doctors at the state hospital in Pueblo, Colorado, heard of his ability as a hypno-therapist and asked him to help them. As a prosperous Pueblo businessman he willingly gave his services free.

Bernstein had a chance to display his business acumen and prolific ideas when he and his wife spent several days at Duke in 1952. Rhine responded enthusiastically and asked Bernstein to be his creative financier, money being perhaps a more urgent necessity at that time than ideas. But Bernstein wasn't interested. He suggested a telepathic experiment in which sender and receiver should be hypnotized. Great idea, thought Rhine, but advised Bernstein to be careful.[1]

The novel telepathic experiment brought no breakthrough information, and Bernstein resumed his therapeutic work, effectively treating several people suffering from psychosomatic illnesses. He developed what seemed like a wild theory, that such illnesses had their origin not only in childhood, as a Freudian might believe, but in the prenatal period. He knew of the apparent ability of people under hypnosis to go back in time to their childhood and reexperience it— what hypnotists called age regression. And when a local young woman named Virginia Tighe came to him for hypnotic treatment to cure her allergies, Bernstein decided to "take her back in time." He put her in a trance and led her back progressively to age one. Then he took a pioneering step—he asked her to imagine herself even further back in time and space. "There are other scenes from faraway lands and distant places in your memory. . . . Now you're going to tell me what scenes came into your mind," he said. "What did you see?" In a whispered and sleepy Irish brogue, Virginia Tighe identified herself as what Bernstein mistakenly thought was Friday Murphy. But later it became clear. She was Bridey Murphy, she announced, born in Ireland in 1798 and died there at sixty-six in 1864.

In six tape-recorded sessions over eleven months, Bridey revealed her life in Ireland 150 years before, then told of her existence after death, in which she escaped purgatory, and "lived" in a boring world where she never ate nor slept, where she rejoined friends and relatives who had died before her, but where there was nothing much to do—except wait to be reincarnated.[2]

Bernstein published the tapes of the age-regression sessions, *The Search for Bridey Murphy*, in 1956, and it became a controversial and much-discussed book, still in print twenty-six years later.

Rhine's *Parapsychology Bulletin* for April 1956 gave it a brief notice:

One of the current best sellers is The Search for Bridey Murphy *by Morey Bernstein (Doubleday). This is an account of what was told by a young woman under hypnosis who was asked to go back in time to a period preceding her own birth. She described what appeared to be a previous existence as an Irish girl, Bridey Murphy, who was born in 1798. Most of the book is Bridey's story, but there is also a series of appendices containing a quantity of straightforward information about parapsychology and the scientific investigations in the field.*

The Chicago *American* implied the book was a hoax, Bernstein a fraud, and that Virginia Tighe was merely relating details of her young life and stories she heard as a child. The Denver *Post* challenged the Chicago *American* exposé, saying that having checked many of the things Tighe (Bridey) had said about life in Ireland a century ago, they found her to be accurate.

When Eileen Garrett persuaded leading parapsychologists to

address the problem for her publication, *Tomorrow*, the experts acted like blind men standing at different vantage points and describing an elephant by touch.

Psychoanalyst George Devereux suggested the event was a cover for romantic passion, and that the married Virginia Tighe was unconsciously trying to disguise her love for Bernstein.

Psychiatrist Dr. Jan Ehrenwald wanted to know who was kidding whom and quoted a noted pre-Freudian Viennese psychiatrist, Professor Wagner Jauregg, "who looked askance at the couch whenever it was used for any purpose other than a legitimate afternoon nap." Jauregg was equally suspicious of hypnosis administered to a vertical or horizontal subject. Ehrenwald believed Bernstein's own emotionally charged interests were telepathically induced in his hypnotized subject.

Psychologist Gardner Murphy admitted there might be some paranormal elements, but otherwise it was typical of autosuggestion. In other words, the woman had imagined her life in Ireland.

Psychoanalyst Dr. Geraldine Pederson-Krag thought Virginia Tighe had been indulging in a lifelong fantasy life, consciously or unconsciously, and Bridey Murphy was just part of it.

Rhine had expert knowledge of hypnosis: "I am glad the question has been raised as to whether the technique of hypnotic regression *could* provide a reliable answer to the question of reincarnation," he wrote.

I do not see how it could. No one has by that method so far come up with any reliable evidence that, in my judgment, even suggests the reincarnation hypothesis. There is always the problem of really knowing to what the hypnotized subject has been exposed throughout her own life, what traces of memory there may be. Then, on top of that, it is not easy to see a limit to the possibilities there may be for the subject to draw upon sources of knowledge beyond the senses or ESP, for he is under pressure to give the hypnotist the sort of story the hypnotist has suggested when he talked about earlier incarnations. . . . More interesting evidence would be a clear case of the presentation in hypnotic regression (or trance) of a really fluent and reliable knowledge of a foreign language, especially a more remote tongue and even an archaic form of it, which would be extremely interesting if properly recorded and studied by competent experts.[3]

Bernstein did not claim Bridey Murphy was absolute proof of reincarnation, but evidence that might point the way to further exploration. Of the thousands of age-regression experiments he has studied since, he has never come across a superior one.[4]

Virginia Tighe, now Mrs. Ginni Morrow, giving a talk to members of the Texas Society for Psychical Research on November 7, 1976, told how, after she was identified as "Bridey Murphy," harassing phone calls forced her to change her phone number thirteen times in three months. But she was grateful that through Bernstein's hypnosis she had obtained physical relief from her allergies.

Does Ginni Morrow believe she was Bridey Murphy in another life?

"I'm slowly finding that I'm a believer more than a non-believer in reincarnation," she says.

"*Life* magazine [March 19, 1956] did an excellent article about the whole matter," concludes Bernstein, "then they followed it on the last page by a so-called 'fact page.' Every goddamn one of their facts that refutes Bridey is factless. It's plain, old-fashioned B.S. And I proved it. It's in Chapter Twenty of my new counterattack edition of *The Search for Bridey Murphy.*"

A leading parapsychologist, Dr. Ian Stevenson, Carlson Professor of Psychiatry; director, Division of Parapsychology, Department of Psychiatry at the University of Virginia Medical Center, takes a special interest in reincarnation. He gives Bridey Murphy high marks, writing:

The hypnotized subject mentioned recondite details about life in Ireland of which it seems extremely unlikely that she could have had normal knowledge. This case has not been improved upon in the many books since written for the general public that have reported experiments with hypnotic regression. Most of these contain absurd anachronisms and other solecisms. Nevertheless, the few substantial results from the use of hypnosis in such experiments justify a more extensive exploration of the technique with better controls. [5]

Well aware of Stevenson's views Rhine, in his quest, stuck to a narrower and firmer path.

42

THE PARAPSYCHOLOGICAL ASSOCIATION 1957

For twenty years Rhine had conducted and encouraged scores of successful psi experiments at Duke and other universities in the United States and abroad. Yet many scientists ignored the findings or supported Dr. Price's view that positive results could only be explained by experimenter fraud. Parapsychologists had resented this charge when it first appeared in the pages of *Science* and discovered to their annoyance that the editor of the official publication of the American Association for the Advancement of Science would not print their angry rebuttals.

Rhine thought to make use of this first sign of unity among parapsychologists. He believed that a group effort might, among other things, help to get parapsychology accepted as a legitimate scientific pursuit. During a summer workshop at Duke in 1957, Rhine proposed the formation of an international association of professional parapsychologists. His staff, visiting students, and scholars thought it a great idea, and agreed that the *Journal of Parapsychology* should be the affiliated publication.

On June 19 Dr. R. A. McConnell was made first president of the new Parapsychological Association; Dr. Gertrude Schmeidler, vice-president; and Rhea White, secretary-treasurer. Rhine staffers, past and present, formed the rest of the council—Dr. Margaret Anderson, Dr. Remi Cadoret, Dr. Karlis Osis, and W. G. Roll.

The stated aim of the association was "to advance parapsychology as a science, to disseminate knowledge of the field, and to integrate the findings with those of other branches of science," on a worldwide basis.[1] The members soon showed that they would keep each other informed and in line; clip the wings of those who tried to fly too fast, too soon; pounce on the fuzzy-minded; yet generally present a united but democratic front against critics. They felt free to attack, defend, and encourage each other. They also assured potential recruits that parapsychology, though still embattled and derided, was an expanding field of promise and opportunities, especially in universities.

One hundred and three joined the association the first year. This group, smaller than the staff of a physics department at a medium-sized university, represented most of the world's active, full-time parapsychologists, with the exception of those working in Communist countries.

Although Rhine was absorbed in his work, he was very much a man of the immediate world. He had been deeply affected by an article in *Life* magazine revealing the traumatic early days of school integration. Photographs showed black children being threatened by a mob of whites outside a schoolhouse. Rhine's letter in response was published in the magazine on September 30, 1957, under the heading *The Children's Crusade*. It was prefaced by an editorial explanation:

One of our readers, Professor J. B. Rhine of Duke University—the famous experimenter in extrasensory perception—has written us a letter urging us to write an editorial. But his letter is such a fine editorial in itself that we prefer to let him speak:

"Thank you for recording for history the account in words and pictures of these brave Negro kids going off to face the mob waiting for them at the schoolhouse. Brave they must be, for they know they will be taunted with abuse that will hurt more than physical injury itself. But still they dare not strike back or even reply, for they all know that a lad of their age was murdered in Mississippi for merely whistling at a white woman. It is not as though they were worked up to it. The desperate courage of the storming of the Bastille and the riots of Poznan burst spontaneously from the ignition of group emotion. But these children have to walk calmly and coolly out to meet tormenting and humiliating attacks that hurt the very soul. I cannot recall that there has ever been a more inspiring demonstration of courage by the children of any race, in any age. Open, then, if you will, your editorial page to these courageous youngsters of America! Their example is at least one redeeming feature in all this horrid chapter of our country's history. Salute them and I think others will take heart and go over and stand beside them. It may help us to believe this is the home of the brave, perhaps more than it is the land of the free."

43

SONG OF THE SIREN
1958–1960

Stanley Krippner often recalled with relish how Rhine crossed the storm-swept campus at the University of Wisconsin in 1953, strode past the frigid faculty, and gave a lively, reasoned lecture that brought the audience in the packed hall to its feet, muffling even the storm with almost wild applause. Rhine must surely have won some adherents then, converted some skeptics to at least an agnostic position, persuaded a few to read his reports. Five years later Krippner was a graduate student at Northwestern University, still engaged in booking provocative speakers. He knew that the psychology department generally regarded the father of parapsychology as an aberration, but Krippner felt they could not help but be impressed by him if Rhine talked to them. Would he be willing to address another college crowd containing hostile elements probably out to humiliate him? Rhine would.

Several members of the education department accepted invitations to meet Rhine at a dinner for him before the lecture. But the psychologists made it known that they would ostracize him. Some were intimidated, no doubt, by their chairman, who announced that anyone dining with Rhine would be a disgrace to the department. Two brave souls went anyway. One of them had an engrossing discussion with Rhine, during which he listed three reasons for his skepticism: Different researchers couldn't be guaranteed to produce identical results; he knew of no mechanism to explain psi; and Rhine's claim that distance did not effect telepathy violated the physical law that an effect diminishes in a predictable proportion over distance.

This irrefutable criticism did not prevent the dinner from being a stimulating and friendly affair, nor did it cause Rhine to recant: All these things, he believed, were puzzling aspects of psi which did not obey known laws. One of the two psychologists at the dinner, Professor Donald Campbell, was later elected president of the American Psychological Association. Rhine's lecture again was a rousing affair. It rekindled Krippner's interest in parapsychology and he became a volunteer investigator.

Rhine phoned Krippner in 1960 to ask if he would look into reports of poltergeist phenomena in the nearby town of Guttenberg, Iowa, where the home of an elderly couple was subject to explosions, as well as furniture that flew through the air of its own volition, or so it seemed. A sailor who had stayed with the couple claimed that as he lay in bed his mattress rose in the air, throwing him to the floor. And he weighed 265 pounds.

Krippner and a fellow student, Arthur Hastings, arrived at the house after it had been tramped through by the curious and by acquisitive souvenir hunters. The gawkers and collectors had been followed by physicists and geologists who used a whole range of instruments from an ion counter and an oscilloscope to a Geiger counter and argon radiation counter, in a vain attempt to pin down the cause of the phenomena.

Both Krippner and Hastings took a simpler approach. By questioning the old couple and their grandson who took care of them, the investigators established where the three of them were when most of the poltergeist outbreaks occurred. The old couple remembered each occasion vividly although they were rarely close to the disturbances they witnessed. The grandson, on the other hand, was always suspiciously near the trouble spot, or couldn't remember where he had been at the time of the outbreak. If anyone had faked the phenomena, he was clearly the one.

But if the grandson were responsible for the explosions and flying furniture—using normal and not supernormal force—what was his motive? Krippner and his partner discovered that before he became virtually a babysitter for his grandparents, the young man had lived a carefree, fun-filled existence. When the old couple fled the intimidating home, their grandson was free to resume his life of leisure. That was the simplest explanation for what had happened, except that it failed to account for the sailor guest and his flight on the flying mattress. Gullible or careless investigators had taken his word for it. But Krippner and Hastings questioned him more thoroughly and eventually learned from him that the night he was thrown from the bed his supper consisted of several bottles of beer. The pair concluded that any spirits in the house that night had been inside the sailor and the rest of the poltergeist activity had been fraudulently engineered by the grandson. They also learned to treat mysteries of this kind critically, looking first for simple answers, rather than gullibly accepting the accounts of witnesses and launching a full-scale investigation with modern instruments.

Rhine approved of their methods and agreed with their conclusions. They had, after all, conducted the investigation as he would have done.

If Krippner had any criticism of Rhine, it was that he tended to be overly cautious, wary not only of the genuineness of reported psi phenomena but of the capability or integrity of the researchers.

I know one case of a student who came up with very suspicious-looking statistics and Rhine gave him the heave-ho. At the time, in one way, I was very alarmed because I thought it might have been an innocent error on the student's part. But, on the other hand, I was very impressed, and glad that Rhine wasn't going to let something like this get by.[1]

Rhine's friendly, encouraging, and scientific attitude more than anything else caused Krippner to follow the song of the siren and become a parapsychologist. He thinks of Rhine as a great man who "through perseverance, brought modern parapsychology into the so-called scientific age."[2]

While Krippner was enthusiastically working for Rhine, another psychologist arrived at Duke. He had come from Britain to conduct an investigation that called into question one of the most important ESP experiments, raising the ugly specter of fraud.

44

A SPY IN THE CAMP
1960

A British psychologist put parapsychology to the test in 1960 in a way that irked Rhine and outraged some of his colleagues. The psychologist, Dr. C. E. M. Hansel, behaved more like a spy in enemy territory than what he was—an invited guest. He had accepted Rhine's offer to examine experiments at the laboratory, one of which was the Pearce-Pratt experiment. Hansel's purpose was to demonstrate reasons for disbelieving in ESP. His method of investigation was unorthodox but effective; and judging from the flak it produced, Hansel's raid was parapsychology's Pearl Harbor.

In the Pearce-Pratt distance tests conducted from 1933 to 1934, Pearce had achieved phenomenal and unmatched success. By 1960 it was almost a legend in parapsychological circles. Accounts in Rhine's *Journal* and books indicated that Pearce had stayed in a cubicle in the Duke library while the experimenter, Gaither Pratt, first worked from a room in a different building 100 yards away and then in one 250 yards off. Rhine and Pratt claimed that Pearce's almost unbroken run of high scoring was striking evidence for psi, because the design and execution of the experiment had eliminated any other possible explanation. Hansel did not take their word for it and set out to show how they could have been fooled.

Dr. Hansel's attitude was reasonable. He pointed out that so much fraud and error had been uncovered in psychical research that until a watertight experiment which ruled out such factors had been undertaken, claims to have demonstrated ESP could not be taken seriously.[1]

Hansel listed the requirements Rhine and Pratt had drawn up for a conclusive experiment:

1. Sound measurement.
2. Satisfactory safeguard against normal sensory communication.

3. Care in recording. The responsibility of recording data should be shared between two responsible persons in such a way that no error made by either could go undetected.

4. Precautions against deception on the part of the experimenters themselves.

Then Hansel tried to show that Rhine and Pratt had failed to meet their own requirements.

Hansel was not alone in suspecting Pearce, or at least in raising the possibility that he was suspect. There were rumors on campus at the time he was achieving his high-scoring success that Pearce was faking it because he needed the fifty cents an hour, paltry as it sounds (although it was during the Depression), or from more lofty motives. One school of doubters compared him to a devout priest testifying to a fake miracle to convert disbelievers. Rumors are not direct evidence, but might lead to it, or point in the right direction. Pratt was less suspect, although he was at the start of his career and would profit from success. Even Rhine—and he would agree—should not be considered above suspicion. And was he, despite his reputation, too trusting? He admitted to me that when McDougall suggested special vigilance of some individuals, especially experimenters and subjects who were achieving high scores (and they included Pratt and Pearce), Rhine felt like a man happily married for forty years being asked to watch his wife for signs of adultery.

During his visit to Duke, Hansel discovered that it would have been *possible* for Pearce to sneak out of the library, cross the yard, go into the building where Pratt was handling the cards, climb onto a chair in the corridor, look through the transom window, and copy down the correct order of some ESP cards. Pearce could also have climbed into an attic above Pratt's room and looked down through a hole in the ceiling—if there had been a hole there in 1933–34. But the yard to be crossed and the corridor outside Pratt's room was often teeming with students. Additionally, at any moment Pratt (or at times Rhine) might have glanced through the window and seen Pearce out of place. It is unlikely Pearce would have taken the risk, even more unlikely that if he did, he got away with it. But it *was* possible. More possible, as Hume would surely have agreed, than a miracle.

Hansel even enlisted one of Rhine's staff, W. Saleh, to show how Pearce might have cheated. He told Saleh to sit in a locked room and to duplicate the procedure used by Dr. Pratt during the Pratt-Pearce experiments; that is, to run through a pack of ESP cards and afterward make a record of the order in which they had appeared. Meanwhile, Hansel said, he would be sitting in an office down the corridor. In fact, Hansel surreptitiously stood on a chair outside the locked room and by looking through a crack at the top of the door was able to record the correct order of 22 of the 25 cards. The British psychologist concluded that Saleh had no idea how such a remarkably high score had been achieved until the deception was explained to him.[2]

Hansel also pointed out that Pearce had never made a statement denying trickery.

He criticized other ESP experiments, but the Pearce-Pratt attack stung Rhine and Pratt the most.

Rhine and Pratt's rebuttal, printed in the same issue of the *Journal of Parapsychology*, disapproved of Hansel's methods and revealed Rhine's enviable talent for making the best of a bad situation. He and Pratt wrote:

In spite of the unconcealed eagerness to give the coup de grâce *to a piece of ESP research, Mr. Hansel is entitled to our appreciation for bringing our experiment of twenty-seven years ago momentarily back into the limelight. This acknowledgement may be linked with the information that, although Hansel's negative approach to parapsychology was a matter of public knowledge, he was invited and given a travel grant by the Duke Laboratory to make the visit that resulted in his paper. . . . We cannot, of course, condone Hansel's methods; instead of directly endeavoring to clear up his differences with the authors . . . he has gone off into print without asking the reaction of the authors. . . . Whether he really has the exceedingly strong case this course of action might suggest or is only exceedingly motivated to damage the evidence for ESP on the grounds of his own prejudgment, the reader will be able to determine for himself.[3]*

They emphasized that, as an added precaution, Rhine had joined Pratt for one successful series of 150 trials. They stated that they could see Pearce enter the library at the start of the series and could see him exit when he emerged. But *could* see is not *did* see. For all their skill at argument, they fail to demolish Hansel's charge that the Pratt-Pearce experimental design was flawed—Pearce *could* have cheated, either working alone or with help. Hansel had no proof, but demonstrated how Pearce might have fooled them—if he was daring, dishonest, and very lucky.

Pratt took his pen up for the defense again in 1967:

Hansel grossly exaggerates the difficulty of the observer's task (Rhine's) of keeping an effective lookout for a familiar subject in an open quadrangle in broad daylight and, at the same time, effectively witnessing my shuffling, cutting and handling of face-down cards during the 25 minutes taken for a run. (The subsequent recording of the cards took less than 30 seconds.) It did not require constant surveillance of the quadrangle to detect any unscheduled appearance of Pearce in that area, and I had no way of knowing when Rhine's gaze might again be turned in my direction.[4]

And then Pratt brought out his ace.

It is true that Pearce has kept silent until recently, but apparently he did so only because no one had asked him properly for a statement.

Pearce willingly supplied a statement when he was requested to do so: "In reference to the suggestions made concerning the experiments that Dr. Gaither Pratt and I did at Duke University, I do not hesitate to say that at no time did I leave my desk in the library during the tests, that neither I nor any person whom I know (other than the experimenter or experimenters) had any knowledge of the order of the targets prior to my handling my list of calls to Dr. Pratt or Dr. Rhine, and that I certainly made no effort to obtain a normal knowledge by peeking through the window of Dr. Pratt's office—or by any other means. Hubert E. Pearce."[5]

Parapsychologist Dr. Gertrude Schmeidler refereed the fight and concluded:

My own feeling is that Hansel's argument is the strongest that I have seen against ESP, but it nevertheless is weak. He must dismiss the statistical anomaly of a high variance in scores which he claims to be at chance; he must postulate that repeated across-campus trips by Pearce were unobserved, as were repeated peering through transoms and movements in an attic; and he must accuse someone of willful deceit. This is a long way to go—further than I personally would be willing to do—in order to explain away a body of experimental data.[6]

But Hansel had made a vital point: Pearce should not have been left unobserved during the tests. Because of that mistake the open-minded, let alone the doubters, are justified in questioning the result as a demonstration of ESP.

Hansel also suggested how the British arch-skeptic turned prominent parapsychologist, S. G. Soal, might have faked his results. Later investigations proved Hansel almost certainly right in suspecting Soal.

Parapsychologist Charles Honorton puts the issue of fraud in a reasonable perspective:

In the final analysis an experimental finding is of value and is to be taken seriously only to the extent that it leads to further inquiry. To regard any experiment as an end in itself is to remove it from the domain of the experimental science. It is obvious that hypothetical construct, such as ESP, cannot be validated by any isolated experiment, no matter how well controlled it might be.* Independent replication is a necessary prerequisite.[1]

Professor Hansel, head of the psychology department at the University of Wales, in Swansea, remains a skeptic. In a letter to me on March 11, 1975, he wrote: "Regarding Rhine's experiments, my views are as they were."

Which was no surprise to Rhine. He could have entertained in a small room the once skeptical scientists who admitted to being converted to belief in ESP.

Rhine had another visitor from Britain that same year, 1960, whose response to Rhine's experiments was a welcome antidote to Hansel's. His name was Arthur Koestler.

---

*This was impressed on Honorton by Rhine himself.

45

DRUGS
1960

Writer Arthur Koestler met Professor Timothy Leary at Harvard in 1960 and learned about his experiments with drugs. Koestler traveled from Harvard to Duke

... and took an immediate liking to both Rhines and their closest collaborator over the last thirty years, Professor J. G. Pratt. Rhine's burly figure, his broad, open face, his obvious sincerity made me think of a woodcutter, and indeed, his favorite hobby is to wander into the woods with an axe and chop up a tree. Yet during my whole stay I had a feeling that these admirable people were living under a cloud, have become accustomed to its shadow, and accept it as unavoidable. If visitors from abroad come to Duke—and there is a steady stream of them—they come for the sole purpose of visiting the Parapsychology Laboratory, as pilgrims come to Prado to hear Pablo Casals. Yet to the students in Duke, Rhine's work is practically unknown, mainly, it seems, because their teachers discourage them from getting acquainted with it. Members of other faculties still consider the parapsychologists as beyond the academic pale. To say that the Rhines are ostracised would be to put it too dramatically; but they are lone figures in the landscape, and they are resigned to it.[1]

Koestler brought a message to Rhine. Professor Leary claimed to liberate ESP under the influence of psilocybin, a synthetic substitute for LSD: Why didn't Rhine try it? Now Rhine had never been under the influence of any drug in his life, even alcohol. His parents had so effectively discouraged him from drinking that when they had once tried to give him medicine with the faintest odor of whiskey, he had refused to swallow it. He had, it is true, given harmless narcotic drugs to students who volunteered to take them for psi tests. But he had never taken any himself.

Several years before Koestler's visit, Rhine had heard Aldous Huxley's account of his experiments with mescaline:

I took mescaline, under the supervision of Dr. Humphrey Osmond, the young English psychiatrist at present working in Canada on the problem of schizophrenia. I have just finished an account of the experience, with reflections on its philosophical, aesthetic and religious implications, which I will send you as soon as it is printed.[2]

Osmond hoped to test the effect of mescaline on specially gifted people, believing it might produce information on the nature of the mind. Hearing of this, Rhine naturally wondered if mescaline might enhance or depress ESP.

When Huxley had visited Rhine at Duke one sweltering October day in 1954, he learned that Rhine wanted to "combine ESP work with pharmacological experiments," having so far only used benzedrine and barbiturates. They discussed the recent news that the National Institute of Mental Health was experimenting with lysergic acid (LSD), but Rhine was not yet ready to undertake similar tests.[3]

By 1960, either Koestler was especially persuasive or Rhine had decided to break a lifetime of abstinence for a worthy cause. There had not yet been any alarming reports of suicides under the influence of LSD, and people he respected had used it without ill effect. Rhine's entire staff agreed to take this trip into the unknown with him—with the exception of Gaither Pratt. He was required to remain clear-headed to test all the others for ESP while they were under the influence of psilocybin.

The staff gathered in three rooms of the parapsychology laboratory—the library, a meeting room, and Dr. Rhine's office. They were joined by a visiting doctor from South America who also agreed to be a guinea pig. The experiment is only a hazy memory to Louisa Rhine, who doesn't remember the details. "We were drugged," she explains.[4]

But W. E. Cox took part, and he recalled with a laugh what happened: "We just took enough psilocybin, which, by well-established and documented findings, would give us great mental control and enable us to solve every problem put before us.

"I had given strict injunctions to Dr. J. G. Pratt to give me a PK dice test while I was under the influence. He did so, but he really had to twist my arm and pester me before I would willingly take time out from the interesting psi discussion that I was having on a major matter with some committee in the corner of the room. He got me to do one run of dice—and the results were chance.

"Rhine was with a group in his office and was encouraged by

Pratt to write a letter. 'All right, if you think you're in your right mind, Dr. Rhine, write a letter.'

" 'I haven't time to write a letter, Gaither. Get out of here!'

" 'No, I insist that you do. . . . All right, then, if you don't want to write a letter, go through the motions as if you did.'

" 'All right. Let's see, now. I'll wear my sleeves up and have sharp pencils here. Now let's see if the dictaphone's working. Ah yes, the dictaphone's okay. . . . Listen, Gaither, I don't have any time to do this!'

"Well, Gaither gave up.

"Now Rhine, through the findings of Aldous Huxley and other reporters, had concluded, I think rightly, that drugs do not make that much difference to the success of ESP card guessing. We long ago had the same experience testing under hypnosis. The increase was just a small percentage, it wasn't worth the candle; so we haven't gone in for drugs or hypnosis, though occasionally some of the students have engaged in that."[5]

Cox, a mechanical engineer (now retired) and amateur magician, lived in North Carolina in 1943 when he first met Rhine. "I took a war course at Duke and frequented the parapsychology laboratory. Later, I left business and devoted all my time to psychokinesis as a specialty. The Russians, incidentally, as Rhine would be the first to say, are a generation behind us in psychokinesis."

Although Cox was never on Rhine's staff, he contributed to much of the research work, and they were mutually fascinated. After his early encounters with Rhine, Cox "thought he was an excellent, scholarly, well-trained and -tutored research scientist, and after the positive truth, let the chips fall where they may. And he was thus trained by the inestimable Dr. McDougall, whose works any chapter of which I open and I can see ideas in there, and statements that should have been thought of before McDougall came along to put them to print. But he seems to have had the ability to perceive what his predecessors in psychology did not. And told them what their errors in concepts were. And so does Rhine, only he does it more modestly, and I must say, I'm a Rhinean in all my philosophy and approach."[6]

Not being on the staff explains why much of Cox's work has a certain wild, almost Alice-in-Wonderland quality. How else explain his investigation to see if Nature is benevolent? Or his construction of a bubble-producing machine to test the power of mind over matter? To judge Nature's kindness, Cox chose the St. Patrick's Day parade in New York City. He assumed that through psychokinesis (some power unknown, but presumed to be mind energy able to move objects) rain could be prevented from falling on the city and ruining the parade. So he looked into New York City's St. Patrick's Day weather for the previous fifty years to see how many of those days were sunny compared with the day before and the day after. He found an indication that Nature indeed appeared to be benevolent because "there was significantly less rain on the days of the parade." Cox got similar results in another city where he was also able to obtain detailed weather charts.

Cox's research also indicated that fewer people, on the average, traveled on trains at times of accidents. "But that wasn't benevolent Nature," he explained. "That was simply arbitrary unconscious clairvoyance on the part of those who didn't ride the trains. If Nature had been benevolent [he laughs], she should have prevented the accidents. But that's the other side of the coin.

"I became an honorary associate of Rhine's group. I wanted to be independent and try my own ideas out. I didn't want the authoritarian Rhine directing me. I had some notions of my own and it turned out I was right in most of them. They were rather provocative, but that's okay if they work.

"Sure, Rhine was a dictator, but without that he wouldn't have put PK and ESP on the map as they are today. You need a dictator to steer the ship of fringe science, or frontier science, down a course."[7]

If Rhine was a dictator—and few disagree with that assessment—he seemed in no danger of being overthrown. Parapsychologists, almost without exception, looked to him as leader in the field. His name was linked to parapsychology as surely as Einstein's is to relativity.

The visiting writer Arthur Koestler, on assignment for the British newspaper *The Observer*, did not stay to witness the results of the drug test. Had he done so, his report might not have stressed the "sober . . . down-to-earth" and "antiseptic" aspects of parapsychological research. He surely would have reported that, at his suggestion, the sober experimenters became guests at a Mad Hatter's tea party. Koestler spent three days at the Duke parapsychology laboratory, then continued his journey to investigate more examples of frontier research at American universities.[8]

Self-described as "a rational person with a strong scientific bent," Koestler believed in the reality of psychic phenomena.[9] His picture of Rhine's lab at Duke challenged skeptical scientists to explain how, while using their rigorous methods, Rhine still obtained positive results. That is, if skeptical scientists bothered to read of Rhine's

. . . almost fanatical devotion to statistical method, mathematical analysis, mechanised controls. The card-guessing and dice-throwing

experiments, repeated over millions of experimental runs with thou-
sands of random experimental subjects—often whole classes of
schoolboys who have no idea what the experiment is about; the
increasingly elaborate machinery for mechanical card-shuffling,
dice-throwing, randomising, recording . . . have turned the study of
extra-sensory perception into an empirical science as sober, down-to-
earth—and all too often as dreary—as training rats to run a maze, or
slicing up generations of flatworms. Even the terminology coined by
Rhine: ESP, Psi effect, decline effect, reinforcement, BM (blind match-
ing), BT (calling cards before touching), STM (screen touch matching),
and so forth, is characteristic of the antiseptic atmosphere in
modern ESP labs. This new look in parapsychology is partly a re-
flection of the prevailing fashion in research in general, but there is
also an element in it of bending over backwards to disarm suspicions
and to meet the sceptic on his own empirical-statistical ground.[10]

Some critics were hoping Rhine would bend over so far that
he'd fall flat on his back.

Rhine welcomed suggestions on how experiments could be
improved, simplified, made more convincing. He was never able to be
philosophic about uninformed or partially informed criticism. When
he heard distorted versions of his work and aims, he did not shrug it
off. But his children never saw him angry on that account. At most he
would grab an ax and go out to chop down a tree. There must be
several tree stumps named after unfair critics.

Yet Rhine had mixed feelings about hostile criticism. After a
specially damaging onslaught had received wide play in national
publications, it was not unusual to find a surprise contribution to the
fund from a well-wisher responding like a spectator cheering on a
boxer who has sustained a low blow. So, though he hardly welcomed
sneers, they sometimes served his purpose.

No matter how telling or traumatic the attacks, they could not
deter Rhine from investigations he believed were slowly revealing a
faint and flickering picture of psi. What could stop him was lack of
money.

He had started off at Duke with a pitiful amount to keep him
going: The Duke Research Council gave him four hundred dollars,
and that had to last for three years. In the early thirties Mrs. Ellen
Woods gave what seemed like a fortune—ten thousand dollars. A total
of about one hundred thousand dollars over several years came from
Congresswoman Frances Payne Bolton, especially to investigate
Eileen Garrett. But Mrs. Bolton stopped giving when Rhine decided it
was premature to pursue postmortem survival research and shelved it
for some distant future. Dr. Charles Ozanne, a Cleveland high school

teacher, had given one hundred thousand dollars strung out over several years. He, too, wanted Rhine to probe death's secrets. And he stopped contributing when Rhine explained he knew of no experiment that could prove or disprove that there was life after death. However, Rhine persuaded Ozanne to set up a separate psychical research foundation in 1960 to investigate problems bearing on the survival of bodily death, with William Roll—a former Rhine staffer—as project director.

In the 1950s the Rockefeller Foundation had given Rhine ten thousand dollars a year for four years. And the Rhines themselves had donated property worth one hundred thousand dollars to keep the lab going.

"After we abandoned survival research, we tried to raise funds for the larger program of experimental work, which was making more headway with the scientific world and also was proving more workable," Rhine explained. "Mr. Sloan of General Motors gave us around two hundred thousand dollars, and Mr. Clement Stone gave some hundreds of thousands."[11] Even so, the income from this money could barely support a small, active research program with modest equipment and a poorly paid staff.

Money was to be much less of a problem after 1960. Then an attorney and inventor named Chester Carlson began to take an interest in Rhine's work.

46

CHESTER CARLSON: INVENTOR OF THE "IMPOSSIBLE" MACHINE
1960

Chester Carlson's ingenuity brought us the Xerox method—a speedy, dry way to make use of static electricity in order to copy anything you can lay flat. Previous photocopying machines all used chemicals or heat rays. Carlson's lively interest and research in parapsychology is virtually a secret to all but a few workers in that small field. He was a modest man who did nothing to court publicity except invent a wonder machine.

Carlson's wife, Dorris, first aroused his interest in ESP in the 1940s. At that time, as a physicist as well as an attorney, he shared the mechanistic views of most of his colleagues. But he could not explain how his wife seemed to foretell the future accurately and have waking visions that paralleled his dreams in striking details. She told him that when she sat alone in her home in Pittsford, New York, she had visions of people and events. Sometimes she heard names of people and of places called out.

Carlson did not shrug it off as imagination, but decided to see if he could conjure up a disembodied voice. He tried it one evening at his home as his wife sat on the sofa nearby, reading, and their cocker spaniel lay on the floor, lulled to sleep by the fire.

"He had thought, he told me later," said Mrs. Carlson, "of hearing the sound of a voice. He concentrated for about fifteen minutes and nothing happened. He became discouraged, and decided to give it up. At that instant in the center of the room, away from any wall [and presumably away from the fire] and away from the ceiling and away from the floor, so that it could not be said that the boards were cracking or anything like that, there was an explosive noise.

"This noise sounded somewhat as though a large paper bag had been filled with air and burst. Not only did my husband hear the sound, I also heard it and was startled by it. And the sleeping dog was startled by it and jumped up."[1] It was not the voice he had hoped for, but it was certainly something Carlson could not explain. It charged his interest in the extrasensory, and he often discussed it with his wife.

"One morning," she said, "I jotted down the things that I had heard and the images that I saw. . . . Many hours later, Chester had a dream so vivid that he called out with great emotion in his sleep and I had to awaken him and ask him to tell me what was taking place. As he related the details of this moving dream-experience, I clearly recognized the material which I had received and recorded some sixteen hours earlier."[2]

Carlson corresponded with several leading parapsychologists (Rhine among them), visited their laboratories, and decided to devote much of his time and money to helping their research.

"We did not often discuss business, but we frequently talked about the meaning of life and the possible implications of para-psychological research," said Mrs. Carlson. "We wondered where it might go wrong; how it could be used to the benefit of man; how it could lead to clues to the next step in the possible conscious evolu-tion; what the new discoveries and developments might be."[3]

On July 26, 1960, Carlson wrote to Rhine proposing the use of more delicate and versatile instruments for psi research. Not only might such instruments detect as yet unsuspected physiological or psychological changes in experimental subjects, but their use would appeal to scientists generally. He knew that most psychologists are not mechanical or electrical experts, and had noticed how even the few simple gadgets at the lab that got out of order waited for weeks for someone to turn a screw or twist a wire to make them work again. So he offered to pay for the instruments and for the salary of an additional staff member with electronic or electromechanical know-how.

He suggested equipping Rhine's lab with electroencephalo-graphs; a relaxation instrument; electronic computers and punched-card systems to speed up computations and eliminate human error; a plethysmograph, which detects minute changes in blood volume close to the skin; a brain-wave synchronizer to induce certain states; and a "white sound" machine. He hoped Rhine did not think he was being too mechanistic in suggesting this equipment and not giving enough attention to the psychology of the subject.

Rhine replied on August 12, although it must have seemed like Christmas. Before responding to Carlson's generous offer, he gave him a detailed account of his summer—writing for several publications, including articles for *Chambers Encyclopedia*; running a summer school for psi students; and entertaining many visitors.

Your question about instrumentation is one that has been on my mind for years. . . . I am told that no new inventions are really needed to give us a very effective ESP test apparatus that would be nice to look at, fun to work with, and easy to handle. But the prospect of spending thousands of dollars of money needed for people has kept us from venturing out on this expensive and really highly wasteful type of exploration. (It takes about twenty machines to get a good one, if our experience is typical. Perhaps it would not be if we had the ablest type of men, but the big industries probably have them picked up.)

When you are down the next time, which I hope will not be too long ahead, let us spend an evening, at least talking over the possibilities there may be and how best we can meet them with proper appreciation and enthusiasm. Your offer really is wonderful!

I am glad you and Dorris are coming to the Convention [of the Parapsychological Association]. I am about settled on sending my daughter Sally in my place. It will mean a lot to her and it is better for her to go really than for me. My deafness and my preoccupation with things here make this seem the wiser choice and besides I like to see the way these young people are running this P.A. by themselves. I shall be working on my Ford Foundation application to keep the home fires burning.

On October 22 Rhine sent another letter to Carlson, giving a picture of his life:

This is Saturday afternoon, I am going out to the woods, taking a few of the men from the Laboratory with me. But as we stroll along the river and through the beautiful autumn colored woods one of the persistent and dominant thoughts that will flit like the flashes of sunlight across my mind will be how grateful I am for all these opportunities, the shared interests, the friendships, the devoted efforts, the confidence in the efforts and aims of those who are doing the work and passing the ammunition to others who can use it. Thus will I be reinspired—and tomorrow begins another week.

We have so many good, interesting visitors: One recently was Dr. Ainslie Mears, psychiatrist of Melbourne who had come to this country to accept the Presidency of the International Society of Experimental and Clinical Hypnosis. He was a charming and in-

teresting man and gave a good lecture at the Medical School in Chapel Hill and, of course, talked at our coffee hour. He had spent six weeks in the mountains of Northern India, making a personal search, through conversation, with a few carefully selected Yogis. One of them he said was one hundred and thirty-four years old. He was deeply impressed and believes he learned much that will help him, not only as a psychiatrist but in his own personal search for an understanding of man. . . .

Rhine thanked Carlson for a gift of Xerox stock that had yielded $12,845.88 toward a parapsychology scholarship fund and frankly spelled out some of his disappointments, especially the difficulty of pursuing anything in the field

. . . without limitations. When I let it worry me, as I sometimes do, it has a depressing effect. We start off with something like the combination of hypnosis, EEG and ESP with Cadoret and Fahler. Then . . . we lose the team and that important promising project has to wait. Now, of course, I am more inclined to look back and thank our lucky stars that we were able to make a beginning, get it started and be ready for the next opportunity that comes along to pick up and go on. It is a similar matter with animal work, because at a certain point, Osis lost interest. [Osis says he did not lose interest but that the physics department objected to the smell of the animals' food.] But we really have a very good beginning on this question of psi in animals, and it is a pretty solid corner of the research field. The same is true with the organization of the branch of case study analyses. Louie's contributions are now beginning to shape up, and that branch is ready to become a highly respectable section of the research. But she did have to interrupt to write this book [Hidden Channels of the Mind]. The book was a necessary step in the program itself. I could go on listing still a number of other developments that either are in an arrested development stage or are waiting for personnel or something of the sort. I have just quit worrying about these frustrations, however; in fact, I do not even let them seem like frustrations to me, because I realize that all the while I was just expecting too much. It looked easier than it is. We are trying to push matters faster than they can be pushed with the limitations we encounter. I start fresh the next morning, then looking for what is possible to do to advance the field a little more this particular day, this week, this year and in the few years that remain.

One thing Rhine did do was continue to encourage young enthusiasts. He had just received a letter from a schoolboy wanting to know more about parapsychology than his hometown library could provide.

47

SUBTERFUGE
1960–1963

Thirteen-year-old Charles Honorton had read all the parapsychology books in his library in St. Paul, Minnesota. He wanted to know more and took his high school teacher's advice: He wrote directly to J. B. Rhine. "Within a week I received a very nice personal letter from Rhine," says Honorton. "At thirteen, this made a profound impression on me. Then for about a year and a half I corresponded with him on a weekly basis."[1]

At the end of that time, after Honorton had done exploratory psi experiments at school, Rhine invited him to attend an expense-paid summer course in parapsychology at Duke. It was a tiring two-day and two-night bus trip. Honorton arrived just as Rhine was leaving for the day. He gave Honorton a brief greeting before turning him over to Ed Cox. And in so doing, Rhine almost lost a bright recruit to the field.

"I nearly turned back," recalls Honorton, who had recently read *Illusions and Delusions of the Supernatural and Occult* by Rawcliffe, a skeptic who gave the impression that parapsychologists are little more than spiritualists.

That impression was strongly reinforced by Cox, a maverick and honorary member of the parapsychology lab who instead of talking about the experimental work, preferred to talk of Eusapia Palladino, the Neapolitan medium who was at least partly fraudulent.

Honorton was disenchanted, but stayed rather than make an immediate grueling return journey. His first impression was quickly corrected when he got to know J. B. Rhine, Gaither Pratt, John Freeman, and Ramakrishna Rao, although at fifteen he did not have the scientific sophistication to evaluate their experimental or statistical methods. Instead, he concentrated on the personalities at the Duke lab, to see if they were careful and cautious or if they rushed into print to publicize their work.

Something happened during the month to convince Honorton that these parapsychologists were, if anything, excessively cautious. He stayed at the home of Mrs. William Preston Few, widow of Duke's first president. Another student in the summer program was also a guest in the Few house. He was an undergraduate and psychology major from UCLA, with the first name David. In clairvoyance tests during a two-week period, he scored higher than any other student—about seven out of twenty-five—with W. Saleh as the experimenter.

Honorton recalls: "One Sunday, David came rushing into my room to describe a dream he'd had the night before in which he'd gotten a perfect score of twenty-five. I suggested that he mail an account of the dream to the lab. If it did come to pass, there'd be documentation in the postmark that he had in fact had the premonition before the event.

"A couple of days later I was doing an ESP test with a subject at the lab and David came running in extremely excited: 'I did it! I did it! I got a perfect score of twenty-five!' I thought he was putting me on, but he literally dragged me back to the office where Rhine and Pratt were standing looking very seriously at the record sheet. And, indeed, he had gotten a perfect score of twenty-five out of twenty-five.

"Now the problem was that since the summer students had access to the lab at off-hours and on weekends, and as there was a new secretary in the lab who had neglected to lock up the prepared decks of cards before she went home over the weekend, it was possible for David to have gained access to one or more packs of cards, written down and memorized the order, and then produced the perfect score.

"I have absolutely no reason to believe that he did that. I don't believe that he did. And even if he had, it would not have accounted for his previous high scores, though at less dramatic levels, when the cards had been locked up. But Rhine assumed that David had cheated and this led to his loss of a promised scholarship in the parapsychology lab.

"Rhine had asked for an evaluation of the perfect score of twenty-five by David, and I remember writing a report of the conditions of the experiment and of the failure to lock up the cards, with the comment: 'I can't understand how this could have happened.' Rhine had added in pencil, 'Lab staff too busy teaching parapsychology to me?'

"I went in and talked with Rhine about this and how unfair I thought it was to assume it was fraud without any evidence other than the spectacular nature of the score. He started telling me that in all his years as a clinical psychologist he could spot someone with psychopathic tendencies. I knew he was not a clinical psychologist, and felt this was extremely unfair.

"But at the same time, I might not be in the field today if it hadn't happened in that way.

"Because it made me very dramatically aware of the fact that contrary to Rawcliffe [and many other critics], Rhine was not going to rush into print with something that wasn't adequately controlled.

"As a footnote to this, I met David again for the first time in fourteen years at the APA convention in New Orleans a few years ago. He's now a faculty member and full professor in clinical psychology at one of the University of California schools. He was just getting interested in the field again after the traumatic experience with Rhine.

"My feeling was that David had everything to lose and nothing to gain in perpetrating a fraud. But we will never know the truth. We talked about it briefly. We later corresponded for a year or two and tried a long-distance experiment, with only chance results. But he was so traumatized by the accusation and assumption of fraud that he had left the field. Up until that time, he had been very highly thought of.

"Recently [1979] I talked with Gaither Pratt about this and he felt it was unfair, that it could well have been fraudulent, but the assumption that it was, was not arrived at in a fair way. The dream had ditched it—because that was too impossible.

"There is one mitigating circumstance that I wasn't aware of at the time. About six to eight months before, Hansel was at the lab and pulled a trick on Wadhi Saleh [see Chapter Forty-Four]. And Saleh had also been the experimenter when David got his twenty-five out of twenty-five."[2]

In an interview during the summer of 1978, Rhine remembered very differently the summer of 1962.

"David was caught cheating. He was a brilliant fellow and the one I would have picked out of the group that summer as the one I most wanted. But he was carried away. I had him in mind in one of those paragraphs on cheating [Article on fraud, "A New Case of Experimenter Unreliability," J. B. Rhine, in the *Journal of Parapsychology*, 38, 1974, pp. 218–225].

"In our educational system, we tend in our unlimited and indiscriminate praise to spoil the young people. And that's what evidently had been done with David. The boy had been led to think he had something wonderful and we all kind of went along with that. He brought that from high school. So that when it came to the actual test situation down here, he apparently cooked up, planned something that was going to be phenomenal. There was something—I don't remember now—that gave away the fact that it was deceptive.

"I faced him with it; took him out behind the building and we talked about it for some time before I could get the confidence of understanding with him, amounting to a confession. And I took evidence from two or three others. He wasn't necessarily the only one involved, but he was the only one we were sure was involved.

"When it came up then, to see whether we could overcome something like this, to continue working with him, it was too much like dynamite.

"At the time Chuck [Honorton] and he were rooming together, and Chuck listened to him. It struck him emotionally that this boy was going to be ruined. David had a fellowship coming up on the West Coast. We didn't interfere with that. He had admitted enough so that we didn't have to make any public point of it.

"He went home and told his parents a story that made them feel belligerent towards us. I had a little trouble with his father over the telephone, but that's when I was tough. I just had to be. But nothing in my whole life hit me any worse than having to go through that with this boy. He was an attractive fellow, very able, and he had just the kind of skills we would want.

"Under the circumstances we couldn't take Honorton into our confidence. The situation was too complicated. I had to handle it with a certain autocratic authority. I took some risk. You'll find that working in this field, there sometimes come out strong feelings you wouldn't expect people to harbor. It makes people drive to the limit, and drive to the limit of cheating, if they're weak in that way."[3]

Honorton stayed in the field. The shock treatment worked and made him, if anything, overcautious.

"I was informally doing a lot of self-testing," he recalls. "And I didn't report to Rhine some of the more striking results—I got an occasional sixteen or seventeen out of twenty-five—for fear he'd think I was cheating.

"The first full day I was there was when the name Foundation for Research on the Nature of Man was adopted [for the new Rhine organization that would be housed on the edge of the Duke campus, but no longer be part of it].

"When I went back home to Minnesota I did a large number of card-guessing experiments. I was obsessed, I guess, with the field."[4]

Honorton became almost a self-made parapsychologist, slowly working his way through books on statistics and scientific methodology. When he started at the University of Minnesota, Rhine gave him a small grant to found the Minnesota Society for Parapsychological Research, based in a suite of rooms on the top floor of a factory. Honorton did a good number of experiments, some involving hypnosis, others involving psi and creativity, and when Rhine invited him to continue his work at the Duke lab, Honorton dropped out of college, planning to resume his college studies in North Carolina. But he never completed his college education, and that became a source of contention between him and Rhine. Rhine feared Honorton's credibility would suffer without academic credentials. It apparently has not in parapsychological circles.

Honorton found that whenever he suggested to Rhine an exciting idea for an experiment, he would come out of Rhine's office having agreed to undertake a different experiment. So, knowing Rhine was disillusioned with hypnosis as a source of psi and eager to do a hypnotic dream study, Honorton waited until Rhine had left for the day and began experimenting in secret. Because his office was in the basement, he was able to continue his hypnotic-dream study under cover of working on something else that met with Rhine's approval. It was published in the *ASPR Journal* eventually.*

Honorton was not alone; other lab workers pursued their own experiments by stealth. Their subterfuge was a hint of storms to come, and the undercurrent of dissatisfaction soon began to come to the surface.

Rhine was damned by some psi researchers for being too rigid and almost paranoid about possible cheating by experimenters and subjects. Others, Honorton among them, damned him for over-riding their complaints and for publishing the work of a researcher whom they mistrusted.

*Charles Honorton and John P. Stump, "A Preliminary Study of Hypnotically-Induced Clairvoyant Dreams," JASPR, 63 (1969), pp. 175–184.

48

UPTON SINCLAIR
1963

Upton Sinclair's wife, Craig, died in 1961, and six months later, at eighty-three, he married a seventy-nine-year-old widow, Mary Willis. He and Rhine continued to exchange mutually supportive letters, and in 1963 Sinclair sent his autobiography.* Rhine replied before he was able to finish it: "I have just received and read your autobiography. It is marvelous to see the force in your pen after all these years. There is still the forward, positive, constructive thrust of the great intellect, as Professor McDougall would have put it." Then Rhine went on to write of his own affairs—how the Indian government proposed setting up a parapsychological research center at a leading university. "It is good to see state support coming to the aid of this branch of research. If it could not, as you had hoped, be done in California, at least India now will lead the way."[1]

When Rhine finished Sinclair's autobiography, he wrote to him on February 25:

I feel deeply stirred and moved to write to you again about this book. But, of course, it is more what the book conveys and symbolizes that I am thinking and writing about. I cannot think of another book representing another life that touches on more points of the compass of life's experiences than does this one. It is because you had more windows open to human problems and social concerns than anyone else I can think of. Perhaps it is a kind of range that could only be possible to a writer with complete freedom of subject matter and a great interest in man and society. You have a great readiness to look at new claims, and it is not your fault that they have not all turned out to be what might have been hoped at first approach. Where would the

---

*The Autobiography of Upton Sinclair, 1962. It was a slightly rewritten version of his American Outpost, 1932.

world be if there were not this willingness to look? I would insist a man be judged as much by his willingness to look at something that may be misleading or even deceptive as by the actual score of his accomplishments.

Not entirely unconsciously, perhaps, Rhine was also writing about himself.

In referring to Sinclair's remarriage, Rhine commented:

I am so glad you have this happy ending, and that I have seen evidence of it with my own eyes. I can believe all you say about this new companionship.

49

FOUNDATION FOR RESEARCH ON THE NATURE OF MAN 1962–1965

One of Gaither Pratt's last major tasks for Rhine in 1962 and 1963 was a trip west across the United States—lecturing as he went, consulting parapsychologists in Texas and California—and then around the world, stopping at psi research centers in Japan, India, and Czechoslovakia.

Pratt had previously visited the state-supported laboratory in Leningrad, where scientists were engaged in ESP experiments. In June 1962 he spoke with a few mavericks in Moscow who were working on their own and at some risk. In Prague he met Dr. Milan Ryzl, soon to blaze forth as a remarkably successful experimenter, able to elicit high ESP scores from Pavel Stepanek after training him under hypnosis.

The good will visit to India was clouded by the strong suspicion that an experimenter, H. N. Banerjee, was cheating. Banerjee, director of the Seth Sohan Lal Memorial Institute of Parapsychology in Sri Ganganagar, was partly financed by Rhine, and had reported outstanding results in experiments with mothers and children. He was asked to send his record sheets to Duke. Researchers there used what Rhine considered an almost fool-proof method of detecting fraud: They looked for evidence of U curves and other common features of ESP. They found none. On the contrary, there were signs that the results had been faked.

Reporting the incident, staff member K. Ramakrishna Rao concluded:

Having considered these possibilities and looked into Mr. Banerjee's personal record, the Parapsychology Laboratory decided to withdraw its support of him. The only way parapsychology can be helped in any part of the world is by solid scientific work with high precautionary standards, and India is no exception.[1]

Rhine reached the mandatory age for retirement, sixty-five, in 1960, but no one at Duke reminded him of it, so he kept going. The administration made it quite clear, though, that he would be retired in 1965 when he was seventy. He knew that the world's first university to accept a parapsychology laboratory now planned to sever all connections with it. If he felt bitter he never expressed it. His reputation and credibility had not suffered. Despite the young rebels who scorned to stick to his methods, Rhine, now seventy, still remained the dominant force in parapsychology throughout the world, his name synonymous with the field.

His departure from Duke could have been a debacle, but it was more like a triumph. Thanks to the foresight of Rhine and his wealthy supporters, especially Chester Carlson and Clement Stone, his organization was in good shape. He took three hundred thousand dollars with him that had been raised by and for the parapsychology laboratory. Rhine and his staff shifted everything across the road to a large white frame house which was to be the headquarters of the Foundation for Research on the Nature of Man (FRNM). It had been officially founded on July 30, 1962, in anticipation of the move.

The name had been suggested by Rhine's friend and supporter William Perry Bentley of Dallas, Texas. He had decided to investigate postmortem survival after his brother died in the 1918 flu pandemic. Bentley came to believe that the study of ESP was necessary to penetrate the mystery of death, and backed Rhine's efforts. FRNM is known colloquially as *Fernam*. The title implies that Rhine was expanding, not contracting, his studies. In fact, FRNM intended to explore fully and carefully all the unusual types of experiences known to man that suggest underlying capacities or principles as yet unrecognized. The research unit was renamed The Institute for Parapsychology. The building was so close to the Duke campus that it hardly appeared separate, cut off merely by a low stone wall and narrow road.

Gaither Pratt did not join Rhine in the new organization. They had worked together for some thirty years. He left Duke to continue as a parapsychologist at the University of Virginia. Pratt's friends say he was deeply disappointed when he left Rhine, and each has a different explanation for his leaving, including frustrated ambition (wanting to take over from Rhine as director), lack of tenure at Duke University and no hope of getting it, an ambitious wife seeking broader horizons, and a growing critical attitude toward Rhine.

Rhine pointed out that working with him for thirty years "enabled Pratt to stay in the field and get a good position," but he would not admit he had fired Pratt.[2]

Pratt's thirty-odd years with Rhine was a remarkable record. Most assistants had lasted a year or two. Five years was unusual. It had been an enchanted voyage for some of them; for others, a short, choppy trip; for a few, a roller coaster ride. Their stories conflict at times: Rhine was too strict, Rhine was too lax. They may all be right, reporting his changing methods to try to grasp his elusive quarry. Those who survived the Rhine treatment and stayed in parapsychology often chose areas he had avoided, or attempted and abandoned. Rhine graduates moved into dream research, into investigating altered states of consciousness through hypnosis, drugs, meditation, and out-of-body experiences. Others attempted to pin down poltergeists, hurrying to the sites of these strange disturbances, hoping to arrive before the victims had been overrun and badgered by inquisitive strangers, police, and journalists.

William Roll specialized in poltergeists, Robert Van de Castle in dreams, Karlis Osis in survival research. Osis interviewed doctors and nurses in America and India who had been deathbed witnesses and concluded that there was a case for survival after bodily death.

Most of these former Rhine researchers rejected the use of ESP cards and favored free-choice targets like paintings. Their subjects were encouraged to guess not five symbols on cards, but an out-of-sight painting or photograph. Then they were asked to describe, by speaking, drawing, or writing, what they "saw." Such targets, of course, appeal more to the imagination than the familiar ESP cards. The drawback with free-choice targets is the difficulty in judging the results. With Rhine's cards, the subject is either right or wrong, and the score can be statistically and unambiguously tallied. But if the free-choice target is Van Gogh's sunflower and the subject describes it as "bright, colorful, sunny," or draws a wheel, what score do you give? Ten out of ten? Seven out of ten? Or nothing?

Rhine kept a wary eye on this new school of parapsychologists, unwavering in his belief that the way to discover the nature of psi and to have it recognized by the scientific establishment was through a narrower and more precise focus. And he needed scientific recognition, because with it would surely come more funding and a greater chance of ultimate success.

Money not only meant more experiments and more sophisticated equipment, but the funds for extensive and more frequent travel. When Rhine heard that the Russians were into ESP research, he realized that even if they confirmed his experiments, they would dispute his conclusions. He believed there was no physical basis to psi. The Russians, in order to reinforce their political philosophy, were trying to prove him mistaken.

He was eager to contact the scattered groups of parapsychologists throughout the world—so rare they were almost an endangered species—to exchange views and information, and to do what he could to support and encourage them. But the danger of extinction was nearer home, in his own lab.

50

THE REVOLT
1966–1969

The nationwide student revolt in the 1960s spread to Rhine's lab. No fires were set, bombs exploded, or equipment smashed, but the effect was almost as devastating when more than half his staff walked out. The trouble began with an experiment to see if people's thoughts affect plants.

Bob Brier was the experimenter. He was well versed in the evidence from Dr. Louisa Rhine's collection that described spontaneous happenings apparently caused by psychokinesis. These included wide ranges of "targets," such as clocks that stopped, pictures that fell, glasses that shattered, and doors that opened and closed inexplicably. Witnesses claimed such events had coincided with death, injury, or dangerous situations involving friends or relatives.

The question was: Did people affect the inanimate objects? Had the minds of the bereaved, the dying—or even the dead—caused objects to move, to stop moving, or to break?

Cleve Backster, a polygraph (lie detector) expert, had made the astonishing claim that a plant reacted with apparent terror when he merely thought of harming it.

Comics and cartoonists spread his claim faster than the scientific press. They could not have asked for an easier subject to ridicule. Backster's findings intimated a world where forests react in fear to a man with an ax, and flowers read men's minds.

But Rhine took Backster's claims seriously enough to send Bob Brier to investigate.

Brier observed Backster conducting his experiment and judged that he was honest, but kidding himself.

He reported this opinion to Rhine, who accepted it as a reasonable conclusion. But when he heard the verdict, Backster asked Brier what kind of experiment would convince him otherwise. Brier designed a double-blind experiment and told Backster that if he followed that and got positive results, it would be convincing.

Not long after that Brier read an account of such an experiment by Backster. It was published in the *International Journal of Parapsychology*, an Eileen Garrett publication.[1]

Brier reviewed the article at one of the lab meetings. His opinion was that although all of his observations of Backster indicated that he was deluded, "if this article is true and Backster in fact has done the experiment as he's reported it—he's got something."[2]

Rhine disagreed, saying he had no confidence in Backster's work: "When he came here he couldn't demonstrate it unless we were out of the room or out of the picture, and that allowed him the possibility of trickery. Now that wouldn't have had to be conscious, deliberate, deceitful trickery. It could have been fooling himself. Backster had less evidence of acceptable status in the way of a claim of recognition than anything I've seen in this field.*

"I don't think he would know the difference between a genuine effect and a nearly genuine effect."[3]

Nevertheless, Rhine supported Bob Brier's attempt to see not if a plant can respond emotionally to human thought, but if human thought can, through psychokinesis, affect a plant.

On his visit to Cleve Backster's lab, Brier had learned how to use the polygraph. In some respects his experiment followed Backster's—the polygraph attached to philodendron plants, the reading of the printout as evidence. But in most other details, it was different.

It worked like this at first: Two plants, A and B, were attached to a polygraph machine, and plant activity was registered on a running strip of paper as squiggles above and below a horizontal line. The higher and lower the squiggles reached, the greater the plant activity was assumed to be. Each human subject in turn sat a few feet from the targets—the two plants—and was asked to try to affect the activity of the plants. Whether the thought should be "Have a nice day" or "I'm a hungry tortoise" was not spelled out. That was left to the subject. The subject opened sealed orders and was told that when a nearby light bulb came on he was to concentrate in thirty-second bursts on either A or B. The sealed orders had been prepared by someone other than Brier, who sat in a nearby room monitoring the polygraph, supposedly unaware of which plant the subject was concentrating on at any given time.

After the experiment, Brier and another person judged if the moments of concentration on targets A and B matched with special activity—if any—on the polygraph printout.

---

*At Cornell, K. A. Horowitz, D. C. Lewis, and E. L. Gasteiger tried and failed to replicate Backster's experiment. Two others who also failed were R. V. Johnson of the University of Washington and John Kmetz of Science Unlimited Research Foundation in San Antonio.

Brier's results were promising and he went on to further experiments with greater safeguards. But the howls from Brier's colleagues caused a showdown. They claimed that he was not unaware of the targets as he should have been, because one of the subjects had inadvertently identified them; that his use of statistics was faulty; that he set out to do pilot studies and after they proved successful, called them formal experiments. Several researchers complained to Rhine and eventually demanded what amounted to a trial.

"I was accused of not presenting my data in a straightforward manner," said Brier. "Some of the younger men like Chuck Honorton tried to cook up a case against me. J.B. called me in and said, 'There have been accusations. What are you going to do about it?'

"I said, 'The thing to do is have a clearing of the air. We should take the charges one by one and see where I stand. And then when I've cleared myself I'm going to quit.' I didn't want to work with these people any more, but J.B. very much wanted me to stay. At that point I don't think he was one hundred percent sure that I would clear myself. I was not going to kid myself into thinking J.B. was madly in love with me and therefore would stand behind me no matter what. He was a very cautious guy and did not commit himself to any one person except J.B. He just said, 'Let's see what happens.'

"So there was a meeting held in J.B.'s office with Sally, J.B., myself, Mrs. Rhine, Chuck, Rex, and maybe John Stump. We were emotional then, I know I was. It was a big thing in my life. Here I was accused of all kinds of terrible things. J.B. was very straightforward. He said, 'We've got to find out.'

"And the accusations were things like I'd said that I'd been technical editor of the *American Institute of Chemical Engineering Journal*, and that I hadn't been. So what I wound up doing was writing to the journal and getting a letter from my boss saying I had been a manuscript editor."

What was a triviality to Brier was an indication of sloppy thinking to Honorton and several of the others.

"J.B. was very impartial," said Brier. "My feeling was he very much wanted me to be vindicated because I was the fair-haired boy, and also he was ticked off at these people for the way they had done this thing, like a kangaroo court.

"One accusation was that I had claimed to have built a birdhouse that I hadn't actually built. The guy I lived with—Ben Feather, Sally's husband—had built it. And Rex Stanford had been over to my house and asked something about the birdhouse. And apparently he thought I'd said I'd built the thing. I was curious as to how such a misunderstanding could have happened, and I think I figured it out. Ben and I were around, and Rex is a southerner. And I think he'd used the phrase: 'Did y'all build the birdhouse?' Meaning the people here. That's the best I could figure it out. The birdhouse sticks in my mind the most because it's so bizarre.

"It took about two weeks to get letters from people to clear myself. I couldn't leave under those accusations. So I said to J.B., 'the thing to do is to replicate the experiment [with the polygraph] under very tight conditions. Let's have Mrs. Rhine as the second experimenter.' Which he agreed to do. And I did replicate the experiment, with Mrs. Rhine handling the targets. [Results were generally positive though not significant. The polygraph-philodendron experiments have not been replicated.]

"When I told J.B. I was resigning after clearing myself, he came over to my office. He said, 'Bob, you don't want to do this. We're all going to be working together for years.' He told me how he had been accused wrongly in the thirties when somebody said of his research things like, 'Rhine keeps his door open so people can peek and look at the experimental cards.' And J.B. said, 'Maybe I left the door open, but not intentionally so that people could peek.' And he tried to show me how he had been accused and he hadn't resigned. He wanted to smooth it over so that Rex, Chuck, and I would still work together."[4]

So Brier stayed, but neither he nor his accusers were satisfied with the atmosphere of suspicion.

Charles Honorton's view is from the other side of the looking glass. "We all liked Bob Brier," he said. "We thought he was very enthusiastic but a little sloppy. We constantly tried to bring the sloppiness to his attention to get him to straighten out, to no effect. When he first came down to Durham, Brier told Rhine he had been editor of a chemistry journal in New York. It turned out that he'd been a manuscript editor. And there were a lot of little things like that which led us to the conclusion that this guy's not just sloppy, he's fooling about with the data. We're not getting any satisfaction from him by giving him feedback and trying to correct it. He's misrepresenting a study that started out to be a pilot study, as a formal one. He's misrepresenting it as having been evaluated on a blind basis, when it wasn't. If the experiment calls for a blind evaluation of a polygraph squiggle and it's not blind, the interpretation of the result is totally meaningless. You don't decide on the basis of your results after the experiment, whether the experiment is a pilot study or a formal experiment. But when the experiment came to be reported at our staff meeting it was no longer a pilot study—it was an official experiment."[5]

When Brier's colleagues pointed out to Rhine their complaints, especially the reporting of a pilot study as a formal experiment, Rhine's initial reaction was total shock and denial. He said he would talk with Brier and remedy the situation. "But Brier somehow won him over," says Honorton, "and we started having these totally crazy meetings in Rhine's office at ten o'clock in the morning, where Rhine never dealt with the issue directly, but in hypothetical terms—in terms of hypothetical people, even though we were all sitting there.

"And he built up this scenario where Brier represented the young J. B. Rhine and I was Carl Zener, his former friend, who had now turned against him. And Bob Morris was Helge Lundholm, another of Rhine's early collaborators. And, I guess, Rex Stanford was Donald Adams. He gave us those names. I remember it being so crazy.

"The upshot was that he wanted Brier to get together with Bob and Rex and John Stump and myself to iron out our differences. We had a session with Brier in which we went point by point—we had a list of forty or fifty items, mostly dealing with experiments. And Brier just threw a tantrum in the middle of that—stormed out and went into Rhine's office. The next thing, we were all on probation.

"The reason for the probation was never made clear, but we were put on probation in 1967. By this time I was tired of living in a paranoid setting, not being able to do the kind of research that I felt was most productive."[6]

Rhine had wanted the researchers at FRNM built into a close group, but failed to see he was encouraging a Frankenstein monster that would turn on him. The group had agreed, knowing the prior stories of personnel problems in the lab, that if Rhine unfairly picked on one of them and fired him, the others would all resign. Honorton was being called into Rhine's office for little sessions a couple of times a week, and he'd been clued by people who had been there for many years that this was Dr. Rhine's way of getting someone to quit. But he did not want to resign. Only if Rhine fired him would Honorton be assured the others would live up to their agreement. So he provoked Rhine into dismissing him.

"I refused to carry out one of his instructions and he stamped his fist on his desk and said, 'Chuck, if you can't get along with me, why are you here?' My response was, 'Dr. Rhine, for the last six months I've been here in spite of you, not because of you.' He asked me if I wanted to type out my resignation and I told him he'd have to take the initiative. So he stamped his fist on the desk again. I was almost in tears at that point because I really loved the man."[7]

When Honorton was fired in the fall of 1969, five others kept their promise to resign as a group—Bob Morris, Joanna Morris, John Stump, Rex Stanford, and John Palmer. Rhine's lab staff was decimated, leaving him with his wife, daughter, and Bob Brier.

A week after he quit, Honorton accepted an offer from Stanley Krippner and Montague Ullman to join them at the Maimonides Dream Laboratory as a full-time research associate.

Rhine recalled, "The group was formed, I was told, over the feeling that they couldn't do enough with me, I was too strong-minded or something. The one who was doing this was Chuck [Honorton], who was very good at pulling people together. He would have made a good labor leader. They thought they had me over a barrel. Now they weren't doing this deliberately to ruin me. But they thought I was wrong, and they'd been looking for years for a case to get me."[8]

This is Louisa Rhine's viewpoint: "Brier was a very bright and competent young fellow and J.B. was trying to figure out how to handle that case. He didn't need to have these kids tell him how they thought Brier wasn't quite straight. They overinterpreted some things too that were against him. If they'd just minded their own business and gone about their own affairs, J.B. would have handled Brier without any help from them, as he had done plenty of others. But they jumped in and we found out they were trying him. All of this was insurrectionary, the beginning of the student unrest in the sixties, as I realize now. It was pretty much a tempest in a teapot. J.B. knew that Brier wasn't careful. Brier hadn't had a thorough scientific background. I worked with him on one plant experiment, but I never caught him at any kind of fraud. He was all right. But these other kids just took a dislike to him."[9]

Ten years after the battle, Honorton reflected, "I had always enjoyed challenging Rhine, arguing with him, and he seemed to enjoy it, too—as long as I was coming down for the summer. Once I was part of the official family, he did not enjoy it. Rhine is the most rigid, stubborn man I have ever known. Jarl Fahler, a Finnish parapsy-chologist, put it very well when I met him at a conference in Europe and we talked about his days at Duke. He was comparing Rhine and Stalin: 'Both Rhine and Stalin have thick white hair. Both are very stern, autocratic, very powerful.' He paused for a moment, then said, 'But Stalin, I think, has more tanks.'

"Rhine demanded one hundred percent loyalty and I don't think he ever trusted anybody completely except Louisa and Sally [wife and daughter]. One of the sources of entertainment in Durham for years was the question: 'Is J. B. Rhine's paranoia inherited or learned?' "[10]

Yet Honorton conceded that Rhine was justified in being tough and cautious. "I can certainly understand more now than I could when I was under his thumb, where a lot of that was coming from in terms of many, many years of struggle and controversy, accusations of incompetence and fraud. Having my own lab and staff now, I can understand some of his toughness. [Honorton was director of the sleep and dream laboratory at Maimonides and is now, in 1982, director of the Psychophysical Research Laboratories, Princeton Forrestal Center, Princeton, New Jersey.] There's only a certain amount of time, money, and number of people. It's still a very precarious field and still under attack."[11]

Honorton felt continued affection for Rhine, but there is no question Rhine would have sacrificed some affection for greater understanding.

"Rhine had a tremendous amount of charm," said Honorton, "but he could also be totally ruthless with the lives of other people, depending on what his goals and needs were. I think he felt very deeply and I don't think he enjoyed doing a lot of the things he did, but he managed to justify them. He had a tremendous capacity to rationalize.

"His authoritarianism and restrictiveness held the field to a very narrow and not very suitable methodology for thirty years, but it did provide a basis for developing standards and terminology, to get it off the ground. And nobody else had been able to do that.

"He established a beachhead in the field and set up at least a primitive way of classifying phenomena and the beginning of a quantitative methodology. And he was a very inspirational writer at times."[12]

The Bob Brier incident, which precipitated the revolt at FRNM, illustrates the underlying atmosphere of suspicion and tension and emotional involvement that only a Solomon could have eliminated. Brier, feeling he was getting nowhere, left a few years after Honorton. Today he teaches philosophy and a course in experimental parapsychology at The New School for Social Research.

Despite the criticism, Rhine reprinted the Brier experiment in a book, *Parapsychology Today*, The Citadel Press, 1968, which he coedited with Brier. In the introduction Rhine noted that "the main objective of research workers today is to discover psychological conditions and factors that will increase the subject's control over his ability and improve his psi-test performance." He adds:

The plant experiment reported by Robert Brier as an exploratory step is a completely novel one even though it falls between the familiar PK tests with moving objects and the attempts already made (with whatever conclusiveness) on PK with living organisms.

And then a note of caution from both editors, clearly a response to the accusations of Brier's former colleagues:

This report is correctly presented by the author as "encouraging," rather than conclusive, for it is essentially a pilot research and needs confirmation. It was included in this volume because it is a new advance of method into PK tests on living target material that invite trial by others. The author will be glad to discuss later technical innovations with anyone pursuing a similar project.

"There is some justification for referring to the post 1965 era as the 'genital period' of parapsychology," wrote John Palmer in his review in the *ASPR*, April 1975, of an unpublished master's thesis by Paul D. Allison.

During this period there was a marked rebellion (largely triggered, conveniently enough for the analogy, by the younger parapsychologists) against the "Father figure" of Rhine. It is noteworthy that these younger parapsychologists were not outsiders, but trainees of Rhine's laboratory. The increasing emphasis on altered states of consciousness, inspired largely by the subjective reports of psychics and mediums, is in clear opposition to the direction of research Rhine advocates.

During Rhine's futile attempt to pacify the rebels on his staff, he accepted an invitation to address the annual convention of the American Psychological Association in Washington, D.C., in 1967. The title for his talk was "Psi and Psychology: Conflict and Solution," referring to the work in parapsychology up to the 1950s. Psychologists who thought they had seen the last of him when he appeared, dry-mouthed and anxious in 1938, saw a poised, calm speaker who betrayed no signs of the conflict currently taking place in his laboratory and for which as yet he had found no solution. He confidently claimed: "The findings of this research period (1930–1950), both at Duke and elsewhere, were substantial. One by one the major claims, based originally only upon spontaneous human experiences, were subjected to laboratory test and experimentally verified. Independent confirmations both in and out of the Duke center followed. . . . Certain general characteristics of the psi process became clear during this period. The most revealing of these is the subject's lack of conscious control over any type of psi ability, a characteristic which accounts for its elusive nature. This discovery showed the importance of learning to measure a genuinely unconscious mental process accurately and quantitatively. It was a new methodological ground, even for psychology. Also, we were surprised to find that psi ability is widespread, probably even a specific human capacity rather than a capacity possessed by a few rare individuals as had been the popular belief. Evidence that psi is not linked with illness or abnormality was another welcome advance."

Though Rhine had the aftermath of a rebellion to contend with and the problem of restaffing the lab, his money worries were soon to be considerably relieved. When Xerox inventor Chester Carlson died in 1968, he left 12 percent of his twenty-three-million-dollar fortune for psychical research, and Rhine's organization was one of the beneficiaries. Five percent (over one million dollars) went to the University of Virginia to be used to support "parapsychological and psychical research and related investigations by Dr. Ian Stevenson and his successors." Carlson left another 5 percent to the American Society for Psychical Research, and 2 percent (close to half a million dollars) to Rhine's Foundation for Research on the Nature of Man.

Apart from his gift of two and a half million dollars to organizations investigating the extrasensory world, Carlson gave no hint in his will of his beliefs. But after his death an envelope was found with "Funeral Arrangements" written on it. Inside was a piece of paper, blank except for the mathematical sign for infinity.[13]

Upton Sinclair's death that same year robbed Rhine of his last living hero—a man whose writing Rhine compared to Lincoln's Gettysburg Address and whose character he compared implicitly to Jesus Christ's. Rhine eulogized his favorites as excessively as he excoriated those he despised, and was not afraid to put it in writing. No wonder Sinclair had kept up a constant and frequent exchange of letters. For his part, Rhine had saved Sinclair from being taken in by doubtful psychics like Arthur Ford and Frederick Marion, cautioned him about Edgar Cayce, and pointed him toward those who had proved themselves in rigorous tests, psychics like Eileen Garrett and Leonore Piper. Sinclair had done his best to immortalize Rhine by featuring him twice in the Lanny Budd series of books—twelve volumes of a blend of fact and fiction. Sinclair was so determined to be accurate in these novels when describing actual events that he wrote "a thousand letters to persons who were eyewitnesses of this or that scene, or who had access to information," revealed his biographer, Leon Harris. Rhine was included in those Sinclair questioned, along with J. Edgar Hoover, President Truman, and Albert Einstein. And George Bernard Shaw applauded the results, saying to Sinclair, "When people ask me what happened in my long lifetime I do not refer them to the newspaper files and to the authorities, but to your novels."[14]

Sinclair had shown that he believed J. B. Rhine was an important figure in contemporary history.

Upton Sinclair's last years had been happy and "for a man who had been in turn ignored, ridiculed, and maligned, it was sweet now on occasion to see himself apotheosized," wrote his biographer, Harris. Sinclair died peacefully on November 25, 1968.[15]

51

BISHOP PIKE
1966–1969

Celebrities often made a beeline for Rhine's lab when in the area. Actors Eddie Albert and Burl Ives, on the Rice diet at Duke (parapsychology wasn't the university's only attraction), took the opportunity to talk with Rhine and see some of his experiments in operation. Comedian Jackie Gleason asked Rhine for advice about a projected TV series on ESP. "He wanted to do thirteen shows," recalled Rhine. "He charmed me into spending all day in New York answering his questions."[1] In his biography of Gleason, Jim Bishop wrote that Rhine was locked in an office with the comedian for several hours. The joke of Gleason's TV staff was that the two men were floating a couple of women into the office through the window.[2] Rhine had planned to spend that day with Eileen Garrett, "and when she heard where I was she wanted me to bring Gleason over to see her."[3] He would have gone had he not been preoccupied with his TV plans. The ESP series never reached the screen, but Gleason's day with Rhine sharpened his interest in the subject, of which he became an enthusiast.

Rhine's celebrity visitors and contacts further alienated Duke's psychology department. Its members responded with growing irritation to such wisecracks from other psychologists as: "Oh, you're from the place where they hunt ghosts!"

He would have welcomed the support of Duke's psychologists, although he was no longer a member of the department, but by now the breach was too wide, and he knew that only a new generation could be expected to take an unbiased look at his results.

Rhine never had a visitor more anxious to know the facts about psychic phenomena than Bishop James A. Pike.

He had shown no special interest in parapsychology until 1966 when his son, Jim, committed suicide and appeared to be the cause of poltergeist activity. Pike had lived in more than his fair share of church residences said to be haunted by former departed tenants, had heard footsteps on the stairs when no one seemed to be there, faced a cold blast of wind that suddenly sprang up inside a church and snuffed out the candles he carried. The church was reputedly haunted by a previous minister who wanted a different lighting arrangement. Pike had also reported a macabre battle with a bat that seemed determined to prevent him from tending to the dying needs of a parishioner.

But Pike was very much a man of this world. He took such events none too seriously, realizing they could be explained rationally. He had led a turbulent life with two wives and several mistresses. He had beaten his alcoholism and had justifiably earned the reputation as America's most controversial clergyman. But it was his urge to know the truth that most characterized the man. Pike had two things in common with Rhine. "If there was anything central to Pike's very being as a person," wrote his friends and biographers William Stringfellow and Anthony Towne, "it was his passion for the truth empirically related and verified. . . . And he was, in his life, a target for ridicule and condescension."[4]

The questions he intended to ask Rhine were literally a matter of life and death.

On February 4, 1966 (at about 3:20 P.M., according to the police), Pike's twenty-year-old son, Jim, shot himself fatally through the head while he was staying in a New York City hotel. He had been taking a drug, Romilar, and was distressed over his homosexuality. The previous four and a half months the bishop and his son had lived together in an apartment in Cambridge, England.

Sixteen days after the young man's death, Pike walked into the apartment they had shared and noticed two postcards face up on the floor between the twin beds. The postcards formed an angle of 140 degrees.

The cleaning woman denied responsibility, and so did Pike's two colleagues, his secretary, Maren Bergrud, and chaplain David Barr. Pike was sure that he had not left them there. It was mildly puzzling. He would normally have given them just a moment's thought. But he kept remembering that his son had bought these postcards. On the off chance a stranger had been in the room, the bishop asked the cleaning woman to make sure from then on that she always locked the apartment before she left. And the bishop took the same precaution. So when he and his two colleagues returned soon afterward from a trip to London and he unlocked the apartment door, Bishop Pike was more than a little surprised to find two books lying between the twin beds exactly where the postcards had been and also making an angle of 140 degrees.

Pike himself had a flair for the dramatic. Here was a man who had flagged down a train in a snowstorm to take himself and a busload of stranded passengers on to their destination. Was his dead son, Jim, using a dramatic way to capture his attention and proclaim death was not the end? Pike had noticed after hearing of Jim's suicide that his son's alarm clock in Cambridge had stopped at 12:30. Someone pointed out that the clock now showed 8:19, the hands being at an angle of approximately 140 degrees.

The police reported Jim had died at about 3:20 P.M. New York time—8:20 P.M. British time. Was this the explanation for all the objects indicating 140 degrees?

That was not the end of the poltergeistlike activity in the bishop's Cambridge apartment. A mirror fell slowly off a shelf, so that there was time to catch it—a shelf that sloped down to the wall. Clothes last seen on hangers were found in a tangled mess at the bottom of a wardrobe.

Pike's response was to attempt to communicate with his son. He went to mediums in Britain and America, even taking part in a highly publicized séance on Canadian television in September 1967 when medium Arthur Ford went into a trance and relayed messages to Pike that seemed to come from his dead son.

In his search for more evidence that his son had communicated with him, Pike called on Rhine in 1968. Rhine took a neutral stance as regards Arthur Ford, who had agreed to be tested at Duke but always had a reason for failing to turn up. However, Rhine was willing to talk at length about what seemed to be psychokinetic activities that Pike had witnessed after his son's suicide.

"He came over from Duke's school of religion, where he'd been lecturing," Rhine recalled. "We had corresponded. He told me about the fantastic physical effects that had happened to him of an apparent psychic nature in England, involving his dead son. We had a very long, earnest talk with his secretary, a Norwegian girl [Maren Bergrud]. We were discussing the way to appreciate, approve, and confirm, to be more sure about those physical things that were happening to him. What questions would you raise, from the point of view of psychology, as to whether or not those things fell when there was nobody near them? Was it an example of psychokinesis or not? I'd ask Pike, 'Were you really awake? If you were awake, were you alert and cautious? When you start thinking back to it you can almost make it more real if you want it to be. Or you can make it less real, if you're afraid of it,' and so forth."[5]

Rhine kept it an open question. But Pike's final conclusion was to believe in life after death, and he wrote:

I have examined and re-examined the events which led me to become convinced that Jim lived on—and therefore, that we all do—and although I am aware of some alternative explanations for most of the

*whole body of phenomena I myself experienced, nevertheless, these
same events and phenomena led me into a vast field of study which
has enabled me to affirm, on a basis of quite independent, well-
established and scientifically assessed data, that men—even now
before death—do indeed transcend the time-space continuum, and
that this conclusion, plus much reliable psychic phenomena, makes
plausible the inference that it is of the nature of man to survive
death.*[6]

Later evidence revealed in Pike's biography that the bulging
leather case Arthur Ford carried around with him, secured by a thick
leather strap and padlocked, contained some of the information
others thought to be paranormal. It was stuffed with biographical
material and obituaries of people—the facts of their lives and deaths,
which Ford revealed "supernormally" at séances.

Rhine did not know that the bishop's secretary, Maren Bergrud,
was his mistress—and mentally disturbed. She might have been the
normal source of the "poltergeist" phenomena. Pike's biographers
suggest that "Maren Bergrud, the bishop's disgruntled mistress, herself sick of mind and body, her faculties distorted by a habit of drugs
and destined less than a year later to drug herself to death, had been
driven by some wild distraction to perpetrate a cruel hoax."[7]

But it has not been proved that Maren Bergrud caused all the
poltergeist activity that sent Bishop Pike to séances with mediums on
both sides of the Atlantic. In fact, she was nowhere near the scene
when some of the phenomena occurred—in David Barr's presence,
for example. And Arthur Ford cannot be completely discredited as a
tricky old fraud trading on the emotions of a bereaved father. Investigators who knew Ford well, including a leading parapsychologist, Dr.
Ian Stevenson, of the University of Virginia, knew that he sometimes
cheated. But they also believe he was a gifted psychic. Deceit and the
gift of mediumship, say the experts, are not incompatible.

Only a year after speaking with Rhine, Bishop Pike found out
if there is a life after death. He was on another search for the truth in
1969, this time to discover the historical Jesus Christ stripped of myths
and moonshine. Pike lost his way and died in the Judean wilderness.

AAAS
1969

Rhine's brainchild, the Parapsychological Association, had been rebuffed in attempts to join the American Association for the Advancement of Science in 1963, 1967, and 1968. The parapsychologists had gone to considerable trouble to meet all the terms of the application, had confirmed that two thirds of the members of the P.A. had Ph.D. degrees, and had some fifty master's and Ph.D. degrees for research in parapsychology. Members had also submitted many of their parapsychological research papers. But the twelve scientists on the AAAS committee repeatedly turned them down, saying that parapsychology is not a true science.

In 1969 the P.A. tried for a fourth time, with E. Douglas Dean and R. A. McConnell leading the effort in academic lobbying. The application was accepted. But there were other hurdles. The AAAS council had first to approve the application, and that was in considerable doubt. Then the council membership had to vote for or against.

The crucial meeting of the AAAS took place at the Statler-Hilton Hotel in Boston on December 30, 1969. When the P.A.'s application for membership was announced, two outraged members in the audience declared that psychic phenomena were impossible. The chairman of the screening committee waited to see if there were more protesters, then said, "The Committee on Council Affairs considered the P.A.'s work for a very long time. The Committee came to the conclusion that it is an association investigating controversial or non-existent phenomena. However, it is open in membership to critics and agnostics, and they were satisfied that it uses scientific methods of inquiry—thus, that investigation can be regarded as scientific."[1] Another hurdle overcome. One more to go.

Before the council members took a vote, Dr. Margaret Mead, the much-loved anthropologist, encouraged by E. Douglas Dean, made an impassioned appeal: "For the past ten years we have been arguing about what constitutes science and scientific method, and what societies use it. The P.A. uses statistics and blinds, placebos, double-blinds and other standard devices. . . ." She concluded, "The whole history of scientific advance is full of scientists investigating phenomena that the establishment did not believe were there. I submit that we vote in favor of this Association's work."[2]

The chairman suggested that because of the controversial nature of the motion, there should be a show of hands. The P.A. members, who had seen their hopes dashed three times, waited tensely.

About 170 hands were raised in their favor. "Against?" About thirty hands went up.

The P.A. had joined—after much effort—some three hundred affiliated scientific, medical, and engineering societies.

Science still held out against the newcomer. And behaviorist Professor B. F. Skinner threw cold water on the parapsychologists who regarded their acceptance as of great consequence. "The American Association for the Advancement of Science, being open-minded, allowed parapsychology to make some presentations at a meeting, and immediately this is twisted to say that now the AAAS recognizes it as a scientific field," he complained. "This is not true. It's the kind of thing I object to. Anyone can become a member of the AAAS; there are almost no qualifications. It's not so easy to become a Fellow of the AAAS."[3]

Skinner's view on the unimportance of being AAAS members was not shared by several of his colleagues, who were soon committed to throwing the newcomers out.

53

AAAS CONVENTION
1970

Rhine sent his new director of research, Dr. Helmut Schmidt, to the annual convention of the AAAS in Chicago two days after Christmas. There was to be a symposium in which members of the Parapsychological Association would have a chance to advance their cause and describe their research before, they hoped, their most articulate critics. Many ex-Rhine staffers were there: Dr. Van de Castle, who chaired the symposium; Charles Honorton; Gaither Pratt; and Karlis Osis among them. The expected atmosphere of intelligent comment and challenging questions from the audience did not materialize.

Thomas R. Tietze, an associate editor of *Psychic*, a popular but informed magazine, noted that scientists the speakers had hoped to attract never showed up. He guessed that many were diverted by a group of young protesters down the hall. The youngsters had created a fracas when they tried to present Dr. Edward Teller, "father of the hydrogen bomb," with a "Dr. Strangelove" award. Teller resisted the dubious honor, as Strangelove was a scientific character in fiction and film with maniacal urges that threatened to destroy the world. One thing is sure, Dr. Teller had not been on his way to listen to the parapsychologists.

Rhine's representative, Dr. Schmidt, revealed to an audience of about two hundred how the Institute for Parapsychology had brought psi research into the space age. Formerly a research physicist with the Boeing Aircraft Company in Seattle, Schmidt had a long-standing interest in parapsychology and had used his daughter, among others, as a subject in ESP and PK tests. Now he told of the advances in Rhine's lab. Schmidt had used a quantum mechanical random generator, which depended on the radioactive decay of a particle of strontium 90, to generate numbers in a random and unpredictable manner. He then asked eleven people to guess the numbers (one, two, three, four) in advance of their appearance. All told, they made ten thousand guesses. By chance, they should have been right 25 percent of the time. They were right 26.4 percent, beating the chance odds of one in a thousand.

Dr. Schmidt described another of his experiments to see if animals could cause a physical effect with their minds. He chose cockroaches because a supply was at hand, left over from a previous experiment. His experimental equipment comprised a plastic box with greased walls so that the creatures couldn't escape. The box had an electrified grid floor connected to a random generator. The cockroaches were subject to mild electric shocks at random intervals. His test was to see if the cockroaches used psychokinesis to decrease the number of seconds in which the electric shock was on, from its normal fifty-fifty times on and off. Because the cockroaches occasionally flipped over on their backs, Schmidt kept watch in order to put them on their feet.

The physicist-turned-parapsychologist had to admit that the result of this exploratory test of 6,400 trials was somewhat baffling. More electric shocks occurred than could be expected by chance. If, as indicated, PK had been demonstrated, the result could be explained in a number of ways, among them: The cockroaches *liked* mild electric shocks; they reacted unnaturally to a novel experience; or the experimenter might unintentionally have caused the increased shocks.[1]

Psychologist Dr. Gertrude Schmeidler of New York's City College had recently been elected president of the Parapsychological Association, and she brought the subject back from cockroaches to people. She stressed that it was not possible to "build a theory of ESP until we can find out what shields it, what stops it." She hoped that when personality concomitants of ESP success and failure were discovered, then one could predict "with considerable accuracy when ESP success will occur."[2]

Rhine was already strongly in agreement with her. He was beginning to see with growing conviction that psychological factors were the key to advancement in uncovering the unconscious springs of psi activity. The psychological mood and motivation of both experimenter and subject had to be much more fully explored. In time, he speculated, there might be schools to train experimenters how to elicit and subjects how to produce psi phenomena.

Despite the yawns and frowns noticed in the audience and one man who ignored the speakers to work on his manuscript about a personal encounter with flying-saucer pilots, the crowd generally showed polite interest. But that was almost ominous. Parapsychology seemed to thrive on conflict.

Fortunately one man stood up to complain that there was

still no theory to explain ESP and that "in science one observes an orderly progression of facts and then constructs a theory to explain those facts." Dr. Van de Castle replied that parapsychology was "still at a data-gathering stage" and that it would be premature to construct a physical theory to explain paranormal phenomena. Dr. Schmeidler added that a psychological theory of sorts was emerging from the accumulation of experimental data. It seemed clear, for example, that psi capacities are not ego-involved.[3]

This meeting was almost Dr. Schmidt's swan song as Rhine's representative. Schmidt had the inevitable clashes with Rhine and began to make plans to join another parapsychological research center. He relinquished his position as director of research, but stayed on to pursue his experiments for several months before leaving to be a research associate at the Mind Science Foundation in San Antonio, Texas. Rhine already had his eye on the next director, who would carry on where Schmidt left off with the promising but puzzling cockroach experiment. It was a bad mistake. Rhine should have followed his instinct to pursue the psychological aspects of the work and not depend on machines, which he and his fellow parapsychologists were lauding as fraud-proof.

54

BETRAYAL
1970–1974

A medical student arrived on the parapsychological scene in 1970, displaying the magic touch of the young J. B. Rhine. His experiments gave positive results with dazzling consistency. In one issue alone of the *Journal of Parapsychology*, December 1970 (Volume 34, Number 4), Walter Jay Levy reported three of his experiments which demonstrated that animals could not only move objects with their minds but were able to see into the future.

To test the precognition theory, Levy gave mice mild electric shocks whenever they jumped into the "wrong" half of a cage. Would the mice use psi ability to avoid the electrified half, which was repeatedly and randomly changed? They did, Levy reported. A second experiment was "designed to see if chicken embryos and young chicks could use psychokinesis to get the heat they needed," and results indicated "that both embryos and baby chicks influenced the random number generator [to turn on the heat] by means of PK."

The third experiment, to test precognition in mice and gerbils, was "designed to repeat, with some procedural modifications, the work of Duval and Montredon in France on precognition in mice." It was an open secret that these were the assumed names of Dr. Remy Chauvin, a Sorbonne biologist, and Dr. J. P. Genthon, who used pseudonyms because of the scorn with which parapsychology was viewed in France.* Again, Levy's results were positive, confirming the psi discoveries of the Frenchmen.

---

*In an interview with Chauvin in the Journal of Parapsychology, *January 2, 1971, Rhine said, "It is a well-known secret that you have done some of your writing on parapsychology under the assumed name of Pierre Duval. What is the present situation with regard to the need for this protective device? Now that parapsychology has spread widely around the world, even behind the Iron Curtain to some extent, and the University of Utrech is offering a professorship on the subject, while the Parapsychological Association has affiliated with the AAAS and other things are happening,*

290

But it was not only Levy's results that cheered Rhine, now seventy-five, but the energy, enthusiasm, and devotion of the young man. He had shown it first while studying medicine in Augusta, Georgia. Every free day or weekend, Levy leaped into his car and drove up to Durham to work with Rhine. Parapsychology engrossed him. His parents were astonished when they saw the mileage on his car's odometer—until he explained his new avocation. And he talked of Rhine in glowing, godlike terms. Rhine, for his part, could not have been more pleased if Levy had levitated at a meeting of the American Society for the Advancement of Science.

Levy's parents watched, slightly stunned, as his graduating class was awarded their medical degrees, knowing that he alone was not continuing in medicine. His training had been expensive. Now he was throwing it all away to work in a questionable field.

With renewed hopes, Rhine welcomed the bright young dynamo. From the first, Levy showed exceptional devotion to his work and a willingness to sacrifice. Although his salary was moderate, it was enough to pay for a room with a bed. But Levy chose to donate part of his money to parapsychology and to sleep in an attic at FRNM alongside the cages of gerbils and electronic equipment—a twenty-four-hour-a-day devotee to the cause.

He was soon rewarded. He had barely been there three years when, in 1973, Rhine appointed this man in his early twenties director of the institute. No longer the up-and-coming heir apparent, he was now the heir in fact. Rhine had made his choice and was preparing to ease himself into semi-retirement.

He put Levy in charge not only of all experiments, but also of the finances, which meant juggling stocks owned by FRNM and heading conferences with accountants. And Rhine sent him out to lecture across the country and to a convention in Scotland. With no managerial or business experience, Levy handled millions of dollars, directed a staff of scientists, and ran and reported his own experiments. The task called for a scientific and financial virtuoso with energy to burn. And Levy appeared to be it.

Naturally his energy and intelligence, which endeared him to Rhine and shot him to the top, did not evoke the same response in those he had overtaken or replaced. One saw Levy as "pathologically ambitious." Another, a psychologist, rejected the word *pathological* to

---

do you still feel that this problem exists for you in your country? Is there that much difference?"

Chauvin replied, "In France we still need protective shelters like assumed names. Nobody can do any harm to me now, but it's easy to harm the academic career of my students in order to punish their teacher. However it is true that affiliation with the AAAS is an enormous event; it could change everything."

describe Levy, characterizing him instead as "a very cool, diplomatic, political animal who knows exactly what he's doing, the direction he's going, and what he wants to accomplish. I have no doubts that he is intensely ambitious." Says another: "Dr. Rhine is attracted to people like that. He's totally one-track, oriented toward his own goals."

Levy was testing mice and gerbils in 1971 when astronaut Edgar Mitchell blasted off for the moon and took ESP cards with him. He arranged a telepathy experiment with three psychics on the ground, but there was a misunderstanding about the exact time Mitchell would be projecting his thoughts, so the results are cloudy at best. Rhine, asked to help judge the scores, noticed that they tended to confirm his belief that ESP is not affected by time or distance. The psychic who made the best score was Olof Jonsson. He had shown impressive psi abilities at Duke before, though Rhine had suspected him of tricks.

The science section of *Newsweek* featured a roundup of parapsychological activities that included both Mitchell and Levy, on March 4, 1974. It reads in part:

"Hard sciences are not used to dealing with subjective phenomena," says ex-astronaut Edgar D. Mitchell, who has emerged as one of the most articulate spokesmen for parapsychological research. "The scientist has to recognize that his own mental processes may influence the phenomenon he's observing. If he's really a total skeptic, the scientist may well turn off the psychic subject."

Some parapsychological groups however—notably that directed by psychologist Walter J. Levy at the Foundation for Research on the Nature of Man—are attempting to make their experiments more respectable by automating the procedures and by using as their subjects small rodents which presumably are less whimsical than humans in exhibiting whatever paranormal gifts they may have. In one experiment designed by Levy and James W. Davis, for example, hamsters or gerbils occupy a divided pen, in one half of which they may at any time be given an electric shock. Selection of the side of the pen to cause the shock is completely automated and random, yet time and time again the rodents have been observed to jump to the other side just before the electric jolt arrives. Levy is convinced that the little creatures learn to beat the statistical odds by somehow fore-telling the future.*

While Levy's triumphs were reported in a national publication, he was working on a new PK experiment. He implanted electrodes in rats' brains, through which their pleasure centers were stimulated. Would they use mind power to increase the stimulation? It was during this Orwellian experiment that Levy's colleagues wondered why he lingered near the equipment when there was no need for him to be there.

Their suspicions aroused, James Kennedy, Levy's coexperimenter, and others secretly arranged to make independent recordings of the rats' performances. Levy's record had shown 54 percent hits. Their duplicate recordings showed 50 percent—or what would be expected by chance.

The researchers agreed among each other to spy on Levy to see if they could catch him cheating. Hiding in the lab and peeking through cracks in doors, they watched him manipulating the apparatus to produce the effects he wanted. The following day the group spoke with Louisa Rhine and then with J. B. Rhine. That afternoon J. B. Rhine confronted Dr. Levy with the evidence. He admitted that he had manipulated the data, and submitted his resignation.

Rhine was deeply shocked and desperately disappointed.

"As my wife and I reviewed this evidence with the men on June 12," wrote Rhine,

... we were left without a doubt that, almost incredible as it seemed, our colleague W* had improperly altered the data, at least in the case of this one rat experiment in PK. I called W in and confronted him with the observations of his colleagues. Within a matter of minutes he acknowledged the charges, and almost without further discussion he offered his resignation. Under the circumstances, of course, I accepted it.[1]

The calm way Rhine recalls this occasion gives no hint of how tense and distressing it must have been for him and Levy. Of course Rhine wanted to know why this man in whom he had put so much trust and hope had betrayed him.

W's answer to my question of how he came to commit this falsification was that this line of experimentation, which had been going so successfully for over a year and which I had been pressing him to try to get independently repeated, had taken a bad turn.... He knew from earlier tests what the general level had been and was impulsively tempted to hold it up artificially in order, as he thought, to

*Rhine used an initial to protect the innocent, he explained. Later he realized he had to identify him fully to warn other parapsychologists to ignore all Levy's experiments as suspect.

stimulate the independent repetitions he hoped would follow. As he expressed his deep regrets, he added a few words about overwork during recent months.[2]

Charles Honorton agrees that Rhine researchers did feel pressure to produce positive results. "I remember being taken to task by Rhine on a number of occasions because I was getting negative results and getting a lengthy discourse on how that related to negative personal attributes in myself."[3]

Levy claimed this was the only work he had faked, but Rhine had to assume that everything Levy had touched was questionable and issued such a warning.

Rhine pointed out that

... at the Duke Parapsychology Laboratory we took the firm position that a subject should not be trusted at all; even if he were a priest or the experimenter's best friend, the conditions must be such that cheating would not be possible. This radical objectivity alienated many workers, but in time it brought dependability on this issue.[4]

Now he asked

Whom can we trust in parapsychology? The answer will have to be: "It is not in any science a question of whom, but of what methods are adequate for confidence." ... My own strongest confidence in parapsychology rests on the vast evidence from the signs of psi, results that are (thus far) unique to this field, and stand out like fingerprints or geologic evidence.[5]

Rhine gave a fuller and more emotional account of the Levy affair in the December 1975 issue of his journal.

W.J.L. had been an extremely enterprising and industrious worker. As the chief administrator of the laboratory and an active leader in almost every aspect of its activities, he well knew all the limits and loopholes in a system he was masterminding seven days of the week—often sleeping in the attic while overseeing the twenty-four hour automatic testing of the animals. [Levy's critics say this gave him more opportunity to cheat.]

As these comments were first written I learned from Dr. Helmut Schmidt of the Mind Science Foundation, who was here at the time of the W.J.L. exposé, that he has since spent two months working with rats with implanted electrodes. Six of the ten rats showed good self-stimulation if they could induce the stimulus by pressing the lever.

Subsequent PK tests under varying conditions ... did not
encourage him to continue the tests.

Others tried to replicate them but failed.

In general, the way parapsychologists received the news of W.J.L.'s
dishonesty was, like our own, one of shocked surprise and amaze-
ment. Why did he do that? How could he ever have felt the need to do
such a thing after all the success he had had? What a careless way to
cheat—not even clever! Was he in his right mind? Had he given other
signs of unreliability or instability? Would this not ruin his career?
How could he possibly stay in parapsychology? Etc., etc.[6]

The extent of the possible damage to parapsychology can be
guessed from a phone call Dr. R. A. McConnell made to fellow
parapsychologist Charles Honorton, immediately on hearing of the
Levy exposé. McConnell's first words were: "What's the worst thing
that could happen to parapsychology?"[7]

But Rhine again displayed his astonishing resilience. Blows
that would have drained or destroyed other men seemed only to
recharge his batteries.

The tragedy of this crisis in parapsychology will not let me lose the
resolve to try to see that an ugly development like this one shall never
again strike our field. . . . One can surely hope that the kind of drastic
effort all of us in parapsychology must now undertake may be all the
more a united one just because W.J.L.'s tragic blunder has brought
the issue home to us all as nothing else conceivably could have done.
    It should now be possible to obtain a more concerted effort all
around than could otherwise ever have been enlisted. A special
obligation of this task I must myself accept since obviously, among all
who shared some responsibility for W.J.L.'s meteoric career in psi
research, I, more than anyone else, could have used greater vigilance
and wisdom by pursuing a policy which would not have permitted a
climax so destructive both to science and the man himself.[8]

Levy resumed his interrupted medical career, and could now
make use of the microscope his parents bought him before he
defected to parapsychology.

Levy's father believed he had his son's confidence: "I discussed it with Jay at length and told him I want to know the facts. 'If
you've committed murder, tell me—it won't go any further.' Jay
absolutely swore to me that the only instance where anything even
resembling that sort of thing happened was in that one experiment
with the rats."[9]

In his father's opinion, Levy had suffered a nervous break-down under the intense pressure of "beating his brains out for Rhine," wanted to quit, but could not face Rhine directly, so that he subconsciously "put a plug in upside down, knowing that he was being spied on, to force a showdown."[10] A secondary consideration was that while Rhine had been ill, Levy had been in complete charge of the institute. When Rhine recovered, says Levy senior, he wanted to resume some of the direction, to young Levy's chagrin. Levy's father thought his son had been overworked and resented the fact that the other researchers had acted like spies. He thought they should have gone to his son with their suspicions and have given him a chance to explain or justify his actions.

But obviously, this would have given Levy a chance to cover his tracks, to fire his accusers, or both.

Rhine was anxious to see if Levy's faked experiments could be honestly replicated. James Terry tried and failed. Nevertheless, Rhine put Terry on the permanent staff. Terry wanted to have his negative results published. Rhine was against publication at that time. When Terry persisted in his efforts to get his work published, Rhine fired him. It was the start of another battle for Rhine, this time with many members of the Parapsychological Association. They believed nega-tive experiments should get full exposure. Rhine thought they were worth only a brief mention, provided those interested in the detailed report could obtain it on request.

When Dr. Irvin Child of Yale failed to replicate another study by Levy, it added "a few more nails to Levy's scientific coffin," wrote reviewer Douglas M. Stokes in the March 1977 *Journal*.

Rhine's long-time critics naturally leaped on the Levy affair as a further demonstration of Rhine's flaws and psi's nonexistence. Rhine hit back at those critics gathering for the kill. They not only threw Levy at him, but also another recently discovered cheating parapsychologist, S. G. Soal. Rhine pointed out that scientific fakes were evenly distributed and not a monopoly of parapsychology. In 1974, the year in which Levy was caught and confessed, William Summerlin, a cancer researcher at New York's Sloan Kettering In-stitute for Cancer Research, had admitted to deceit.

A generous view of these fakers is that they believe in the theories that their fudged data confirmed. Charles Honorton puts Levy in that category. "Other researchers have reported similar types of effects, although not literal replications of Levy's," says Honorton. "I suspect that what was going on with Levy was a genuine effect that was not as reliable as Levy wanted it to be. And that he helped it along."[11]

Rhine's son, Robert, a businessman working abroad, heard

from his mother and sisters about the Levy affair. He was returning to the United States and "passed through Durham just to say 'Dad, I'm sorry it happened.' Because it really hurt him. I could tell he was upset. I know the lab was frequently criticized for tyring to produce results that proved ESP exists. But I recalled a couple of conversations over the years when Dad said, 'In our lab we can't afford any cloud of suspicion. We must work so that nobody can challenge us and make it stick.' But I think he profited from that experience with Levy. He told me as late as this year [1980] that some of his bitterest enemies and harshest critics over the years had written to him after the episode and said, 'We're sorry that happened to you. And we believe you've been telling the truth.' "[12]

55

A TEST OF SURVIVAL 1974

In June 1974 Rhine wrote an article in the *Journal of Parapsychology*, the title of which could have been borrowed from the opposition: "Telepathy and Other Untestable Hypotheses."[1] Rhine did not deny the existence of psi—he proclaimed it. But he stressed the difficulty in proving telepathy, postmortem survival (PMS), and out-of-body experience (OBE). After a century of effort no one had devised a clear way to demonstrate telepathy, for example. What people claimed to be telepathy could be clairvoyance, wrote Rhine, or even psychokinesis—one mind exerting a physical effect on another.

He was amazed that "parapsychology has clung so long to the unanswerable questions in spite of warnings against their futility."[2]

As for out-of-body experience, Rhine asked,

How can it ever be proved that the subject who claims to have projected himself mentally out of his own body and traveled to some other physical location has not simply imagined that he has traveled there? The only meaningful evidence offered us consists of claims of psi effects supposed to have been produced by the traveling mind; but the interpretation is always ambiguous. . . . How could a clear distinction be drawn to show that some personal agency did travel in space to the new location and that it was there that it exercised whatever psi ability was registered? That is the question to be answered, and no one has yet offered a definite design for a way of obtaining an answer.[3]

Rhine had quietly tried some OBE experiments, then dropped them as inconclusive.

Leaving the question of telepathy to be solved in the distant future, Rhine said that it also meant postponing research into postmortem survival. The evidence for that, he maintained, could be explained in terms of psi, and so, he added, could the evidence for reincarnation, "mediumistic communication with the inhabitants of other planets, with theological realms, and such." In fact, the reports of such occurrences "have no more definitive evidential basis than the subject's own imagination."

On the other hand, he admitted that "it could not be said about any of these hypotheses that no method will ever be discovered or invented that could allow a reliable test and thus solve such problems. It is not impossible—or to me even inconceivable—that this should one day occur. All that might be needed for such an advance would be that one or more subjects develop reliable enough tracer-sensitivity to identify reliably the sources of information received."

Rhine would further develop his suggestion of "tracer-sensitivity" as a way of verifying postmortem survival.

But now he chose to end by pointing out to future parapsychologists the path to follow:

The telepathy example, after nearly a century of trial, seems to offer an important lesson for the psi research worker, the necessity of selecting a clearly researchable problem; first, one that does not assume anything the method itself cannot test; and second, one that with significantly positive results can be expected to answer the one question singled out for the test as designed. The lesson of working always with clear and sharp issues, if fully learned and applied at this stage of parapsychology, can multiply the rate of advance for the field as a whole more rapidly than anything else to be compared.[4]

Less than a year later, Rhine, now approaching his eightieth birthday, made what he believed was a step forward in searching for a simple and effective way to test the hypothesis of postmortem survival. In his anguished attempt to defend psi research after Walter Jay Levy had admitted to faking his experiment, Rhine re-emphasized the pattern of evidence in the old tests for ESP and PK that appeared to indicate the presence of psi—evidence that was not discovered until years after the tests were made. So that unless the subjects or experimenters were clairvoyant, they would not have been aware of these signs, or "fingerprints." One such was the overall pattern of scoring. And it was these "hidden" signs which Rhine not only embraced as indicating the existence of psi but which he believed might help in experiments to discover if man does survive bodily death (postmortem survival).

"It can now be made a rather logical question for biology, just as psi ability has logically come to be regarded as a part of an extended psychology," he wrote.[5]

Moreover, the PMS question can now be more neutrally stated: Is there any recordable sign of personal continuity beyond death or does every trace of mind, including psi, disappear? This question allows a fairly good possibility of an answer, yes or no. Up until now there has been only the search for a possible affirmative answer, sufficient for first attempts at exploration. A negative answer could not have been expected. Now it becomes a more basic question as we inquire what the total role of the psi system is in the organism, how it functions on the various levels and stages of life and embryonic development. Does it have any sort of bodily localization, or any necessary physiological accompaniment? Does it show any degree of somatic interdependence in any way? Or any verifiable independence whatsoever? More specifically, what is the relation of psi to sleep (natural or induced)? Does this mental function ebb and flow with the fluctuations of vigor, health, and illness of various types in man and the many animal species that can now be counted on for a broad basis of evidence?[6]

Rhine proposed starting PMS experiments with animals, to study their gradually lowered states of consciousness until their deaths, and later with terminal human patients. They could be undertaken with patients or healthy volunteers under anesthesia. "With advanced psi methods for tracing results to a given source, this ought to have a fair prospect of realization; at least nothing about it is beyond the rational expectation that might follow from the record of psi research, so far as I know it today."[7]

Assuming the animals or humans to possess psi abilities, Rhine suggested recording these along with life processes on a chart, to see if as the life processes diminish up to death or under anesthesia, the psi activities also diminish to the same extent. If they did, this would indicate the unlikelihood of survival after death.

On the other hand, the best possible techniques of psi communication will objectively trace and graph any indications of independent continuity of peculiar personal signs that persist on into and beyond the final stages of declining vitality—if any of them do. We may well hope to have all related sciences working together on the problem— much as has developed in the counterpart study of the origin of life. . . . One little reliable sign of PSM as showing the extrabiological nature of psi, either in animal or human subjects, that would stand out as clearly as its extraphysical nature has done over the years, would electrify the whole field of parapsychology as nothing ever has. However, there is now no firm basis for a prediction either way.[8]

Whether positive or negative, the evidence from such extensive research should be regarded as an equally important contribution to human knowledge, Rhine thought.

In the late sixties and early seventies Rhine had returned to his early interest in survival research. He also resumed his work with people of outstanding psychic ability.

56

PSYCHIC STARS
1969–1974

Psychics appeared at Rhine's door who claimed to have found missing persons, helped the police track down killers, discovered buried treasure. All Rhine had to do, they said, was accompany them on one of their cases and see for himself. Then the scientific world would have to accept ESP.

But this was precisely what Rhine did not want to do. This was the "failed" method, which the modern experimental approach of science in all fields had replaced. It was too uncertain. Who was to know what inside information a psychic had to a crime? His best friend might be the chief detective; a neighbor might be a witness; the newspapers may have given him many clues.

Rhine's intent was to find definitive answers, not maybes. So when psychics arrived at FRNM eager to demonstrate their powers, they were frequently disillusioned by their reception.

Rhine would test them his way, with the cards or dice—not their way. And if they protested that they needed to work with real people and real situations, they received a not-so-fond farewell.

Further, although Rhine believed psychics should be handled with care and consideration, he was always on guard against publicity seekers who planned to use his name to enhance their prestige.

Sean Harribance had become famous in Trinidad as a psychic with a gift for foretelling the future. Like Eileen Garrett, he was curious to have his talent scientifically probed. Psychologist Dr. Hamlyn Dukhan tested him in Trinidad. He put twelve photographs face down on a table and asked Harribance to guess the sex of the subjects. In a thousand trials, he averaged nine right out of twelve, instead of the six expected by chance. Dukhan wrote to Rhine, who invited Harribance to Durham and sent the money for his fare.

Harribance arrived on January 17, 1969, and endured a series of disappointments. Dr. Rhine greeted him on the run. Harribance was housed in an attic room. He found after a long hungry wait that he was expected to buy his own meals. He had no means of transportation. "I had come to Durham with such high expectations," wrote Harribance. "Now, forty-eight hours after my arrival, I was very lonely and depressed. I missed my family and my friends, and I found myself in a situation where no one seemed to care about me."[1]

It is not surprising that a hometown celebrity was shaken by his reception at Durham, where a psychic, after all, was just another guinea pig. After three weeks of testing with ESP cards, Harribance had not scored above chance. Although he had been invited for three months, Rhine suggested that he return home immediately. Rhine explained he was short of staff and money, and obviously did not want to stretch out what seemed fruitless tests. Harribance dreaded returning home a failure. He told Rhine that the cold weather, radical changes in his diet, initial loneliness in a strange country, all could account for his indifferent score. He had a few hundred dollars. If Harribance supported himself, would Rhine continue testing him? Rhine agreed. Eventually Harribance did well on the ESP tests and even better at PK. He was also tested at the Psychic Research Foundation by the project director, William G. Roll. There, Harribance continued to display unusual psychic ability, once getting results better than chance by the one hundred trillion to one.[2] Roll considered Harribance to be one of the most outstanding of all sensitives tested in a laboratory.[3]

Harribance eventually realized the pressure Rhine had been under when they first met and had forgiven what seemed like Rhine's indifferent, almost callous treatment. Harribance now admired and respected him.[4]

Three years after Harribance first arrived at Duke, psychic M. B. Dykshoorn turned up from Australia. He claimed the unique distinction of a passport that described him as a clairvoyant. This Dutch psychic said he had used his powers to find buried silver during World War II, to find a metal box buried for more than three hundred years, to have helped solve two crimes, and to have aided the police find the body of a missing girl.

He told Rhine that he had helped the police to solve a murder. His feats had been confirmed by witnesses and their reports notarized. He explained: "I reenact the murder, go to all the different places where the killer went."[5]

Dykshoorn was living in Australia when he began to correspond with Rhine, and in 1972 left there with his family to submit to Rhine's tests in North Carolina.

Dykshoorn asked Rhine to follow him and record everything he said and did when he attempted to solve a crime. Rhine was only interested in Dykshoorn's ability to call the ESP cards or affect the fall of dice. The psychic protested that he had no psychokinetic powers, was not a telepathist or hypnotist. He wanted his demonstrated talents to be tested. Rhine was adamant. But even if Dykshoorn was willing, said Rhine, he would not be able to fit him in for a month, being short of staff and funds.

The Dutch psychic capitulated. He waited for a month, then submitted to the card tests for eight hours a day. His proposal to distinguish different blood samples was turned down, as was his suggestion that Rhine contact the police and get him a crime to solve. Rhine proposed instead that his staff should "playact" a murder for the psychic to investigate. Dykshoorn said that he responded psychically to genuine human emotions, not make-believe ones. When he was told the card testing would go on for about a month, Dykshoorn walked out, but had a change of heart when he heard that results of his tests had been encouraging.

But when he wrote to Rhine saying he was ready to do more tests, Rhine turned him down. He apparently believed Dykshoorn was being financed or sponsored by someone and was more than anxious not to make his institute a public relations organization for psychics. And when Dr. Rhine found Dykshoorn's visit to FRNM had been written up in a July issue of the Charlotte Focus, he severed their relationship.

Dykshoorn was disappointed. "I feel strongly that confining an analysis of my psychic talents to statistical tests involving cards or other inanimate objects was hardly an adequate determinant," he later wrote. "The ability to identify cards may signify that a person possesses ESP, but there are or should be many other criteria—criteria with more convincing weight—to establish or confirm such powers. . . . I have found human bodies and solved police cases. I solved many cases over long-distance telephone wires. I can also use my gift to tell anyone about his or her past, present, and future, and I can do it at any time, under any conditions. As it happens, I can also identify cards consistently enough to be judged psychic according to tests devised by the parapsychologists, but it gives me no satisfaction to be recognized as genuine by such standards. The ability to identify cards is a very minor aspect of my psychic gift."[6]

However, in a 1974 interview, Dykshoorn had mellowed: "Dr. Rhine speaks very highly about me and I about him. I consider him an outstanding scientist. He has a system that he has been working for thirty years or more and he did not like it when I came in as a termite in his system.* I think he should have made an exception

_____

*Louisa Rhine points out that Rhine's "method was experimental—not anecdotal—and these practitioners seemed not to understand that. It was like going to the doctor and then objecting to the remedy he offered."

for me. But I have no hard feelings. I see Dr. Rhine as one of the pioneers in parapsychology and I'm sure this man has done a lot. I admire him."[7]

Some forty years after the golden era in which Rhine had discovered psychic superstars, a new crop had arrived at his lab to refute or at least give pause to the critics who dismissed the earlier high results as due to loose controls. Now, in the late sixties and early seventies, Dykshoorn and Harribance were joined by a third man, Bill Delmore. All three achieved high scores in rigorously controlled experiments.

Dr. Irvin Child, a Yale University psychologist with only a casual interest in parapsychology, first met Bill Delmore at Yale in 1972. "He was dropping out of law school to explore his apparent psychic talents. That was the first time that I had ever met anybody who seemed to have ESP experiences. His ESP, if it was that, was demonstrated in the form of card tricks which I could not evaluate. Still I found it very impressive. Delmore was interested in getting in touch with people doing research on parapsychology. I had just learned that [Dr. Ed Kelly] a former student from Yale with a Ph.D. from Harvard had just abandoned his research career to go into parapsychology. He was at the Institute for Parapsychology. I told him about this possible subject [Delmore] and found that the institute was interested in having such potential subjects. Delmore did visit there and Kelly took him to Harvard. Delmore made enough impression on the people in the psychology department at Harvard that they voted to provide money to support him at Rhine's Institute for Parapsychology."[8]

In one test with playing cards at Rhine's institute, reported in 1974, Delmore was expected to get 9 hits out of 468 trials. He achieved a phenomenal score of 67 hits.

Harribance was a cooperative subject who thought his gift came from God. Delmore was difficult. "He reported many spontaneous psi experiences and was noted for the 'tricks' (which did not seem like legerdemain) played with cards," wrote Dr. Louisa Rhine.

He did not like formal card tests, but preferred situations in which he could respond more spontaneously. However, in 20 standard ESP card runs, he averaged 8.2 hits per run, a CR [critical ratio: a measure to determine whether or not the observed deviation is significantly greater than the expected random fluctuation above the average] of 7.16. Tested with other devices, including a PK machine, his results often were phenomenally high, but his personal temperament and general impatience made him far from an easy subject with whom to work under acceptably tight conditions.[9]

Rhine concluded, despite the dazzling performances of Harribance and Delmore, that psi ability was not restricted to the gifted few. Dr. Louisa Rhine agreed with him, comparing psi to singing:

Though every normal person can do it, some do it better and easier than others. Singing, however, can be improved by proper teaching, but for psi no teachers yet know the rules. It is a spontaneous, natural gift, much like humor.[10]

57

THE RUSSIANS
ADVANCE
1977–1978

At eighty-two, late in 1977, Rhine suffered a stroke. He was taken to the hospital for rest and for tests, emerging a week later somewhat leaner and with a weakened left leg. But the day he came out of the hospital Rhine climbed the steps to his study to continue his work—"not taking three steps at a time as he used to," said Louisa Rhine. "Now he held the rail and walked a step at a time."[1]

He had appointed Dr. K. Ramakrishna Rao director of the Institute for Parapsychology, the experimental arm of FRNM. Rao was an articulate spokesman for parapsychology, a prolific writer and careful researcher. He had been a lecturer in philosophy at Andhra University, a Fulbright scholar and Rockefeller fellow. On a return visit to India he had helped to uncover what appeared to be fraudulent psi experiments. Rao was promising to be a worthy heir to Rhine. But no one doubted that Rhine was still in overall charge. And when, in the spring of 1978, the Smithsonian Institution invited him to lecture on psi and then publicly debate with a skeptical critic, Rhine did not plead illness and send Rao in his place. The invitation was a better fillip than a week's bed rest.

To present his case at the Smithsonian had a special piquancy, which he shared with his audience there. He had never forgotten that when astrophysicist C. G. Abbot was head of the Smithsonian, he had made an ESP test with himself as both experimenter and subject. His results were significant and he sent a report of the experiment to Rhine for publication. There was one proviso: The report was to be anonymous. And that's how it appeared, under the title: "A scientist tests his own ESP ability."[2] Abbot apparently was afraid that his being linked with Rhine's work might damage the reputation of the Smithsonian, jeopardize his job, subject him to ridicule, or all three.

Abbot's report appeared in the *Journal of Parapsychology* in 1938. Not until eleven years later, when he had retired, did Abbot acknowledge that he was the anonymous author, and then he submitted another article for Rhine's *Journal*, signed this time, and titled: "Further evidence of displacement in ESP tests."[3] Rhine believed that Abbot was one of a number of scientists who had achieved or witnessed positive psi results, but for various reasons had been reluctant to admit it.

Since the stroke, it took Rhine longer to clarify his thoughts. He had always spoken slowly and deliberately, even admitted he was not a quick thinker. But his intensity of delivery and concentration had emphasized not his hesitation, but his earnestness. He listened intensely, too, partly because of his defective hearing. Now the pauses while he searched his memory or marshaled his words were evidence of his illness. But he was improving almost daily.

The trip to Washington on April 19, 1978, proved therapeutic. His limp was less apparent and there was no hint of frailty or hesitation in his speech when he debated Dr. Paul Kurtz, leader of the Committee for the Scientific Investigation of Claims of the Paranormal, an anti-pseudoscience movement. Kurtz was also editor of its publication, the *Skeptical Inquirer*.

In the afternoon the two men were interviewed for a Smithsonian radio program. Kurtz explained his open-minded but critical attitude toward parapsychological research. He was committed to scientific enquiry and objectivity, agreeing with Rhine that there should be research into psychic phenomena. Kurtz was rather disarmed when Rhine said: "I agree with virtually everything you've said." But then followed a sharp give-and-take. After the broadcast they spoke in a hall of the main museum before an audience of Smithsonian associates, parapsychologists, and members of the public. Kurtz read his paper, "Is Parapsychology a Science?"* His major objection was the difficulty in knowing how to replicate the psi findings, and he suggested that attempts at replication should be undertaken by skeptics or neutral observers. He did not think the claims made by parapsychologists had been substantiated by the evidence. Rhine gave an account of past work and future objectives. He had no complaint about Kurtz's attitude, but thought psi had been manifestly demonstrated to occur, whatever the objections of the critics.[4]

Rhine gave as good as he got in his defense of parapsychology in the debate that followed, though Kurtz—a professor of philosophy at the State University of New York at Buffalo—was less vehement in his criticism than others on his committee. Many of its members were among the 186 scientists who had signed a manifesto in 1975 denouncing astrology as a pseudoscience.

However many committees might be organized against him, Rhine knew his position was infinitely better than that of Soviet parapsychologists. For some years he had been corresponding with the Russian Edward K. Naumov, a promoter of parapsychology in the Soviet Union, exchanging views and information. Then Naumov's letters stopped. Rhine soon found out that Naumov had been arrested and sentenced to a period in a labor camp. His crime apparently had been to encourage parapsychological research and lecture about it without official approval. Shortly afterward, Robert C. Toth, a Los Angeles *Times* correspondent in Russia, was arrested. He was released after handing over information he had obtained about Soviet psi experiments.

Rhine was informed of a formerly secret report, prepared for the United States government, which attempted to assess Soviet parapsychology. The report concluded that the Russians accepted telepathy as a fact, and were pressing ahead with their experiments, probably in mental hospitals, where psychics could be surreptitiously tested under the guise of being patients receiving psychiatric treatment. I. M. Kogan was named as one of the most credible Russian researchers. He believed telepathy might have a physical basis and "hypothesizes that the transfer of information is advanced by ultra-long electromagnetic waves in spherical waveguides formed by the surface of the earth and the ionosphere."[5]

The only rival for leadership in the parapsychological world had been University of Leningrad professor L. L. Vasiliev, who died in 1966. He started his parapsychology experiments in the early thirties, almost simultaneously with Rhine. The difference was that Vasiliev's remained secret for twenty-five years.[6] Vasiliev probably scared the Soviet government into supporting an energetic psi research program in the 1960s and '70s by innocently promoting a false rumor: Two French magazines reported successful telepathy experiments on the U.S. submarine *Nautilus*. Vasiliev mistakenly assumed these accounts to be true. On the other hand, he was aware that the U.S. Office of Naval Research had funded Rhine's lab to carry out experiments. Putting one rumor and one fact together, Vasiliev made one big mistake. He concluded that Rhine had directed the *Nautilus* experiments. The money had not been to finance the *Nautilus* work, but to investigate pigeon homing. However, Vasiliev's supposition seems to have been taken seriously by the Soviet government. Vasiliev was given a laboratory for telepathy experiments, where he worked for six years, until his death.

Naturally, Rhine was pleased that the scientific establishment in at least one country took his work seriously and had experimentally confirmed some of it. He expected the Russians to propose a physical basis for telepathy: That was, after all, the party line. He was just as biased in favor of a nonphysical explanation, although his partiality was based on his findings, not his philosophy. What he deplored was the likelihood that accredited Russian parapsychologists were funded by the military or the secret police and that their intent would be to use psi discoveries for repressive or aggressive ends.

The Russians showed their unpredictability in the summer of 1978 and justified Winston Churchill's characterization of Russia as "a riddle wrapped in an enigma," an apt description of psi itself. A headline in the *Christian Science Monitor* for June 27 read: "Kremlin to allow conference on parapsychology." Now the Russians were inviting a public exchange of information between psi researchers in their country and abroad. Naumov was freed—at least until the next change of policy.

Meanwhile, Rhine was being bombarded with letters from his brother Thomas, a staunch Christian who wanted reassurance that J.B. shared his faith. Thomas wrote: "You've got a great name in this country and some of the foreign countries. How about up in Heaven?" Rhine did not reply. "He didn't want to talk about religion," Thomas explained afterward. "I wrote him five letters and all I put in every one of those letters was: 'What's your belief down there?' [Thomas was in Ohio, J.B. in North Carolina.] And finally, after the fifth letter, all he wrote back was: 'My belief is the same as yours, but I dursn't let my light shine down here.' I wrote to J.B.: 'Just think of the rewards and blessings you're missing by not letting your light shine.' He never did answer. I wrote a lot of letters he didn't answer."[7] Rhine was not a believer. His answer was to console his brother, and perhaps to obtain respite from the proselytizing. "*Agnostic* means something rather more negative than J.B. was," Louisa Rhine pointed out. "If by agnostic you mean he didn't subscribe to the religious views that call God the maker of everything, and the man with the beard—then he was an agnostic. J.B. thought there might be a power of some sort with a purpose. And he was trying to find out."[8]

A month after Rhine heard the news that the Kremlin was supporting a conference on parapsychology, I spoke with him. He had agreed to cooperate with me in writing his biography, but had not yet made up his mind how far he would go. On July 31, 1978, we sat with Louisa outside the white frame house he used as an office. To begin with, his chief concern was that we might be disturbing a nesting bird. Assured that we were not, Rhine expressed his reservations obliquely. He said it was important to know what a writer was looking for, because in his experience a writer usually found just what he was looking for. What was I looking for? The facts about his life and work, I said. I told him I would not prejudge him, but that I would seek information from his critics as well as his supporters. He took the equivalent of a deep breath before replying. And then he said, in effect, that he would tell me anything I wanted to know.

58

DR. JOHN A. WHEELER
1979

The case for psi does not depend exclusively on Rhine's work. Careful, intelligent researchers before and since have demonstrated what appears to be psi activity. But his contributions have been such that should anyone expose him or his work as seriously flawed it could cripple the young science still, after fifty years, struggling to be acknowledged as legitimate. Throughout his working life, Rhine's reputation has been that of a stubborn, proud, even paranoid scientist—but one of unassailable integrity.

During the last year of his life, when he was 83, what some regard as the most devastating attack on Rhine's reputation occurred at the annual meeting of the American Association for the Advancement of Science, at Houston, Texas. There, on January 8, 1979, Dr. John A. Wheeler charged Rhine with having launched his career in parapsychology after pushing the key down an uncontrolled time to achieve a successful outcome in a Lamarckian experiment. One parapsychologist at the meeting and several who later heard a tape recording and read a transcription of Dr. Wheeler's remarks, concluded that he had questioned Rhine's honesty. If that was true—and Dr. Wheeler denies it—it was the first time Rhine had ever been accused of fraud.

Dr. Wheeler is unquestionably a great physicist who worked closely with Albert Einstein, Neils Bohr, and Edward Teller. He is known for his theory on the cosmic traps in space, "black holes," from which no matter can escape. For years, while lecturing at Princeton, contact with the lunatic fringe had made him "sad and thoughtful." One student told Dr. Wheeler that he frequently spoke with people who came down from Mars, and invited his teacher to join him on Route 206, ten miles north of Princeton, to meet the Martians. Dr. Wheeler was not curious enough to go see for himself, but he did wonder what spurred people to take a serious interest in Martians, flying saucers, the Bermuda Triangle, and similar fantasies. He was especially interested in the psychology of the investigator. "What is the source of the element of good judgment?" he asked himself. "What distinguished real science from pseudo-science? And in studying these fascinating byways of self-delusion, where did one have to draw the line and say: 'I'm not going to waste any more time on this'?"[1]

Curiously, although he read many works on parapsychology, including two of Rhine's critics, Irving Langmuir and archcritic Dr. C. E. M. Hansel, Dr. Wheeler never went to the source. All his information about Rhine's work came from secondhand sources, proponents and opponents. And after this study of the subject he joined the critics. Never once did he read one of Rhine's books, nor even dip into the *Journal of Parapsychology* to read Rhine's own descriptions of his experiments or answers to his detractors.

A few days before Dr. Wheeler was to address a meeting of the AAAS on his prepared topic, the quantum theory of measurement, he learned that a panel discussion would follow his talk in which several parapsychologists would take part. He knew that some parapsychologists—Rhine was not among them—had cited his work on quantum mechanics, suggesting that such fantastic conceptions as black holes and the weird world of psi have much in common. To prevent his listeners at the AAAS meeting from assuming even the remotest connection between his subject and psi, Dr. Wheeler decided to express his conviction that parapsychology was a pseudo-science and to launch a campaign to disaffiliate the Parapsychological Association from the AAAS. With that in mind he supplemented his prepared paper with two last-minute appendices provocatively entitled "Drive the Pseudos Out of the Workshop of Science," and "Where There's Smoke There's Smoke."

Dr. Wheeler was also stung into attack because pseudo-scientists were raking in large amounts of money from public and private sources that he thought could be infinitely better spent on serious research. Furthermore he was concerned that if parapsychologists succeeded in linking psi with quantum mechanics it would hold the field up to ridicule and possibly discourage promising young scientists from entering it. Those were among the reasons Dr. Wheeler asked AAAS members to reconsider a decision made ten years earlier when they had voted to admit the Parapsychological Association.

"Faith healers can be prosecuted," said Dr. Wheeler, "confidence men can be sent to jail, but no one would propose that parapsychologists be prevented from soliciting for government support. But why should the name 'AAAS-affiliate' be allowed to give those solicitations an air of legitimacy?" He pointed out that in all their years of work, parapsychologists had not performed one battle-tested experiment that could withstand attack from the skeptics.[2]

Charles Honorton, a parapsychologist on the discussion panel,

protested that although Dr. Wheeler had discussed the Bermuda Triangle, occult chemistry, UFOs, and similar subjects, he had not talked
about scientific studies of psi, or of contemporary psi research.

Dr. Wheeler responded to Honorton by giving an account of a
nonparapsychological experiment which took place 50 years previously, but one in which Rhine was involved:

*I think I might only mention one interesting experiment done by the
great psychologist McDougall on rats. Could the children of rats, if
the parents had learned to go through a maze and distinguish
successfully between the food and electric shock, might not the
children of such educated parents, themselves, do better learning? So
the control group of rats with the training were worked out, and then
McDougall had to be away for the summer and left the work to his
post-doctoral associate, on the babies. And sure enough, it turned out
the babies of the educated parents did better going through the maze
than the babies of the uneducated parents. This was so impressive to
McDougall—and the statistics really convincing—that McDougall and
his post-doctoral put the work together in a paper, but they took the
precaution, thanks to McDougall, to submit the work to Tracy Sonneborn, distinguished both in genetics and in statistics. Something
about the work raised the suspicions of Tracy Sonneborn. So he went
to talk to the two men at Duke. And one thing led to another, and it
turned out that the post-doctoral had been so interested in the
success of the baby rats, that when they made a mistake—the baby
rats, children of the educated parents—that when they made a mistake and went to the outlet where the electric shock was, he pushed
down the key a long time and gave them a "lollapalooza" of a shock.
No wonder they learned faster than the others! So the paper was
never published. The only thing that I haven't mentioned here is the
name of the post-doctoral: It was Rhine. Rhine—he started parapsychology that way.*[3]

The parapsychologists on the panel and in the audience were
stunned and silent. How could they refute this accusation? It appeared to be "inside information" from an irreproachable source,
revealing Rhine to have been at least inept and possibly dishonest.
Would parapsychology ever recover from such a blow?

Rhine had been too ill to attend the meeting. His first reaction
on hearing of the attack was to think: "Here we go again!"[4] His second
reaction was disappointment that no parapsychologist at the meeting
had come to his defense. Later, he realized that none of them had the
information to support him. He, alone, knew the facts of the case.

Rhine ordered a transcript of Dr. Wheeler's remarks about his part in the Lamarckian experiment and found that almost every sentence was either inaccurate or misleading. Dr. Wheeler's most serious charge was that Sonneborn discovered that Rhine, in his eagerness to prove the hypothesis, shocked the experimental rats for a longer time than he shocked the control rats. Sonneborn did, in fact, suspect that the intensity and duration of the shock given to the rats was not adequately controlled. But it was Rhine himself who first reported that the results indicated the intensity of the shock could cause differences in the rate of learning of both experimental and control groups. And Sonneborn used this report by Rhine to support his criticism of McDougall's experiments.

Dr. Wheeler claimed the paper was never published. Not true. McDougall published a total of four reports on his Lamarckian experiments, one of them co-authored with Rhine. What is more, McDougall wrote in a footnote to their joint 1933 paper: "My cordial thanks are due for helpful criticism, especially to Drs. F. A. E. Crew, T. M. Sonneborn, J. B. S. Haldane, V. Hazlitt, W. E. Agar, and most especially to Dr. J. B. Rhine, who, in addition to many helpful criticisms and suggestions, has given much skilled and laborious collaboration during the last four years."[5] McDougall considered Rhine to be a "well-trained biologist, a most careful worker,"[6] and in 1934 he characterized Rhine as "a ruthless seeker after truth, almost, I may say, a fanatical devotee of science."[7]

Although recently felled by a stroke, Rhine was slowly recovering. He was anxious and able to respond to Wheeler's attack. He contacted Tracy Sonneborn who explained he had been misquoted by Dr. Wheeler and would immediately write to so inform him. Which he did. When Dr. Wheeler learned that his account had been a distortion, he sent a letter of retraction to *Science*, the official journal of the AAAS. It failed to spell out what he had said about Rhine. Rhine's letter also published in *Science* remedied Wheeler's omission. But, although Rhine had a transcription of Dr. Wheeler's taped remarks, his paraphrase of those remarks, contained in Rhine's letter, overreaches the facts. Rhine wrote in his letter:

According to Wheeler a post-doctoral assistant in the experiment intentionally altered the conditions so as to produce spurious results.[8]

Wheeler never used the word "intentionally" although several parapsychologists and Rhine himself believed that was the sense of Wheeler's accusation. [Wheeler's letter of retraction and Rhine's response are in Appendix C.]

Dr. Wheeler had vividly demonstrated the danger of not going to a primary source for information. When asked how he could have given such an inaccurate account of Rhine's early experimental work, Wheeler explained:

Ten minutes ago my wife and I were talking about this problem of making sure that what one quotes from a conversation is true. It's just too easy to make a good story if one hears a story that's been told two or three times. It can get out of hand. I had carefully prepared remarks, prepared against a time deadline, and I wanted to say something about the topic that we're now discussing. But I had no time to look it up, so I was careful to leave it out of my written remarks. Then, in the question period afterward, I stupidly didn't realize that the tape recorder was still on, and this was going to a larger audience. And I operated within the framework of a second-hand story, which was a mistake.[9]

Dr. Wheeler insisted that he only meant to imply that Rhine had unconsciously manipulated the results.[10]

Rhine and his fellow parapsychologists got support from an unexpected quarter. The Committee for Scientific Investigation of Claims of the Paranormal opposed Dr. Wheeler's proposal to disaffiliate the Parapsychological Association.

"We oppose any effort to expel the P.A. from the AAAS," said Dr. Paul Kurtz, who had recently debated with Rhine at the Smithsonian and was the leader of a group of scientists and skeptics joined together to investigate claims of the paranormal. "We issued such a statement as a group. We are committed to open enquiry."[11]

On the other hand, Dr. Wheeler received backing for his stand from scientists in France and Italy as well as in the United States. Admiral Hyman G. Rickover, who in his eighties was still testing submarines for the U.S. government, telephoned Wheeler to express his support.

But Rhine himself had been vindicated. And he had Dr. Wheeler to thank for the space *Science* had given to both their letters. Getting any positive news about psi in *Science* was in itself a triumph. Ironically, his critics sometimes served as Rhine's best propagandists.

59

THE LAST BATTLE
1979–1980

Rhine was virtually blind by the fall of 1979, but hoped an operation would bring the world back into focus. His vision had clouded rapidly in the past few months. People were mysterious shadows until they came within a few feet of him. Even with his glasses on, print remained a blur, and for Rhine not to be able to read was like slow starvation. He had been diabetic for several years, but resisted going to doctors or when he did go—reluctantly—he failed to follow their advice. "He followed his own advice," said his daughter Rosemary.[1]

A series of strokes had played tricks with his memory, but had not weakened his will to keep active, to continue his work, to scorn being treated as an invalid. However, at eighty-three, the once-rugged J. B. Rhine looked frail and vulnerable. Even his family had been surprised to see how he had reverted to the unscientific opinions of his father on health and medicine. They expected J. B.'s attitude toward medicine to be similar to his attitude toward his own work. "But everyone can't be perfect and I guess that was the one way he wasn't perfect," remarked his daughter Rosemary. "He was the most amazing man. He'd had minor strokes, his vision and his hearing were going, but he was still taking his briefcase to work—though he couldn't do a lot of it."[2]

Now he was ready to do what doctors advised—if only they could restore his sight.

Louisa read aloud to him the letters and news items she knew he would want to hear. One letter came from the British Society for Psychical Research offering him the presidency. He had been sent the same invitation some years before, but then he had been full of vigor and engrossed in his experiments at the lab and had turned it down. At this stage in his life, when he was physically disabled, he responded as if he had been awarded the Nobel Prize. Louisa was surprised by his enthusiasm and his immediate acceptance of the honor, then realized that it was just the lift to his spirits he needed. And now, with a lifetime to look back on, he could see things from a larger perspective. The society knew he was in poor health, but the presidency would not involve a journey to Britain. All he had to do was write a presidential address. Someone else would read it for him.

This accolade from abroad, unlike the Nobel Prize, had no cash value, but it at last put him officially among the titans of psychical research. Past presidents of the SPR had been Henry and Eleanor Sidgwick; Harvard's William James; Arthur Balfour, who was later prime minister; physicist Oliver Lodge; Nobel prizewinners Charles Richet and Henri Bergson; as well as two friends and contemporaries, William McDougall and Gardner Murphy. He had admired some of them enormously and now he was to be one of them.

J.B. never stopped working on his presidential address. He put together a word or two at a time, scrawled on paper to remind him of the line he intended to take or a reference he wanted someone to check for him. He had decided the subject should be parapsychology and religion. He did not quit even when told by the doctors that the operation on his eyes would never take place. He may have had unorthodox ideas about medicine, but he read enough medical journals to know the doctors' decision meant his diabetes was too far advanced for surgery. He would have to face the rest of his life with little or no sight.

In December 1979, J.B.'s son, Robert, flew up from Mexico City, where he was manager of a General Motors assembly plant, to spend Christmas with his parents and sisters at Buzzards' Roost, as they called the family home in Hillsborough. Three days before Christmas, Rhine and his son went for a walk under the trees and down to the lake. Although he knew his father could hardly see, Robert sensed J.B. did not want to be guided. Rhine's one concession to his handicap was to follow his son instead of leading the way as he had always done before. As they walked through the trees, J.B. would occasionally point skyward and say, "See that bunch of birds?" The "birds," according to Robert, were mistletoe.* After J.B. had mentioned the birds a couple of times, Robert replied, "No, I didn't see anything." Then Rhine said, "My eyes are so bad, I could really think they're birds, but I know they're not."[3]

Rhine had always been a positive, optimistic presence, but now for the first time he seemed a little depressed. "He couldn't follow the conversation, nor clearly see his children, grandchildren, or his great-grandchild," said Robert. "He sat at the head of the table,

*They were both wrong. There is no mistletoe on the Rhines' property. They were probably both looking at leaves.

but unless one of his family called out 'Dad, here I am!' he didn't know they were there. He'd say, 'Is that you, Rosie?' She's his youngest daughter. It was kind of pathetic and I think he knew that when you reach that point, it could be that you don't have much longer to go."[4]

Less than two months later, on February 19, Louisa went to a seminar on parapsychology. Rhine was in bed but awake when Louisa returned. She told him about the seminar, but "he didn't seem to focus on it; couldn't any more," said Louisa. "But he did say: 'Well, we must go on. . . . we must go on.' " They were his last words to her before he fell asleep.[5]

At four-thirty next morning, Louisa heard a noise in the bath-room and hurried there. She found J.B. already dead.[6]

Daughter Rosemary was at home on the West Coast when Louisa telephoned with the news. Rosemary wondered why there had been no thunderclap or dream to warn her. Soon afterward she began to compose a poem about "the great and gentle man . . . till the end a fighter." She read the poem at a memorial service for her father at Duke University chapel.[7] All Rhine's children thought they had lost a wonderful father, and the world a great scientist.

A *New York Times* reporter telephoned the director of the Institute for Parapsychology, Dr. K. Ramakrishna Rao, who said: "Dr. Rhine's work will come to be one of the most significant of this century, and he will be classed with Einstein and Freud." Dr. Rao added, "We will try hard to realize his dreams and hopes to find the true nature of man."[8]

When the British Society for Psychical Research committee heard of Rhine's death, they mourned their president, a great para-psychologist who had broken new ground and put parapsychology on a clearer course. They decided to offer the presidency to Louisa. She and J.B. had worked as a team for some thirty years and she was acknowledged to be an outstanding parapsychologist in her own right. At eighty-nine, Louisa took J.B.'s last words to heart. She began to write her presidential address.

60

THE SUMMING UP

While Rhine searched for man's extrasensory nature with a pack of cards and a handful of dice, other scientists had raised the odds against him by finding evidence to support a strictly material universe. Darwin's theory of evolution received fresh blood transfusions and the wild dreams of science-fiction buffs promised to be truly prophetic as geneticists began to create new life forms and hovered on the brink of discovering the secret of life itself.

The world appeared simpler and stranger than previously imagined—"simple enough to be understood by a barmaid"—yet weird as an LSD trip.[1] Bizarre, informed guesses by theoretical physicists, the aristocrats of science, were confirmed by sophisticated instruments. They saw, at times, a house of horror, especially when focusing on "black holes" with cosmic appetites; the outer-space answer to the earth's piranhas, devouring everything in the neighborhood. Yet no matter how way-out, events in the world obeyed physical laws and consequently were credible to the scientific community. Extrasensory activity flouted known physical laws and therefore was a fantasy to all but a few scientists.

Some psi antagonists who were also religious performed remarkable feats of mental gymnastics or double-think, believing in the efficacy of prayer while denying even the possibility of telepathy. Claims for precognition especially aroused the scorn of scientists whose article of faith was that an effect cannot precede a cause. But "cannot" should be struck from the scientists' lexicon. The impossible occurs every few years, and scientific prognosticators awake to find new worlds they declared could never be.

Just six years after physiologist Johannes Peter Muller said no one would ever measure the speed of nerve conduction, Hermann von Helmholtz measured it. Albert Michelson, famous for first accurately measuring the speed of light, maintained that everything there was to know about physics had been discovered. Shortly afterward came the scientific revolution with Einstein's theory of relativity, quantum theories, the isolation of the electron, and detection of radioactivity. In his time Ernest Rutherford probably knew more about atoms than anyone; his experiments revealed that they consisted of protons and electrons. As *the* expert, he declared that man would never tap the atom's energy. Admiral William Leahy agreed, saying in 1945: "The [atomic] bomb will never go off, and I speak as an expert in explosives."[2]

Predictions, even by experts, obviously must be taken with plenty of salt. How much more so when they address subjects with which they are unfamiliar. As physicist Eugene P. Wigner warned after receiving a Nobel Prize in 1963: "It does not make me a person of wisdom. . . . It is a great danger if statements of scientists outside of their field are taken too seriously."[3]

One of Rhine's complaints about his critics was that few of them knew enough about his work to pass judgment. He speculated that had he found no evidence for psychic phenomena, the opposition would have applauded his efforts and endorsed his results. But because he claimed to have uncovered evidence for clairvoyance, precognition, and psychokinesis, in controlled experiments, he endured a harrowing trial by ordeal, which was made more painful because many of the judges declined to examine his findings, let alone undertake experiments for themselves.

He was prepared for incredulity, said Louisa Rhine, even hostility from fellow scientists when he began his work:

But not for the viciousness or durability of it. He did not know then or even faintly foresee that even decades later, what he called in his preface (to Extra-Sensory Perception) *"the inevitable reactionary response to all things new and strange," would be resounding against his investigations just about as stridently as ever, nor could he have guessed that his last effort, even in old age and failing health, would have to be expended in defense even of his own basic honesty. . . . Without that dogged unquestioning devotion to the solution of that question, which he thought of as for humanity, as well as for himself, he might have been discouraged and diverted somewhere along the way. But to a personality combination of hereditary single-mindedness, and early training in meeting adversity head-on, such turning back or away was unthinkable.*[4]

But not all scientists aligned themselves with the opposition. One of the most distinguished supporters was Nobel laureate Wolfgang Pauli. He accepted Carl Jung's view that meaningful coincidences are manifestations of an acausal or extraphysical principle "equal in importance to physical causality." Pauli described it as a "metaphysical" or "absolute order" of the cosmos which provides the background of physical phenomena. And although his physicist friend Dr. Werner Heisenberg was not a believer in psi, he said: "I would never claim that physics and chemistry exclude the possibility of such phenomena."[5]

Neurophysiologist Sir John Eccles won the Nobel Prize in 1963 for his share in discoveries "concerning the ionic mechanisms involved in excitation and inhibition in the peripheral and central portions of the nerve cell membrane."[6] He took an interest in Rhine's work, twice visiting him at Duke, and on May 15, 1978, wrote to me about Rhine:

I appreciated his enthusiasm and integrity. He developed controls so effectively that much of the emotional spontaneity was lost, and that may explain why the card guessing was so close to chance. I was disappointed in the growing interest in psychokinesis, which dominated the Utrecht conference in 1976. I think of all the Psi phenomena telepathy is the most likely to be substantiated.

Two Nobel-prizewinning physicists who take psi seriously are Britain's Dr. Brian Josephson and Dr. Richard Mattick of the University of Copenhagen.

The dean of engineering and applied science at Princeton, Dr. Robert G. Jahn, told *Science News* in 1979 that he had designed psi experiments involving sophisticated technology. He stated: "Once the overburden of illegitimate activity and irresponsible criticism is removed, there is sufficient residue of valid evidence to justify continued research."[7]

That was the legacy Rhine left Dr. Jahn and future parapsychologists—a residue of valid evidence, even when the fraud and fudging are taken into account.

Rhine brought no Einstein-style revolution to psychical research and frequently acknowledged his debt to the nineteenth-century researchers of the SPR, but the cumulative effect of his many changes and innovations proved effective in first finding signs of psi and then in investigating it. He introduced standard five-symbol decks of twenty-five ESP cards, stressed the importance of statistical evaluation, and simplified methods so that almost anyone can design and evaluate psi experiments. He originated a terminology for psi phenomena, psi procedures, and test methods that has been accepted by the field at large. He discovered position effects in the record of psi tests—more correct scores at the start and end of experiments—and this pattern of scoring provided independent evidence for psi, "the fingerprints" as he liked to think of them. In 1933 Rhine was first to undertake a sustained experimental program to see if mind can move matter, and he obtained positive results.

One important change Rhine adopted was not to concentrate on psychic stars, but to test anyone and everyone, sometimes en masse. He concluded that psi, like a sense of humor, is widely distributed and best displayed in a friendly, familiar setting. Why was he so uniquely successful in eliciting psi? Louisa Rhine suggests the answer:

In trying to discover and understand almost any unknown, the first attempts to unravel the secret often seem by hindsight to have been clumsy, if not actually counter-productive. But in J.B.'s attempt to unravel this secret, it did not turn out that way, for the very serious-ness and intensity with which he asked the question of his student subjects affected them with something like contagion, so that they took the task he set for them in the same way. Neither teacher nor student knew the kind of attitude that was necessary, but once they caught the spirit and became involved, the proper attitude resulted and together they got the answer, or what was then at least the promise of the answer. And as it seems now they got it because the spirit they brought to it supplied what one could call the "yeast," the ferment necessary in this recipe.

Later, when other experimenters often failed to duplicate the results, even though they followed carefully all the points of tech-nique J.B. had described, they were baffled and, for a time and to an extent, J.B. was too. But the fact was, that in this recipe the "yeast," the necessary spirit, was not mentioned. I went back to the account of the tests reported in that first book and found not the slightest mention of it.

Possibly, the atmosphere in which these early subjects worked was all the more effective because they and the experimenter too were unaware of this ingredient. But as it appears now it had been unconsciously created by the nature of the experimenter and the combination of hereditary and environmental factors that defined his personality. Together they created the yeast that was such an important ingredient of the test.[8]

From his own experiments and those of subsequent para-psychologists, Rhine obtained a fairly reliable picture of who is most likely to demonstrate psi and what are the most fruitful conditions. The subject must believe in the possibility of psi, want to do the test, be well-rested and at ease. He or she should be enthusiastic and treat the experiment in the spirit of a game or competition. But results do not depend on the subject alone. The experimenter, too, plays a significant role, and will obtain best results if he has the positive, outgoing, and confident personality of a supersalesman.

Psi scoring is usually depressed if the subject takes narcotic drugs, is tired, bored, uneasy, or emotionally disturbed. An unexpected visitor can temporarily lower the score. In his early days with Linzmayer and Pearce, Rhine found that a challenging atmosphere of high expectation produced the most remarkable results.

Rhine pointed out what had previously escaped researchers: There might not be such a thing as telepathy—it could be, for instance, clairvoyance in disguise. He was inclined to believe that all the psi manifestations—retrocognition, clairvoyance, telepathy, precognition, psychokinesis—were different aspects of one phenomenon. And he concluded, from both experiments and anecdotes, that there was considerable evidence that animals too had psi.

Rhine emerged from his long enchanted, and often brutal, voyage like a witness at a trial who has only glimpsed the criminal, but has seen enough to know beyond doubt that the criminal exists. He believed that the early SPR researchers had been on the right track, suspecting that psi ability manifests itself through the unconscious mind. And that was the problem. Psi activity being unconscious—something like dreaming—it is next to impossible to control until the unconscious mind is better understood. Rhine regarded such control as one, if not the greatest, of parapsychology's tasks. Its achievement, of course, would upgrade parapsychology from an inexact to an exact science.

He responded to critics who refused to take his work seriously until he demonstrated psi on demand that due to the unconscious nature of psi, such a demonstration was not yet possible. As early as 1956 he wrote:

The spontaneous, uncontrollable nature of ESP naturally bothers us all, parapsychologists as well as skeptics. But many other erratic, fugitive effects can be found in nature, more especially in the mental sciences, but even in biology and physics. And they are no less "natural" than the more reliable ones, for all man's inability to reproduce them at will.[9]

Rhine had achieved at least some fleeting control over psi. The most dramatic example occurred when he built up Hubert Pearce "to a pitch of performance in a clairvoyance test in which he made twenty-five hits in unbroken succession. But it was a delicate operation, and it must be kept in mind, too, that H.P. eventually lost his capacity to score above chance in psi tests."[10] Nevertheless, Rhine was optimistic then that the problem of psi control would be overcome. Nineteen years later, in 1975, Rhine realized that to unlock the secrets of psi an entirely new approach was needed. Speaking at the annual convention of the American Psychological Association in Chicago, he explained:

The newest problem now coming up . . . is a question of basic method that promises to be the most radical issue yet encountered. The question is this: Since psi is nonphysical, how can the methodology of parapsychology be limited to a physical basis? To experiment with psi ability would seem to require uniquely parapsychic test methods; in other words, nonphysical methods are necessary for experimenting with nonphysical abilities; physical methods suffice only to control against sensorimotor leakage.[11]

Despite the elusive nature of psi, Rhine did not doubt that an extrasensory world exists. He felt confident he had authenticated in his laboratory many of the claims of the nineteenth-century researchers. He died before he was able to write his intended lecture on parapsychology and religion, but it is clear that his evidence confirms some religious teachings. And although he left many mysteries unsolved, he was convinced he had found the answer to the question that had started him on his life's work: Man is not merely a machine but has a transcendental mind able to free itself from the strictures of time and space and possibly to survive bodily death.

Under his single-minded, dedicated, and resolute leadership, parapsychology not only survived attacks meant to destroy it, but prospered and gained credibility. He was almost alone when he started. At the end of his life he had more than two hundred fellow parapsychologists and knew of over eighty schools, colleges, and universities offering parapsychology courses.

A few years before he died Rhine made an appeal for an open-minded attitude, which his poorly informed critics should take to heart:

We are still so vastly ignorant about life and mind and their origin and functioning that I doubt that anyone has a reasonably close guess (or rational inference) as to the great ultimate universal truth about them. It is likely to be beyond present power to comprehend when and if eventually it is revealed to the sciences. What matters most today, in any case, is that we faithfully preserve this indescribably wonderful privilege of exploring as best we can, intelligently and responsibly, on ahead into the great unknowns of human nature and destiny with all the endless reach of curiosity, method, and design the expanding sciences can command.[12]

If time proves Rhine right, as I believe likely, he will be remembered as a great scientist, one "of those who were at home in the unknown and left their footprints there."[13]

APPENDIX A

RHINE-JUNG CORRESPONDENCE

After reading Jung's *Modern Man in Search of a Soul* (1933), Rhine sent the Swiss psychiatrist a copy of his *Extra-Sensory Perception*. William McDougall, a former associate of Jung's, had told Rhine an intriguing story of a knife that had mysteriously exploded in Jung's kitchen. In a November 14, 1934 letter, Rhine asked Jung if he would elaborate.

JUNG TO RHINE, NOVEMBER 27, 1934

I have received a copy of your most interesting book Extra-Sensory Perception, *but I didn't know that I owed the book to your personal kindness. I am highly interested in all questions concerning the peculiar character of the psyche with reference to time and space, i.e., the apparent annihilation of these categories in certain mental activities. I am quite ready to give you any information concerning my own experiences in such matters, but I should like you to tell me exactly what you expect of me.*

Concerning the case of the exploded knife I can only tell you that it happened in 1898 under apparently simple circumstances. The knife was in a basket beside a loaf of bread and the basket was in a locked drawer of a sideboard. My aged mother was sitting at a distance of about 3 meters near the window. I myself was outside the house in the garden and the servant was in the kitchen which is on the same floor. Nobody else was present in the house at that time. Suddenly the knife exploded inside the sideboard with the sound of an exploding pistol. First the phenomenon seemed to be quite inexplicable until we found that the knife had exploded into four parts and was lying scattered inside the basket. No traces of tearing or cutting were found on the sides of the basket nor in the loaf of bread, so that the explosive force apparently did not exceed that amount of energy which was just needed to break the knife and was completely exhausted with the breaking itself.

Within a few days of this fact under very similar circumstances a round table with the diameter of about 130 cm. suddenly tore about 3/4 through. The table then was 90 years old, its shape hadn't been altered and there was no central heating in the house. I happened to be in the adjoining room with the door open in between and it was the same sound as of an exploding pistol.

According to my idea these two facts are connected with an acquaintance I had made just in these days. I met a young woman [his cousin, in fact] with marked mediumistic faculties and I had made up my mind to experiment with her. She lived at that time at a distance of about 4 km. She hadn't come anywhere near to my house then, but soon after the series of seances with her began. She told me that she had vividly thought of these seances just in those days when the explosions occurred. She could produce quite noticeable raps in pieces of furniture and in the walls. Some of those raps also happened during her absence at a distance of about 4 km.

I am going to send you a photograph of this knife. Thanking you again for your most valuable book.

JUNG TO RHINE, MAY 20, 1935

I was glad to be able to contribute to your researches, but being of a less optimistic outlook than you Americans I never put my experiences on show. I have learned too much from the past in that respect. There are things which are simply incomprehensible to the tough brains of our race and time. One simply risks being taken for crazy or insincere, and I have received so much of either that I learned to be careful in keeping quiet. I would ask it as a favour from every psychologist in Europe not to put that photograph [of the exploding knife, which he had sent to Rhine, who wished to display it] on the wall, but since North Carolina is very far away from Europe, so far away, indeed, that probably very few are even aware of the existence of a Duke University, I shall not object. I have found that there are very few people who are interested in such things from healthy motives and fewer still who are able to think about such and similar matters, and so in the course of the years I arrived at the conviction that the main difficulty doesn't consist in the question how to tell, but rather in how not to tell it. Man's horror novi is so great that in order not to lose his modest brain capacity he always prefers to treat the fellow who disturbed him as crazy. If you are really serious in teaching people something good, you must do your best to avoid such prejudices. Those are the reasons why I prefer not to communicate too many of my experiences. They would confront the scientific world with too upsetting problems.

JUNG TO RHINE, APRIL 1, 1948

Your experiments [with long-distance card-guessing and dice-throwing] have established the fact of the relativity of time, space and matter with reference to the psyche beyond doubt. The experimental proof is particularly valuable to me, because I am constantly observing facts that are along the same line.

JUNG TO RHINE, FEBRUARY 18, 1953

The work I am planning on ESP does not concern the fact itself (which you have demonstrated up to the hilt), but rather the peculiar emo-tional factor that seems to be a very important condition deciding the success or failure of the ESP experiment. . . . I have observed a great many ESP cases with my patients in the course of time.

The two men corresponded about parapsychology for more than two decades. Jung expressed his confidence in Rhine's work in a January 26, 1959, letter to Dieter Meyer, a German singer, who had told Jung of his ESP experiences. "These ESP phenomena are much more common than is generally assumed," Jung wrote. "They point to a quality of the unconscious which is outside the categories of time and space. Rhine's experiments, conducted with large numbers of people, offer irrefutable proof of this."

On November 23, 1971, ten years after Jung's death, Rhine wrote to the psychiatrist's secretary, Aniela Jaffe:

One of the reasons for my sincere admiration of Dr. Jung came from his forthright devotion to the findings of parapsychology with which he came into experience long ago before I began to give attention to them at Duke. When the experimental studies helped to bring the findings into a firm status he made no bones about taking the con-sequences seriously. Not many people in science are so straightfor-ward in their intellectual life; they wait for someone else to stand in the front lines.

APPENDIX B

THE RHINE-SINCLAIR LETTERS

Upton Sinclair's account of his wife's telepathic ability and the experiments he undertook to satisfy his curiosity had intrigued McDougall and Walter Franklin Prince. They tested her, too, even more rigorously, and the results were positive.

Rhine inherited Sinclair as a correspondent when McDougall and Prince, through ill health, began to fade from the scene. The Rhine-Sinclair correspondence drew them together into a lifelong friendship.

The parapsychologist was not only interested in Sinclair as an ESP aficionado, but also in the man's novels and his efforts as a social reformer.

SINCLAIR TO RHINE, DECEMBER 22, 1932

I am of course tremendously interested in what you tell me about your experiments. Unfortunately, you do not tell me the one important thing, which is what percentage of success you are getting. You must be getting some percentage beyond that of chance or you would not be so much encouraged over the matter. I am tremendously interested to know, because Mencken, and other such friends, now have telepathy and clairvoyance listed as the latest of my inanities; and while I can manage to endure being considered mentally unbalanced, I do not enjoy it especially, and will be glad of your support.

I had not heard that McDougall's son had died, and am sorry indeed to hear of this sorrow in their lives.

RHINE TO SINCLAIR, JUNE 30, 1933

I hope yet this summer to be able to prepare a report on the telepathy phase upon which I am now working. A good way to state my results for brevity and simplicity is to state the average number of hits per 25 trials. The chance expectation is 5 in 25. I have now about 54,000 trials which average above 7 in 25. This may seem like a small margin but it is mathematically of tremendous significance. It is 71 times the probable error, whereas to be significant, 4 times the probable error is required by most conservative judges. One man, my best subject, has guessed 11,000 with an average of very close to 9. Another, a girl, has guessed 2,000 with about the same average. Still another has guessed 5,000 with an average of over 8; still another has guessed 4,000 with an average slightly under 8, and so on, downward. I find that with pure telepathy, in which there are no objective conditions used by the agent, that the results run about the same as pure clairvoyance in a given subject. I have found both capacities in four subjects.

The special experiments are showing up some interesting things too. The presence of a stranger means a sure drop in ability. Narcotic drugs depress and stimulant drugs improve; illness depresses; the introduction of new conditions depresses function. There are a number of interesting curves which have shown up but which cannot be briefly stated. I have now several thousand results obtained by calling the cards in a pack that remains unbroken until the end, i.e., the subject calls down through the pack without anybody removing the cards. These results are on an average between 7 and 8 and are very significant indeed, but are not quite so high as some of the others. This seems to me to throw out our wave mechanics theory of present day physics, since an X-ray photograph of such a pack of cards could only show a blotch.

We had here at Duke what I think will be an historical event in the history of psychical research. Mr. J. F. Thomas, Assistant Superintendent of schools in Detroit, a man of about 58, was given the degree of Ph.D. for a thesis on studies in trance communication, mainly with Mrs. Leonard of England. I have had the pleasure of working with him for about 5 or 6 years and am fully convinced of the genuineness of his work. This is the first time, of course, that mediumistic studies have been any way favorably considered by graduate school research directors. The responsibility, of course, was on Dr. McDougall and to him belongs the credit.

RHINE TO SINCLAIR, APRIL 13, 1946

Yes, I recall your suggestion that I investigate Cayce, and we made an effort to do so. I wrote him, he came to see me when he visited his son at Duke, and we sent a coworker, Dr. Warner, to Virginia Beach to see him. Dr. Warner could not pin anything down in the time he was

*there. We gave Cayce one trial on diagnosis, and he missed com-
pletely. Worse still, the thing looked like a racket—twenty dollars a
trial, and forty for medicines which only Cayce's supply house at
Norfolk could furnish. Even so, we would have gone on, had not
Warner become ill so that he had to give up his study. I was planning
another effort when Cayce died. Thank you for the clipping about
Dickens. Did you ever read the story of Dickens' precognitive dream?
In a dream he met a woman who was a complete stranger, and the
next day she appeared at tea and said exactly what she had said in the
dream. I believe this is told in Walter Franklin Prince's Noted Witnesses for Psychic Occurrences.**

RHINE TO SINCLAIR, JULY 10, 1946

*I was in New York a few weeks ago, and met Sugrue† at Town Hall.
He is still confined to a wheel chair, but has strong hopes of getting
out of it within a few years. He claims that Cayce saved his life, and he
on his part is giving a great share of his energies to the foundation set
up to promote Cayce's work—that is, a scientific study of the records
Cayce left. I was deeply impressed by the sincerity and fine spirit of
the man, but I could not see any way to get a scientific grip on Cayce's
ability at this stage.*

SINCLAIR TO RHINE, MARCH 8, 1948

*I happened to be talking with Charlie Chaplain [sic] on the telephone
yesterday, and I mentioned that you were coming. It will interest you
to know that he knew all about your work and said eagerly that he
would get up something in the way of a party for you. He is very good
fun to meet because he enacts the story which he is working on or
preparing, and that way you get a free show!*

RHINE TO SINCLAIR, AUGUST 9, 1951

*I do not think much of the Borley Rectory‡ story. I am inclined to give
enough credence to the reporter's story about Harry Price, that he
caught him throwing stones surreptitiously as he was showing people
about in the rectory, and I have a profound distrust for Harry Price,
based upon a good bit of secondhand acquaintance. If I were going to*

---

*It is.

†Thomas Sugrue, author of There Is a River, a book about Edgar Cayce.

*‡Borley Rectory was considered Britain's most haunted house. It eventually
burned to the ground. Price wrote two books about his investigations: The Most
Haunted House in England, 1940, and The End of Borley Rectory, 1945.*

use a story* I would take Dr. Prince's "Carbon Monoxide or Carbon Monoxide Plus," as the title went—a bulletin of the old A.S.P.R. describing the hauntings in one of those old Beacon Street places.

SINCLAIR TO RHINE, AUGUST 16, 1951

I was greatly shocked by what you tell me about Harry Price. I have never heard anything of the sort about him, and I was entirely convinced by the "Borley" story. I cannot see how conceivably all those complicated phenomena can have been produced as tricks. I would rather doubt the word of a newspaper reporter. Apparently you don't know that I prepared an elaborate motion picture scenario out of the "Borley" story, and had it mimeographed and offered it to the studios. But ever since the days of the EPIC campaign they have all been disinterested in my work. I had taken this "Borley" scenario and made it over into one of the stories that I put into my "Arabian Nights' Entertainments." I don't know what to do about it now: I might let it go as a work of fiction.

SINCLAIR TO RHINE, JULY 28, 1953

About Ford: I have heard various reports about him, and, of course, all I can say is our personal experiences. McDougall, myself, and my wife had a seance with him, and he told us many things which he could not possibly have found out in libraries—the Los Angeles Library couldn't find them out because I asked them to try. We three went away afterwards and sat down to have lunch, and we went over the entire seance in accordance with my notes, and I made fresh notes conforming to the statements of my wife and McDougall. I then wrote my seance up, and it was published in the "Psychic Observer." It was many years ago. What was still more significant was what happened in my home. Ford came there and we invited half a dozen friends, and Ford had no means of knowing who was invited (my wife wouldn't even let me use the telephone). They were Bob Wagner, editor of "Script," and his wife, Theodore Dreiser and his wife, and my wife's younger sister and her husband. When Ford arrived I took him out in the garden and then I took him into a darkened room and did not introduce him to any of those persons. He had no means of knowing who they were, and he told them the most amazing things. My brother-in-law, Brabour Irwin, is the man you read about in "Mental Radio," and he had a younger brother who was killed in an accident in a very extraordinary way. He was struck by the pole of a

---

*Sinclair was thinking of writing a book about ghosts and poltergeists.

wagon hauled by two galloping horses. His name was Elwood, and I have never heard that name and didn't know the brother had existed. Bob Wagner was told about a younger brother who had died of a ear infection caused by concussion from the firing of big guns on a battleship. Dreiser was told about an old journalist friend, and he said he couldn't remember. Dreiser had been drinking and was half asleep, but his wife helped him to remember. He wrote us afterward that it was all correct. I wrote that affair up also, and it was published in the "Psychic Observer." I forgot to add one extraordinary detail. Mrs. Gartz came in unannounced and brought a young nephew whom we had never heard of before, and Ford said there was a strong Catholic influence there—something most unlikely in the case of Mrs. Gartz. He was told there was domestic trouble, and this embarrassed him because it hadn't been made known. I could not imagine a more perfect test than that. The young man denied it, but there was a divorce soon afterwards.

RHINE TO SINCLAIR, FEBRUARY 17, 1954

Say what we will about the British, they have put their psychical research, as they call it, on the map of the world, as they have done with other things, too. It [a British-published book on parapsychology] would reach the Australians and Canadians and South Africans where there are more people per thousand interested in the subject than anywhere else except Britain and Holland.

RHINE TO SINCLAIR, MARCH 1, 1954

Do you know Bill Wilson of Alcoholics Anonymous? I have met him a few times and corresponded with him . . . he is deeply involved with mediums and, trusting chap that he is, he doesn't know wheat from chaff, but he does know his alcoholics.

RHINE TO SINCLAIR, NOVEMBER 25, 1959

At this stage of parapsychology, anything that cannot be tested experimentally had better be left to the individual. It is hard enough to get acceptance of the best established facts, but, as you know, we are making a little progress on those lines.

APPENDIX C

THE WHEELER-RHINE LETTERS

Dr. John A. Wheeler's letter of retraction dated 12 April 1979 was published in *Science*, the magazine of the AAAS. It reads:

I am writing to correct what I said about Professor J. B. Rhine of Duke University in the question and answer period following my paper, "Not Consciousness, but the Distinction Between the Probe and the Probed, as Central to the Elemental Quantum Act of Observation," following the paper of E. P. Wigner at the panel session on "Physics and Consciousness" on 8 January 1979, at the annual meeting of the AAAS in Houston. The tapes of that session, distributed under the sponsorship of the AAAS, carried my prepared paper. They also carried two appendices I prepared for my paper, when I discovered to my dismay that the other three participants were speaking on the so-called field of "parapsychology," one of these appendices called "Put the Pseudos Out of the Workshop of Science," and the other called "Where There's Smoke, There's Smoke" (both being reprinted in the 13 April issue of The New York Review of Books, *along with my February letter to the board of directors of the AAAS suggesting that the AAAS disaffiliate the Parapsychological Association).*

In response to one of the questions from the floor, I unwisely repeated a secondhand, and as it turned out, incorrect account of the experiments of Rhine and McDougall purporting to show that descendants of "educated" rats do better at mazes than the descendants of "uneducated" rats. Rather than repeat here my inaccuracies, let me give references to the literature in which the interested reader may get the story correctly:

Robinson, Roy. "Genetics of the Norway Rat." Pergamon Press, 1965. Chapter XVII, Acquired Inheritance, pp. 697–720.

Sonneborn, T.M. "McDougall's Lamarckian Experiment." The American Naturalist, *Vol. LXV, November–December 1931; pp. 541–550.*

Rhine's letter to *Science,* dated June 27, 1979, reads:

I am glad to see Dr. John Wheeler's letter of retraction of the charge he made against me in Houston on January 8, and am pleased to have the opportunity to reply. It is also good to know that his statement of retraction will be sent to all those who have already purchased tapes containing a record of Wheeler's charge against me, and further that the Wheeler charge will be deleted from tapes and records of the symposium being distributed by the AAAS in the future.

As may be seen, however, Dr. Wheeler's letter does not identify just what it is that he retracts; it could be any little thing; he vaguely calls it "inaccuracies." I have therefore to insert here a brief abstract of this missing part of the story condensed from the official taped record:

After Dr. Wheeler ended his critical remarks on the Parapsychological Association (PA) he was asked to be more specific. In reply he gave an account of an experiment from McDougall's rat research at Duke 50 years ago, work in which I had a part. According to Wheeler a post-doctoral assistant in the experiment intentionally altered the conditions so as to produce spurious positive results. However, subsequent consultation with Dr. S., a distinguished geneticist (whose name was given to the audience) led to the disclosure to McDougall of these false positive results and in consequence they were never published. Dr. Wheeler concluded his story at this point by saying: "The only thing I haven't mentioned here is the name of the assistant who did the experiment. It was Rhine—Rhine! He started parapsychology that way!"

No one was present at the seminar who was prepared to respond to this unscheduled accusation; so it went unchallenged. It was some weeks before I got it from the transcription of the AAAS tape of the seminar and sent it first to Dr. S., the witness whom Wheeler cited, and he responded at once (February 19). He rejected the charge against me as wholly untrue.

I sent his letter (which is necessarily confidential) to Mr. Wm. D. Carey, Executive Officer of the AAAS, and received on March 19 a prompt and cooperative response from him. In the meantime, Dr. S. wrote Dr. Wheeler directly to set him straight. Finally Dr. Wheeler wrote me a note of apology (February 20), and on April 12 he wrote the note of retraction in Science, *to which I am responding now.*

An acceptance of Wheeler's retraction might be expected at this point to wind up this "Houston affair," but for one more item so far not discussed: this is a letter from Wheeler to Carey, dated January 12, in which he pursued his plan announced at Houston to "run the 'pseudos' out of the workshop of science." This letter, only four days after the blast-off at Houston, was of course based on the impressive case Dr. Wheeler was evidently still confident he had made at the seminar in identifying parapsychology as "pseudo," and for which I was chosen as an example. The dates show Dr. W. could hardly have known of his mistake as the time he made the appeal to Mr. Carey. The collapse of his plan, right on the launching pad as it were, may reasonably be assumed to have left the "Houston affair" to history.

But in science mistakes are seldom completely fruitless. No sooner had the PA been "read out of the status of eligibility" for affiliation with the AAAS than the new president of the association, Dr. Kenneth Boulding, was asked in an interview by the Washington Star *(9 January) where he stood on the issue of the attack on the PA by Dr. Wheeler. These few courageous words of President Boulding, quoted by the* Star, *will I think make the Houston meeting of the AAAS a memorable one long after the controversy over the PA affiliation is deservedly forgotten. This is the Boulding Declaration, as I should like to call it:*

"The scientific community must always be kept open. We cannot just discard the evidence of parapsychology out of hand. One has to subject their methodology to something. I am in favor of keeping them in."

These words put new meaning into AAAS affiliation and give this great organization an added responsibility for the advancement of its more difficult, venturesome sciences such as parapsychology.

The letter by Dr. Wheeler and the response by Dr. Rhine were both published in *Science*, July 13, 1979, Vol. 205, No. 4402, p. 144, and headed "Parapsychology—A Correction."

NOTES AND SOURCES

INTRODUCTION

1. Interview with J. B. Rhine (hereafter cited as JBR), September 24, 1970.

THE LEGACY

1. Morton Prince, *The Dissociation of a Personality* (New York and London: Longman's Green and Co., 1906). Prince was one of Rhine's Harvard instructors.

2. Gardner Murphy and Robert O. Ballou, eds., *William James on Psychical Research* (New York: The Viking Press, 1960), p. 319.

3. Alan Gauld, *The Founders of Psychical Research* (London: Routledge & Kegan Paul, 1968), p. 138.
      The purpose and scope of the Society is still printed on the inside cover of the Journal of the American Society for Psychical Research (hereafter cited as JASPR), as follows:
      1. The investigation of claims of telepathy, clairvoyance, precognition, retrocognition, veridical hallucinations and dreams, psychometry, dowsing, and other forms of paranormal cognition; of claims of paranormal physical phenomena such as telekinesis, materialization, levitation, and poltergeists; the study of automatic writing, trance speech, hypnotism, alterations of personality, and other subconscious processes; in short, all types of phenomena called parapsychological, psychic, or paranormal.
      2. The collection, classification, study, and publication of reports dealing with the above phenomena. Readers are asked to report incidents and cases. Names and places must be given, but on request will be treated as confidential.
      3. The maintenance of a library on psychical research and related subjects. Contributions of books and periodical files will be welcomed.
      4. Cooperation in the above tasks with qualified individuals and groups who will report their work to the society.

4. Nandor Fodor, *Encyclopedia of Psychic Science* (Secaucus, N.J.: University Books, 1966), p. 271.

5. *PSPR*, Part XVII, Vol. VI (1890).

6. R. Hodgson and S. J. Davey, "The Possibilities of Malobservation and Lapse of Memory from a Practical Point of View." *PSPR*, LV (1887).

7. William James, Presidential Address to *SPR. PSPR*, Part XX, Vol. XII (June 1896).

8. Fodor, op. cit. p. 5. Results of the Census of Hallucinations, involving 32,000 responses, appeared in *PSPR*, Vol. X (1894).

9. Alan Gauld, op. cit. p. 315.

10. Ibid. p. 338.

11. Sir Oliver Lodge, "University Aspects of Psychical Research," *The Case For and Against Psychical Belief* (Worcester, Mass.: Clark University Press, 1927), p. 6.

1. THE ULTIMATE MYSTERY

1. Interview with JBR, July 31, 1978.

2. Louisa E. Rhine, at a memorial meeting, quoting an autobiographical sketch by JBR, Durham, N.C., Nov. 28, 1980.

3. Interview with Paul Rhine, March 15, 1980.

4. Interview with Thomas Rhine, March 15, 1980.

5. Ibid.

6. Ibid.

7. Interview with Paul Rhine, March 15, 1980.

8. JBR, *New Frontiers of the Mind* (New York: Farrar & Rinehart, 1937), p. 52.

9. Interview with Thomas Rhine, March 15, 1980.

10. Interview with Paul Rhine, March 15, 1980.

11. Interview with Thomas Rhine, March 15, 1980.

12. Interview with Paul Rhine, March 15, 1980.

13. Ibid.

14. JBR, op. cit. pp. 52–53.

15. Interview with Louisa E. Rhine (hereafter cited as LER), July 21, 1980.

16. Ibid.

17. Interview with JBR, July 31, 1978.

18. Interview with Paul Rhine, March 15, 1980.

19. Ibid.

2. UNIVERSITY OF CHICAGO—BATTLES WITH THE BEHAVIORISTS

1. *The Encyclopedia of Philosophy*, Vols. 7 and 8 (New York: Collier-Macmillan, 1967), pp. 279–280.

2. *Current Biography* (Detroit: Gale, 1942), pp. 869–870.

3. Interview with JBR, July 31, 1978.

4. Ibid.

5. Ibid.

6. Charles Higham, *The Adventures of Conan Doyle* (New York: Pocket Books, 1976). And from the *Chicago Tribune,* April 17, May 22, 24, 25 and 27, 1922.

7. JBR, *New Frontiers of the Mind* (New York: Farrar & Rinehart, 1937), pp. 53–54.

8. Interview with JBR, July 31, 1978.

9. Sir Oliver Lodge, *The Survival of Man* (New York: George H. Doran, 1909).

10. "Interview: Dr. J. B. Rhine." Jean Shinoda Bolen, M.D., *Psychic* (July 1972), pp. 7–34.

11. JBR, op. cit. pp. 10–13.

12. Ibid.

13. Carl Murchison, ed. *A History of Psychology in Autobiography* (Worcester, Mass.: Clark University Press, 1930).

14. JBR, op. cit. p. 42.

15. Bolen, op. cit. p. 9.

16. Ibid. p. 7.

17. Raymond Van Over and Laura Oteri, eds. *William McDougall: Explorer of the Mind* (New York: Helix: Garrett, 1967) and *A History of Psychology in Autobiography.*

18. Ibid.

19. Rhine, op. cit. pp. 50–51.

20. LER, "Man and Scientist," at a memorial service, Durham, N.C., November 28, 1980.

21. Ibid.

3. LESSONS IN DECEPTION

1. JBR, *New Frontiers of the Mind* (New York: Farrar & Rinehart, 1937), p. 23.

2. Thomas R. Tietze, *Margery* (New York: Harper & Row, 1973), pp. 32–39.

3. JBR letter to James Malcolm Bird, 1926.

4. JBR letter to Bird, April 20, 1926.

5. Tietze, op. cit. pp. 25–26.

6. Interview with JBR, October 30, 1978.

4. MARGERY THE ENIGMA

1. Interview with JBR, September 24, 1970.

2. The source for much of the material in this chapter is Thomas R. Tietze's lively biography *Margery* (New York: Harper & Row, 1973).

3. L. R. G. Crandon, "The Margery Mediumship," *The Case For and Against Psychical Belief* (Worcester, Mass.: Clark University, 1927), pp. 90–91.

4. Interview with LER, August 3, 1980.

5. JBR and LER, "One Evening's Observation on the Margery Mediumship," *Journal of Abnormal and Social Psychology*, No. 21 (1927), pp. 401–421.

6. Interview with JBR, September 24, 1970.

7. *Time* (February 21, 1938), p. 61.

8. Tietze, op. cit. pp. 184–185.

9. Interview with Dr. John Crandon, October 22, 1977.

10. Ibid.

11. Interview with Marian Nester, May 23, 1978.

12. Interviews with Hudson Hoagland, April 30 and May 27, 1978. Also: Hudson Hoagland, "Science and the Medium: The Climax of a Famous Investigation," *Atlantic Monthly* (November 1925), pp. 666–681.

13. Ibid.

14. Interview with JBR, September 2, 1970.

15. JBR and LER, op. cit.

16. *JASPR*, Vol. 68, No. 4 (1974), pp. 417–424.

17. *JASPR*, No. 21 (1927), pp. 401–421.

5. HARVARD

1. *ASPR Proceedings*, Vol. 1 (1886).

2. *Biographic Dictionary of Parapsychology* (New York: Helix Press, 1964), p. 156.

3. Gardner Murphy and Robert O. Ballou, "The Last Report: Final Impressions of a Psychical Researcher," *William James on Psychical Research*, (New York: The Viking Press, 1960), p. 322.

4. Ibid.

5. Ibid.

6. Rev. Elwood Worcester, *Walter Franklin Prince, A Memorial* (Boston: BSPR, 1935), p. 10.

7. WFP, "The Doris Case of Multiple Personality," *Proceedings of the ASPR*, Vols. IX and X (1916).

8. Interview with LER, May 31, 1980.

9. Arthur Conan Doyle, shortly after Houdini's death. Quoted in Doug Henning with Charles Reynolds, *Houdini: His Legend and Magic* (New York: New York Times Books, 1977).

10. Interview with JBR, September 27, 1970.

11. Interview with Anthony Westerhof, May 3, 1978.

12. Interview with Hudson Hoagland, May 27, 1978.

13. *The Case for and Against Psychical Belief* (Worcester, Mass.: Clark University Press, 1927), p. 150.

14. Ibid.

15. JBR letter to WFP, November 23, 1927.

16. Gardner Murphy, "Autobiography of Gardner Murphy," *Journal of Parapsychology* (hereafter cited as *J of P*), p. 167.

17. R. Laurence Moore, *In Search of White Crows* (New York: Oxford University Press, 1977), p. 175.

18. Interview with Dr. Lois Murphy, April 22, 1978.

6. LADY WONDER

1. Milbourne Christopher, *ESP, Seers & Psychics* (New York: Thomas Y. Crowell Co., 1970), p. 47.

2. Ibid. pp. 46–47.

3. Fred S. Keller, *Learning: Reinforcement Theory* (New York: Random House, 1954), p. 31.

4. JBR and LER, "An Investigation of a 'Mind-Reading' Horse," *Journal of Abnormal and Social Psychology*, Vol. 23, No.4 (January–March, 1929), pp. 449–466.

5. Interview with LER, November 14, 1977.

6. *Life* (December 22, 1952); *Popular Mechanics* (March 1952).

7. Interview with LER, August 17, 1980.

8. JBR and LER, op. cit.

9. JBR and LER, "Second Report on Lady, the 'Mind-Reading' Horse," *Journal of Abnormal and Social Psychology*, Vol. 24, No. 3 (October–December 1929), pp. 287–292.

10. JBR letter to WFP, March 28, 1928.

11. Interview with Dr. Harold Gulliksen, April 30, 1978.

7. COMMUNICATIONS WITH THE DEAD?

1. Interview with LER, December 22, 1979.

2. JBR letter to WFP, November 23, 1927.

3. JBR letter to WFP, March 31, 1928.

4. John F. Thomas, Ph.D., *Beyond Normal Cognition* (Boston: BSPR, 1937). Thomas revealed his principles and procedures as follows:

     1. To hold all experiments in places distant from my home, which has been in Detroit for a number of years.

    2. To select sensitives who had never known the trance person-alities.

    3. To hold a series with my name unknown.

    4. To make arrangements for this series through recognized societies.

    5. To vary the observer, as well as the sensitives.

    6. To conduct a number of experiments with no observers, as such, but with a recorder in charge who had also never known the trance personalities.

    7. To have a sensitive do automatic writing with no one else present.

    8. To use extreme care in conversation and correspondence not to give information to the sensitives or recorders, and contra, to give casual facts at times, intentionally, to see whether they later would be given in the trance.

    9. To conduct carefully, record accurately, and analyze critically all experiments.

    10. To have a study of the records made by critics of scientific training who would be free from emotional bias.

    11. To study the records at a university as a problem in abnormal psychology.

    12. To set up experimental tests, ultimately, for awareness, for evidential memories, for facts unknown to me, and for instances of con-tinued purposes; that is, to make a departure from purely spontaneous material.

5. JBR letter to WFP, March 31, 1928.

6. Thomas, op. cit.

7. *JASPR* (January 1941).

8. *RATS*

1. D. J. West, "The Strength and Weakness of the Available Evidence for Extrasensory Perception," *Extrasensory Perception*. (New York: The Citadel Press, 1956). p. 21. Published version of talk given at a CIBA Foundation Symposium in 1955.

2. Interview with Anthony Westerhof, May 3, 1978.

3. Ibid.

4. Interview with LER, December 22, 1979.

9. *HYPNOSIS*

1. Henri E. Ellenberger, *The Discovery of the Unconscious* (New York: Basic Books, 1970), pp. 116–117.

2. Ibid. pp. 337–338; and F. W. H. Myers, *Human Personality and Its Survival of Bodily Death* (New York: University Books, 1961), pp. 141–143.

3. JBR, *New Frontiers of the Mind* (New York: Farrar & Rinehart, 1937), p. 58.

4. JBR, *Extra-Sensory Perception* (Boston: Bruce Humphries, 1964), p. 46.

5. JBR, *New Frontiers of the Mind*, op. cit. p. 56.

6. Interview with Anthony Westerhof, May 3, 1978.

7. Ibid.

8. Ibid.

10. BREAKTHROUGH

1. JBR, *Extra-Sensory Perception* (Boston: Bruce Humphries, 1964), p. 4. Rhine uses the term *extrasensory perception* to mean "perception in a mode that is just *not* sensory."

2. Interview with Adam Linzmayer, November 6, 1977.

3. JBR, *New Frontiers of the Mind* (New York: Farrar & Rinehart, 1937), p. 78.

4. Ibid. p. 79.

5. Ibid.

6. Ibid. p. 81.

7. Interview with Adam Linzmayer. op. cit.

8. Ibid.

11. UPTON SINCLAIR AND ALBERT EINSTEIN

1. Upton Sinclair, *Mental Radio* (New York: Collier Books, 1972), p. 16.

2. Ronald W. Clark, *Einstein: The Life and Times* (New York: Avon Books, 1972), pp. 744–755.

3. Ibid. p. 37.

4. Interview with Helen Dukas, June 16, 1980.

5. *Saturday Review* (April 14, 1956).

6. *Time* (April 21, 1923).

7. Leon Harris, *Upton Sinclair: American Rebel* (New York: Thomas Y. Crowell Co., 1975), p. 356.

8. Interview with JBR, July 31, 1978.

9. Mary Craig Sinclair, *Southern Belle* (New York: Crown, 1957).

10. Ibid.

11. Leon Harris, op. cit. p. 272.

12. THE HUMAN GUINEA PIG

1. JBR, *New Frontiers of the Mind* (New York: Farrar & Rinehart, 1937), p. 86.

2. Ibid. pp. 85–89; and interviews with JBR.

3. JBR, *Extra-Sensory Perception* (Boston: Bruce Humphries, 1964), pp. 213–214.

13. THE GOLDEN ERA

1. J. Gaither Pratt, *Parapsychology: An Insider's View of ESP* (New York: E. P. Dutton, 1967), p. 55.

2. JBR, *New Frontiers of the Mind* (New York: Farrar & Rinehart, 1937), pp. 95–96.

3. Pratt, op. cit.

4. Ibid. p. 58.

5. JBR, op. cit. pp. 102–105.

6. JBR letter to WFP, June 28, 1932.

7. JBR, *Extra-Sensory Perception* (Boston: Bruce Humphries, 1964), p. 77.

8. Ibid. Preface, 1964 ed.

9. Ibid.

10. R. A. McConnell, *ESP Curriculum Guide* (New York: Simon and Schuster, 1970), p. 23.

11. Interview with LER, November 14, 1977.

12. McConnell, op. cit. p. 24.

13. JBR, *New Frontiers of the Mind*, op. cit. p. 109.

14. JBR, *Extra-Sensory Perception*, op. cit. Preface, 1964 ed.

14. TRANCE MEDIUM EILEEN GARRETT

1. Eileen J. Garrett, *Many Voices: The Autobiography of a Medium* (New York: Putnam, 1968), pp. 52–57; Allan Angoff, *Eileen Garrett and the World Beyond the Senses* (New York: William Morrow, 1974), pp. 93–101.

2. Garrett, op. cit. pp. 162–164.

3. Eileen Garrett letter to JBR, Spring 1934.

4. JBR, *New Frontiers of the Mind* (New York: Farrar & Rinehart, 1937), pp. 224–225; JBR, "Telepathy and Clairvoyance in the Normal and Trance States of a 'Medium,' " *Character and Personality*, Vol. 3 (1934), pp. 91–111.

5. WFP letter to JBR, March 1934.

6. Garrett, op. cit. p. 97.

7. William R. Birge and JBR, "Unusual types of persons tested for ESP. A professional medium," *J of P* (1942), pp. 85–94.

8. JBR, *New Frontiers of the Mind*, op. cit. pp. 224–225; JBR, "Telepathy and Clairvoyance in the Normal and Trance States of a 'Medium,' " op. cit. pp. 91–111.

9. J. G. Pratt, *On the Evaluation of Verbal Material in Parapsychology* (New York: Parapsychology Foundation, Inc., 1969).

10. Naomi A. Hintze and J. Gaither Pratt, Ph. D., *The Psychic Realm: What Can You Believe?* (New York: Random House, 1975), pp. 217–218.

11. Pratt, op. cit.

12. JBR, *New Frontiers of the Mind*, op. cit. p. 228.

13. John G. Fuller, *The Great Soul Trial* (New York: Macmillan, 1969), p. 215.

14. Ibid. p. 359–361

15. THE STAB IN THE BACK

1. JBR, *New Frontiers of the Mind* (New York: Farrar & Rinehart, 1937)

2. Ibid. pp. 131–133.

16. LIFE AFTER DEATH AND MIND OVER MATTER

1. *Walter Franklin Prince: A Tribute to His Memory* (Boston: BSPR, 1935).

17. FRIENDS AND CHAMPIONS

1. JBR letter to Rev. Hubert Pearce, December 8, 1934.

2. Hubert Pearce letter to JBR, December 18, 1934.

3. Interview with Robert Rhine, June 14, 1980.

18. QUESTIONS AND ANSWERS

1. JBR, *New Frontiers of the Mind* (New York: Farrar & Rinehart, 1937), pp. 231–233.

2. LER, *ESP in Life and Lab* (New York: Macmillan, 1967), p. 19.

3. John L. Randall, *Parapsychology and the Nature of Life* (New York: Harper & Row, 1975), pp. 82–84.

4. W. Whatley Carington letter to JBR, January 13, 1935.

5. JBR letter to W. Whatley Carington, February 1935.

6. JBR letter to E. R. Dodds, 1935.

7. Robert H. Thouless letter to JBR, 1935.

8. JBR letter to H. F. Saltmarsh, April 3, 1935.

9. JBR letter to G. N. M. Tyrell, April 4, 1935.

10. Interview with Adam Linzmayer, November 6, 1977.

11. Ibid.

19. EDGAR CAYCE—THE SLEEPING PROPHET

1. JBR letter to Dr. Lucien Warner, January 28, 1935.

2. Thomas Sugrue, *There Is a River* (New York: Henry Holt, 1942); Hugh Lynn Cayce, *Venture Inward* (New York: Harper & Row, 1946); Jess Stearn, *Edgar Cayce—The Sleeping Prophet* (New York: Doubleday, 1967).

3. Edgar Cayce communication to JBR, April 7, 1936.

4. Edgar Cayce letter to JBR, April 7, 1936.

5. JBR letter to Dr. Lucien Warner, April 9, 1936.

6. JBR letter to Hugh Lynn Cayce, April 13, 1936.

7. Hugh Lynn Cayce letter to JBR, May 6, 1936.

20. A MENTAL PATIENT AND DREAM TELEPATHY

1. JBR letter to Professor Hornell Hart, March 23, 1936.

2. LER, *Hidden Channels of the Mind* (New York: William Sloane Associates, 1971), p. 18.

3. Ibid. p. 144.

21. HOLLYWOOD

1. JBR letter to Eileen Garrett, 1936; interviews with JBR.

2. Paul Tabori, *Harry Price: The Biography of a Ghost-Hunter* (London: Athenaeum Press, 1950).

22. THE VANISHING WOMAN

1. Interview with Dr. Bernard F. Riess, April 25, 1978.

2. Ibid.

3. B. F. Riess, "A case of high scores in card guessing at a distance," *J of P* (1937), pp. 260–263.

4. C. E. M. Hansel, *ESP and Parapsychology: A Critical Re-Evaluation* (Buffalo, New York: Prometheus Books, 1980), pp. 102–103.

23. DR. GARDNER MURPHY AND THE JOURNAL OF PARAPSYCHOLOGY

1. Grover Smith, ed., *Letters of Aldous Huxley* (New York: Harper & Row, 1969), p. 729.

2. Dr. Gardner Murphy, "Notes for a Parapsychological Autobiography," *J of P*, No. 21 (1957), pp. 165–178; letter to author from Dr. Lois Murphy, June 20, 1980.

3. Ibid. Dr. Gardner Murphy.

4. Interview with Dr. Lois Murphy, April 22, 1978.

5. JBR letter to Gardner Murphy, November 2, 1936.

6. Interview with JBR, July 31, 1978.

24. RHINE, JUNG, FREUD

Much of the material in this chapter comes from Paul J. Stern, *C. G. Jung: The Haunted Prophet* (New York: George Braziller, 1976) and Barbara Hannah, *Jung: His Life and Work* (New York: Putnam, 1976), as well as from conversations with Dr. J. B. Rhine, Dr. Louisa E. Rhine, Dr. H. A. Murray, and Dr. Henri E. Ellenberger.

1. From a study by Aniela Jaffe on Jung's family, compiled from family documents; C. G. Jung, *Erinnerungen Traume, Gedanken* (Zurich: Rascher

Verlag, 1962), pp. 399–407; and C. G. Jung, *Memories, Dreams, Reflections* (New York, Pantheon, 1963).

2. Ernest Jones, M.D., *The Life and Work of Sigmund Freud: The Last Phase* (New York: Basic Books, 1957), p. 391.

3. Ibid. p. 395.

4. Ibid. pp. 395–396.

5. C. G. Jung, *Memories, Dreams, Reflections*, op. cit. Introduction.

6. Interview with JBR, July 31, 1978.

7. JBR, "Nature and Psyche," *Tomorrow*, Vol. 4, No. 2 (Winter 1956), p. 43.

8. JBR, *The Reach of the Mind* (New York: William Sloane, 1947), pp. 89–90. Also Jung letter to JBR, November 27, 1934.

9. *Ten Years of Activities* (New York: Parapsychology Foundation Inc., 1965), pp. 99–100.

10. JBR, "Nature and Psyche," op. cit.

11. Ibid. p. 44.

12. Jung letter to Stephen I. Abrams, June 20, 1957.

25. THE OPPOSITION

1. Chester Kellogg, "New Evidence (?) for Extra-Sensory Perception," *The Scientific Monthly* (October 1937), pp. 331–341.

2. JBR et al., *Extra-Sensory Perception After Sixty Years* (Boston: Bruce Humphries, 1940), p. 146.

3. Ibid. p. 142.

26. IN THE LION'S DEN

1. Interview with JBR, July 31, 1978.

2. Ibid.

3. *Time* (April 11, 1938).

4. Interview with Dr. B. F. Skinner, November 19, 1977.

5. Interview with Dr. Steuart Henderson Britt, April 30, 1978.

6. Interview with JBR, July 31, 1978.

7. JBR et al., *ESP After Sixty Years* (Boston: Bruce Humphries, 1940).

8. "ESP Symposium at the APA," *J of P* (1938), pp. 247–272.

9. Ibid.

10. Interview with Dr. Bernard F. Riess, June 13, 1978.

11. Interview with Dr. Steuart Henderson Britt, April 30, 1978.

12. Interview with Dr. Bernard F. Riess, June 13, 1978.

13. William James, "The Final Impressions of a Psychical Researcher," *The American Magazine* (October 1909).

27. HIDDEN EVIDENCE

1. Interview with JBR, May 21, 1978.

2. JBR, *The Reach of the Mind* (New York: William Sloane, 1947), pp. 107–108.

3. JBR et al., *ESP After Sixty Years* (Boston: Bruce Humphries, 1940); and JBR, *The Handbook of Parapsychology* (New York: Van Nostrand Reinhold, 1977), p. 168.

4. Interview with LER, August 3, 1980.

5. Interview with Rosemary Rhine, May 16, 1980.

6. JBR letter to Mrs. Upton Sinclair, November 23, 1943.

7. Interview with Dr. Betty [Humphrey] Nicol, August 26, 1978.

8. Interview with JBR, July 31, 1978.

9. Grover Smith, ed., *Letters of Aldous Huxley* (New York: Harper & Row, 1969), pp. 484–485.

10. JBR letter to Upton Sinclair, January 20, 1943.

11. Ibid, July 21, 1945.

28. SPONTANEOUS ESP

1. JBR letter to Upton Sinclair, June 27, 1947.

2. Author's correspondence with Louisa Rhine, 1980.

3. Robert Thouless letter to author, August 18, 1979.

29. EXORCIST

1. Interview with Reverend Luther Miles Schulze, September 29, 1980.

2. Ibid.

3. Washington *Post* (August 20, 1949).

4. William Peter Blatty, *William Peter Blatty on The Exorcist* (New York: Bantam, 1974), p. 21.

5. Interviews with JBR, October 30, 1978, and July 8, 1979.

6. William G. Roll, *The Poltergeist* (New York: Signet, 1972), p. X.

7. Upton Sinclair, *O Shepherd Speak!* (New York: The Viking Press, 1949), pp. 538–539.

30. DOWSING

1. JBR, "Some Exploratory Tests in Dowsing," *J of P*, No. 14 (1950), pp. 278–286.

2. Kenneth Roberts, *Henry Gross and His Dowsing Rod* (New York: Doubleday, 1951), pp. 149–161.

3. JBR, op. cit. p. 284.

4. Roberts, op. cit. p. 219.

5. Gardner Murphy et al., "A Field Experiment in Water Divining," *JASPR*, No. XIV (1951), pp. 3–16.

6. R. J. Cadoret, "The Reliable Application of ESP," *J of P*, No. XIX (1955), pp. 203–227.

7. K. Osis, "Some Explorations of Dowsing Techniques," *JASPR* (1960), pp. 141–152.

8. Interview with JBR, July 31, 1978. Also see Martin Ebon, ed., "Dowsing in Vietnam," *The Psychic Reader* (New York: World, 1969), pp. 45–47.

31. AN UNEXPECTED SUPPORTER

1. Wilder Penfield, *The Mystery of the Mind* (Princeton: Princeton University Press, 1978), p. 21.

2. Ibid. p. 88 and p. 85.

32. KARLIS OSIS

1. Interview with Dr. Karlis Osis, November 13, 1977.

2. Interview with Olga Worrall, December 20, 1977.

3. Interview with Dr. Karlis Osis, November 13, 1977.

4. Interview with Dr. Karlis Osis, February 5, 1978.

5. Interview with Dr. Karlis Osis, June 17, 1979.

6. Ibid.

7. Ibid.

8. Ibid.

33. PIGEONS AND PSI TRAILING

1. J. Gaither Pratt, *Parapsychology: An Insider's View of ESP* (New York: E. P. Dutton, 1967), pp. 240–249.

2. Interview with Dr. Robert Van de Castle, September 12, 1978.

3. JBR and S. R. Feather, "The Study of 'Psi Trailing' in Animals," *J of P*, Vol. 26 (March 1962), pp. 1–22.

4. Interview with Dr. B. F. Skinner, June 8, 1980.

5. Allan C. Fisher, Jr., "Mysteries of Bird Migration," *National Geographic* (August 1979).

34. SECRET WORK FOR THE ARMY

1. JBR, "Location of hidden objects by a man-dog team," *J of P*, Vol. 35 (1971), pp. 18–33.

2. Ibid.

3. Ibid.

4. Robert L. Morris, "Parapsychology, Biology, and ANPSI," *Handbook of Parapsychology* (New York: Van Nostrand Reinhold, 1977), p. 700.

5. JBR, op. cit.

6. JBR, "Parapsychology and Scientific Recognition," J of P, Vol. 16 (December 1952), pp. 225–232.

35. SUGAR THE CAT

1. JBR and S. R. Feather, "The Study of 'Psi Trailing' in Animals," *J of P*, Vol. 26 (March 1962), pp. 1–22.

2. Ibid.

36. JONSSON

1. Interviews with J. B. Rhine and Karlis Osis, November 13, 1977, and Olof Jonsson, November 20, 1977.

2. Interview with Karlis Osis, November 13, 1977.

3. Ibid.

4. Interview with W. E. Cox, March 30, 1978.

37. KRIPPNER'S ODYSSEY

1. Letter from Albert Einstein to Stanley Krippner, September 22, 1953.

2. Ronald W. Clark, *Einstein: The Life and Times* (New York: Avon, 1972), pp. 641–642.

3. Interview with Helen Dukas, June 16, 1980.

4. Stanley Krippner, *Song of the Siren* (New York: Harper & Row, 1975), p. 7.

5. Ibid.

6. Ibid. p. 8.

7 Ibid. p. 10.

8. Ibid. pp. 10–11.

9. Interview with Stanley Krippner, March 29, 1978.

10. George R. Price, "Science and the Supernatural," *Science*, Vol. 122 (1955), p. 359.

11. G. R. Price, "Apology to Rhine and Soal," *Science*, Vol. 175 (1972), p. 359.

12. Interview with JBR, July 31, 1978.

38. DR. REMI CADORET AND CHRIS THE WONDER DOG

1. Interviews with Dr. Remi Cadoret, February 11 and 19, 1978.

2. Ibid.

3. Interview with Rosemary Goulding, December 11, 1977.

4. Interview with Dr. Martin Kaplan, December 11, 1977.

5. Interview with Rosemary Goulding, December 11, 1977.

6. Interviews with Dr. Remi Cadoret, February 11 and 19, 1978.

7. Ibid.

8. Ibid.

9. Interview with Rosemary Goulding, December 11, 1977.

10. Interviews with Dr. Remi Cadoret, February 11 and 19, 1978.

11. Interview with Rosemary Goulding, December 11, 1977.

12. Interviews with Dr. Remi Cadoret, February 11 and 19, 1978.

13. Ibid.

14. Ibid.

39. RHINE AND HIS STAFF

1. Interview with Dr. Remi Cadoret, February 19, 1978.

2. Interview with Dr. Betty [Humphrey] Nicol, August 26, 1978.

3. Interview with JBR, March 21, 1978.

4. Interview with Dr. Karlis Osis, February 5, 1978.

5. Ibid.

6. Ibid.

7. Ibid

40. THE FIRE BUILDER

1. Interview with Dr. Robert Van de Castle, June 8, 1980.

2. Ibid.

3. Ibid.

4. Ibid.

5. Interview with W. E. Cox, July 16, 1978.

6. Interview with Dr. Robert Van de Castle, June 8, 1980.

7. Ibid.

8. Ibid.

9. Interview with Rhea White, March 29, 1978.

10. Gertrude Schmeidler, ed., ExtraSensory Perception (New York: Atherton Press, 1969), p. 91.

11. Interview with Dr. Margaret Anderson, March 29, 1978.

12. Interview with Rhea White, March 29, 1978.

13. Sybille Bedford, Aldous Huxley (New York: Knopf, 1974), pp. 560–561.

14. Grover Smith, ed., Letters of Aldous Huxley (New York: Harper & Row, 1969), p. 719.

41. REINCARNATION AND BRIDEY MURPHY

1. Interview with Morey Bernstein, May 2, 1979.

2. Morey Bernstein, The Search for Bridey Murphy (New York: Doubleday, 1965).

3. "Symposium of Seven Questions," Tomorrow, Vol. 4, No. 4 (Summer 1956), p. 25–48.

4. Interview with Morey Bernstein, May 2, 1979.

5. Ian Stevenson, "Reincarnation: Field Studies and Theoretical Issues," *Handbook of Parapsychology* (New York: Van Nostrand Reinhold, 1977), p. 636.

42. THE PARAPSYCHOLOGICAL ASSOCIATION

1. *Proceedings of the Parapsychologial Association*, No. 1 (1957–1964), p. 4.

43. SONG OF THE SIREN

The sources for much of this chapter comes from Stanley Krippner's autobiography *Song of the Siren* (New York: Harper & Row, 1975).

1. Interview with Stanley Krippner, March 29, 1978.

2. Ibid.

44. A SPY IN THE CAMP

1. C. E. M. Hansel, *ESP: A Scientific Evaluation* (New York: Scribner's, 1966), pp. 19–22.

2. Ibid. p. 78.

3. JBR and J. G. Pratt, "A Reply to the Hansel Critique of the Pearce-Pratt Series," *J of P* (June 25, 1961), pp. 93–94.

4. Gertrude Schmeidler, ed., *ExtraSensory Perception* (New York: Atherton Press, 1969).

5. Ibid. pp. 56–57.

6. Ibid. p. 57.

7. Charles Honorton, "Error Some Place," *Journal of Communication*, Vol. 25:1 (1975), p. 112.

45. DRUGS

1. Arthur Koestler, *Drinkers of Infinity—Essays 1955–67* (New York: Macmillan, 1969), pp. 230–234.

2. Grover Smith, ed., *Letters of Aldous Huxley* (New York: Harper & Row, 1969), letter to JBR, July 19, 1953, pp. 678–679.

3. Ibid. Aldous Huxley letter to Humphrey Osmond, October 16, 1954, p. 713.

4. Interview with LER, July 31, 1978.

5. Interview with W. E. Cox, July 16, 1978.

6. Ibid.

7. Ibid.

8. Arthur Koestler, *The Roots of Coincidence* (London: Picador, 1974), p. 12.

9. Ibid.

10. Ibid. pp. 12–13.

11. Interview with JBR, July 31, 1978.

46. CHESTER CARLSON: INVENTOR OF THE "IMPOSSIBLE" MACHINE

1. Lecture Forum Honoring the Memory of Chester F. Carlson, New York City, December 4, 1968.

2. Ibid.

3. Ibid.

47. SUBTERFUGE

1. Interview with Charles Honorton, June 21, 1978.

2. Ibid.

3. Interview with JBR, July 31, 1978.

4. Interview with Charles Honorton, June 28, 1978.

48. UPTON SINCLAIR

1. JBR letter to Upton Sinclair, February 12, 1963.

49. FOUNDATION FOR RESEARCH ON THE NATURE OF MAN

1. K. Ramakrishna Rao, review of "Five Years Report of Seth Sohan Lal Memorial Institute of Parapsychology," by S. C. Mukherjee, in *J of P*, Vol. 28, No. 1 (March 1964), pp. 59–62.

2. Interview with JBR, July 31, 1978.

50. THE REVOLT

1. C. Backster, "Evidence of a primary perception in plant life," *International Journal of Parapsychology*, Vol. 10 (1968), pp. 329–348.

2. Interview with Bob Brier, May 20, 1978.

3. Interview with JBR, July 31, 1978.

4. Interview with Bob Brier, May 20, 1978.

5. Interview with Charles Honorton, June 21, 1978.

6. Ibid.

7. Ibid.

8. Interview with JBR, July 31, 1978.

9. Interview with LER, May 31, 1980.

10. Interview with Charles Honorton, June 21, 1978.

11. Ibid.

12. Ibid.

13. Lecture Forum Honoring the Memory of Chester F. Carlson, New York City, December 4, 1968.

14. Leon Harris, *Upton Sinclair—American Rebel* (New York: Crowell, 1975) p. 335.

15. Ibid. pp. 355–356.

51. BISHOP PIKE

1. Interview with JBR, July 31, 1978.

2. Jim Bishop, *The Golden Ham* (New York: Simon & Schuster, 1956).

3. Interview with JBR, July 31, 1978.

4. William Stringfellow and Anthony Towne, *The Death and Life of Bishop Pike* (New York: Doubleday, 1976), pp. XII–XIII.

5. Interview with JBR, July 31, 1978.

6. James A. Pike with Diane Kennedy, *The Other Side* (New York: Doubleday, 1968), p. 126.

7. Stringfellow and Towne, op. cit. p. 153.

52. AAAS

1. Nona Coxhead, *Mindpower* (New York: Penguin, 1976), p. 24.

2. Ibid.

3. Interview with Dr. B. F. Skinner, November 19, 1977.

53. AAAS CONVENTION

1. Thomas R. Tietze, "Science Officially Meet Psi," *Psychic* (June 1971), p. 20.

2. Ibid.

3. Ibid. p. 21.

54. BETRAYAL

1. JBR, "Comments: 'A New Case of Experimenter Unreliability,' " *J of P*, Vol. 38, No. 2 (June 1974), pp. 215–225.

2. Ibid.

3. Interview with Charles Honorton, June 3, 1980.

4. *J of P*, op. cit.

5. Ibid.

6. Ibid.

7. Interview with Charles Honorton, June 3, 1980.

8. *J of P*, op. cit.

9. Interviews with Walter Jay Levy's father, April 11 and April 15, 1978; July 5, 1979.

10. Ibid.

11. Interview with Charles Honorton, June 3, 1980.

12. Interview with Robert Rhine, June 14, 1980.

55. A TEST OF SURVIVAL

1. JBR, "Telepathy and Other Untestable Hypotheses," *J of P*, Vol. 38, No. 2 (June 1974), pp. 137–153.

2. Ibid.

3. Ibid. pp. 147–148.

4. Ibid. p. 152.

5. JBR, "Comments: Psi Methods Examined," *J of P*, Vol. 39, No. 1 (March 1975), pp. 38–58.

6. Ibid.

7. Ibid.

8. Ibid.

56. PSYCHIC STARS

1. Sean Harribance, as told to the Reverend H. Richard Neff, *This Man Knows You* (San Antonio, Texas: The Naylor Co., 1976), p. 60.

2. W. G. Roll and J. Klein, "Further Forced Choice ESP Experiments with Lalsingh Harribance," *JASPR* (January 1972), pp. 103–112.

3. Norma Bowles and Fran Hynds with Joan Maxwell, *Psi Search* (New York: Harper & Row, 1978).

4. Interview with Sean Harribance, September 24, 1977.

5. Interview with M. B. Dykshoorn, April 12, 1978.

6. Ibid.

7. Ibid.

8. Interview with Dr. Irvin Child, April 24, 1978.

9. LER, *PSI: What Is It?* (New York: Harper & Row, 1975), p. 67.

10. Ibid.

57. THE RUSSIANS ADVANCE

1. Interview with LER, November 14, 1977.

2. C. G. Abbot, "A scientist tests his own ESP ability," *J of P*, Vol. 2. (1938), pp. 65–70.

3. C. G. Abbot, "Further evidence of displacement in ESP tests," *J of P*, Vol. 13 (1949), pp. 101–106.

4. Interview with Dr. Paul Kurtz, October 30, 1979.

5. *Novel Biophysical Information Transfer Mechanisms* (NBIT), January 14, 1976, Section 3, p. 1.

6. J. G. Pratt, "Soviet Research in Parapsychology," *Handbook of Parapsychology* (New York: Van Nostrand Reinhold, 1977), pp. 883–903.

7. Interview with Thomas Rhine, March 15, 1980.

8. Interview with LER, May 31, 1980.

58. DR. JOHN A. WHEELER

1. Interviews with Dr. John A. Wheeler, July 12, 1979 and December 20, 1981.

2. From Dr. Wheeler's remarks at a meeting of the AAAS, in Houston, Texas, January 8, 1979.

3. Transcription of Dr. Wheeler's comments, tape recorded, at AAAS meeting on January 8, 1979.

4. Interview with JBR, July 8, 1979.

5. JBR and William McDougall, "Third report on a Lamarckian experiment," *British Journal of Psychology* (1933), 24, pp. 213–235.

6. William McDougall, "Second report on a Lamarckian experiment," *British Journal of Psychology* (1930), 20, p. 210.

7. William McDougall, Foreword in JBR's *Extra-Sensory Perception* (Boston: Bruce Humphries, 1964), p. XV.

8. JBR letter to *Science*, dated June 27, 1979.

9. Interview with Dr. John A. Wheeler, July 12, 1979.

10. Ibid.

11. Interview with Dr. Paul Kurtz, October 30, 1979.

59. THE LAST BATTLE

1. Interview with Rosemary Rhine, May 16, 1980.

2. Ibid.

3. Interview with Robert Rhine, June 14, 1980.

4. Ibid.

5. Interview with LER, May 31, 1980.

6. Ibid.

7. Interview with Rosemary Rhine, May 16, 1980.

8. *The New York Times* (February 21, 1980).

60. THE SUMMING UP

1. The great British physicist Sir John Joseph Thomson, who developed the famous Cavendish Research Laboratory at Cambridge University, maintained that scientific theories should be simple enough to be understood by a barmaid.

2. Morris Goran, *The Future of Science* (New York & Washington: Spartan Books, 1971), pp. 87–88.

3. Ibid. p. 63.

4. LER, "Man and Scientist," at a memorial meeting, Durham, N.C., November 28, 1980.

5. Alister Hardy, Robert Harvie and Arthur Koestler, *The Challenge of Chance* (New York: Random House, 1973), pp. 192–193.

6. *Nobel: The Man and His Prizes* (New York: Elsevier, 1972), p. 258.

7. *Science News*, Vol. 116, No. 21 (November 24, 1979), pp. 358–359.

8. LER, "Man and Scientist," at a memorial meeting, Durham, N.C., November 28, 1980.

9. JBR, "The Experiment Should Fit the Hypothesis," *Science*, Vol. 123, No. 3184 (1956), pp. 203–204.

10. JBR, "ESP: What Can We Make of It?" *J of P*, Vol. 30, No. 2 (June 1966), pp. 103–104.

11. JBR, "Parapsychology and Psychology: The Shifting Relationship Today," *J of P*, Vol. 40, No. 2 (June 1976), pp. 132–133.

12. JBR, "Comments: Psi Methods Reexamined," *J of P*, Vol. 39, No. 1 (March 1975), p. 57.

13. The definition of a great scientist by Dr. Albert Svent-Gyorgyi, who was awarded the Nobel prize for discovering vitamin C. *The Way of a Scientist* (New York: Simon and Schuster, 1966), p. 113.

INDEX

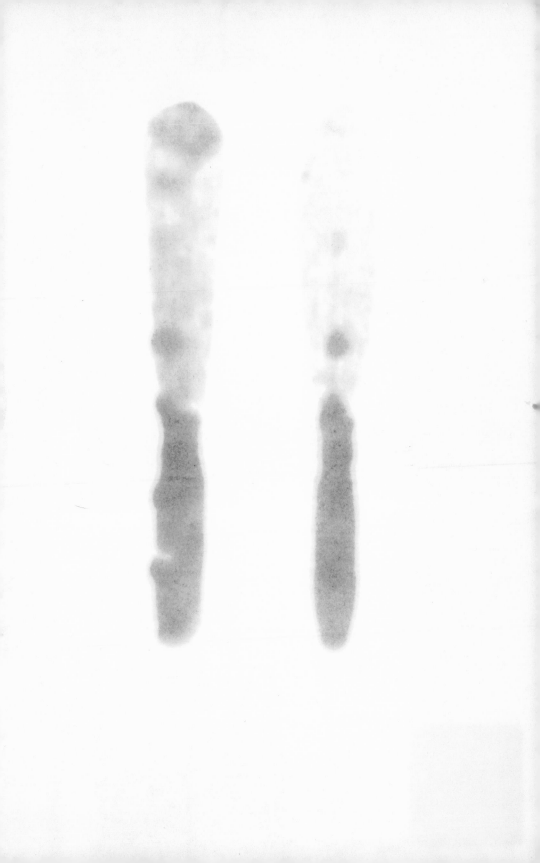